FAMILIES *and* WORK

FAMILIES
and WORK

New Directions in the Twenty-First Century

Karen I. Fredriksen-Goldsen
University of Washington

Andrew E. Scharlach
University of California, Berkeley

New York • Oxford
Oxford University Press
2001

Oxford University Press

Oxford   New York
Athens   Auckland   Bangkok   Bogotá   Buenos Aires   Calcutta
Cape Town   Chennai   Dar es Salaam   Delhi   Florence   Hong Kong   Istanbul
Karachi   Kuala Lumpur   Madrid   Melbourne   Mexico City   Mumbai
Nairobi   Paris   São Paulo   Singapore   Taipei   Tokyo   Toronto   Warsaw

and associated companies in
Berlin   Ibadan

Published by Oxford University Press, Inc.,
198 Madison Avenue, New York, New York, 10016
http://www.oup-usa.org

Library of Congress Cataloging-in-Publication Data
Fredriksen-Goldsen, Karen, I., 1957–
Families and work: new directions in the twenty-first century / Karen I.
Fredriksen-Goldsen, Andrew E. Scharlach.
p.   cm.
Includes bibliographical references and index.
ISBN 0-19-511272-5 (cl : alk. paper) – ISBN 0-19-511273-3 (pbk: alk. paper)
1. Work and family–United States.   I. Scharlach, Andrew E. II. Title.
HD4904.25 .F74 2000
        306.3'6'0973–dc21   99-058504

Printing (last digit): 9 8 7 6 5 4 3 2 1

Printed in the United States of America
on acid-free paper

To our families

· C O N T E N T S ·

Preface

As we enter the twenty-first century, we have the opportunity and challenge to rethink the relative balance between family and work. We are living in a time when the pace of life is escalating, demands are increasing, and time has become a scarce commodity. Under such circumstances, it is not surprising that while work and family remain central to the lives of most Americans, combining them often creates strain and stress for many of us.

The balance between work and family is likely to continue to change due to significant demographic transformations, including shifts in the age and ethnic structure of the population, in the composition of the family, and in the nature of work and the work place. Such significant social and demographic changes occur against a backdrop of strong cultural values, including familial responsibility, the American work ethic, self-determination, and the pursuit of wealth through capital accumulation.

This book is a study of the experiences and needs of employees with the entire range of family care responsibilities. Through an exploration of the synergistic relationship between work and family, we examine the impact of demands and resources in our working lives and our families. Further, we consider the role of the work place and the larger community in responding to the needs of Americans as they attempt to balance their work and family care responsibilities

A central theme of this book is the necessity to form a partnership between family, business, government, and the larger community to address work and family issues, recognizing that the various stakeholders have similar as well as differing interests. It is our hope that through an examination of how such a partnership might be developed, we will find ways for work and family roles to more effectively support and enhance one another.

The material presented in this book builds upon much earlier work that has explored these two pivotal life domains. The bodies of literature on work and family, as well as caregiving, have provided us with many insights for further exploring how employees integrate their work and family responsibilities. We, the authors, collaborated on all aspects of this book, and the ideas presented were developed through our ongoing research.

We want to thank the many people who have contributed directly to the development of this book. First, we want to thank the Lawrence Berkeley Laboratory (LBL) employees who participated in the survey, for it was their willingness to share their experiences that made this book possible. We also want to acknowledge the support of LBL management and staff, including Michael Goldstein, Harry Reed, Kathleen Handron, Rod Fleischman, and Charles Shank.

Financial support was provided by LBL, the University of California Academic Senate Committee on Research, and the Eugene and Rose Kleiner Chair for the Study of Aging. The study was based in part on our earlier survey of adult care responsibilities among employees of the University of California at Berkeley, conducted in collaboration with the Chancellor's Advisory Committee on Dependent Care.

We want to thank our research assistants who helped us at various phases of this project, including: April Gilbert, Blanche Grosswald, Ha Pham, Teresa Dal Santo, Jill Schlesinger, Sandy Shrager, Heidi Spence, and Judie Svihula. We want to thank Virginia Senechal and Natalie Goldstein for their assistance with copy editing. We would like to acknowledge the support and assistance of our editors at Oxford University Press, Jeffrey Broesche, Layla Voll, Benjamin Clark, and Gioia Stevens. Karen would also like to extend a special thanks to Andrew Scharlach, who was an outstanding mentor, teacher, and dissertation chair during her doctoral program at UC Berkeley.

We are deeply indebted to our families, Jayn, Tenaya and Bryce, and Ilene, Rebecca and Emily, for their patience and support through the writing of this book. They truly provide the impetus for us to consider mindfully our own relationship to family and work.

· PART ONE ·

Family and Work

· 1 ·

FAMILY CARE AND WORK

INTRODUCTION

As we enter the twenty-first century, family and work are undergoing immense transformation. More persons than ever before are combining family care and employment outside of the home. Of the more than 69 million American parents with children under the age of 18 (Famighetti, 1998), almost 90 percent are employed (U.S. Bureau of the Census, 1998). Indeed, working parents constitute approximately 40 percent of all workers in the paid U.S. labor force.

The number of women in two-parent families who are in the paid labor force has increased dramatically in the past 50 years. In 1960, only 18 percent of mothers with children under the age of six were working. Today more than 60 percent of mothers and 80 percent of fathers with children under the age of six are employed (U.S. Department of Labor, 1997). Seventy-five percent of mothers with children ages 6–17 are now employed, an increase from 39 percent in 1960 (U.S. General Accounting Office, 1992b). Fifty-three percent of all mothers return to work before their child is a year old, up from 38 percent only 15 years ago (U.S. Bureau of the Census, 1996b). It is estimated that four out of five children under one year of age now have a working mother (Krajicek & Moore, 1993).

More than one in seven adults are currently involved in the care of ill or disabled relatives or friends (Marks, 1995). Patients are being released "quicker and sicker" from hospitals. With the advent of Diagnostic Related Groupings (DRGs), average hospital stays have been substantially reduced from nearly 10 days in 1983 to 8.0 days by 1993 (U.S. Health Care Financing Administration, 1996). Policy changes such as these have placed added responsibility on families and communities to provide ongoing assistance to ill and disabled family members, often with inadequate supports.

The majority of such assistance is provided informally by family members (Pavalko & Artis, 1997; U.S. Bureau of the Census, 1997b), primarily wives and daughters. For example, it is estimated that more than 85 percent of the care of disabled older adults is provided by family members and other unpaid helpers. More than 50 percent of these caregivers are working full-time jobs (NAC/AARP, 1997). Approximately 25 percent of family caregivers are part of the "sandwich generation," providing care for children as well as disabled adults (U.S. Senate, 1994).

Family care and employment remain normative adult roles in this society, impacting the overall quality of life of American families. Family care involves dependencies, responsibilities, obligations, and entitlements, as it interfaces with working life. At the end of the twentieth century, the commitment to provide family care remains high, despite unprecedented change. The United States is experiencing tremendous shifts in its work force and economy, in the age and ethnic/racial structure of its population, in the increasing heterogeneity among its families, and in changes in its communities. These changes are impacting as well as defining new relationships between work and family.

This book addresses the critical juncture between work and family. While integrating work and family responsibilities results in both positive and negative consequences, we will explore how recent changes in family care, as well as the work place, have resulted in increased demands upon employed family caregivers. To understand these changes more fully we will examine the synergistic relationship between employees' demands and resources, as well as the larger context, including private and public responses to work and family issues. In doing so, we draw upon an integrative model that enables an examination of the interface between family care and employment across the full range of employees' family responsibilities—from child care to elder care.

Changing social and demographic factors combined with longstanding American values form the societal backdrop for work and family issues. In this chapter we will examine the changing nature of our population, our families, employees, businesses, and the larger community in which we live. We will also highlight some of the central work and family issues and the cultural values that frame the current work and family debate. Lastly, we will present an overview of this book; how it will explore the interrelationship between work and family; and the components necessary to form a partnership between workers, families, businesses, and communities in order to balance our personal and societal commitments to family and work in the twenty-first century.

The U.S. Population

The U.S. population is aging dramatically, with an equally dramatic shift in the nature and longevity of familial relationships. Primarily influenced by fertility rates, mortality, and migration, the proportion of elderly in our society is rising rapidly. In fact, since the turn of the century, there has been more than an eleven-fold increase in the number of persons 65 and older (U.S. Bureau of the Census, 1996a). In 1800, every second person was under the age of 16 and only a few lived beyond the age of sixty. The proportion of the population that is 65 and older, which was slightly under 13 percent in 1995, is projected to rise to more than 20 percent by 2040 (Hagen, 1999). As a result of the aging of the "baby boomers," there will be a tremendous surge in the proportion of elderly between the years 2010 and 2040, when the number of persons 65 and older is projected to increase from approximately 39 to more than 65 million.

The proportion of the population that is 85 and older is growing especially quickly, more rapidly than any other segment of the population (U.S. Bureau of the Census, 1996a). While in 1991 about 1 percent of the total U.S. population was 85 or older, by the year 2040 this group is projected to increase to almost 4 percent and to number approximately 14 million persons; by 2050, it will reach nearly 5 percent and number 19 million persons.

As older Americans have come to represent an ever larger proportion of the U.S. population, families are increasingly becoming "top heavy" with a growing number of relationships across generations. This phenomenon will create both benefits and challenges for the American society. Older adults possess tremendous resources, and population aging will likely result in an increase in beneficial exchanges between generations. For example, parents often continue to provide support and care for children even into late adulthood, and most older adults provide more assistance to younger family members than they receive.

However, concomitant with the aging of the U.S. population is a significant increase in the number of elderly in need of long- term care assistance. After the age of 85, for example, more than half of the population have mobility and self-care limitations impacting their ability to meet personal care needs such as bathing and dressing (U.S. Bureau of the Census, 1990). The shift from hospital-based care to more extensive community and home-based assistance has resulted in increased reliance on family members and personal supports. Further, advances in medical care have increased the number of patients sent home to families for care. Unlike popular stereotypes, few elderly live in nursing homes. Only about 5 percent of persons over 65 reside in nursing homes at any given time (Roy & Russell, 1992). The ongoing care needs of disabled adults are generally met informally by family members, the majority of whom are working.

The Family

During the last several decades, the American family has undergone dramatic changes that impact work and family. Similar to trends reported in the majority of developed nations, the American family has become increasingly heterogeneous. Due to increases in individuals living alone, single-parent households, and persons living together in other nontraditional family arrangements, the "first-married nuclear family" no longer predominates; it has become but one of numerous family types.

Other notable changes impacting the American family include a decrease in overall fertility, an increase in family dissolutions, and a shift in economic roles within the family. American families are generally smaller today than ever before; women are bearing fewer children and doing so later in their reproductive years.

The U.S. Bureau of the Census (1992a) projects a continuing trend of decreased fertility. The total number of U.S. births declined about 9 percent during the 1990s, although there was considerable variation by race. While, overall, the white population may begin to decline within 30 years, most racial and ethnic minority groups are projected to experience substantial growth. For example, by the year 2030 it is estimated that the African-American population will increase by 50 percent (14 million persons) and that Asian, Pacific Islander, and American Indian populations may triple in size, increasing by approximately 16 million persons.

The U.S. currently leads all developed nations in the number of single-parent families. While marriage remains the primary source of family formation, the number of single-parent families has increased significantly and is the second most common type of family form. In 1994, 26 percent (3.9 million) of all births in the U.S. were to unmarried women (including widowed, divorced, and never married women) (U.S. Bureau of the Census, 1995a).

In comparison to other developed nations, the U.S. also has the highest rate of divorce. In 1974, the termination of marriage through divorce had for the first time in U.S. history become more common than dissolution through the death of a spouse. Although the divorce rate has recently declined slightly, it is estimated that more than 50 percent of all marriages that occurred in the 1970s will be terminated through divorce, approximately double the rate of divorce in 1950s marriages (Wetzel, 1990).

Given these high rates of divorce and the number of children born outside of marriage, close to one-third of all families in the U.S. are headed by unmarried women (U.S. Bureau of the Census, 1993a). The Census Bureau reports that single parents constitute 31 percent of all family households, up from 13 percent in 1970 (U.S. Bureau of the Census, 1996b), and represent about 25 percent of all working parents (Ferber, O'Farrell & Allen, 1991). Fifty-nine percent of single mothers with children under the age of six and 79 percent of those with children between 6 and 17 are in the work force (Mulroy & Pitt-Catsouphes, 1994). Twenty-six percent of children live in single-parent homes at any one time (Smith, 1991), and almost half of all children will live in a single-parent home at some point in their childhood (Heymann, Earle & Eagleston, 1996). By comparison, fewer than 10 percent of children lived in single-parent families between 1940 and 1960 (Hofferth, 1992). There are about four times as many single working mothers as single fathers, although households headed by single fathers represent the fastest growing household form.

There is a growing disparity in income distribution in the U.S., with a widening gap between low- and high-income families. Peckman (1990) found that the total share of income received by the nation's wealthiest families (top one-fifth) decreased from 1948 to 1952, remained relatively unchanged from 1952 to 1981, but rose steadily in the late 1980s. In 1993, the share of income of the top 5 percent of wealthiest families was the highest ever recorded in U.S. history (U.S. Bureau of the Census, 1997b).

Female-headed families tend to be one of the most economically vulnerable segments of the population. For example, in 1995 married-couple families had an average yearly income of $47,000 ($55,000 if wife employed; $32,000 if wife not employed), male-only head-of-household families had an income of $30,000, and female- only head of household families, $19,000 (U.S. Bureau of the Census, 1997b). In 1992, 46 percent of female-headed families were living in poverty compared with 7 percent of married-couple families (U.S. Bureau of the Census, 1994b).

While female-headed families have high rates of poverty, the majority of single mothers with children are in the labor force. In 1992, 62 percent of female heads of household worked compared with approximately 50 percent in 1960 (U.S. Department of Labor, 1994). These figures in part include a substantial increase in the number of single mothers who are officially seeking work but are currently unemployed. The number of unemployed single mothers has increased by approximately one-third during this time period. Given public policy regarding welfare reform and the various welfare initiatives that mandate employment, we will likely see a further increase in the number of single mothers seeking employment.

The increase in other types of nontraditional families also significantly impacts the nature of family care and employment. For example, there has been a substantial increase in the number of unmarried cohabiting couples, as well as gay and lesbian couples with children. It is estimated that more than 4 million lesbians and gay men are raising children (Ettelbrick, 1993). The proliferation of nontraditional families raises important questions regarding the definition of family in relation to family care.

As demographic trends, such as the aging of the population, increase the need for familial caregivers, the decline in birth rates and the changing composition of the American family will likely limit the availability of informal caregivers. Smaller families tend to produce fewer relatives to assist in the care of dependents. Given the high rates of divorce and remarriage, the U.S. is also developing rather complex and fluid kinship networks. Following divorce, for example, many children lose contact with one of their parents, most often the father.

Factors such as these may limit the availability and involvement of family members as informal care providers, and will likely increase the utilization of nonfamily members in the care of dependents. Given the recent changes in income distribution in the U.S. and the relatively high numbers of impoverished single women as family care providers, however, many families may have limited access to the economic resources necessary to purchase high-quality care. Accompanying the increase in family heterogeneity is a corresponding pressure for accommodation of a variety of family types with potentially varying needs.

The Labor Force

As we continue to shift from a manufacturing to a service-based economy, with a corresponding lack of increase in real wages over the last 20 years, American families are becoming increasingly dependent on two incomes. In 1997, approximately 54 percent of all families had dual wage earners, both husband and wife working; sixty-five percent of married couples with children under the age of 18 were dual-earners (U.S. Bureau of Labor Statistics, 1998). In comparison, in 1920 only approximately 9 percent of "traditional families" (married with wife and husband present) had dual wage earners (Hayghe, 1990).

During the last several decades, there has been a more than 200 percent increase in the number of women working (U.S. General Accounting Office, 1992b). Although historically, the majority of women have worked inside the home, the participation of women in the formal labor market has steadily increased—from approximately 20 percent of the female population (5 million women) in 1900 to nearly 60 percent in 1996 (U.S. Department of Labor, 1997). Women aged 25 to 34, who are in their prime child-bearing and child-rearing years, have demonstrated the largest increase in labor-force participation—73 percent in 1991 compared with 45 percent in 1970 (U.S. Department of Labor, 1994).

It is estimated that at the beginning of this century, women account for approximately two-thirds of the growth in the American labor market. In the year 2000, more than 75 percent of women between the ages of 45 and 60 are employed outside of the home. There has not been a corresponding adjustment in the participation rate of men. In fact, the formal labor-market participation rate among men has declined only slightly over the last several decades (U.S. Department of Labor, 1997).

Despite their increased involvement in the labor force, the earnings of women consistently lag behind those of men. Most women are in relatively low-paying positions and report seeking work out of financial necessity. In 1996, women's annual full-time earnings were only 74 percent of men's (U.S. Department of Labor, 1997). Furthermore, women's career advancement and salaries do not progress at the same rate as do those of men in comparable positions, and they tend to have higher turnover rates (U.S. Department of Labor, 1995b; Stroh, Brett & Reilly, 1996).

Schwartz (1989), in her controversial discussion of the "mommy track," suggests that women do not advance as quickly as men and tend to leave their positions to accommodate family needs. Others maintain that women have higher turnover rates due to lack of career opportunities and the "glass ceiling" effect (U.S. Department of Labor, 1995b)—that is, women do not advance in their careers because of organizational barriers that constrain them. The lower wages and lack of career advancement experienced by women likely reduce available resources to assist them in meeting their work and family responsibilities.

Some evidence suggests that men, particularly younger men, desire more time with their families (New Ways to Work, 1995, as cited in Lewis & Lewis, 1996). Yet both women and men report encountering barriers to balancing career and family responsibilities. Such barriers include the marginalization of work and family issues as women's issues, work-place cultures that do not support family roles, and high levels of work demands. In a survey of large companies with work and family benefits, it was found that less than two percent of the workers used available work-place benefits such as job sharing, telecommuting, or part-time options. Reasons cited for not using such benefits included penalties for using them (e.g., job loss) and excessive work demands (Holmes & Friedman, 1995).

The expanding number of women entering the labor market and families' increased reliance on two incomes will likely have profound implications for the work place and for family care in this country. The net effect of these changes is that an increasing number of persons in the U.S.—particularly women—will be combining familial care and employment roles.

Regardless of their participation in the labor market, family care remains primarily "women's work." Reflecting existing societal norms and gender roles, research consistently demonstrates that compared to men, women have primary responsibility for family care. It is estimated that women provide 80 percent of the informal care that their families receive (U.S. Senate, 1996). When working, women basically assume a "second shift" to meet their additional homemaking and family care responsibilities (Hochschild, 1989; 1997).

Due to shifts in fertility and the increased labor-force participation of women over the last several decades, there is expected to be a gradual slowdown in the expansion of the labor force during the next decade. Several significant changes in the ethnic and racial composition of the labor force are expected, with considerable growth among African- and Hispanic-Americans (Jacobs, 1998). While non-Hispanic whites are expected to remain the largest share of the labor force, their growth rate is considerably below that of other racial and ethnic groups. For example, whites are expected to account for 73 percent of the labor force in 2006 compared to 75 percent in 1996 and 80 percent in 1986. By the year 2006, Hispanics are expected to be the second largest group in the labor force, surpassing African-Americans. The increasing number of racial and ethnic minorities in the formal labor market has important cultural implications for the integration of work and family responsibilities.

Hispanics and African-Americans are both significantly more likely than whites to be employed in the service sector or as operators, fabricators, or laborers, while whites are more likely to be employed in managerial and professional positions. It is also important to consider differences by race and ethnicity in terms of income and poverty rates as they relate to access to formal support services to assist family members providing care. In 1996, the median household income was $43,276 for Asian and Pacific Islanders, $37,161 for whites, $24,906 for Hispanics, and $23,482 for African-Americans (U.S. Bureau of the Census, 1998). In 1997, the poverty rate was approximately 27 percent among Hispanics and African-Americans, 14 percent among Asians and Pacific Islanders, compared to 11 percent among whites (U.S. Bureau of the Census, 1998).

The Work Place

As we enter the postindustrial era, this society is experiencing tremendous changes in the nature of the economy and the composition of the formal labor market. With more manufacturing occurring in developing countries with lower wages and cheaper production costs, the United States is increasingly relying on a service-based economy, which tends to offer lower wages.

Given the increasing globalization of the economy and rapid technological changes, there is an increased emphasis on productivity and cost control in business. American businesses are responding to these pressures through increased industry consolidation, specialization, organizational delayering, and re-engineering to reduce fragmentation and duplication and streamline business and production processes. As part of this effort, downsizing has become more common among American businesses. Based on a recent survey of major U.S. companies, downsizing is now characterized as a strategic rather than a reactive response of the private sector (Raber, 1996).

It is estimated that as a result of downsizing, two out of every three American workers will be forced to leave their jobs at some point during their work lives (Kates, Grieff & Hogen, 1990). Although companies may experience an initial increase in productivity, there often is a decrease in worker satisfaction and morale. The National Study of the Changing Work Force (Holmes & Friedman, 1995) found that 42 percent of those surveyed had experienced downsizing at their place of employment and as a result, employees were working more hours and felt more burned out. Although the employees remained committed to performing their jobs well and in some cases took increased initiative, they experienced less satisfaction, loyalty, and commitment to their jobs and their employers.

Recent research indicates that the portion of employees involved in contingent employment is growing more rapidly than permanent, full-time positions. Of the various types of contingent employment (part-time, temporary, and independent contractual work), part-time work is increasing the most rapidly (Drury & Almand, 1990). Involuntary part-time work has accounted for the greatest growth since 1970.

The use of the contingent labor force tends to cut labor costs and enhance staffing flexibility. The contingent labor force, however, also reduces the stability of the labor market, results in lower wages, and decreases the protection of workers in terms of workplace benefits such as insurance, retirement, sick leave, and other social benefits. Part-time and temporary workers tend to receive lower pay and fewer benefits than permanent, full-time employees. Part-time workers earn approximately 60 percent, and temporary workers earn about 77 percent, of the wages earned by full-time workers. It has been estimated that almost one-fifth of the American work force is involved in part-time work (Kahne, 1993), especially prevalent in the service industry and largely impacting women and low-skilled segments of the work force.

Technological advances such as computers, robotics, and automation are also radically altering the landscape around work and family. As technology continues to generate more information and opportunities, the pace of life is escalating. The complex web of technological supports that link individuals to a vast array of systems and information creates both opportunities and constraints for the American worker. As workers are linked from work to home by e-mail, cell phones, and beepers, there are more opportunities and fewer boundaries between work and family, with all of life's domains becoming more permeable. Never before has the worker had such opportunities for flexibility and autonomy, nor been so easily accessible, with potential on-call access 24 hours a day. The increasing demands as well as opportunities resulting from the growing technological advances must be considered in the work-family equation.

As business responds to technological advances and global competition, a new "contract" is emerging between employees and employers (Holmes & Friedman, 1995). With the shifting emphasis on cost control and efficiency, there is less commitment to job security, internal career advancement, and benefits. At the work site today, skill and performance are generally more highly valued than loyalty and tenure. And with the trend toward job elimination and organizational de-layering, there is pressure on employees to meet organizational demands by increasing their commitment and time. American employees today are likely to experience heightened demand and responsibility, as well as more autonomy.

The appropriate role of business in work-family affairs continues to be debated. How companies respond to work and family issues depends on a number of factors such as organizational change (e.g., downsizing, merger, acquisition), current and anticipated labor shortages, membership in the service sector, percentage of female workers, and degree of unionization. As the work place becomes increasingly fluid, it will likely shift the role of business in responding to work and family needs.

The Community

The U.S. is a geographically mobile society. In the single-year period from 1993 to 1994, approximately 43 million U.S. residents (nearly 17 percent of the population) moved (U.S. Bureau of the Census, 1994a). Although the majority made a local move, 8 million persons moved between counties in the same state, nearly 7 million moved to another state, and 1.2 million moved to the U.S. from abroad.

Such mobility often creates distance between family members and limits the availability of relatives to provide direct hands-on assistance, potentially changing the nature of family care and the interrelationship between family and work. For example, in some cases grandparents are no longer available to assist working parents in the care of their children. And although the majority of adult Americans still live close to their parents, adult children are increasingly coordinating care at a distance for their elderly parents. The greater geographic dispersion of family members is likely to strain the capacity of informal networks to provide care.

Adapting to such movement and the shifts in the economy, our communities have undergone tremendous change. For example, recently it has been suggested that community is no longer defined by geographic proximity, but rather by technological linkages (American Association of Retired Persons [AARP], 1998). As American neighborhoods are becoming more transient, evidence suggests that Americans are investing less time in their communities and civic responsibilities. A national poll found that in 1993 only 13 percent of Americans in the past year "attended a public meeting on town or school affairs" compared to 22 percent in 1973 (Putman, 1995). Today, fewer Americans are participating in Parent-Teacher Associations, church-related groups, and other volunteer organizations.

With the majority of parents in the work force and most children being cared for outside of the home, residential neighborhoods have been denuded of people during work hours. Thus, even parents who do stay home with children are often isolated and without the support and backup of other neighbors in similar circumstances. Child-care exchanges, still a useful babysitting option for parents (versus full-time child care), are now arranged through organized parent-support groups as often as through casual neighborhood efforts. The current trend toward more people working at home could reverse this emptying of neighborhoods, but only if some of the time saved by workers not commuting is focused on neighborhood and not work-related pursuits.

While many communal structures and institutions may be changing in relation to work and family care, many American values are not. The commitment to provide care for family members remains high. Research demonstrates that in this country, family responsibility is a robust value. And because such cultural values as the American work ethic, self-determination, and individualism are equally strong, there is ambivalence about how to address the integration of family care and employment.

The debate centers around several basic value dilemmas such as the role of the family, businesses, and government in providing assistance to families and their dependents, and the appropriateness of the public versus private sectors in addressing work and family issues. Often implicit in such policy discussions is the issue of supplanting private family care with public financing. Concern has been expressed that formal support services would create a "substitution" effect and supplant no-cost family care with costly taxpayer-supported assistance. There is also tension between publicly provided programs and market economy service development. All of these issues reflect a basic ambivalence regarding private versus public responsibility in providing assistance to families and their dependents.

Family Care and the Work Place

In summary, several trends are significantly impacting the relationship between family care and employment:

- Composition of the labor force. The expanding number of women entering the labor market is resulting in more persons (particularly women) combining family care and employment. Today there are more dual-earner couples as well as more employed single parents. Furthermore, future growth in the labor market will result in a labor force that is younger and more ethnically and racially mixed.

- Availability of family members. As the population ages, the need for familial caregivers is increasing. Yet the changing composition of the American family and increased geographic mobility may limit the availability and involvement of family members to provide care. As families are becoming more diverse, they have varying needs and experiences combining work and family responsibilities.

- Changes in the nature of work. With the impact of technological advances and global competition, skill and performance have become generally more valued than loyalty and tenure in the American work place. Many workers are experiencing more autonomy with increased demands and responsibility.

- Changing communities. With the composition and function of our neighborhoods changing, our communities are undergoing transformation. As more parents work, more children are receiving care outside of their homes. With increased geographic mobility, more families are assisting chronically ill and disabled members from a distance.

- Family and gender roles. Despite tremendous demographic change, several facets of American life have remained relatively constant—for example, the central role of the family and the continued relevance of gender in the distribution of family-care responsibilities. There continues to be limited societal recognition of those providing family care, combined with ambivalence regarding the role of the private and public sectors in addressing work and family issues.

Structure of this Book

In this book, we will examine these current social and demographic changes in terms of their implications for American families and work places, and the opportunity they provide to create new ways to integrate work and family responsibilities. The following chapters will analyze existing knowledge regarding family care and employment, synthesize existing research, and introduce a model for understanding the integration of work and family across the diverse range of family-care responsibilities.

Although in the past, most discussions of work and family have focused on issues relevant to young children and parents, more recently the debate has been expanded to encompass the care needs of the elderly. There have been relatively few attempts to examine other intergenerational care arrangements or caregiving across the lifespan. Yet family care occurs throughout the life course. In this book, we will examine the full range of family-care relationships, including children, chronically ill and disabled working-age adults, and the frail elderly.

The following two chapters review existing knowledge about child and adult care as they interface with the work place. In Chapter 2, we discuss the characteristics of working parents, the types of child care they use, and the problems they experience. In Chapter 3, we examine the prevalence of adult care responsibilities, characteristics of family members providing such care, and the types of care responsibilities. Both chapters explore the impact of family responsibilities on work, as well as how work affects family life.

Chapter 4 provides a critical review of conceptual approaches that have been used previously in the work and family and caregiving literature. The models reviewed range from those that define work and family as separate spheres to those that highlight their interaction. Those that utilize an individual perspective are compared to those that incorporate a macro-level perspective. We also explore the differing underlying assumptions that have guided conceptual approaches to the care of children in contrast to those that have primarily focused on the care of the elderly.

Persons combining family and work responsibilities vary substantially in their ability to manage those roles and in the work and family outcomes they experience. Yet many previous studies have tended to generalize about the work and family experience without examining the impact of specific work and family characteristics and their integration. Chapter 5 provides an innovative family-care paradigm for understanding the inter-relationship between family care and employment characteristics. This framework highlights the interactive nature of employment and family care by providing a model for examining the interplay between social and demographic characteristics, demands, and resources in both the family and occupational domains.

Chapters 6 and 7 discuss the experiences of working parents and employees who assist ill and disabled adults, including the prevalence of care responsibilities, the impact of combined work and family-care responsibilities on work activities and family commitments, the stresses experienced by caregivers, and the programs and benefits utilized and considered helpful in alleviating conflicts between family and employment responsibilities. We draw upon the findings of a comprehensive study of work and family experiences among nearly 2,000 diverse employees of a large technology research center. The study achieved a 76 percent response rate (higher than that obtained by any previous dependent-care survey). Gorey, Rice, & Brice (1992), for example, found that most studies of employed caregivers had a relatively low response rate, on average only 45 percent.

In Chapter 8, the findings from the family-care model are discussed in relation to the characteristics of those providing family care and to the demands and resources in both family and occupational domains. We also compare the experiences of employees with differing types of family care responsibilities, including those with child-care responsibilities, those assisting ill and disabled adults, and those with multigenerational care responsibilities (providing assistance to both children and adults).

Although the majority of the work and family literature has focused on corporate concerns and the needs of white, high-level career women and men, it is likely that the difficulty in combining work and caregiving is accentuated for racial and ethnic minorities in low-status occupational positions. In order to provide a more comprehensive analysis of the experiences of employed caregivers, Chapter 9 explores the important influences of gender, race and ethnicity, and occupational role, and the interactive relationship between family and employment responsibilities in these diverse groups.

Chapters 10 and 11 review and evaluate a variety of work-place programs, benefits, and polices that have been designed to support employees in meeting their family-care and employment responsibilities. Specifically, in Chapter 10 we examine work-place programs currently available to employed caregivers and evaluate the efficacy of the various approaches. In Chapter 11, we analyze various public policies, including child care, long-term care, tax incentives, and family leave as mechanisms to assist employees with their combined work and family-care responsibilities. In Chapters 10 and 11, we also discuss necessary components of a public and private response to build a community-based infrastructure that supports employees with family-care responsibilities. In Chapter 12, we outline a research agenda to further advance current thinking about work and family.

In the concluding chapter of this book, we discuss the need to form a partnership between families, businesses, government, and communities to insure a balance between our societal commitments to family and work roles. In light of changing work and family environments, we suggest directions that are necessary to develop a public response that addresses the challenges facing those with combined family and employment responsibilities.

SUMMARY

The relationship between work and family is undergoing transformation as the U.S. experiences dramatic shifts in the aging and racial and ethnic structure of its population, in the composition of its families and labor force, and in the nature of business, as well as the availability of communal structures. As we enter the twenty-first century, these changes will require us to reconsider and reconceptualize the interrelationship between family care and employment. As family members, as employees, and as members of a community we must ask ourselves what we value: What is a relative balance between family and work?

· 2 ·

CHILD CARE AND
THE WORK PLACE

INTRODUCTION

The availability of families to provide care for their children during working hours declined dramatically during the second half of the twentieth century, attributable primarily to the changes in women's work patterns, in family composition, and in the nature of work and communal life. In this chapter, we examine the situation faced by today's working parents. We will see how changes in employment patterns and family support structures, coupled with inadequate public and private responses, have combined to create unique challenges for employed parents. Adequate, affordable, dependable child care is difficult to find, and certain types of care are particularly hard to secure. We will also discuss the continued role that gender plays in the care of children, despite the increasingly similar work patterns of men and women.

In this context, it is not surprising that many employed parents, especially women, experience substantial amounts of role strain. Some, however, are able to make accommodations in their work or family roles that enable them and their children to benefit from the combined demands of working and parenting. How these employees manage their potentially competing family and work roles will be of central interest in this chapter and throughout the book. Of particular interest is the balance between the magnitude of family and work demands and the adequacy of potential resources such as social support as it impacts the experiences and needs of working parents and their families.

WORKING FAMILIES

Characteristics of Working Parents

As discussed in the previous chapter, the number of women in two-parent families who are in the paid work force has increased dramatically in the past 50 years, without an equivalent change in the work patterns of fathers. Today, more than 60 percent of U.S. women work for pay, as compared to 30 percent in 1950 (U.S. Bureau of the Census, 1993b). Changes in men's work patterns have not kept pace: while the percentage of working mothers has almost tripled in the past 50 years, the percentage of working fathers has declined by less than 5 percent (Heymann et al., 1996).

Working parents (individuals with children under the age of 18) represent about 40 percent of all workers in the paid labor force in the United States (Ferber et al., 1991; Galinsky, Bond & Friedman, 1996). The Family and Work Institute's 1992 telephone survey of a randomly selected national sample of working men and women (Galinsky et al., 1996) found that employees with children had an average age of about 37, slightly younger than nonparents' average age of 40 years. Twenty-five percent of parents and more than 30 percent of nonparents had a bachelors degree. Eighty-six percent of parents were married or living with a partner, as compared to 53 percent of nonparents.

Eighty-six percent of working parents worked full-time and 14 percent worked part-time. Mothers were more than twice as likely as fathers to be employed in part-time or temporary positions. Working parents worked an average of 43 hours per week, with fathers working significantly more hours outside of the home than mothers. Approximately one-third of working parents held managerial or professional positions. Parents and nonparents did not differ with regard to personal or household income, occupation, number of hours worked, part-time or contingent employment. Nor did they differ in terms of their access to benefits such as personal health insurance, pension plans, paid or unpaid leave, or flex-time.

Types of Child Care Utilized by Working Families

A variety of child-care forms has developed along with the increase in mothers' participation in the labor force. These include care by parents, care by grandparents and other relatives, care by friends including child-care exchanges, care by paid in-home care providers including nannies and au-pairs, family day care, child-care centers, and no care or "self-care."

In 1993, according to the *Survey of Income and Program Participation* (Casper, 1996), 30 percent of preschool children with an employed mother were in organized child-care facilities as their primary care arrangement, while 16 percent were cared for by their father, 17 percent by grandparents, 9 percent by other relatives, 21 percent by nonrelatives, and 6 percent by the mother herself, including mothers working at home.

Seventy-five percent of school-age children live in families without a parent at home during the day (Seligson, Fersh, Marshall, Marx & Baden, 1990). The 1990 *National Child Care Survey* found that, among school-age children with an employed mother, 11 percent were in center-based programs,

7 percent were in family day care before and after school, 19 percent were in lessons or sports, 3 percent were with a nonrelative in their own home, 3 percent cared for themselves, and 2 percent had other arrangements. By age 12, 32 percent cared for themselves at least some time during the day.

Care in formal child-care centers has increased dramatically during the past 30 years, while care by relatives and nonrelatives has declined. By 1993, the Children's Foundation estimated that there were more than 90,000 child-care centers and more than 270,000 regulated family day-care homes in the United States. The growth in out-of-home child day care can be attributed to a number of factors, including increased female labor-force participation; improving economic conditions; decreased availability of grandparents, non-working family members, and other informal sources of child care; increased numbers of single-parent families; and changing attitudes regarding the acceptability of nonfamilial day care for preschoolers (Casper, 1996). Indeed, the majority of all three- to five-year-old children now attend nursery school, regardless of whether or not their mothers are in the labor force (U. S. Bureau of the Census, 1993b).

Care in the home, whether by relatives or paid care providers, remains a preferred child-care option for many families. Since the majority of center-based programs and family day-care homes do not accept children under two and a half, parents who can afford in-home care are especially likely to choose this option when children are young. Care by relatives is particularly common in some ethnic communities, where larger, extended families live close together.

In 1987, it was estimated that 7 percent of all 5- to 13-year-olds, about 2.1 million children, were home alone on a regular basis (U.S. Bureau of the Census, 1987). A more recent article suggests that there may be between 3 and 12 million American latchkey children (Soloman, 1994). Some reports suggest that close to 5 million children age 6 and older regularly receive no care or supervision after school (Seligson, 1997).

A survey of 5,000 families in the Boston area with children in grades K through 5 revealed that 75 percent of parents who were working or in school were not able to be at home when their children returned from school (Seligson et al., 1990). Yet only 14 percent of these children attended after-school programs. Most were taken care of at home by relatives; more than 36 percent spent some time every day cared for by an older sibling. Seven percent of children (aged 9 to 10 years) spent some time home alone each week. An additional 13 percent spent some time alone occasionally.

Time before school presents yet another problem. Twenty-four percent of parents in the survey had to leave for work before their children went to school. Of these children, only 1 percent attended a before-school program. The rest divided into the following categories: 40 percent stayed at home alone, 35 percent went to other peoples' homes, and 18 percent went to school before any teacher or adult supervisor arrived (Seligson et al., 1990). Most of the working parents who left their children alone did so unwillingly. About one-third of the entire group surveyed had looked for school-age child care and could not find it.

Quality of Child Care

In seeking child care for their children, parents generally place highest priority on convenience, safety, and affordability (Miller, 1990; Roche & Camasso, 1993). Finding child care that is located near home or work, open during the mother's normal working hours, dependable, and provides a safe environment are often a parent's primary concerns (Sonnenstein, 1991). By comparison, the characteristics typically identified by child development experts as indicators of quality child care may be secondary. These include group size, staffing ratios, caregiver training and experience, caregiver stability, types of daily activities, and adequacy and age-appropriateness of activity areas (Hayes, Palmer & Zaslow, 1990).

However measured, the quality of many child-care centers and family day-care homes is low. Observational studies of the quality of teacher-child interactions indicate that fewer than 15 percent of children are in child-care centers or family-care settings considered to be of high quality. Between 12 and 21 percent are in settings whose quality is so low that care is considered to be unsafe or developmentally deleterious (Helburn & Howes, 1996). Quality has been found to be especially poor in centers serving infants and toddlers. Infants require significant attention and personal contact but are unable to articulate their needs to care providers or parents, making the quality of the provider especially critical. Preschool children have significant interaction with other children at the child-care location, while infants are totally reliant on care providers for all of their needs. In addition, state-mandated ratios for infant care mean that it may be even more difficult for infant-care providers to be economically viable, possibly resulting in even greater underpayment of staff.

While relatives with child-care experience who want to care for children can be among the best care providers, not all are, and studies on the quality of care by relatives are not reassuring about the consistency or quality of care children receive. Moreover, while many view relatives as safer, more concerned care providers than impersonal centers, relatives are often chosen because of cost and availability rather than for quality reasons. Similarly, paid in-home child care varies in quality with the care provider.

Cost of Child Care

Child care costs about 7 percent of a family's weekly income, on average (U.S. Bureau of the Census, 1991). This percentage varies with the age of the child. Those with preschool-age children spend an average of 10 percent of family income on child care, an amount comparable to what they spend on food. Those with school-age children spend about 5 percent. The most expensive child care arrangement is a paid in-home care provider, followed by center-based care, family day care, and finally, care by relatives. Not surprisingly, families with higher household income are more apt to use nonrelative child care (Dawson & Cain, 1990). Emlen (1991) found that in a study of bank employees, those with incomes of $50,000 or more were twice as likely to use center care, while family day care was used equally by families with high and low (under $25,000) incomes.

Single mothers and poor families spend a larger share of their budget on child care and are most likely to experience problems paying for child-care arrangements. Families with incomes of less than $15,000 spend one-fourth of their family income on child care, while those with higher incomes spend less than 7 percent (U.S. Bureau of the Census, 1991); moreover, one-third of those in the higher income group receive an income tax credit for dependent care (Willer, Hofferth, Kisker, Divine-Hawkins, Farquhar & Glantz, 1991). One child's care costs about 10 percent of an average family's budget, but costs one-third to one-half of most single mothers' incomes (Stipek & McCroskey, 1989).

The Department of Labor's 1994 *Working Women Count!* survey of more than 250,000 working women found that 56 percent of mothers with children under the age of five identified "finding affordable child care" as a serious problem (U. S. Department of Labor, 1995b). Difficulty paying for child care has been associated with problems finding child care, more frequent changes in care arrangements, greater child-care worries, higher absenteeism at work, and greater work-family conflict (Emlen & Koren, 1988). The higher the cost of child care, the greater the likelihood of employee turnover and the lower the rates of maternal labor-force participation (Blau & Robins, 1989; Maume, 1991). The resource gap between the actual cost of decent quality child care and the needs of working parents is met in large part through inappropriately low salaries and other economic and in-kind contributions by providers. In this way, child-care providers essentially provide hidden subsidies to parents (Kisker & Maynard, 1991), contributing to staff burnout and high staff turnover rates in the child-care industry.

The lack of affordable child care poses a substantial barrier to finding jobs or attending school for many parents. Indeed, one study of Boston area families with school-age children found that the lack of affordable child care prevented one-third of low-income women and about one-half of moderate-income women from attending school or looking for a job (Seligson et al., 1990). A 1991 Bureau of Labor Statistics study concluded that lack of affordable, quality child care prevents more than one million young mothers from entering the paid labor force (Cattan, 1991).

Problems with Child Care

Adequate, affordable, accessible child care is not easily found, at any price. In Fernandez's 1986 study, 25 percent of mothers and 10 percent of fathers reported that obtaining high-quality child care was a problem. In a study of 4,000 DuPont workers, more than 25 percent of whom relied on child care, a majority of parents reported having trouble finding child care, especially infant care and summer programs for school-age children (DuPont, 1989). Even finding out about child care can be problematic. In a survey of 1,470 parents employed in a communications company, 39 percent reported that it was either difficult or very difficult to find out about available child care (Galinsky, 1988).

AVAILABILITY OF ADEQUATE CHILD CARE

The quality of child care is central to its impact on children and their working parents. Yet a national study examining the quality of care provided in the 1970s and 1990s by child-care centers and family day-care providers found that group size, staff turnover rates, and most other measures of quality had declined during that period (Kisker, Hofferth, Phillips & Farquhar, 1991). A *Wellesley School-Age Child-Care Project* in 1987 found that the supply of child-care services available in Boston was only enough for about 5 percent of Boston school-age children at the time (Seligson et al., 1990).

Finding child care can be particularly difficult for employees who work evening, night, or weekend shifts, which are predicted to represent the greatest increase in job growth (Hayes et al., 1990). Already more than seven million mothers of children under the age of 15 have nonstandard work hours (U. S. Department of Labor, 1995a). Nonstandard work schedules are especially prevalent among low-income mothers, nearly one-half of whom work rotating or changing schedules and one-third of whom work weekends (Hofferth, 1996). Without matching child-care services, this presents a major problem for the present and an even greater one for the future (McEnroe, 1991). Organized child-care facilities, which often are not open in the evening or on weekends, are used by 37 percent of women who work day shifts, but by only 22 percent of women who work other schedules (Casper, 1996). Women who work nonstandard shifts are much more likely than other mothers to rely on the child's father or other relatives. Moreover, nonstandard work shifts are increasingly staffed by employees with the lowest incomes, benefits, and other resources with which to pay for adequate child care.

CHILD-CARE BREAKDOWNS

Even when available, child-care arrangements are subject to breakdowns and other disruptions, which can be extremely stressful for parents and children alike. In a 1987 Fortune survey, 40 percent of families with children under 12 experienced at least one breakdown of child-care arrangements in the previous three months; nearly a quarter of these families had two to five breakdowns during this time. The leading causes of such breakdowns included having sick children and having a child-care provider who quit or was sick (Galinsky & Hughes, 1987).

The *National Study of the Changing Workforce* found that 32 percent of employed parents with children under the age of 5 had experienced child care arrangements falling through at least once in the previous three months, as did 20 percent of parents with children aged 5 to 12 (Galinsky, Bond & Friedman, 1993). Because of child-care breakdowns, some parents decide to bring children to their work places, feeling they have no other choice. In one company, the number of children at work was so high that a rule was instituted prohibiting parents from bringing their children with them to work (Burden & Googins, 1987).

Problems with child care can affect employees' personal lives and job performance. One study of 2,000 women found that only 34 percent of mothers who had experienced serious problems arranging child care reported being very satisfied with their lives, compared with 49 percent of mothers who experienced no such problems arranging child care (National Council of Jewish Women, 1987). Dissatisfaction with existing child-care arrangements has been associated with higher levels of stress, more stress-related health symptoms, more work-family spillover, and tardiness (Shinn, Galinsky & Gulcur, 1990). In addition, parents may experience greater personal stress, and children may suffer from the consequences of inadequate care (Emlen & Koren, 1984; Fernandez, 1986; Galinsky & Hughes, 1987; Ferber et al., 1991; Hofferth, Brayfield, Deich & Holcomb, 1991; Neal, Chapman, Ingersoll-Dayton, & Emlen 1993).

The type of child-care provider seems to impact the likelihood of child-care breakdowns and related work interference experienced by working parents. Work interference seems to be particularly low when one parent can stay at home to provide child care, producing absenteeism rates significantly lower than those experienced by working parents who use child-care centers or nonfamily child care. Indeed, some studies have found that fathers with a spouse at home have absenteeism rates similar to those of men without children (Emlen & Koren, 1984). Families with a parent at home also experience fewer child-care problems than those using nonfamilial care (Kossek, 1990). However, there is some evidence that these findings may be most salient when the parent staying home is the mother. A study by Maume and Mullin (1993), for example, found that women who depended primarily on their children's fathers for child care were significantly more likely to quit their jobs than mothers who had other child-care provisions. This association was strongest for low-wage mothers. Child care provided by family members is generally less apt to be associated with high levels of stress than care provided by friends (Sheppard, 1994). Unsupervised child care, in which children are cared for by a sibling or are left alone, is most likely to result in absenteeism (Emlen & Koren, 1984).

Stability of child care also can be a problem. One study of the durability of child care for preschool children of welfare mothers (Wolf & Sonenstein, 1991) found that care by relatives in the child's home was a particularly unstable form of child care, sometimes ending and being replaced by no child care at all. This study also found that there were more disruptions in the child care of African-American children than in the care of Latino and white children. These findings suggest that current efforts to push single parents from welfare into work should not depend on family members to replace parents as child-care providers.

ILL CHILD CARE

The lack of adequate sick child care is one of the most common problems with child-care arrangements. Indeed, one early study of working parents found that two-thirds of mothers and one-third of fathers reported missing work because of a child's illness (Burden & Googins, 1987) In the 1990 National Child Care Survey, more than half of the respondents who reported a sick child during the past month missed at least one day of work to stay home and care for their child (1991). Moreover, Fernandez's study of 5,000 workers in five corporations found that caring for a sick child was the cause of 80 percent of absenteeism among women with four or more absences from work during the previous year (Fernandez, 1986). Sick care is particularly an issue for single, minority, low-income mothers (Landis & Earp, 1987).

Landis and Earp (1987) asked working mothers their preferences for child care when their children were ill: 84 percent preferred in-home care by parents, 76 percent preferred in-home care by relatives or friends, and 53 percent preferred a separate sick room or infirmary at the child's regular child-care center. Mothers who chose "out-of-home care" were more likely to be minority women, single parents, or low-income (less than $10,000 annual income in 1985); that is, those most likely to experience the greatest difficulty in securing assistance with sick children.

CHILDREN WITH SPECIAL NEEDS

It is estimated that at least 10 percent of children of working mothers have special needs (Green & Widoff, 1990), although it is difficult to estimate the number of children affected, since "special needs" can range from minor, temporary conditions to life-threatening illnesses (Butler, McManus & Newcheck, 1986). However, data from the 1987 *National Medical Expenditure Survey* indicate that approximately 12 million children, representing one-fourth of all children under the age of 18, have one or more chronic health conditions (Hoffman, Rice & Sung, 1996). In addition, more than one-third of families each year experience child illnesses lasting at least two weeks, and one-fourth experience child illnesses lasting three weeks or more (Heymann et al., 1996).

Nearly half of all mothers with disabled infants or preschoolers work outside the home (Klein & Sheehan, 1987), resulting in approximately 1.5 million working parents who require child care for young children with disabilities and chronic conditions (Fewell, 1986). Moreover, the General Accounting Office estimates that approximately 400,000 children are so disabled that they require long-term care on an ongoing basis from parents and other care providers. The most common conditions requiring ongoing care are asthma and other respiratory disorders, mental retardation, and neurological disorders (U.S. General Accounting Office, 1995b).

Parents of children with special needs can have a particularly difficult time finding adequate child care (Neal et al., 1993). In one survey of 70 day care centers (Berk & Berk, 1982), only 58 percent expressed a willingness to accept children with disabilities into their programs. Moreover, in a survey of child care supply in several cities (Kisker, Maynard, Gordan & Strain, 1989), only 4 out of 10 family day-care providers would accept children with special needs.

It is evident that difficulty in locating affordable and accessible child care is a significant pressure experienced by today's working parents. In Chapter 6 of this book, we will further explore how problems with care arrangements relate to the strain experienced by parents, as well as to the accommodations they make when managing multiple work and family responsibilities. In the fourth section of this book, we will examine the types of child-care programs that are currently made available by employers and outline a public-policy framework necessary to create a community-based infrastructure that supports high-quality, accessible child care.

IMPACT OF FAMILY AND WORK RESPONSIBILITIES

Impact of Work on Parents' Personal Life

Work and family responsibilities can affect one another in many ways, both positive and negative. Parents attempt a variety of strategies at home and at work to enable them to provide the best possible care for their children while performing as effectively as possible on the job. Although combining work and family roles can yield many benefits for parents and employers, there is a potential for substantial role conflict as parents make the accommodations necessary to achieve a workable balance.

A substantial body of research has pointed to both positive and negative consequences for working mothers responsible for two jobs (i.e., one working for pay outside the home, the other doing the vast majority of household chores and child care) (Biernat & Wortman, 1991). Some of the differences in findings have to do with the group to whom employed mothers are compared. When employed mothers' mental health is compared to that of mothers who don't work, they fare well; but when compared to employed fathers, they fare more poorly. Research on men and work has typically focused on the negative results of job loss and unemployment compared to men who are employed. Little attention has been paid to fatherhood and how its interaction with work affects men's personal lives. Thus the impact of work on parents' personal life can be framed in a positive or negative fashion depending on one's focus. Following is a discussion of some of these findings.

For many parents, involvement in the work force appears to be positive, resulting in little or no distress as a result of combining work and family responsibilities (Emlen & Koren, 1984; Barnett & Marshall, 1989; Waldron & Jacobs, 1989). Mothers who are in the paid labor force, for example, generally report higher levels of physical and mental well-being than mothers who are not working outside of the home (Barnett & Baruch, 1985; Barnett & Marshall, 1989; Repetti, Matthews & Waldron, 1989; Waldron & Jacobs, 1989). The nature and intensity of the work and family responsibilities, rather than employment or parenthood per se, appear to be the critical factors that determine the impact on working parents (LaCroix & Haynes, 1987; Repetti et al., 1989).

That working mothers have been found to experience greater psychological well-being than nonworking mothers may be due to a variety of advantages that working provides. In addition to income and health insurance, parents benefit from the additional social support that may come from coworkers or other people encountered through work. Just as family can be an emotional buffer against work stressors, so can work be an emotional buffer against family difficulties. By providing some time away from the demands of children, spouse, and household, work can provide a much needed respite. And finally, work may be a source of achievement and recognition that supports a parent's self-esteem in ways that housework and parenting may not. Hochschild (1997) has argued that some parents may find more satisfaction at work than at home, resulting in a tendency to work long hours as an escape from the demands of family and household responsibilities. This in turn may make the family a less pleasant place to be, as its needs are compressed into fewer and fewer hours per day.

Another factor that may influence how mothers and fathers cope with the combined demands of work and family is their attitude toward work. For mothers especially, commitment to their jobs can influence satisfaction and role strain. For example, mothers with high levels of work commitment who stay home for at least five months after the birth of their children have been found to have greater irritability and depression than do mothers with low levels of work commitment (Lerner, 1994). High levels of job satisfaction are associated with lower levels of work-family conflict (Voydanoff, 1988) and more positive mother-child interaction patterns (Lerner, 1994).

Role Strain

The term "role strain" is used to describe "the experience of discomfort, pressure, worry, anxiety, tension, or frustration that may arise when people function in both work and home life" (Bohen & Viveros-Long, 1981). Work and family role strain is associated with reduced physical and mental well-being, as measured by depression, life satisfaction, and absenteeism (Googins & Burden, 1987). For example, among working parents in an American Express survey of 30,000 employees in 30 sites, 71 percent reported experiencing stress as a result of conflict between their work and family roles (Thomas & Thomas, 1990). Burden and Googins (1987) found that almost one-half of nearly 700 working parents surveyed experienced "a lot of stress" or "extreme stress" in balancing their work and family responsibilities (Googins, Gonyea & Pitt-Catsouphes, 1990). However, the 1992 Families and Work Institute study found that only 17 percent of working parents reported a lot of conflict between their work life and family/personal life (Galinsky et al., 1996). In Chapter 8 of this book, we analyze how characteristics of both work and family-care responsibilities relate to increased strain, as well as accommodations at the work place and in personal relationships among working parents and others with family-care responsibilities.

Existing evidence suggests that levels of role strain are especially high for working mothers (Barnett and Baruch, 1987; Rosenfield, 1989; Galinsky et al., 1996), most likely because they generally retain primary responsibility for home life and its responsibilities. Many studies have shown that employed mothers work more total hours than employed fathers when both the job and the housework (including child care) hours are counted (Pleck, 1984; Rexroat & Shelan, 1987; Scarr, Phillips & McCartney, 1989). Higher levels of child-care responsibility also seem to be associated with higher stress levels and lower levels of psychological well-being in working mothers (Ozer, 1995). Steil and Turetsky (1987) also found that high levels of child-care responsibility were associated with depression and somatic stress symptoms in working mothers. Shared responsibility was associated with less depression and lower levels of anxiety. The best predictor of a working mother's psychological well-being was her perceived ability to enlist the father's help in child-care duties.

Perceived role strain has been associated with a wide variety of health and mental health consequences (Burden & Googins, 1987; Kasl & Cooper, 1987). Neal et al. (1993) found that female employees, older employees, and those with multiple caregiving responsibilities showed consistently more personal health stress. Googins and Burden (1987) found that women, particularly mothers, reported lower levels of health and energy than men. Employed mothers exhibited reduced levels of physical and emotional well-being compared with men; however, the key factor associated with decreased well-being was work-family role strain, not gender. Male employees who had similar family responsibilities as females appeared likely to experience the same work-family role strain and lower levels of physical and emotional well-being.

In Seligson's (1997) needs assessment of Boston child-care services for school-age children, parents cited inflexible work policies as a major problem interfering with their child-care responsibilities. About one-half of the working mothers surveyed could not call or receive phone calls from their children, even in emergencies. One-third could not take time off when their children were sick. About two-thirds could not take time off for a school holiday. Fewer than one-half had any input in determining their own work schedules. Jobs and training programs of low- and moderate-income parents were highly correlated with inflexible schedules, e.g., no time off and/or no phone calls.

A major source of role strain for both fathers and mothers is overtime hours (Burke, Weir & Duwors, 1980; Staines & Pleck, 1983; Voydanoff, 1984).

And even if the total number of work hours does not exceed 40 per week, the schedule itself is significant in its effect on role strain. Nonstandard shifts, changing shifts, and unpredictable schedules have all been associated with role strain (Quinn & Staines, 1979). With an increase in national and global emphasis on a service economy, nonstandard work schedules and work patterns are developing at an increasing rate, blurring the temporal and geographic separation between work and family roles and creating increased demand for nontraditional forms of child care. It is the nature and intensity of demands facing employed parents that tend to determine the impact of combining family and work responsibilities. Throughout this book, we will explore how excessive demands can lead to incompatibility between family and work responsibilities. Difficulties managing multiple work and family-care responsibilities are most likely to occur when work and family demands are high and resources are low.

Impact of Work on Children

The literature on the impact of parental employment on children's welfare generally concurs that the consequences are neither consistently positive nor negative. Parents in dual-earner households spend about the same amount of time with their preschool children as do parents in households where only one parent works, although the parents sacrifice leisure time with one another in order to do so (Parcel & Menaghan, 1994). Moreover, the economic advantages of parental employment can have important benefits for family well-being and children's development (Parcel & Menaghan, 1994).

As summarized by Alison Clarke-Stewart (1992), the research on nonparental day care suggests that adequate child care is not harmful to children and may even be beneficial for their development. Studies show that children in day care score higher on IQ tests, are more advanced in their hand-eye coordination, and are more creative in play. Existing research also shows, however, that children in day care can be less polite, less agreeable, less compliant, louder, and more aggressive than children who are not in day care (Belsky, 1992), although these differences are slight and tend to disappear by the ages of five and six (Harvey, 1999).

Early studies by Belsky (1988) suggested that during the first year of a child's life, nonparental child care for more than 20 hours a week posed a risk for developmental problems. In Belsky's research, regular nonmaternal child care was found to be associated with insecurity and lack of bonding to the mother during infancy and increased aggressive and noncompliant behavior later on. However, infants in day care have also been found to display signs of more advanced social and intellectual development, which persist until about age five (Clarke-Stewart, 1992). There is some evidence as well that children whose mothers work have a less sex-stereotyped perspective, possibly because of the role modeling, and fathers are somewhat more involved in child care (Hoffman, 1989). Such early research suggested both positive and negative effects of maternal employment on child development.

More recent research suggests that maternal employment does not lead to permanent negative effects on the behavior, academic achievement, and psychological health of children (Scarr, 1998; Harvey, 1999). For example, a comprehensive, longitudinal study conducted by Harvey (1999) found that there was no consistent evidence of substantial effects of early parental employment (including both maternal and paternal employment) on children's later development, and any positive and negative consequences counteracted one another. In some cases, the income earned by mothers was found to be of particular benefit to children and their families. Overall, current research suggests that the quality of family life and parenting, including the mental stability and maturity of the parents, is more important in the development of children than the employment status of the mother.

An important mediator of the impact of employment on children's welfare is the quality of care they receive while the parents work. Ratios of caregivers to children, stability of care, and size of the group are all significant in determining care quality. For children older than one year, the literature shows that high-quality child care is equivalent or in some cases even better for children than being at home with mothers. Some children, especially those from low-income families, seem to do better in a child-care setting than at home in terms of intellectual development (Slaughter, 1983). A series of studies by researchers at the Wellesley College Center for Research on Women (Marshall, 1991) found that children in care settings marked by higher levels of language stimulation and positive caregiving during their first three years of life had greater language abilities at 15, 24, and 36 months, received higher scores on measures of infant development at age two, and displayed more school readiness at age three.

The impact of parental employment on children also appears to be associated with various work-related factors such as parents' attitudes toward their jobs, whether it is their choice to work, and the nature of job demands (Ferber et al., 1991). When mothers work outside the home because they wish to do so and when child care is at least satisfactory, the evidence suggests that stress on the family is not high and children are as healthy as children with mothers who are full-time homemakers (Ferber et al., 1991). When fathers work long hours or hold jobs that are especially stressful, on the other hand, they may be less physically or psychologically available to their children (Crouter & Perry-Jenkins, 1986), potentially contributing to lower vocabulary development in young children (Parcel & Menaghan, 1994).

Impact of Family Responsibilities on Work

As with research on the impact of work responsibilities on families, findings regarding the impact of families on the working lives of parents and other caregivers are mixed. There are a number of potential advantages for employers who have employees with families, including increased employee stability due to the economic and geographic requirements of families, workers' knowledge of family markets (e.g., children's products), and the potential for employees' increased life satisfaction. Family relationships may function as a form of emotional support or buffer to stressors in the work place, potentially giving spouses and parents an advantage over nonparents and individuals living alone (Keita & Sauter, 1992). In support of the notion that there is some advantage to workers with families, married men historically have earned more than their nonmarried counterparts, after controlling for demographic and educational variables (Hill, 1979; Korenman and Neumark, 1991). Married women, however, have never enjoyed this income advantage over single women, and some studies have shown a negative association between children and earnings for women (Korenman & Neumark, 1992).

Despite the argument that employees with families may provide potential advantages for employers, most research on how employees' family responsibilities affect their work behavior has focused on the potential deleterious sequelae of family responsibilities. For example, in their efforts to accommodate their family and work responsibilities, parents may make accommodations in their work patterns that result in absenteeism, unscheduled time off, telephone calls home, reduced concentration on work, and decreased work-place productivity (Fernandez, 1986; Galinsky & Hughes, 1987; Meisenheimer, 1990; Hofferth et al., 1991; Neal et al., 1993). More than two-thirds of employed parents report experiencing work interference associated with their child-care responsibilities (Fernandez, 1986; Lucas, 1986). Working parents may spend work time making child-care arrangements, thinking or worrying about a child while at work, leaving early or arriving late because of child-care problems, or missing work entirely because of an ill child or a breakdown in child-care arrangements.

A 1989 study by the U. S. Bureau of Labor Statistics (BLS) found that married women with young children had absenteeism rates that were double those of married women without children (Meisenheimer, 1990). In a 1984 study of 5,000 management and crafts workers at five large companies, Fernandez (1986) found that employees with children under the age of 12 were 50 percent more likely to be absent from work than were employees without children. One study of female aerospace workers found that women with children under the age of six were three times as likely as other women to experience occupational injuries (Wohl, Morgenstern & Kraus, 1995). Increased risk of occupational injuries was particularly apparent for slightly older mothers (women ages 30–39), for grandmothers (women ages 50 and older), and for African-American women.

A 1990 *Child Care Survey* by the U.S. General Accounting Office found that 51 percent of employed mothers who reported having a sick child in the last month took time off to care for the child. Estimates of time missed from work due only to children being sick range from 5.6 to 28.8 days per worker per year (Doyle, 1976; Carpenter, 1980), resulting in an estimated financial loss to employers of between $2 and $12 billion a year (Landis & Earp, 1987).

Problems with child-care arrangements are an especially potent contributor to absenteeism. Child-care problems have been called "the most important of any job or family predictors of work-family conflict" (Shinn et al., 1990). Difficulty finding child care has been associated with absenteeism (Galinsky & Hughes, 1987), tardiness, stress, and higher levels of work-family conflict (Emlen & Koren, 1984; Fernandez, 1986; Galinsky, 1988). Fernandez (1986) found that 48 percent of women and 25 percent of men spent unproductive time at work because of child-care problems. Hofferth et al. (1991) reported that child-care failures caused 15 percent of employed mothers to take time from work and 7 percent to miss at least one day of work during the past month.

Data from the U. S. Bureau of Labor Statistics indicate that 774,000 part-time workers give child-care problems as their reason for working part-time (U. S. Bureau of the Census, 1996b). In addition, many low-income jobs do not provide flexibility in work schedules, resulting in a higher incidence of absenteeism among low-income workers with child-care problems.

CONTRIBUTORS TO WORK INTERFERENCE

Employees with the highest rates of absenteeism are generally single women with children younger than five years old. The rates increase with the number of children per family (Galinsky, 1988; Ferber et al, 1991). Klein (1986) found that women with a child under 6 years old missed an average of 12.8 days of work per year, while women with a child between the ages of 6 and 17 missed only 6.7 days per year.

Neal et al., (1993) found that having a child with a disability was associated with greater absenteeism. Moreover, the severity of the child's disability tends to be inversely related to the likelihood of maternal participation in the labor market (Breslau, Salkever & Staruch, 1982); mothers of children with disabilities usually work because of the added financial burdens associated with raising children who have special needs (Bagnato, Kontos & Neisworth, 1987; Urdent, 1987; Scarr et al., 1989; Betz, Unger, Frager, Test & Smith, 1990; Crowley, 1990). However, the impact of a child's disability on the mother's labor-force participation has been found to vary by race and income. Disability has a greater negative impact on maternal employment among African-American and low-income families than among white and high-income families (Breslau, et al., 1982).

As mentioned earlier, gender-role divisions in modern society produce differences in the child-care responsibilities and work-place experiences of working mothers and working fathers. Probably as a result of these differences, work-place interference associated with family responsibilities is found in 39 percent of women (Fernandez, 1986) but only 13 percent of men (Galinsky & Hughes, 1987). A BLS study found absenteeism rates of women workers aged 25 to 34 to be 9.7 days per year, compared to 4.8 days per year for men in the same age group (Hedges, 1977).

Burden and Googins (1987) found no gender differences when the extent of family duties were controlled, suggesting that a primary reason for women's higher levels of absenteeism is the fact that they tend to have primary responsibility for child care and other family responsibilities (Bonilla, 1989). From this perspective, men's lower absenteeism rates may result from the women in their families taking the bulk of the responsibility for child care and child-care arrangements, i.e., "absenteeism for men was low because the women's was high" (Emlen and Koren, 1984, p. 6). To what extent are such gender differences impacted by characteristics both at work and within the family? In Chapter 9, we will examine the important influence of gender, as well as race and ethnicity and occupational status as they relate to the strain experienced by working parents and others with family-care responsibilities.

SUMMARY

The interface between work and parenthood has changed dramatically during the latter half of the twentieth century. Changes in women's work patterns, increased numbers of single parents, increased intrafamilial and interfamilial mobility, and the deterioration of traditional communal support structures have contributed to pressures on working parents. At home, parents experience the time pressures of combining work and family as well as the psychological and financial benefits that work affords. For many parents, involvement in the work force is positive, with working mothers generally reporting higher levels of psychological and physical health than nonworking mothers.

Working parents remain vulnerable to role strain and other stresses at work and at home. At work, parents struggle to complete their job responsibilities in the face of children's illnesses and breakdowns in child-care arrangements. Women are especially vulnerable to absenteeism and other work-place impacts, given societal gender-role expectations that women retain primary responsibility for child care. Child-care resources have not expanded sufficiently to meet the needs of working parents. For most parents, high-quality day care is unavailable or unaffordable, and even adequate child care remains "hard to find and difficult to manage" (Emlen & Koren, 1988). At the same time, job demands remain high, and the American work place affords parents little chance of accommodating their work activities to support their roles as parents.

Society is now faced with the challenge of identifying and supporting strategies that have the potential to yield productive workers, produce healthy children, support well-functioning families, and enhance individual well-being. These goals can be accomplished only by further understanding the interactive relationship between work and family and the conditions that result in effectively integrating satisfying work and family lives.

· 3 ·

ADULT CARE AND
THE WORK PLACE

INTRODUCTION

In this chapter, we examine the situation faced by workers who are providing assistance to elderly and/or disabled adults, an expanding and sometimes hidden group, which comprises nearly one out of every four persons in the U. S. labor force. The term "caregiver" has been used to refer to individuals who provide direct or indirect physical assistance, financial aid, or emotional support to adult family members or friends who have physical, cognitive, or emotional disabilities. Existing research indicates that employed caregivers experience emotional and financial strain, as well as salutary consequences, as a result of their adult-care responsibilities. Working caregivers, like working parents, are faced with the challenge of combining potentially competing family-care and job responsibilities, frequently making substantial accommodations in one or both of these roles.

Most of the existing literature on caregiving focuses almost exclusively on caregivers for elderly persons, typically ignoring those who give care to disabled recipients under age 65. In this chapter, we examine both of these groups of caregivers. We will also examine the accommodations made by employees in their effort to provide care for an elderly or other disabled adult while fulfilling their work responsibilities and the factors that impact their success in balancing these dual roles.

The Need for Care

The General Accounting Office estimates that more than 12 million adults have physical or mental disabilities necessitating ongoing assistance with day-to-day activities. Approximately 2 million of these disabled persons live in nursing homes or other institutions, while more than 10 million are cared for at home or in the community, primarily by family members. Moreover, some demographers estimate that the number of persons requiring long-term care may double within the next 25 years, as the baby boom generation grows older (U.S. General Accounting Office, 1995a).

The need for assistance is especially great among older adults. Data from the 1993 *National Health Interview Survey* (Crimmins, Saito & Reynolds, 1997) indicate that 6.4 percent of community-dwelling elderly persons (age 70 and older) are functionally disabled, requiring assistance with one or more activities of daily living (ADLs), such as bathing, eating, walking, and dressing (Katz, Ford, Moskowitz, Jackson & Jaffee, 1963). Another 13.8 percent need assistance with instrumental activities of daily living (IADLs), such as using the telephone, shopping, cooking, doing laundry, driving, taking medicines, and budgeting (Lawton & Brody, 1969; Doty, 1986).

While the likelihood of disability increases with age, it should be noted that, at any particular time, more than 75 percent of people aged 65 or over do *not* need assistance with any activities of daily living. Contrary to popular conceptions, only about 5 percent of older adults are receiving assistance in nursing homes or other residential care facilities, while about 18 percent are disabled and managing in noninstitutional settings. Of the 18 percent receiving care in noninstitutional settings, two-thirds require assistance with IADLs only, and only 19 percent are seriously disabled with five or six ADL limitations (Brody, 1985).

While most research on caregiving has targeted the caregivers of recipients aged 65 and older, about 40 percent of adults with disabilities are younger than 65. The General Accounting Office estimates that about 5 million adults age 18–64 require assistance with day-to-day activities, including 710,000 who reside in institutional settings and 4.4 million who live in the community and are assisted primarily by family members (U.S. General Accounting Office, 1995b).

There is some evidence that disability rates are declining. The *National Long-term Care Survey* found that the proportion of the elderly population with chronic disabilities dropped from 23.7 percent to 22.6 percent between 1982 and 1989 (Manton, Corder & Stallard, 1993). Data from the *National Health Interview Survey* (Crimmins et al., 1997) of noninstitutionalized persons in the United States, which has been administered annually since 1957, found that the percentage of community-dwelling elderly persons (age 70 and older) who are disabled with regard to ADLs or IADLs declined from 21.1 to 19.5 percent (a proportional decline of 8%) between 1982 and 1993, adjusting for changes in sample composition over time. The prevalence of work disability, defined as the inability to perform work because of a physical, mental, or other health condition, also declined between 1980 and 1990, from 85.2 to 81.5 per 1000 adults ages 18 to 64 (Manton et al., 1993). However, the overall number of Americans requiring assistance is increasing, largely as a result of demographic changes that are resulting in increasing numbers of older adults.

PREVALENCE OF CAREGIVING

About one-sixth of U.S. households provide care to an elderly or disabled adult, although estimates vary based on the population studied and the manner in which care is defined. A 1996 National Council on Aging (NCOA) telephone survey of a representative sample of 10,000 Americans over the age of 18 found that 13 percent, representing 25 million Americans, had provided either direct or indirect assistance to someone age 55 or older within the past 12 months (NCOA, 1997). Another telephone survey of a representative sample of English-speaking adults conducted at about the same time by the National Alliance for Caregiving and the American Association of Retired Persons (NAC/AARP) estimated that approximately 16 percent of respondents, representing about 15 million U. S. households, were currently providing assistance to someone aged 50 or older, and another 6 percent had done so within the past year (NAC/AARP, 1997).

According to the 1996 NAC/AARP survey, 64 percent of these caregivers are working, 52 percent full-time and 12 percent part-time (NAC/AARP, 1997). These findings are somewhat higher than previous estimates. The 1987 AARP/Travelers survey, for example, found that 55 percent of caregivers were employed (42 percent full-time and 13 percent part-time) (AARP/Travelers, 1988). In 1982, the *National Informal Caregivers Survey* found that only about 31 percent of caregivers were employed (Stone, Cafferata & Sangl, 1987).

Similar prevalence rates of caregiving have been found among employee groups. A 1992 meta-analysis of studies of caregiving employees found a mean prevalence rate of 21.1 percent (Gorey, et al., 1992). Neal and her colleagues found that 23 percent of workers responding to a survey distributed at 33 Portland-area businesses reported providing care for an elderly person, and 4 percent reported providing care for a disabled adult under the age of 65 (Neal et al., 1993). A survey of a randomly selected stratified sample representing more than 10,000 employees at the University of California, Berkeley, estimated that 20 percent of all employees were providing assistance to an adult family member or friend who had a health problem or disability; approximately 9 percent were caregivers for someone aged 18–64; and approximately 14 percent were caregivers for someone age 65 or older (Scharlach & Fredriksen, 1994). In addition, 12 percent of employees indicated that they had provided care in the previous year, and 31 percent anticipated having care responsibilities in the ensuing five years. These findings suggest that, for a majority of employees, caregiving will be an issue at some point during their work lives.

Employed women are as likely as nonworking women to become caregivers (Moen, Robison & Fields, 1994; Stern, 1996). Moreover, some studies have found that employed caregivers are no more likely than nonworking caregivers to relinquish their caregiving responsibilities (Boaz & Muller, 1992). It also is important to note that the number of years spent providing adult care is typically considerably less than the number of years spent working. For example, Moen and her colleagues found that women born between 1905 and 1934 spent an average of 17.5 years in paid work between the ages of 18 and 55, but only 2 years providing caregiving (Moen et al., 1994).

WORKING CAREGIVERS

Characteristics of Caregivers

According to the 1996 NAC/AARP survey, the typical caregiver is "a married woman in her mid-forties who works full-time, is a high-school graduate, and has an annual household income of $35,000" (NAC/AARP, 1997, p. 8). Compared to same age noncaregivers, caregivers are less likely to be employed, more likely to be below the poverty line, and their self-reported health is lower (Biegel, Sales & Schultz, 1991).

Employed caregivers tend to differ somewhat from this profile. Caregivers engaged in full-time employment tend to be younger than their nonworking counterparts, more likely to be male, college educated, have higher incomes, and have secondary rather than primary caregiving responsibilities (AARP/Travelers, 1988). They also tend to care for individuals who are less impaired, they are less likely to reside with the care recipient, and they tend to spend less time providing direct care.

Although most employed caregivers provide care to just one person (almost 70 percent), 23 percent take care of two people, and 8 percent take care of three or more people (NAC/AARP, 1997). Asian and African-American caregivers are especially likely to be involved in caring for more than one person (NAC/AARP, 1997; Travelers, 1985). The 1996 NAC/AARP study found that 35 percent of caregiving employees were the primary caregiver, down from almost 60 percent in 1987 (Wagner, 1997).

CAREGIVER AGE

The average age of employed caregivers is about 47 years (Gorey, Brice & Rice, 1992; NAC/AARP, 1997); the median age at which women begin caregiving is 42 years (Moen et al., 1994). Asian and Hispanic caregivers have average ages of about 40, and more than one-third are under 35 (compared with only one in five of white caregivers who are under 35) (NAC/AARP, 1997).

GENDER

Women are more likely than their male counterparts to take on care responsibilities for disabled family members; indeed, two-thirds to three-fourths of all caregivers are female (Barr, 1990). Caregiving women are less likely than male caregivers to be employed full-time. There is some evidence that caregiving is more common among women whose lifestyles have been more traditional, such as women who married earlier, had more children, and participated in volunteer roles rather than paid employment (Robison, Moen & Dempster-McClain, 1995).

RACE/ETHNICITY

There is a relatively small body of research on racial and ethnic variations in caregiving; most of the existing studies examine the experiences of white and African-American caregivers only. Although the evidence is somewhat equivocal, there seems to be a slightly higher prevalence of caregiving among African-American and Hispanic employees than among White employees (Fredriksen, 1993b), particularly for care recipients younger than 65. Hispanics are three times more likely than other ethnic groups to be taking care of an adult child. Hispanics and African-Americans are more likely than whites or Asians to be providing care to an adult aged 18–64 (Fredriksen, 1993b).

Ethnic and racial differences are seen also in the percentages of caregivers who are employed full-time (NAC/AARP, 1997). Fewer than 56 percent of white, African-American, and Hispanic caregivers are employed full-time, compared to more than 63.3 percent of Asian caregivers. Hispanics have the highest proportion of nonemployed caregivers (28 percent), followed by African-Americans at 20.3 percent, whites at 18.9 percent, and Asians at 18.2 percent.

Care Recipient Characteristics and Impairment

Care recipients are an average age of 77 years old, with 64 percent over age 75. Care recipients are typically female relatives: 31 percent of caregivers take care of their own mothers, 9 percent care for a mother-in-law, and 12 percent take care of a grandmother (NAC/AARP, 1997). Elderly care recipients are most likely to be the employee's parent or parent-in-law, while care recipients under the age of 65 are about as likely to be a parent, a spouse, a child, or another relative (Neal et al., 1993; Scharlach & Fredriksen, 1994). Of all racial/ethnic groups, Asians are the least likely to be caring for a spouse (only 1 percent) and the most likely to be assisting a father (18 percent) (NAC/AARP, 1997).

The 1996 NAC/AARP survey found that only 17 percent of care recipients lived with their caregivers, down from 32 percent in the 1987 survey (NAC/AARP, 1997). More than one-fourth of the care recipients lived at least 100 miles away from the caregiver (National Council on the Aging, 1997). Asian care recipients were more likely to live in the same household as their caregiver than were African-Americans or whites (NAC/AARP, 1997). Other studies have found that younger care recipients (ages 18–64) are more likely to share a residence with their caregiver than are older care recipients (65 and older) (Scharlach & Fredriksen, 1994).

In contrast to some popular stereotypes, the percentage of U.S. households containing elderly parents and their adult children is approximately the same as it was at the end of the nineteenth century. One popular image of family history is that until recently, there were many multi-generational families living under one roof. However, until the 1900s, most grandparents did not live long enough to require intensive caretaking. According to a study in Massachusetts by Hareven and Adams (1996), the cohort of children born between 1920–1929 and coming of age around World War II was the first to experience caring for "old old" parents. When more than one parent needed assistance, typically each parent would live with a different sibling. Even when parents did not live in the same household as adult children, the caregiver, usually the daughter, would still do many household tasks for her parents, often balancing the needs of parents, her own family, and work. There is evidence that more recent cohorts of caregivers are actually more likely to reside with disabled family members than were caregivers born earlier in this century, perhaps reflecting the increased likelihood of chronic, disabling conditions, as well as the increased number of years during which individuals can expect to live with those conditions (Moen et al., 1994).

CARE RECIPIENT HEALTH CONDITIONS

A variety of health crises and chronic conditions create a need for long-term care. In elderly persons, arthritis and heart disease are the two most common conditions (U.S. General Accounting Office, 1995b). Younger care recipients, by comparison, tend to suffer from a wider array of disabling conditions including cancer, heart conditions, AIDS, psychiatric conditions, and degenerative diseases such as multiple sclerosis. On average, older care recipients of employed persons are more disabled physically and cognitively than younger care recipients (Scharlach & Fredriksen, 1994). For the most part, recipients' conditions are long-term or chronic; only about 10 percent have conditions that are expected to last three months or less (NAC/AARP, 1997).

DEMENTIA

Approximately 20 percent of caregivers say they take care of someone with Alzheimer's disease or another dementia as the primary or secondary illness. Dementia is especially likely to be identified among African-American care recipients, and least likely among Asian care recipients. The cognitive impairment and behavior disorders often associated with dementia create unique stressors for caregivers. Further, cognitively impaired elderly persons living in the community have been found to be more likely than the cognitively intact to be ADL disabled (Spector, 1991), thus necessitating greater levels of care. Virtually all Alzheimer's and other dementia caregiving studies published in the last decade have reported high levels of burden and distress (Schulz, O'Brien, Bookwala & Fleissner, 1995). Specific problems related to the care of Alzheimer's patients include feeling overwhelmed, being depressed or anxious, having strained relationships with other family members, and feeling that life is uncontrollable (Zarit, Reever & Bach-Peterson, 1980; Barnes, Raskind, Scott & Murphy, 1981; Rabins, Mace & Lucas, 1982; Morycz, 1985). The 1996 NAC/AARP survey reports that those caring for someone with dementia are more likely than other caregivers to have had less time for other family members or leisure activities (66 percent) (NAC/AARP, 1997).

DEVELOPMENTAL DISABILITIES

Cognitive and behavioral disabilities are also often a feature of developmental disability. Family members are the most consistent source of care for people with developmental disabilities throughout the lifespan (Heller, 1993). Approximately 85 percent of persons with mental retardation live with their parents (Fujiura, Garza & Braddock, 1989). As people with developmental disabilities age, family coping often becomes more difficult, and the likelihood of out-of-home placement can increase, perhaps due to the non-normative nature of the caregiving (Farber, 1959; Myers, Borthwick & Eyman, 1985). The key characteristics associated with caregiver burden among persons caring for adults with developmental disabilities are poor physical health of the care recipient, maladaptive behaviors, severe retardation, and low adaptive behavior (Black, Cohn, Smull & Crites, 1985; Heller & Factor, 1988; Seltzer & Krauss, 1989).

MENTAL ILLNESS

Caregivers of mentally ill adults face many of the same dilemmas as caregivers of adults with developmental disabilities: non-normative care, the realization that their child will not experience a normal life, concerns about what will happen when they are no longer able to provide care (Greenberg, Seltzer & Greenley, 1993). In addition to these, caring for a mentally ill adult poses some special problems for the caregiver. The course of mental illness is unstable, and caregivers cannot be certain how the recipient will react in everyday situations. In their comparison of caregivers of adults with mental illness and adults with developmental disabilities, Greenberg et al. (1993) found that mothers of mentally ill adults were more burdened, had poorer relationships with the care recipient, had fewer social support resources, and had a greater likelihood of unrelenting contact with the care recipient, as only about half left during the day for a job or day program. Jones and Jones (1994) reported a number of behaviors bothersome to caregivers of mentally ill adults, including embarrassing behaviors such as talking inappropriately or throwing things, and excessive demands and attention-seeking behaviors.

TYPES AND AMOUNTS OF ASSISTANCE PROVIDED

Caregivers provide a range of direct services to their care recipients, including help with personal care activities (ADLs) such as bathing, grooming, dressing, feeding, and toileting; and with instrumental activities (IADLs) such as household chores, errands, arranging care, financial management, and direct financial help. Existing research suggests that working caregivers provide less assistance and also spend less time in caregiving activities than nonemployed caregivers. More than half of all caregivers (employed and nonemployed) help with at least one ADL, and 29 percent help with at least three. In comparison, some studies have found that only about 3 percent of employees provide assistance with ADLs (Travelers, 1985; Scharlach & Boyd, 1989).

The vast majority of assistance provided by employees is less intensive instrumental care. More than one-third of employed caregivers assist with home maintenance activities and repairs, and more than one-fourth do housecleaning, make phone calls for care recipients, and/or manage the care recipient's finances (Wagner, 1997). An additional 10 percent provide only financial assistance (Scharlach, 1988).

Employed caregivers tend to spend less time providing direct assistance than do nonemployed caregivers. In general, the average caregiver provides care for 18 hours per week. Close to one in five provides either "constant care" or at least 40 hours of care per week (NAC/AARP, 1997). Caregivers who work full-time, on the other hand, spend an average of 6 to 10 hours per week providing services to their disabled parents or other family members (AARP/Travelers, 1988). Still, a number of employees do spend a significant amount of time providing care. Twenty-seven percent spend more than 20 hours per week providing care and about eight percent spend 35 hours or more (Travelers, 1985; AARP/Travelers, 1988). In general, the number of hours of care provided was substantially lower in 1996 than in 1987 (Wagner, 1997).

Some studies suggest that having a job may contribute to decreased amounts of caregiving by men but not by women (Stoller, 1983). A study of pairs of sisters, one of whom was employed and one of whom was not employed, found that the two groups did not differ in the amount of care they provided for their elderly parents (Matthews, Werkner & Delaney, 1989). Similar findings were obtained by Brody in a study comparing employed and unemployed caregiving daughters (Brody & Schoonover, 1986). Differences in employment status do affect how women attend to caregiving responsibilities. Employed daughters typically share the responsibilities of personal care and cooking with other family members or paid caregivers, whereas unemployed daughters usually perform those activities single-handedly, perhaps because they have fewer financial resources with which to purchase paid caregiving assistance (Noelker & Poulshock, 1982; Archbold, 1983; Kinnear & Graycar, 1984).

A study by Steuve and O'Donnell (1984) revealed a more complex relationship between employment of caregiving daughters and the effect on their parents. Employment had little or no impact on the amount of caregiving when the parents were extremely sick; both employed and unemployed daughters assisted their parents when they were seriously ill. However, employed daughters provided less care when parents were only moderately sick or disabled.

The amount of care required is directly related to the extent and type of care recipient disability. One study that utilized daily diaries to track the amount of care provided to demented elders found that severely cognitively impaired elders received an average of 8 hours per day of care, while mildly and moderately impaired elders received about 3 hours per day (Hu, Huang & Cartwright, 1986). One exception is the care of nonelderly adults. Employees who care for adults under the age of 65 provide more hours of direct assistance per week, even though care recipients under the age of 65 tend to be less functionally and cognitively impaired than elderly care recipients (Scharlach & Fredriksen, 1994). In addition, they provide more intensive personal care, spend more time housekeeping and administering medications, and incur greater financial costs, even though they have lower incomes on average than caregivers of older persons.

Direct versus Indirect Services

Although almost three in four caregivers (73 percent) report that someone else helps provide care to their recipient, only about one-sixth of workers who provide care for elderly relatives receive assistance from a paid provider, such as a home-health worker. About one-half receive help from family members or friends. The remaining third receive no outside assistance (Stone et al., 1987; Scharlach, 1988). Formal care services (those provided by persons other than family members) have been estimated to provide less than 15 percent of the total number of care days for services such as home-health care, housework, and adult day care (Doty, Liu & Wiener, 1985), although caregiver use of such services seems to have increased dramatically in the past decade (Wagner, 1997).

Gender, economic status, and race affect whether a caregiver provides care directly or arranges for someone else to do so. Arranging for an outside care provider involves finding out what resources are available and assisting dependent family members in acquiring the appropriate kinds of assistance. Among university personnel, faculty and administrators were more likely to arrange for care, whereas clerical, service, and trade staff were more likely to provide direct care, including transportation, housekeeping, administering medications, and providing personal care (Fredriksen & Scharlach, 1997). In addition, proportionally more support staff were women and they were more likely to be non-white, unmarried, in fair or poor health, and have lower incomes than professionals and administrators.

Financial Support

In 1993, Americans spent almost $108 billion for long-term care of persons with disabilities. Although federal and state spending accounted for 64 percent of this total, the remaining 36 percent, amounting to more than $38 billion, was paid directly by individuals and their families (U.S. General Accouting Office, 1995b). Estimates of the percentage of adults who assist their parents financially—in addition to in-kind assistance (clothes, food, and the like)—vary from 10 to 50 percent (Horowitz, 1985).

Families with a care recipient have an average of $100 to $200 a month in extra expenses (Scharlach, 1988; Brody, 1990), representing about 5 percent of the typical monthly income of caregivers who are employed full-time (*Fortune* and John Hancock, 1989). Employed caregivers provide about the same amount of financial assistance as those who are not employed, although it represents a smaller proportion of their household income. When the amount of care provided is translated into market value (using the approximate median wage of a professional Home Health Aid of $8.00 an hour as a proxy), caring for a severely demented elder costs caregivers the equivalent of about $64 a day, while caring for a mildly or moderately impaired elder costs about $24 (Hu et al., 1986).

A small but still significant percentage of caregivers experience financial strain. Data from the 1987–1988 *National Survey of Caregivers* indicate that more than 60 percent of working caregivers incur added costs associated with providing care, spending an average of 5 percent of their monthly income on caregiving expenses (AARP/Travelers, 1988). Only 7 percent of caregivers define their expenses as a financial hardship; however, some groups of caregivers experience a more severe financial impact than others. These include those who tend to more severely disabled care recipients and spend more time performing caregiving tasks, those who care for nonelderly adults, those who lack a college education, and those who earn $15,000 a year or less (Hirst 1985; Scharlach & Fredriksen, 1994; NAC/AARP, 1997). Twice as many African-American and Hispanic caregivers report financial hardships as white and Asian caregivers.

IMPACT OF CAREGIVING
AND WORK RESPONSIBILITIES

Positive Impact on the Caregiver

Whether or not caregivers work, the experience of providing care for an ill or disabled family member can impact individuals and families in a variety of ways. Of special interest in this book is how the balance of work and family demands combined with available resources relates to employed caregivers' positive or negative experiences.

Although adult care can be extremely stressful, many caregivers find the overall experience to be quite positive. A study of caregiving employees at Transamerica Life Insurance Companies, for example, found that two-thirds of the employees evaluated the overall experience of caregiving as mostly positive, while 31 percent saw it as mostly negative, and 2 percent as neutral (Scharlach, 1994). Among caregivers responding to a national survey of family caregivers (NAC/AARP, 1997), 75 percent used positive words to describe their caregiving experience, such as "rewarding," "helpful," "happy," "thankful," "grateful," "enjoyable," and "love." Positive attributes of caregiving included fulfillment from caring for a loved one, the sense of fulfilling one's responsibilities, being able to repay care to a former caretaker, knowing that the care recipient is receiving good care, the opportunity for physical and emotional closeness with the care recipient, and financial benefits of pooling income or assets (NAC/AARP, 1997). Helping others, moreover, has been found to increase one's sense of personal control over life, contributing to better personal psychological well-being (Krause, Herzog & Baker, 1992).

Caregiving Strain

The majority of employed caregivers, however, also experience some negative impacts associated with their care responsibilities, including emotional strain, family conflict, health problems, financial hardships, work disruptions, and job terminations. Multiple roles have been associated with increased caregiver burden, fatigue, depression, and other symptoms of emotional stress (Horowitz, 1985a; Brody, 1990; Neal et al., 1993; Brody, 1995), and feelings such as anger, anxiety, and self-blame (Sizemore & Jones, 1990). Among respondents to the NAC/AARP (1997) survey of family caregivers, one-third of caregivers describe their experience in negative terms such as "stressful," "burdened," "tired," and "exhausting." While we have information that describes the extent of strain experienced by employed caregivers, we still know relatively little about how the interplay between work and family characteristics impacts caregiving strain.

Studies of ill or disabled persons provide extensive evidence of the strains that can be experienced by their caregiving family members. Women caring for a severely disabled adult son or daughter, for example, experience higher levels of psychiatric disturbance and chronic illness than women of comparable age and marital status in the general population (Hirst, 1985). Studies of adults with cancer (Wellisch, Jamison & Pasnau 1978; American Cancer Society 1979; Lewis 1986; Northouse & Swain 1987), heart attacks (Dhooper 1983; Ell & Northen 1990), and strokes and other neurological injuries (Lezak 1978; Brown & McCormick 1988; Schultz, Tompkins & Rau 1988) indicate that their spouses experience increased emotional distress, sleep disturbance, eating disorders, and restricted social activities. The demands of providing care to a disabled person can put caregivers at increased risk of becoming depressed (McLanahan & Monson, 1990). Clinical depression is typically found in more than 18 percent of caregivers, compared with fewer than 6 percent of noncaregivers (Schultz et al., 1995). Family members of persons with AIDS may be particularly at risk for emotional distress and social isolation (Macklin, 1988; Turner, Pearlin & Mullan, 1989).

A number of factors contribute to the emotional strain of caregivers. These include watching a loved one experiencing an illness or disability, the stress of relating to care recipients who are depressed or uncooperative, and care recipient behavior problems such as wandering, screaming, and destroying property (Scharlach, 1994). Caregivers also experience emotional strain from such factors as lack of free time, socioeconomic pressures, and the caregiver's own health problems.

Much of the literature on caregivers with dual (work and caregiving) roles emphasizes the role strain experienced by the caregivers. Working caregivers report higher levels of stress in combining work and family responsibilities than do noncaregivers. Scharlach and Boyd (1989) found that 25 percent of employed caregivers experience job-family conflict as compared to 11 percent of noncaregiver employees. Seventy-five percent of employed caregivers find that their work and family responsibilities are in conflict with each other to some extent (Travelers, 1985; Gibeau, Anastas & Larson, 1987; Scharlach & Boyd, 1989).

Role strain experienced by working caregivers can have secondary effects on their care recipients, although caregivers' employment status does not, in and of itself, seem to predict increased likelihood of institutionalization of disabled elders (Kasper, Steinbach & Andrews, 1990). Caregiver burden has been implicated as a significant contributor to institutionalization of disabled elderly persons (McFall & Miller, 1992). Increased caregiving demands, particularly when they entail greater performance of physical tasks, can increase the caregiver's desire to seek institutional placement for the care recipient (Morycz, 1985). Care recipients whose caregivers are employed and experience high levels of caregiving stress are apt to experience a significantly higher than average risk of institutionalization. To what extent are levels of role strain impacted by the relative balance of employed caregivers' work and family demands and the resources they have available to them? In Chapter 7, we will examine the interaction between family care responsibilities and work demands as they relate to the stress and strain experienced by employed caregivers.

Impact on Family Relationships and Personal Life

Caregivers also report higher levels of stress in family relationships than do noncaregivers (Neal, et al. 1993). More than 40 percent report that their caregiving responsibilities leave them less time for other family members than before. An equal proportion say that caregiving has necessitated giving up vacations, hobbies, or other personal activities. Those with the most intensive caregiving responsibilities, both in terms of hours of care and types of assistance provided, experience the most family conflict. Younger caregivers experience more family conflict than older caregivers, perhaps because they are more likely to have young children and spouses (NAC/AARP, 1997).

Impact on Caregiver Health

Caregiving can affect caregivers' health and physical well-being. Caregivers tend to report more physical ailments than noncaregivers, including arthritis, back trouble, hearing problems, insomnia, rectal problems, and diabetes (Pruchno & Postashnik, 1989; Scharlach, Runkle, Midanik & Soghikian, 1994; Schultz et al., 1995). Some groups of caregivers have been found to exhibit poorer immune function, more respiratory tract infections, lower antibody and virus-specific T-cell responses to influenza, and slower rates of wound healing (Vitaliano, Schultz, Kiecolt-Glaser & Grant, 1997).

Physical strain is especially great among caregivers with the heaviest care responsibilities, including those who care for family members with Alzheimer's disease and those who provide 40 or more hours of care per week and assist with at least two ADLs (NAC/AARP, 1997; Scharlach et al., 1997). Caregivers with heavy caregiving demands do not get as much exercise as other caregivers, for example, putting them at risk for future health problems (Scharlach et al., 1997). Lack of social support also increases the likelihood that caregivers will experience age-related heart problems (Vitaliano et al., 1997).

Deleterious health consequences of caregiving are far from universal, however. Self-rated health is not generally found to be lower in caregivers than other members of representative adult samples (Scharlach, Sobel & Roberts, 1991). Moreover, more than half of caregivers report no physical strain as a result of their caregiving activities (NAC/AARP, 1997). Some studies suggest that caregivers might go to greater lengths to prevent health problems than do non-caregivers. For example, caregivers are more likely than comparison groups of noncaregivers to eat breakfast every day, get flu shots, and pneumonia vaccines. They are also less likely to smoke and they drink less alcohol than the national average for their age group (Scharlach et al., 1997). Caregivers do not typically utilize health-care services to a greater extent than noncaregivers (Scharlach et al., 1994), although this might be because they do not have time to attend to their own conditions, or they underestimate their medical needs by comparing them to the relatively more serious circumstances of their care recipients.

Impact on Work

WORK-PLACE ACCOMMODATIONS

Employed caregivers are frequently forced to make substantial accommodations in their work activities, to balance effectively the potentially competing demands of work and family roles. Indeed, more than half the respondents to a national survey of family caregiving (NAC/AARP, 1997) had made changes at work to accommodate caregiving. However, the types and extent of accommodations vary greatly, and the majority of caregiving employees do not experience substantial amounts of time away from work because of their adult-care responsibilities. In Chapter 7, we will explore how both family and work characteristics impact the level of work-place accommodations made by employed caregivers.

Caregiving responsibilities can necessitate taking time from work for such tasks as taking the care recipient to a doctor's appointment, completing errands, or arranging services for the care recipient. Among employed caregivers responding to the 1996 NAC/AARP survey, more than one-half reported losing time from work as a result of their caregiving duties (NAC/AARP, 1997). This was up from only about one-third in 1987 (AARP/Travelers, 1988). Women caregivers work between two and four fewer hours per week, and between one and three fewer weeks per year, than other female employees (McLanahan & Monson, 1990). Women caring for disabled elders lose more work time than women with school-age children, but less than those with preschool children.

In addition to losing time at work, 30 percent of employed caregivers reportedly change their work schedules to accommodate caregiving responsibilities (Stone et al., 1987). Some reduce their hours to the extent that their jobs change from full-time to part-time employment, as was reported by 7 percent of respondents to the NAC/AARP survey (NAC/AARP, 1997). Female employees are more likely to make these adjustments than their male counterparts (McLanahan & Monson, 1990). Female caregivers are also less able to work overtime, and are more likely to reduce their work hours or quit work altogether.

Most of the evidence of work impact is based on employee self-reports, which have been criticized as subjective and based on the possibility of reverse causality (that changes in work activity promote caregiving activity rather than vice versa). To address these issues, Stern utilized nonlinear estimation techniques to examine the relationship between caregiver status, caregiver characteristics, and working arrangements among adult children of elderly persons (Stern, 1996). Stern found unequivocal evidence that providing care for an elderly parent significantly impacts the number of hours worked. Work status, on the other hand, was found to have little or no impact on the decision to provide care. Other research suggests that caregiving may have the greatest impact on reducing work hours from full-time to part-time, with little or no impact on reductions from part-time to no work (Boaz & Muller, 1992).

EFFECTS ON PRODUCTIVITY

The most frequently cited work-related effect of adult-care responsibilities is decreased productivity (Scharlach, 1994). It is estimated that the average amount of constructive work lost, including time away from work and reduced productivity, is about 8 hours per caregiving employee per month. Caregiving employees attempt to compensate for missed work and reduced productivity by working after hours during the week, working weekends, working at home, and working harder (Scharlach, 1994). However, caregivers' responsibilities can put greater demands on coworkers, as well as absorbing the time of supervisors, who may be called on to arrange coverage for absent employees, counsel about benefits, or provide emotional support. The Metropolitan Life Insurance Company estimates that work disruptions associated with employee caregiving responsibilities affect 25 percent of full-time employees and result in productivity losses of $1,142 per year per employee, for a nationwide total of more than $11 billion. When part-time employees are included, the number rises to $29 billion.

On the positive side, there is also evidence that employees' adult-care responsibilities can have a salutary effect on job performance, which may not be so easily quantified. For example, caregiving employees may be more sensitive and effective in their interactions with customers, have greater self-confidence, and have increased feelings of competence (Scharlach, 1994). Some caregiving employees find their work more enjoyable because they perceive it as a respite from the demands of caregiving.

LEAVE-TAKING, EARLY RETIREMENT, AND QUITTING

Some employees are forced to take a temporary leave of absence or quit work altogether to accommodate their caregiving responsibilities. A national survey of family caregiving found that 20 percent of all caregivers left their jobs either temporarily or permanently because of care responsibilities: 11 percent took a leave of absence, 4 percent took early retirement, and 6 percent gave up work entirely (NAC/AARP, 1997). One study of women caring for their elderly mothers found that 28 percent of the nonworking caregivers had quit their jobs in order to provide care, and 26 percent of the employed caregivers were considering leaving their positions due to their caregiving duties or had already reduced the number of hours they worked (Brody, 1995). Moreover, some caregivers report postponing or abandoning the search for employment because of a family member's ill health (Matthews, et al., 1989). Thus, women who care for a disabled adult son or daughter are much less likely to be in the work force than are other women their age (Hirst, 1985).

Those employees who are caring for the most disabled care recipients are most likely to have to leave their jobs to provide care. Among family members caring for terminally ill cancer patients, for example, more than 25 percent left their jobs to care for their dying loved ones, and almost 67 percent of those who did not officially quit spent time away from work and did not collect salaries (Muurinen, 1986). Quitting one's job to provide terminal care is especially likely among employees who are female, have lower incomes, and/or have fewer years of education. Unfortunately, these are the very employees who most need to work and who are least likely to have substantial financial reserves to see them through a period of unemployment.

Although most caregivers are not forced to make significant changes in career plans or leave their jobs because of the demands of providing care to a disabled adult, those who must do so are apt to suffer long-term economic repercussions, which is one of the factors contributing to the high incidence of poverty among elderly women. Quitting paid jobs, reducing the number of paid working hours, and not seeking or accepting job promotions in order to be a caregiver for an adult disabled relative can entail significant opportunity costs for employees. Leaving a job to provide care to a parent is associated with a reduced salary on the last job, as well as a decrease in total years worked. Women who leave employment for a caregiving role make $3,965 less per year than those who retire for another reason. Lost wages and lost opportunities for promotion detrimentally affect women caregivers' financial situation as they themselves grow older, resulting in reduced social security benefits for female caregivers (since amount of payment is based on lifetime earnings) (Kingson & O'Grady-LeShane, 1993).

Positive Impacts of Working and Caregiving

Although employed caregivers experience higher levels of role strain than their nonworking counterparts, they are not necessarily more depressed or under more stress. An analysis of data from the 1982 *National Long-term Care Survey* by Giele, Mutschler, and Orodenker (1987) found that those caregivers who were employed experienced significantly less stress than did those who were not employed. Some studies have found that working caregivers are less depressed than nonworking caregivers (Tennstedt, Cafferata & Sullivan, 1992). Moreover, working women who have been caregivers display higher levels of mastery, self-esteem, and life satisfaction than those who are not in the labor force (Moen et al., 1995).

At least for some employees, then, working and caring for a disabled adult can have a mutually beneficial impact. In a study by Scharlach (1994), 38 percent of respondents claimed that their job had no negative effects on their caregiving activities. The positive impacts of work on caregiving mentioned by these respondents included the financial benefits, a better relationship with the care recipient due to their job satisfaction, and receiving emotional support from coworkers. More than half of those surveyed described the overall impact of work on caregiving as positive, 27 percent evaluated it as negative, and 18 percent said it was neutral. A number of studies have suggested that working can provide a welcome respite from caregiving (Brody, Kleban, Johnson, Hoffman & Schoonover, 1987; Petty & Friss, 1987; Stone & Short, 1990). It also seems likely that those individuals who are able to take on and maintain caregiving responsibilities while continuing to work may have more psychological, social, and economic resources than many of their nonworking counterparts. Moreover, the experiences of caregiver strain and satisfaction can be understood as two relatively independent psychological processes. Satisfaction, for example, does not mitigate caregiver strain and depression, while burden does not reduce the caregiver's positive affect (Lawton, Rajagopal, Brody & Kleban, 1992).

SUMMARY

As a result of the aging of the population and longer life expectancy, increasing numbers of family members will be providing assistance to an ill or disabled adult relative. Existing research indicates that caregiving employees experience both detrimental and salutary consequences as a result of their multiple responsibilities. Most caregiving employees are able to make the accommodations necessary to balance their work and caregiving responsibilities, with limited impact on their jobs or those that they assist. However, they often do so at some personal cost in terms of physical fatigue, emotional strain, interference with personal relationships and social activities, or financial hardship.

To date we have considerable information that provides a descriptive overview of the caregiving experience and underscores many of the characteristics of caregivers and adult-care recipients. Yet we know relatively little about the interaction between work and adult caregiving and the ways in which caregivers can integrate their work and caregiving responsibilities to minimize the detrimental impacts while maximizing the positive consequences for themselves, their families, and their jobs.

PART TWO

Theory and Research

Conceptual Perspectives on
Family Care and Work

_____

INTRODUCTION

There has been an extensive historical debate regarding the interplay between work and family in American life. The relationship has been characterized at times as symbiotic; at other times it as been described as predominantly conflictual. While scholars from many fields—sociology, psychology, social welfare, demography, law, economics, and others—have entered the debate, there is relatively little agreement about how these two pivotal life foci interface and interact.

This chapter will examine various theoretical approaches that have been employed to describe and understand the interrelationship between family care and employment. The bodies of research addressing the care of children and the care of adults have generally been based on differing underlying assumptions. Role theory, spillover, compensation, and conflict-based conceptual approaches have generally been applied to the care of children. The majority of research on elder care, on the other hand, has incorporated a stress and coping theoretical perspective. This chapter will review these theoretical frameworks as well as life-span approaches and macro-level theories, and examine how they have been utilized to understand the needs and experiences of employees caring for children and ill and disabled adults.

Through examining the various conceptual approaches, theoretical constructs will be highlighted that are most useful for understanding the interplay between work and family. These dimensions of work and family will then be integrated into a family-care model, as outlined in Chapter 5, that can be applied across the range of family-care responsibilities.

WORK AND NONWORK

Early theoretical writings generally viewed work as interdependent and inseparable from other social roles and institutions, although these writings often differed in their analyses in terms of consequence. For example, some theorists viewed the relationship between work and other social roles as inherently alienating (Marx and Engels, 1939), while others advanced a varied, potentially integrative relationship (Durkheim, 1947; Weber, 1947). The majority of recent research has supported the notion of interdependence between work and other life domains (Wilensky, 1960; Swanson, 1992), although a few studies have supported separate, independent relationships (Dubin, 1976; Payton-Miyazakazi & Brayfield, 1976).

Historically, most theoretical and empirical developments in the field have treated work as the primary variable, examining it in relationship to a number of social roles and institutions, including the family. For example, it has been found that certain job characteristics (e.g., status, prestige, tenure, and working outside of the home) correlate positively with overall life satisfaction (Hunt, Near, Rice, Graham & Gutteridge, 1977; Near, Rice & Hunt, 1980), and are related to levels of political participation (Near et al., 1980) and leisure time activities (Parker & Smith, 1976; Near et al., 1980).

Conversely, work-place satisfaction and involvement have been found to be related to various nonwork factors, including employee demographic characteristics (e.g., age, education, race, and religion, but not gender) (Locke, 1976; Near et al., 1980), health status, leisure activities, and type of community (Near et al., 1980). In a comprehensive review of the work-nonwork research, Near et al. (1980) found consistent support for the fact that there are multi-directional interrelationships between work and nonwork roles and behaviors. Specifically, they determined that work-place structures impact attitudes and behaviors outside of work, and that nonwork structures impact work attitudes and behaviors. Although research has demonstrated numerous associations between work and nonwork variables, little is known about the nature and complexities of these relationships (Near et al., 1980; Zedeck & Mosier, 1990; Frone, Russell & Cooper, 1992a; Swanson, 1992).

Work and Life Perspective

Recently there has been a resurgence of interest in the work-nonwork approach. For example, it has been suggested that the work and family field should be redefined and expanded to incorporate a broader work and life perspective. Basically, this approach has been advanced to ensure equity between employees with and without family-care responsibilities and to ensure that all employees have the opportunity to pursue their individual interests and leisure activities regardless of family-care responsibilities.

Although the broader perspective achieves better recognition of the importance and influence of other life domains in relation to work and overall life satisfaction, it has several limitations. First, the work and life perspective reinforces the notion that the care of family members is the sole responsibility of individual families rather than a community concern. Second, the work and life approach advances work as the primary variable, with other social roles and activities assessed in relation to participation and involvement in the work domain. As such, it reinforces a primary limitation of existing research.

WORK AND FAMILY CONCEPTUAL APPROACHES

Separate Spheres Models

In some of the early literature on work and family, an independence or separate spheres model was advanced (Parsons, 1970; Chow & Berheide, 1988). For example, the segmentation theory (Payton-Miyazakazi & Brayfield, 1976; Zedeck and Mosier, 1990) or theory of independence (Burke, 1986) presents a compartmentalized approach to work and family. According to this perspective there is an inherent separation between the two domains, and involvement in one arena does not necessarily impact the other. The two roles are seen as having disparate functions—the family meeting primarily expressive and affective needs, while work serves instrumental purposes within a competitive environment (Parsons, 1970).

Interactive Models

Kanter (1977), in a seminal analysis of the work and family literature, criticized the "myth of separate worlds" and identified key aspects of both spheres that were likely to impact one another. Dimensions of the work experience impacting families included *relative absorptiveness* (demands of work), *time and timing* (scheduling and time requirements of work), *work rewards and resources*, *world view* (work culture), and *emotional climate* (psychological aspects of work). Within the familial domain, the impact of *family culture* (ethnic and cultural traditions) and *family relationships* on work orientation, motivation, and goals were highlighted.

In order to understand the interrelationship of work and family processes such as those outlined by Kanter, a number of theoretical models have been advanced:

> The *instrumental approach* presents work and family as having a symbiotic relationship, each domain serving as a means for obtaining something needed in the other (Payton-Miyazakazi & Brayfield, 1976; Burke, 1986; Zedeck & Mosier, 1990). For example, work provides economic sustenance and material gain for the family.

> *Spillover theory* postulates that the various spheres of life (such as work and family) have the potential to impact one another both positively and negatively (Champoux, 1978; Near et al., 1980; Staines, 1980; Zedeck &

Mosier, 1990; Barnett, 1994; Williams & Alliger, 1994). It is assumed that attitudes and behaviors cross over between work and family, such that (for example) satisfaction at the work place creates satisfaction at home and vice versa.

Compensation theory presents a compensatory approach to the interrelationship between work and family. This theory posits that deficits in one domain (e.g., work) are offset or made up by fulfillment in another (e.g., family) (Champoux, 1978; Near et al., 1980; Staines, 1980; Burke, 1986; Zedeck & Mosier, 1990; Hochschild, 1997). For example, if one's family provides limited stimulation or reward, it is assumed that other life roles or activities (e.g. work involvement) will provide challenge and fulfillment.

According to *conflict theory*, the differentiation between work and family results in dissension. This perspective maintains that the domains of work and family are generally incompatible, given their differing demands, responsibilities, expectations, and norms (Payton-Miyazakazi & Brayfield, 1976; Zedeck & Mosier, 1990; Burke, 1994). For example, it is assumed that a satisfying and demanding occupation will inevitably result in sacrifices in the family domain.

Research on Work-Family Models

Research examining the relationships proposed by these theoretical perspectives is limited in scope, and has focused primarily on the applicability of spillover, compensation and conflict theories (Champoux, 1978; Staines, 1980; Small & Riley, 1990; Hochschild, 1997). A spillover effect from work to family has been documented in a number of studies (Staines, 1980; Crouter, Huston & Robbins, 1983; Small & Riley, 1990; Higgins, Duxbury & Irving, 1992; Barnett, 1994). Small and Riley (1990), for example, found time, energy, and psychological processes evident in work spillover into family and personal life. In another study (Higgins et al., 1992), work conflict was found to be the strongest predictor of family conflict. Further, Williams and Alliger (1994) found that juggling multiple roles and demands impacted mood in both work and family, with unpleasant mood spilling over from work to home and home to work.

In an early review of the literature, Staines (1980) concluded that the majority of existing research supported a spillover effect between work and nonwork roles, including the family. However, under variable circumstances there was also evidence of a compensatory effect between work and nonwork roles. For example, Piotrkowski (1979) noted that within working-class families men who lacked satisfaction at the work place tended to seek it from their family life. More recently, Hoshchild (1997) found that time is a scarce commodity among most American workers, and corporations are increasingly able to absorb more family time in part because women feel more rewarded and appreciated at the work place than they do as a result of their family and home responsibilities.

Several studies have analyzed areas of the conflict resulting from the juxtaposition of work and family functioning (Barling, 1990), including family and psychological well-being (Olson & Hamilton McCubbin, 1983; Matthews, Conger & Wickrama, 1996), marital functioning (Scarr et al., 1989; Barling, 1990; Pittman, 1994; Burley, 1995; Matthews et al., 1996), child development (Scarr et al., 1989) and gender roles and responsibilities (Matthews & Rodin, 1989; Scarr et al., 1989; McBride, 1990; Burley, 1995).

The majority of this research has focused on the prevalence, degree, duration, and consequences of conflict, work strain, and stress overload between work and family-care responsibilities. For example, in a study that analyzed work-family conflict and marital outcomes, Matthews et al. (1996) found that work-family conflict resulting from husbands' and wives' work is positively related to their psychological distress, which is related both directly and indirectly to marital outcomes through their marital interactions, e.g., greater hostility, less warmth and supportiveness.

Integrating work and family results in great variation, each role affecting the other in potentially positive and negative ways (Frone, et al., 1992a). Each can create difficulties as well as have positive impacts on the other life domain, and can do so simultaneously. For example, difficulties at home can lead to problems at work, and vice versa. Based on a national probability sample, Forthofer, Markman, Cox, Stanley and Kessler (1996) found that marital distress was associated with work loss, especially among men. In addition, family-care responsibilities predict higher rates of absenteeism among those providing various types of family care (Neal et al., 1993). Evidence also strongly suggests that difficult experiences on the job can spill over to the family. Pressures and overload at work have been associated with increased withdrawal, anger, and arguments at home (Piotrkowski & Katz, 1983; Bolger, DeLongis, Kessler & Wethington, 1989; Repetti, 1989; Repetti & Wood, 1997). While both men and women experience spillover from work to home, women are significantly more likely then men to compensate by increasing their work at home when their husbands have a difficult day at work (Bolger et al., 1989).

Family and work also impact each other in positive ways, and greater satisfaction at home seems to lessen the impact associated with problems on the job. For example, the quality of men's and women's marital and parental roles has been found to buffer the psychological distress associated with work-related difficulties and poor experiences on the job (Barnett, Marshall & Pleck, 1992; Barnett, 1994). Good experiences at work can have positive impacts on family life. For example, mothers' involvement in complex types of work is associated with providing an enriched home environment that promotes child development (Menaghan & Parcel, 1995). Support from supervisors regarding employees' nonwork demands and responsibilities has been found to be positively associated with job satisfaction and health outcomes (Thomas & Ganster, 1995).

Moreover, employed family members can simultaneously experience both strain and satisfaction as a result of their dual responsibilities. For example, working mothers often report high levels of strain (Neal et al., 1993), but also high levels of income, satisfaction, and social support, when compared with nonworking mothers (Scarr, 1998). Caregivers of ill and disabled adults also report high levels of stress (Neal et al., 1993) as well as positive consequences gained from their work and family care responsibilities (Scharlach, 1994).

Work-Place Characteristics

Various work-place characteristics have been found to be related to work and family conflict (Frone et al., 1992a). In a study of working parents, for example, work-related variables had the strongest association with job and family tension (Kelly & Voydanoff, 1985). Among the work-place factors found to be associated with conflict between employment and family-care responsibilities are an unsupportive relationship with one's supervisor (Fernandez, 1986; National Council of Jewish Women, 1987; Thomas & Ganster, 1995); decreased job autonomy; increased job demand and overload (Piotrkowski & Katz, 1983; Burke, 1986; Fredriksen & Scharlach, 1997); inflexible work schedules (Thomas & Ganster, 1995); and increased number of hours worked (Staines & Pleck, 1983; Burke, 1986).

Burke (1988) found work and family conflict to be most strongly associated with work-place orientation, workload, stimulation, scope of client contacts, institutional goals, autonomy, leadership, supervision, and social isolation. Individuals with higher perceived control have been found to have less work-family overload and interference (Duxbury, Higgins & Lee, 1994).

Family Characteristics

Fewer studies have examined the impact of family behaviors and attitudes on work-family conflict. In an investigation of the relationship between work-family conflict and marital adjustment, Burley (1995) found that spousal social support and equity in the division of labor in the home had a small but significant mediating influence. Child-related support, in terms of adequate child-care facilities (Sahoo & Bidyadhar, 1994), has also been found to be a highly significant predictor of work-family conflict and harmony.

In a cross-sectional survey at a work site, Emlen and Koren (1984) found that parents with heavier family responsibilities, especially women with children under 12 years of age, reported significantly higher rates of interference and conflict between work and family. Thirty-eight percent of women with children under 12 reported some degree of difficulty combining work and family roles. Perceived levels of stress were associated with such factors as the age of dependent children, the gender and marital status of the worker, the type of child care utilized, and the distribution of care responsibilities.

Work-Family Interdependence

In the early work of Greenhaus and Beutell (1985), they suggested the importance of addressing both work-to-family and family-to-work conflict, since the predictors and consequences might differ. Although the majority of previous studies have examined the influence of work on the family, more recent studies are focusing on the reciprocal nature of the relationship (Gutek, Searle & Klepa, 1991; Frone et al., 1992a; Netemeyer, Boles & McMurrian, 1996). For example, Frone et al. (1992a) demonstrated that conflict between family and work was related to work distress, and among blue-collar workers in particular was related to family distress. Gutek et al. (1991) found that the more hours spent in either domain, the more likely that interference originated there.

While an interdependent relationship may exist between work and family, the nature and impact of the two domains may be different. Frone, Russell, & Cooper (1992b), for example, found that work interfered with family life more often than family life interfered with work. Thus, the boundaries between work and family are likely asymmetrical, with family boundaries being more permeable than work boundaries.

Work and Family Support

Although the emphasis has been on conflict between the two domains, there is increasing evidence of the significance of support in work and family. Adams, King and King (1996) found that work and family can be simultaneously characterized by interrelational conflict and support, and that the nature of the relationship is influenced by the level of involvement in both domains, which can significantly impact work and life satisfaction. For example, high levels of work interference with family were significantly associated with lower levels of emotional and instrumental familial support. Conversely, higher levels of family support were correlated with lower levels of work interference.

Studies have illustrated that familial support serves to buffer work-related stress (House, 1981) and increases work commitment (Orthner, 1980; Orthner & Pittman, 1986). In a study of the military, degree of work commitment was strongly associated with perceived levels of familial support and organizational support for families (Orthner & Pittman, 1986). In addition, positive experiences as a partner or parent have been found to moderate the relationship between job role quality and psychological distress, regardless of gender (Barnett, 1994).

Limitations of the Work and
Family Conceptual Approaches

As a body of knowledge, the various conceptual approaches suggest a complex multi-directional relationship between family and work, with potentially varied ways of integrating the two domains. It is evident that the ways in which the roles are integrated can lead to various outcomes, including conflict and compatibility. Each role can create difficulties as well as have positive impacts on the other life domain. The extant literature illustrates the significance of the interplay and complexity between work and family. Although the various approaches are generally treated as conceptually distinct, evidence suggests that spillover, compensation, and segmentation may in fact be operative simultaneously.

The work and family conceptual approaches we have described here tend to be limited by a number of shortcomings, including: emphasis on work as it affects the family rather than utilizing a multi-directional approach; treating the individual as the primary unit of analysis rather than the family or work group; focusing primarily on dual career families or male earners rather than incorporating the full diversity of family constellations, such as single female earners, gay and lesbian couples, and extended families; and, reporting only associations between variables, with a lack of attention to the complexities of interrelationships, processes, and experiences involved. That most of the existing work and family literature has failed to incorporate an examination of the contextual background has in effect perpetuated gender, race, and class biases (Chow & Berheide, 1988). In addition, the vast majority of the work and family literature has focused on employment as related to families with children, with comparatively little attention to the care of ill or disabled adults.

ROLE THEORY

Role theory provides a social context and structure for many of the work-family conceptual models described above. Goode (1960), in a classic analysis of role theory, advanced that social structures and institutions were comprised of roles and role relationships. One of the earliest applications of role theory (Woodworth, 1934) illustrated the normative expectations that were aligned with particular social positions, including attitudes, values, functions, obligations, and behaviors.

Social Roles

Persons function within roles, as part of institutions, operative for the maintenance of society (Pearlin, 1983). Roles, as a dynamic aspect of social positions, refer to expectations as well as actual behaviors, and to coherent sets and patterns of behaviors rather than single acts; roles are culturally oriented, proscribed and sanctioned by a group or society (Jacobson, Charters & Lieberman, 1951; Sarbin, 1954; Bates & Harvey, 1975). From a role theory perspective, the informal provision of family care involves performance in a social role—parent or caregiver—that incorporates various familial and cultural attitudes, values, obligations, and normative behaviors.

Within the broader context of specific cultures (Heiss, 1981), social role performance involves the occupancy of multiple roles with differing obligations and the participation in role sets—a cluster of relationships where multiple occupants share a single role (Merton, 1957; Goode, 1960). Employed parents and family caregivers are actively involved in two pivotal social spheres: family, one of the primary centers of role involvement (Goode, 1960); and occupation, in which persons derive varying levels of status, personal esteem, and economic resources (Pearlin, 1983). Some have maintained that work and family are the two most central roles in life (Campbell, Converse & Rodgers, 1976).

Role Strain

Defined as "the felt difficulty in fulfilling role obligations" (Goode, 1960, p. 483), role strain manifests as the inability or perceived inability to adequately meet expectations of responsibility in a given social role. Goode maintains that through "role bargains," a manner of deciding and selecting among various role behaviors, individuals work toward adjusting role demands and reducing role strain. In terms of work and family role involvement, role strain has often been proposed to result from inter-role conflict, impacted by both incompatible role responsibilities (Hirsch & Rapkin, 1986) and incompatible role expectations (Secord & Backman, 1964).

In an analysis of work and family-role conflict, Greenhaus and Beutell (1985) specified *time-based* conflict (insufficient time to meet the demands of both roles), *strain-based* conflict (strain in fulfilling one role makes it difficult to meet the responsibilities of another), and *behavior-based* conflict (behavioral styles supported in one environment may be incompatible with behaviors needed in another). Problems for parents and employed caregivers may arise if they have insufficient time to meet both their family-care and employment responsibilities, are providing care during late evening hours, or if the work environment supports authoritarian decision-making, which conflicts with the participatory model more useful in the provision of family care.

Pearlin (1983) identified other potential sources of role strain including: "*role captivity*" (incompatibility between an individual and the specific role tasks one is expected to execute); *role overload* (time expenditures involved in meeting role obligations) (Coverman, 1989); *role ambiguity* (lack of defined or explicit normative expectations regarding role fulfillment) (Thomas, 1968); and, *role frustration* (structural elements inhibiting role performance) (Komarovsky, 1976).

Existing research suggests that outcomes associated with combining multiple roles are impacted by a number of factors, including the magnitude of dual-role responsibilities (Googins & Burden, 1987; Gutek et al., 1991), the adequacy of social support (Repetti et al., 1989; Burley, 1995), adaptation and coping styles, role identification, sense of self (McBride, 1990), and the sequencing of career and family goals (Statham, 1986). Among university employees, for example, Schultz, Chung and Henderson (1988) found evidence of both time- and strain-based conflict, with gender, age, number of children, and employment status of spouse impacting the nature of the work and family relationship.

Role Gains

Although the majority of theoretical and empirical work has illuminated the negative consequences of work and family involvement, the multiple-role enhancement perspective suggests that mastery and well-being may be achieved through engagement in varied roles (Biegel et al., 1991). Existing research demonstrates that multiple-role performance can result in a variety of salutary outcomes, including increased psychological well-being, autonomy, and personal growth (Hirsch & Rapkin, 1986; Barnett & Marshal, 1989; Biegel et al., 1991). Over two-thirds of men and women in one sample (Marshall & Barnett, 1993) reported that combining work and family responsibilities had definite gains, including making them better parents, and one-quarter experienced no work and/or family strain. Major predictors of work and family gains included positive experiences with work and family, social support, and sex-role attitudes (Marshall & Barnett, 1993).

Although women tend to report higher levels of work and family-role interference than men, compared to nonworking women, working women do not generally report higher levels of life stress (Crosby, 1987), and both career and noncareer working women are generally committed to and satisfied with their multiple roles (Hiller & Dyehouse, 1987). Some women with combined work and family roles report better health (Waldron & Herold, 1986; Repetti et al., 1989) and a more autonomous sense of self (Meisenhelder, 1986).

Balanced Role Commitments

Some argue that the psychological commitment to various social roles is most salient, although the majority of research has examined the impact of objective demands, such as time and energy, on multiple role performance. For example, Marks (1977) hypothesizes that "balanced, positive commitments" lead to lower role strain. He argues that cultures that value equally positive commitments to all of life's roles will evidence low levels of role strain, while those that value some roles more highly than others will result in increased levels of strain (Marks, 1977; 1994).

According to this framework, the emphasis is on the subjective interpretation of role involvement rather than the objective demands of various roles. In a study that sought to assess the impact of balanced commitments, Marks and MacDermid (1996) found that individuals who had more balance across all of their roles and activities had lower levels of role strain and depression and higher levels of well-being, such as role ease and self-esteem. O'Neil and Greenberger (1994), however, did not support the notion that balanced commitments to work and parenting necessarily lead to lower role strain, although they concluded that the relationship between role strain and role commitment is likely impacted by the "occupational and social context" of people's lives.

Limitations of Role Theory

Role theory effectively illustrates the interactive nature of work and family roles, the importance of the social properties of family caregiving and employment, and the significance of role resources versus demands in family-care outcomes. However, the theory is limited by its lack of attention to contextual factors and specification among theoretical constructs.

Role theory perspectives generally give limited attention to gender, race and ethnicity, and occupational role, as factors potentially impacting the interrelationship between family and work. In addition, the distinction between role antecedents and consequences is often vague. For example, outcome measures often incorporate potential indicators of role demands and resources, as well as role strain. Moreover, the majority of role theory research has examined the care of children, with limited attention to the care of ill and disabled adults.

STRESS AND COPING

The majority of research on care of the elderly has implicitly or explicitly utilized a stress and coping theoretical perspective (Gatz, Bengtson & Blum, 1990; Zarit, 1990a). Stress, as a theoretical construct, has been conceptualized in a number of different ways: as a nonspecific response (Cannon, 1932; Selye, 1950), in relation to specified stimuli (Elliot & Eisdorfer, 1982), and as an interactive, transactional process (Lazarus, 1966; Lazarus & Folkman, 1984; Aneshensel, Pearlin, Mullan, Zarit & Whitlatch, 1995).

Initially borrowed from the field of physics, the conceptualization of stress was, in one of its first applications to humans, utilized by Cannon (1932) in an examination of the impact of environmental stressors on biological systems. During the last several decades, there has been a proliferation of stress-related research (Goldberger & Breznitz, 1982; Hobfoll, 1989), and the field has expanded to include the examination of everyday, routine stressors (Stephens, Norris, Kinney, Ritchie & Grotz, 1988; Kinney & Stephens, 1989), stress-related adaptations, outcomes and coping strategies (Holroyd & Lazarus, 1982), and interventions to negate the harmful impacts of stress (Meichenbaum & Jeremko, 1982).

Transactional Stress Paradigm

Departing from response- and stimulus-driven definitions of stress, Lazarus and Folkman's (1984) transactional stress paradigm places an increased emphasis on the interactive, relational nature of the stress process, which is conceptualized broadly to include stressors (originating outside of the individual), appraisals, responses, and outcomes. According to this formulation, stress is defined "relationally" (Holroyd & Lazarus, 1982) as "any event in which environmental demands, internal demands or both tax or exceed the adaptive resources of an individual or social system" (Monat & Lazarus, 1985, p. 3).

Applied to the study of family care, the transactional stress paradigm provides a framework to illustrate the impact of stress on both psychological and physical health (McCubbin, Cauble & Patterson, 1982; Chiriboga, Weiler & Nielsen, 1988/89). Several recent theoretical models of family care illustrate the impact of caregiving stressors, given meaning through the appraisal process and mediated through social and psychological mechanisms, such as social support and coping (Zarit, 1990a). McCubbin et al. (1982), for example, developed the "double ABCX" model. This conceptual framework breaks down the impact process into stressful event (A), family resources (B), family's appraisal of the stressor (C), amount of strain and crisis associated with the stressor (X), and the cumulative impact of secondary problems created with the original stressor.

Barling (1990) suggested using a general open systems approach to study the interaction between stress processes, family functioning, and employment. In one such application, Eckenrode and Gore (1990) outlined the interactive nature of stressors and resources, with stress-mediating and stress-moderating processes as sets of mechanisms linking work-family boundaries. Each of these relationships is proposed to have the potential of both positive and negative outcomes. Such a model highlights the significance of functioning within both family and occupational domains, and it explicates various relationships inherent in the culmination of work and family responsibilities.

Building upon stress models such as these, Pearlin, Mullan, Semple and Skaff (1990) and Aneshensel et al. (1995) have developed one of the most comprehensive conceptual frameworks for the study of caregiving. According to this formulation, the caregiving stress process is influenced by the following four domains: *background and context of the stress* (e.g., demographic factors, family composition and history, and prior caregiving experience); *stressors* (e.g., health and cognitive impairment of the care recipient); *stress moderators* (e.g., social support and coping styles); and *outcomes of stress* (depression, anxiety, and changes in physical health) (Aneshensel et al., 1995).

CONTEXTUAL FACTORS

Research indicates that contextual factors such as the caregiver's gender (Cantor, 1979b; Fredriksen, 1995), social class (Archbold, 1983; Cantor & Little, 1985), race and ethnicity (Mui, 1992; Fredman, Daly & Lazur, 1995), and the relationship between caregiver and recipient (Horowitz & Shindelman, 1983) are likely to impact the caregiving experience.

For example, women, racial and ethnic minorities, and persons employed in staff-level positions have been found to provide relatively high levels of caregiving assistance with few work-place resources. Women formally employed in a caregiving role in addition to providing informal care are at increased risk for emotional and physical distress (Marshall, Barnett, Baruch & Pleck, 1990). The quality of the mother and daughter relationship has also been found to be a strong predictor of a daughter's commitment to caregiving (Pohl, Boyd, Liang & Given, 1995). Himes, Jordan and Farkas (1996) found that age, education, and marital status are also important caregiver characteristics that influence the provision of care.

STRESSORS

The stress process and related outcomes are hypothesized to be influenced by specific active stressors—both *primary* (e.g., the illness and limitations of the care recipient) and *secondary* (e.g., role strains, family conflict, employment and caregiving conflict, restrictions on social activities). The stress event, as the primary stressor, resides outside of the caregiver and encompasses the change in circumstances that results in stress.

Existing research indicates that those primary stressors most likely to cause strain for the caregiver include the care recipient's physical, behavioral, and/or cognitive malfunctioning (Deimling & Bass, 1986; Friss, Whitlatch & Yale, 1990; Starrels, Ingersoll-Dayton, Dowler & Neal, 1997)—particularly behavioral disturbances (Stone & Short, 1990); and the nonpredictability of care needs (Pruchno & Resch, 1989). In one study of the impact of care recipient impairment on adult children caregivers, Starrels et al. (1997) found that cognitive and behavioral problems were more stressful than functional disability. Impairment level directly impacted stress level via the amount of caregiving provided.

Secondary stressors, both objective and subjective, include caregivers' feelings toward caregiving and the various resulting work and family conflicts. Secondary stressors in one's social relationships and work context (Chiriboga et al., 1988/89) include changes in social participation (George & Gwyther, 1986) and accommodations at the work place (Scharlach et al., 1991; Starrels et al., 1997). In one longitudinal study, caregiving was found to most frequently impact a caregiver's personal life (61 percent), followed by family life (18 percent) and employment (15–20 percent) (McKinlay, Crawford & Tennstedt, 1995).

MODERATORS

Parallel to the secondary stressors are moderators, influencing both primary stressors and the stress appraisal process. Moderators include such factors as the availability of resources and support for the caregiver (George & Gwyther, 1986) and the caregiver's coping mechanisms (Pearlin et al., 1990). For example, positive reappraisal and active coping styles have been associated with increased psychological well-being, while feelings of helplessness have been associated with higher levels of depression (Fleishman & Fogel, 1994). Feelings of mastery and high levels of social support have also been associated with increased well-being. For example, employed caregivers with better social and economic resources tend to experience lower levels of caregiving stress and strain (Brody, Litvin, Hoffman & Kleban, 1992).

Limitations of Stress and Coping Theories

Transactional stress paradigms incorporate the interactive nature of the stress process and have provided one of the most comprehensive theoretical approaches for the study of adult caregiving; yet, their application is limited by a few considerations. First, they have been utilized primarily to examine the experiences of caregivers of the elderly, with limited attention to the care of working-age adults or children. Further, the vast majority of this research has examined only caregiver outcomes, with extremely limited attention to the needs and experiences of the care recipient.

Stress and coping frameworks have been criticized for being tautological in form, overly complex, and not applicable to empirical rejection (Hobfoll, 1989). In addition, many of the existing transactional stress theories do not adequately address the interplay and impact of social structures and relationships in the caregiving process. Stress-related factors have often been treated as independent and noninteractive entities (internal or external stimuli).

Although some caregiving models treat employment as a secondary stressor, they do not delineate the structural relationships or psychological or social processes between family and work domains. In general, such factors as social roles, relationships, and norms have not been adequately incorporated into transactional stress paradigms when applied to the provision of informal adult care by employed caregivers.

LIFESPAN APPROACHES

To date there have been notably few attempts to examine work and family or caregiving across the lifespan (Biegel et al., 1991; Friss & Whitlatch, 1991;

Ansello & Eustis, 1992; Neal et al., 1993). In fact, as illustrated in the review of the various conceptual approaches, the majority of theoretical perspectives have examined either the care of children or the care of adults, with relatively limited attention across types of care.

Caregiving occurs across the life span, and individuals often vary the degree of family and work involvement at different points in their life. Utilizing a life-course approach (Elder, 1992), caregiving can be viewed "as a life contingency, a consequence of the interdependence of life paths of family members," responsive to changing circumstances and ongoing family needs (Moen et al., 1994, p. 177). This approach emphasizes the changing landscape of people's lives: the restructuring of lives through time, incorporating both contemporary and historical influences.

The life-course perspective is closely aligned with the developmental perspective, which has been advanced in the work and family field (Sekaran & Hall, 1989; Lambert, 1990; Swanson, 1992; Chi-Ching, 1995). This perspective utilizes a dynamic, longitudinal approach, incorporating individuals' experiences across the life span. It recognizes that in accordance with differing developmental stages, individuals may link work and family differently at varying points in their careers and lives.

Both developmental and life-course perspectives highlight the importance of timing, sequencing, and duration of life events and transitions (George, 1993), in relation to both normative and nonnormative life changes (Ryff, 1986; Pittman & Blanchard, 1996). Although a life-course framework has rarely been applied to the familial care of dependents, it highlights the need to develop a family-care paradigm that can be applied across the variety of types of care, the need to incorporate both contemporary and past experiences, and to link employment and family caregiving experiences.

MACRO-LEVEL THEORIES

Feminist Perspectives

Whereas the theories that have been discussed thus far generally incorporate a micro-level perspective, which emphasizes the individual, other theoretical approaches have extended the discussions of work and family and caregiving by utilizing a macro-level analysis. Feminist theorists, for example, focus on the effects of patriarchy, both in the work place and in the family. Such an approach illustrates the constraining and oppressive nature of institutionalized gender relationships, which reflect women's position in the larger social system. The structural components of family care are linked to power relations and the allocation of economic and social rewards. From a feminist perspective, one must examine the impact of the provision of care on the economic independence and equality of women in society.

As a dimension of our social structure, women predominate as unpaid providers of family care. Feminists note that women provide the majority of caregiving, both paid and unpaid, to children as well as to elders, in all types of settings ranging from care in the home to formal settings. Generally most family care is provided privately in the home, and remains largely invisible. As found repeatedly, women continue to do the vast majority of family care and household work, even when they are participating in the paid labor force.

Focusing on the work place, researchers such as Milkman (1987) have noted the resilience of gender segmentation and continued earning differentials among men and women with comparable human capital. The continuation of women as the primary nurturers and caregivers makes it difficult for them to compete with men in the work place. Similarly, women's lower earnings in comparison to men and ongoing societal expectations make it more likely that they will be the ones, in heterosexual couples, who minimize their work in favor of caregiving. Providers of paid caregiving services are also predominately female, receiving relatively low wages and often having poor working conditions. The majority of paid providers of child care and long-term care, for example, receive wages at a level that places them near or below the poverty line. Looked at together, these contributions emphasize how women's roles at home and in the work place are intertwined.

Some feminists argue that women perform the majority of family care because of "the societal ideology of separate public and private spheres for men and women in our society, the low value placed on the work of women in the home, societal disregard of the economic costs of caring to women, and the lack of public support for governmental and corporate policies to meet the needs of dependent citizens" (Hooyman & Gonyea, 1995).

Psychoanalytic feminists such as Chodorow suggest that some of the continued sexual divisions in society stem from the fact that both boys and girls are nurtured by women instead of men (Chodorow, 1978). Other feminist theorists highlight the differences in the psychological development of men and women. For example, research findings suggests that men tend to view themselves as more separate than do women, while women tend to define themselves more through their interpersonal relationships and relational capacities (Gilligan, 1982; Josselson, 1992). In terms of moral orientation, Gilligan found that males are more likely to value individual rights and responsibilities, while women tend to place an increased emphasis on the care of and concern for others.

Abel and Nelson (1990) identify the two rather divergent perspectives that tend to inform the feminist analysis of caregiving. The first approach views caregiving primarily as labor and as oppressive, contributing to women's secondary status. The other perspective accentuates the social connections and reciprocity inherent in family caregiving. Abel (1986) maintains that neither of these perspectives is adequate, rather that caregiving encompasses both significant personal experiences and relationships, and is an oppressive institution that maintains economic inequalities and the subordinate status of women.

The feminist perspective attends to the interconnectedness of family care and work, and the important role of social and economic structures in maintaining the gendered division of labor. Martin (1990a) points out that the tendency to ignore the work-place emphasis on full-time commitment and the lack of attention to the interdependence of work and family responsibilities distorts reality in a way that penalizes women (Bose, Feldberg & Sokoloff, 1987; Martin, 1990b). Furthermore, a feminist analysis incorporates the social and cultural context in which women live, illustrating the diversity of women's experiences, shaped by gender as well as by race and ethnicity, class, and sexual orientation.

Marxist Theory

In studying the relationship between the paid work place and the family in the United States, sociologists relying on Marxist theory have pointed to the influence of capitalism and its inherent power structure (Zaretsky, 1976; Dizard & Gadlin, 1990). From this perspective, changes in the nature of family life can best be understood as responses to the dictates of the market. When the production system was based primarily in the home or on the family farm, large, extended families were efficient and useful, and men, women, and children all were considered to be doing "productive" work. When production moved to the factory, women were left at home to tend to children and create a home that would support the "worker," so that the worker could be most productive.

   When work required greater mobility, extended families were no longer as useful, and the nuclear family with the stay-at-home wife became the mobile family unit of choice. Now that women have entered the work force in large numbers, families are no longer seen as a support for workers but are, instead, a hindrance. Capitalism during the current postindustrial information age appears suited to and dependent on unattached, individual workers rather than those burdened with the demands of family life. From this perspective, it is no accident that work and family issues tend to be framed primarily in terms of how to alleviate work-place interference caused by family responsibilities.

Resource Dependence and Institutional Theories

Resource dependence theories postulate that actors will behave according to the nature of their exchange relationships. From a political-economic perspective, for example, organizations are likely to act in ways required by powerful exchange partners. This is pertinent to work and family research to the extent that the level of effort an organization is willing to expend to change work patterns, corporate culture, or programs in order to accommodate employees with family responsibilities will be related to whether or not those employees are perceived as important exchange partners.

While much of the work and family literature insists that employers must recognize the growing importance of this issue for workers and the importance of employees for the future of the organization, companies remain reluctant to engage in significant change. This perspective suggests that the lack of involvement of the corporate sector reflects that one of the following must be operating: that those who would benefit from the changes are not perceived as critical exchange partners by those in charge; that those who would benefit from changes are not making their own needs known in a manner that is perceived as meaningful to their corporate audiences; or that other, more powerful, exchange partners are not supportive of such changes. It is interesting to note that the number of female managers, not the number of women employed as a whole, has been found to be significantly associated with corporate responsiveness to work and family issues (Ingram & Simons, 1995).

Institutional theory emphasizes that organizations are permeable and, therefore, can be strongly influenced by their environments (Scott, 1992) as they attempt to insure their own survival. As such, many of the relevant forces in organizational life are due to social and cultural pressures to conform to conventional beliefs and thus gain legitimacy, rather than to pursue rationally more effective performance (Zucker, 1988; Powell & DiMaggio, 1991).

Ingram and Simons (1995) examined institutional and resource-dependence theories in explaining organizational responsiveness to work-family issues and found that organizations do, under specific circumstances, respond in a calculated manner to institutional pressure. Thus, institutional theory emphasizes the importance of culture, socialization, and roles, as well as formal institutions such as government, on the work place and the family.

Googins (1997) reiterates this emphasis by pointing out that, in relation to the realms of work and family, the community is both an important stakeholder and has significant influence. Support structures outside of employing organizations and family units can have a large impact on how well individuals integrate their responsibilities, whether children and others in need of care receive it, and whether work organizations are well served by caregivers in the paid labor force. He suggests that research on work and family interaction cannot be complete without taking into account the community context within which the work place and the family exist, including government, schools, churches, clubs, recreation centers, and other community resources.

Limitations of Macro-level Theories

Macro-level theories are clearly relevant to the question of how work and family interrelate and illustrate the important contribution of social structures and societal factors as they influence family and work arrangements. Several of the macro-level perspectives highlight important equity issues and demonstrate how the current configuration of work and family responsibilities maintains the status quo and the subordinate position of those providing family care. Such perspectives, however, have not been adequately examined and can be relatively difficult to apply in the empirical analysis of family care and employment.

SUMMARY

The conceptual approaches reviewed in this chapter provide insights and raise a myriad of issues pertinent to the interrelationship between family care and employment responsibilities. It is interesting to note that the bodies of research addressing the care of children and the care of elderly adults have generally utilized divergent theoretical approaches with differing underlying assumptions. The majority of the literature in the area of work and family historically developed with an emphasis on work, while informal caregiving primarily originated from a gerontological perspective.

The historical evolution of these related, although often seemingly disparate, fields has resulted in several significant differences. The work and family literature has generally treated work as the primary variable of interest and then examined it in relationship to the family. In contrast, the informal caregiving literature has focused almost entirely on the needs and experiences of caregivers serving the impaired elderly, with limited attention to the care of other family members or the needs of the care recipients. Even the term "caregiving" tends to reduce familial relationships to the act of providing care, rather than capturing the context and broader dimensions of familial relationships and the experiences involved in receiving and providing family care. Moreover, the care of working-age adults has rarely been addressed in the literature, regardless of the theoretical perspective. Perhaps this reflects a tendency to view dependency and the need for family care at the two extremes of the age continuum, rather than across the life cycle.

Although none of the existing perspectives may be adequate to explore the full range of family-care responsibilities, each perspective offers important insights. The various work and family conceptual approaches demonstrate the interactive nature of work and family domains, while role theory highlights the social context of care and the impact of demands and resources. Stress and coping perspectives illustrate the importance of background, contextual, and mediating factors in the care of family members. Highlighting the important contribution of social structures and the larger community as they impact the intersection between work and family, the macro-level theories underscore issues regarding equity and the economic costs associated with the current configuration of work and family responsibilities.

Research findings based on these various conceptual approaches support the premise of a complex relationship between family and work, impacted by individual, familial, work place, as well as community- and societal-level influences. Although various models of work and family have highlighted differing aspects of the relationship, over time such conceptual approaches have increasingly integrated more varied dimensions of each domain. In the next chapter, we will build on these theories and propose a resource and demand conceptual framework to increase our understanding of the diverse types of family care in relation to the work place.

· 5 ·

RESEARCH MODEL
AND METHODOLOGY

INTRODUCTION

As we have seen, work and family have been viewed from a variety of perspectives that highlight differing aspects of the interaction of employment
and family caregiving. The various conceptual frameworks discussed in the
last chapter highlight the interplay between such factors as the structural
characteristics of people's lives, stressors and demands, and mediators and
resources, and their impact on the interrelationship of family care and work.

To date, the vast majority of research on these conceptual models has
been descriptive rather than evaluative. Existing research, moreover, has
been limited by a number of methodological constraints, including the application of the models to only one type of care, the use of multiple definitions of family care, and the use of unrepresentative samples. Of the few
existing studies that have examined the entire range of family caregiving experiences, most have attained relatively low response rates.

This chapter will discuss the blending of role theory and stress and coping theoretical frameworks to develop a resource and demand family-care
model that can be applied across all types of family care. This family-care
model will be examined utilizing findings from a comprehensive examination of family and work experiences among nearly 2,000 employees of a technology research center. In this chapter, we review the conceptual model
guiding this study, discuss operationalization of key constructs, and describe
our research methodology.

RESOURCE AND DEMAND MODEL

The conceptual model utilized in this research incorporates several theoretical constructs from stress and coping and role theory (as described in the
previous chapter) to begin exploring the culmination of caregiving and employment responsibilities: background characteristics and personal life impact (accommodations) constructs from transactional stress theories, and a

73

demand and resource formulation from role theory. A transactional stress and coping model illustrates the context of stress, the impact of primary and secondary stressors (both objective and subjective components), stress-related mediators, and personal life impacts resulting from the stress process.

Rather than separating the stress event, stress mediators, and secondary stressors, as is the case in most transactional stress theories, this model incorporates them using the role theory constructs of family and work-role demands and resources. Role theory highlights the impact of resources and demands on caregiving outcomes, incorporating the social properties inherent in the culmination of family-care and employment responsibilities.

Romeis (1987) developed a conceptual framework of role strain and caregiving that illustrated the impact of role demands and resources. Caregiver strain was conceptualized as a function of the imbalance between caregiving demands (e.g., functional limitations of the care recipient) and caregiver resources (e.g., available social support). Although the model linked caregiver strain to demands and resources, it neglected the context of caregiving, e.g., gender and race, and the accommodations or changes caregivers make in the work place or family to meet caregiving responsibilities.

A demands and resources formulation, as applied to work and family, is preferred over other existing conceptual frameworks because it emphasizes the interactive nature of the relationship and allows for an assessment of role demands and resources in both domains. Such an approach can be applied across various types of care and offers a means to ensure congruence in the examination of work and family domains. In some of the early work and family models that incorporated demands and resources, workplace characteristics such as number of hours worked, work schedule, job involvement and satisfaction, work control, pressure, and flexibility were examined. Family characteristics initially assessed included such variables as the presence of children and spouse employment and support.

In a study of working parents, Kelly and Voydanoff (1985), for example, presented a resource and demand model of role strain, in which both strain overload and strain interference were identified as potential outcomes for working parents engaged in multiple roles (Voydanoff, 1981, as cited in Kelly & Voydanoff, 1985). They identified individual, family-related, and work-related demands and resources impacting the degree of role strain. Their model moved beyond a simple work-family dichotomy to advance the idea that work and family role strain results from factors incorporating "multiple levels of social structures and process." For example, they found that job tension was particularly high for female single parents and those caring for young children (under the age of six). Degree of job tension was also associated with amount of overtime worked, degree of dissatisfaction with hours worked, and scheduling.

Warren and Johnson (1995) applied a resource and demand formulation to examine the impact of work-place support on work and family role strain among employed mothers with preschool children. In their study there was additional attention paid to the impact of work-place behaviors and characteristics on role strain. Perceptions of work environment support, supervisor flexibility, and utilization of work and family benefits were associated with lower levels of strain, after controlling for family demands.

Neal and her colleagues (1993) surveyed the employees of 33 companies in Oregon to examine the range and impact of family-care responsibilities in relation to personal characteristics, demands, and resources in both family and work domains. This research made an important contribution to the resource and demand formulation by incorporating all types of family care. Furthermore, the research demonstrated that both demands and resources are important constructs in assessing the degree of strain experienced by family members providing assistance. However, the research was limited by a number of factors, including an overall response rate of only 34 percent and the underrepresentation of ethnic minorities and nonprofessional and nonsupervisory staff positions.

FAMILY CARE AND WORK MODEL

As illustrated in Figure 5-1, the resource and demand family-care model utilized for this research postulates that role strain and work and family accommodations are impacted by **background characteristics, family and work role demands, and resources**. This conceptual framework incorporates the following domains: caregiver characteristics (gender, age, race/ethnicity, marital status, job classification, health status); caregiving demands (number of care recipients, type and extent of hours of care provided, age and disability status of care recipients); employment demands (number of hours worked, work demand); caregiving resources (income, assistance with caregiving); employment resources (work support, control, flexibility); work accommodations (missed days from work, changes at the work place due to caregiving responsibilities); family accommodations (changes in family relationships, social activities); and role strain. It is hypothesized that role strain

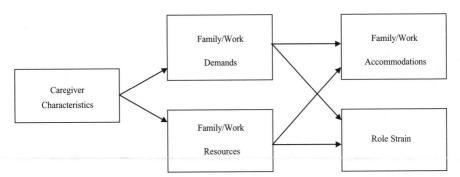

Figure 5-1 A resource and demand family-care model incorporating caregiver characteristics, family and work demands, resources, accommodations, and role strain.

and work and family accommodations can be understood in light of the levels of demands and resources, and certain background characteristics.

Background Characteristics

People combine family care and employment within the contexts of their lives, influenced by background characteristics, as well as social, cultural, and political factors. Background characteristics have been found to affect the likelihood of exposure to stressors, the availability of resources, and subsequent outcomes among various subgroups in the population (Aneshensel et al., 1995). The background characteristics examined in this model include gender, race/ethnicity, age, marital status, job type, and health status of the caregiver.

Among both working parents (Emlen & Koren, 1984; Neal et al., 1993; Duxbury & Higgins, 1994) and caregivers of ill and disabled adults (Kramer & Kipnis, 1995; Fredriksen, 1996), women tend to provide higher levels of assistance and report higher levels of strain. The provision and consequences of familial caregiving are also likely impacted by race/ethnicity, age, health, job type, and marital status, given the likely association between such background characteristics and various family and work demands and resources.

Family and Work Demands

Family role demands include such factors as the caregiver's overall number of dependents, care recipient age, disability of children, impairment level of adult care recipients, and problems experienced with care arrangements. Work-place demands include the caregiver's number of hours worked per week and perceived level of work demands. Based on the resource and demand family-care paradigm, family and work demands are proposed to impact work and family accommodations and the extent of role strain experienced among the employed caregivers.

The number of children and their ages (Fernandez, 1986; Klein, 1986), the age of the adult care recipient (Scharlach & Fredriksen, 1994), and the disability of a child (Deiner, 1992) or adult care recipient (Deimling & Bass, 1986; Friss & Whitlatch, 1991) have been frequently identified as contributors to strain in meeting family-care responsibilities. Difficulty locating and maintaining adequate child-care or adult-care assistance has also been associated with higher levels of work-family conflict, including higher levels of personal strain and work disruptions (Emlen & Koren, 1984; Anastas, Gibeau & Larson, 1987; Neal et al., 1993; Fredriksen & Scharlach, 1996).

Such work-place variables as work demand (Burke, Weir & DeWors, 1980; Fredriksen & Scharlach, 1997) and lack of job flexibility (Ferber et al., 1991) have been associated with higher levels of role strain and work and family conflict. High workload and lack of control and flexibility at the work place have been found to contribute to high stress and strain levels in general (Karasek, 1981).

Family and Work Resources

In much of the caregiving research, analytic attention has focused primarily on caregiving demands, with more limited attention to the caregiver's available resources. The conceptual framework utilized in this study analyzes both. Family resources include income and satisfaction with care arrangements; work-place resources include support, flexibility, and control. It is hypothesized that lower levels of family and work resources combined with higher family and work demands will result in higher levels of accommodations and role strain.

Previous research supports this hypothesis. Lower levels of strain have been found to be associated with higher social and economic resources (Orthner & Pittman, 1986; Brody et al., 1992), with caregivers' satisfaction with care arrangements and ease in obtaining and managing assistance for dependents (Galinsky et al., 1993; Neal et al., 1993), with a supportive relationship with one's supervisor (Fernandez, 1986; Hughes & Galinsky, 1988), with high decision-making control, and with social support from one's coworkers (Karasek, 1981).

Family and Work Accommodations

Accommodations, as a theoretical construct, are the adaptations that caregivers make, given the constellation of their family and work-role demands and resources. In this conceptual framework, work accommodations include missing days from work and turning down extra work opportunities due to care responsibilities. Family accommodations include changes in a caregiver's family, social, and personal activities as a result of caregiving.

Previous research has found that such accommodations include missing time from work, missing work promotions, decreasing social activities, and giving up free time (Emlen & Koren, 1984; Scharlach & Boyd, 1989; Fredriksen, 1993a; Neal et al., 1993). Compared to those without family-care responsibilities, employees caring for a dependent child or adult are more likely to be absent or lose time from work (Scharlach, Lowe & Schneider, 1990). The concept of accommodations is related to such concepts as personal life impacts (Pearlin et al., 1990) or work interference (Scharlach et al., 1991) in transactional stress paradigms.

Role Strain

The primary outcome assessed in this family-care model is role strain. Bohen and Viveros-Long (1981), utilizing an ecological and family systems approach, defined work and family role strain as "the experience of discomfort, pressure, worry, anxiety, tension, or frustration that may arise when people function in both work and home life." In this study, the concept of role strain, encompassing role performance demand (Wallace & Noelker, 1984) and role expectations (Clark & Mills, 1979), will be utilized to assess a caregiver's perceived level of conflict when combining the two normative roles of employment and familial caregiving.

RESEARCH METHODOLOGY

Study Site and Sample

In order to examine this resource and demand family-care model, we conducted a study of the work and family experiences of a representative sample of employees at one work place. The study site, Lawrence Berkeley Laboratory, is a prominent, well-established technology center funded by the U.S. Department of Energy, located in Berkeley, California. There are 2,528 persons employed at least half-time on a permanent basis at this work site. The employees include scientists and engineers, administrative professionals, administrative clerical staff, and technical personnel. Seventy-three percent of the employees are male and 27 percent are female. In terms of race and ethnicity, 75 percent of the laboratory's work force is white, 12 percent is Asian or Pacific Isander, 7 percent is African-American, 5 percent is Hispanic, and 1 percent is American Indian.

The study utilized a cross-sectional survey design. Data were obtained from all personnel holding appointments of at least 12 months and currently employed 50 percent time or more. Survey questionnaires were distributed in July 1992 to 2,528 employees. Of these, 31 subjects did not meet the criteria for inclusion in the study (e.g., no longer employed at the work place, on sabbatical, or temporary visitors) and were dropped from the sample. From the remaining 2,497 subjects, a total of 1,888 usable surveys were returned, for an overall response rate of 76 percent, higher than that achieved in any previous dependent care survey.

Table 5-1 displays the sociodemographic characteristics of the survey respondents, as compared to the entire population of Laboratory personnel employed at least 50 percent time. When comparing the survey respondents to the overall employee population, respondents were found to differ significantly by gender and job classification, but not by age or race/ethnicity.

Approximately 30 percent of the survey respondents were women, compared to 27 percent of the Laboratory sample population. This slight over-representation of women among respondents is most likely attributable to the frequently observed tendency of men to have a lower participation rate in employee surveys such as this. In addition, administrative professionals were slightly more likely to respond to the survey than were the other employee groups.

TABLE 5-1 Characteristics of the respondents, compared to all laboratory personnel

	Respondents	LBL Personnel
Sample size	1888 (76%)	2497
Gender		
Male	70%	73%
Female	30%	27%
Age		
Under 30	8%	8%
30–39	29%	29%
40–49	34%	35%
50–59	24%	24%
60 and over	5%	5%
Race / Ethnicity		
White	77%	75%
Asian / Pacific Islander	13%	12%
Black / African American	6%	7%
Hispanic	4%	5%
American Indian	<1%	<1%
Job Category		
Scientists and Engineers	38%	40%
Administrative Professional	29%	25%
Administrative Clerical	11%	11%
Technical	23%	25%

In order to obtain more accurate estimates of the employee population and correct for the differential response rates, the sample was weighted by gender. The following gender weightings were utilized: men, 1.04; women, 0.91. All subsequent figures used in this book are based on these weighed adjustments. After adjusting for differentials by gender, survey respondents were strikingly similar to the population values in terms of race/ethnicity and job classification.

The research design utilized in this study was selected for several reasons. By using a cross-sectional design at a work-place setting, information was gathered on a large number of employed caregivers in a variety of caregiving situations, with diverse caregiving and employment demands. Unavailable in most settings, this sample represented a diverse work force by gender, race/ethnicity, and job type.

Data Instrumentation and Collection

Data were collected using a self-administered questionnaire (See Appendix 1). Part I was completed by all respondents, whether or not they were currently providing child-care or adult-care assistance. They were asked to indicate whether or not they currently had children for whom they had care responsibilities, or expected to have children in the next five years. This section of the survey also asked respondents whether they were assisting an adult family member or friend with a health problem or a disability, had done so in the past five years, or expected to do so in the next five years. Examples of assistance were offering emotional reassurance, providing or arranging for housekeeping or personal care, monitoring the health of an elderly person, and assisting with financial matters.

Part II was completed only by those employees with child-care responsibilities. Included in this section were questions regarding the ages of the children, current and preferred child-care arrangements, problems with existing child-care arrangements, and child-care programs that might be offered at or near the Laboratory. Part III was completed by those employees who were currently caring for a disabled or ill family member or friend, age 18 or older. Included in this section were in-depth measures of current adult caregiving demands and behaviors and personal strains associated with caregiving. Part IV examined the work behaviors and opportunities affected by child-care and adult-care responsibilities, asked about programs and benefits that might alleviate any deleterious impacts of family responsibilities, and requested basic sociodemographic information.

This survey differed from those utilized in previous studies of caregiving employees in a number of ways: 1) the measures were conceptually consistent and had either statistical or face validity; 2) child care and adult care were defined broadly to include employees who had any child-care responsibilities or provided any kind of assistance to an ill or disabled family member or friend, age 18 or older; 3) respondents were asked to report on their child-care and adult-care responsibilities and the extent of interference between their family and work responsibilities; and 4) all measures were tied as closely as possible to psychologically distinct markers to increase reliability and between-subject comparability.

Measures

The measures used in this study collected information in the following areas: demographics, current and previous caregiving experiences, nature and type of child-care responsibilities, nature and type of adult-care responsibilities, family and work characteristics, personal and occupational impacts of combining work and family responsibilities, and utilization and perceived helpfulness of various work-place programs and benefits.

The variables used in this research were operationalized as follows:

BACKGROUND CHARACTERISTICS

The social and demographic characteristics assessed included the caregiver's age, gender, race/ethnicity, job classification, marital status, and self-reported health status (measured by a single-item, 1 = poor to 4 = excellent (Maddox & Douglass, 1973).

FAMILY AND WORK DEMANDS

The family and work demands assessed were the number and age of care recipients, type of assistance provided, disability of care recipient, and problems with care arrangements. In addition, information on the number of hours of assistance provided, relationship between the caregiver and care recipient, and the living arrangement of care recipient was obtained for adult-care responsibilities. Work-place demands assessed were hours worked and work demand.

Disability. Respondents were asked whether they had any children who had special needs such as a physical, mental, or emotional disability. For adult care recipients, functional, cognitive, and behavioral impairment levels were assessed.

Based on the short versions of the physical and instrumental ADL indices of the Philadelphia Geriatric Center Multi-level Assessment Instrument (Lawton, Moss, Fulcomer & Kleban, 1982), an eight-item measure was developed to assess functional impairment of adult care recipients. Respondents checked if they assisted the care recipient with such tasks as chores, taking medications, and performing personal care. Personal care items (ADLs) were weighted by a factor of three; the mean was then calculated for the eight items (Cronbach's Alpha reliability coefficient = 0.79).

Cognitive impairment was measured by two items assessing if the adult care recipient had difficulty making common sense decisions or remembering things recently heard (based on a scale developed by Horowitz & Dobrof, 1982). The mean was calculated for the two items (Cronbach's Alpha reliability coefficient = 0.77).

Behavioral disturbances of adult care recipients were measured by responses to three items assessing if during the past month the care recipient had become very agitated or depressed, uncooperative with care providers, or had behaved in ways that were embarrassing or unsafe. These items were based on a measure developed by Poulshock and Deimling (1984). The mean was obtained for the three items (Cronbach's Alpha reliability coefficient = 0.68).

Problems with care arrangements. Problems with child-care arrangements that were assessed in this study included cost, care for sick child, emergency care, schedule, location, quality, dependability, care for child under 2, care for child 2–5, care before and after school, care during vacations, and care for special needs children (each rated from 1 = no problem to 3 = major problem).

Problems with adult-care arrangements that were assessed included understanding regulations, accessing local services, learning legal options, quality of care, cooperation from family members, cost of care, and breakdowns in arrangements (each rated from 1 = no problem to 3 = major problem).

The scores for cost, location, dependability, and quality were summed (Cronbach's Alpha = 0.80) across the four items to develop a measure that could be applied across both child and adult care.

Work demand. Work demand was measured by the number of hours worked per week by the employee and self-reported work demand. Level of work demand was determined by the extent to which respondents agreed with the following statement: I have enough time to get my work done (1 = strongly agree to 4 = strongly disagree) (Karasek, 1987).

FAMILY AND WORK RESOURCES

Measures of family and work resources included household income, satisfaction with assistance provided, assistance received, and work-place resources.

Income. Information on household income per year before taxes was obtained in six ordinal categories, ranging from less than $20,000 to $100,000 or more.

Satisfaction with care arrangements. Level of satisfaction with care arrangements was assessed through a single item rating level of satisfaction with child or adult arrangements (1 = not satisfied to 4 = extremely satisfied).

Assistance received. Level of assistance with adult-care responsibilities was assessed through a single item rating how much assistance overall the caregivers received with their adult-care responsibilities (1 = none at all to 4 = a great deal). In addition, respondents indicated if the care recipient received any paid help or other assistance beyond that provided by the caregiver.

Work-place support. Work-place support was assessed by responses to two items: The people I work with take a personal interest in me and My supervisor is interested in my welfare (Karasek, 1987). The two questions were scored on four-point Likert scales, ranked 1 = strongly agree to 4 = strongly disagree.

Flexibility. Work-place flexibility incorporated three items (based on Scharlach et al., 1991) assessing characteristics of the work place: I can adjust my work schedule; I can take time off for personal reasons; and I can work at home if necessary. The three measures were scored on four-point Likert scales, ranked as 1 = strongly agree to 4 = strongly disagree.

Control. Work-place control was assessed with two items: I have a lot of freedom to decide how to do my work and I have a lot to say about what happens on my job (Karasek, 1987). The two questions were scored on four-point

Likert scales, ranked 1 = strongly agree to 4 = strongly disagree. An over-all measure of work-place resources was constructed by taking the mean of the scores obtained on the work-place support, flexibility, and control variables (Cronbach's Alpha reliability coefficient = 0.70)

FAMILY AND WORK-PLACE ACCOMMODATIONS

Work time missed. Time missed from work was assessed by asking respondents to indicate how many days of work they had missed in the previous two months because of their family-care responsibilities, as well as the total number of hours missed in the previous two months because of disruptions during the work day for family-care responsibilities. Number of days missed was multiplied by eight and added to the total number of hours of interruptions to yield an estimate of the total number of hours of productive work missed in the previous two months.

Work accommodations. Based on Scharlach et al. (1991), the frequencies with which respondents reported seven types of work accommodations—e.g., missing part of a work day, missing an entire work day, reduction in productivity or hours worked, or missing a promotion, work-related trip or other work opportunity—were obtained. The mean was obtained for the time missed and work accommodation measures (Cronbach's Alpha reliability coefficient = 0.73).

Family accommodations. Family accommodations were assessed by asking respondents the degree to which their family-care responsibilities interfered with social activities and spousal or partner relationships. Each item was scored on a four-item Likert scale, 1 = none at all to 4 = a great deal. The mean was obtained for the two items (Cronbach's Alpha reliability coefficient = 0.81).

OUTCOME VARIABLES

Caregiving strain. Types of personal strain experienced by the caregivers were assessed by asking respondents to rate separately the extent to which they currently experienced physical, financial, or emotional strain as a result of their family-care responsibilities. The items were scored on a four-point Likert scale (1 = none at all to 4 = a great deal). A single item was used to rate the extent to which their family care responsibilities interfered with their personal free time (1 = not at all to 4 = a great deal).

Role strain. Derived from five items, based on Bohen and Viveros-Long (1981), the role strain measure was designed to take into account all work and family responsibilities. Respondents were asked the extent to which they had more to do than they could comfortably handle, lacked enough time for themselves, were exhausted when going to bed at night, and did not have a good balance among or were not meeting their work, family, and personal responsibilities (1 = strongly agree to 4 = strongly disagree). The mean was obtained for the five items (Cronbach's Alpha reliability coefficient = 0.83).

WORK-PLACE BENEFITS, PROGRAMS, AND POLICIES

To assess the utilization rate and perceived helpfulness of various work-place benefits and programs, respondents were provided with a list of policies and programs available at the work site (e.g., flex-time, dependent care account, employee-assistance program (EAP), counselor, resource guide). Respondents were asked to indicate whether they had utilized each benefit and the extent of its helpfulness (1 = not at all helpful to 3 = very helpful).

Respondents also were provided with a list of other policies, programs, and benefits an employer might offer to assist employees with their family-care responsibilities (e.g., part-time work, ability to work at home, ability to use donated sick leave, support groups, seminars), and were asked to indicate those they would be likely to use.

Limitations of the Study Design

The design used in this study was an effective, pragmatic approach, given the objectives of the research, resources, and time considerations. However, the limitations of the design must be considered. Given the lack of an appropriate control group, it is impossible to determine causality between variables. Moreover, the research design and sample used in the study do limit the generalizability of the findings to the Laboratory's work force, which likely is not representative of the U.S. work force as a whole. The caregivers were predominately middle-class and may have had fewer care demands than some other types of caregivers, e.g., those not working who are caring full-time for family members with severe health and cognitive impairments. Caregivers with the heaviest demands may, in fact, have already terminated employment to meet their family-care responsibilities.

The unique nature of the employment site needs to be considered. As research laboratory employees, it is likely that the respondents have greater levels of work-place flexibility and autonomy than is available to parents and caregivers in many other employment settings. Furthermore, the work site exists in a community with a comprehensive service network for individuals with disabilities.

It also should be noted that self-report data are subject to several potential distortions. For example, in this study, some respondents may have overstated the impact of family care to support the need for additional programs, or they may have understated their situation, concerned that they would suffer some negative ramifications if their responses were disclosed. In addition, self-reports are based on subjects' perceptions and interpretations rather than behaviors, and do not replace actual objective measures of the variables under study such as the functional limitation of the care recipient, days off from work, or reduced time alone.

Data Analysis

To assess associations among nominal and ordinal level variables such as gender and type of care, contingency tables and Chi Square statistics were calculated. Inferential techniques such as ANOVA were used for variables treated at the continuous and ordinal or nominal level of measurement. For example, one-way ANOVAs were utilized to examine such relationships as degree of role strain by race. In the event that significant differences were found, statistical techniques such as Bonferroni's were used to compare differences among groups.

T-tests were calculated when one variable was treated at the continuous level of measurement and the other was categorical and dichotomous, e.g., degree of role strain by gender. To assess the degree of bivariate association between dependent and independent variables treated at the interval or continuous level of measurement, correlations and linear regressions were calculated.

To control for background characteristics and evaluate the impact of the independent variables on the various dependent measures, multiple regressions were completed. As part of the multivariate analysis, all bivariate relationships were assessed for multicollinearity. Initially, a matrix of bivariate correlations was created and inspected for high levels of association (higher than 0.80). A more stringent test was used to regress each independent variable on all other independent variables, to check for R-squares close to 1.00, an indicator of a high degree of multicollinearity. All scales used in the study were tested for reliability using Cronbach's Alpha reliability coefficients.

These various univariate, bivariate, and multivariate methods were utilized to provide a preliminary analysis and description of the variables, and to eliminate from further multivariate analysis those variables with poor distributional qualities, prohibitive numbers of missing data, and limited association with the outcome variables. Through these steps there was a reduction in the number of variables to be tested, although sufficient measures remained to test all of the specified domains in the conceptual framework.

Linear regressions were then run to assess the impact of the following predictor variables on work and family accommodations and role strain: background characteristics (caregiver's health status, age, gender, race, and job category); family and work-role demands (number of care recipients, care recipient age, level or impairment of the care recipient, and work demand); and family and work resources (household income, help received with caregiving, work-place support, control, and job flexibility).

SUMMARY

The demand and resource framework used in this research builds upon the various conceptual approaches that have been developed in the work and family and caregiving fields. By combining aspects of stress and role theories, both the psychological and social aspects of family care are emphasized, illustrating the significance of combining dual role responsibilities in the provision of informal family care.

Incorporating constructs from both perspectives, the research discussed in this book analyzes the interactive nature of the following factors: background characteristics, work and family role demands, work and family resources, work and family accommodations, and role strain. In the next chapter, we will describe research findings based on the application of the resource and demand family-care model.

PART THREE

Employee Family-Care Responsibilities

· 6 ·

Employees with Children

FINDINGS

INTRODUCTION

In Chapter 2, we documented the pressures on today's working parents as they attempt to balance the potentially competing demands of employment and child rearing. We found that many, but not all, working parents experience substantial amounts of personal stress in balancing their work and family responsibilities, and that conflict between job and family can affect a parent's physical and psychological well-being. Incompatible family and work responsibilities can also contribute to work-place impacts such as excessive absenteeism, unscheduled time off, telephone calls home, lost concentration, and reduced productivity.

We also noted substantial variability in the type and amount of work-family conflict working parents experience: many report considerable role strain, others little or none. Many mothers who are in the paid labor force, for example, report higher levels of physical and mental well-being than those who are not working outside of the home. This suggests that it is the nature and intensity of employees' work and family responsibilities, rather than employment or parenthood per se, that determine the impact on parents of working outside the home.

In this chapter, we examine those specific characteristics of employees' work and family situations that are most apt to require accommodations at home and at work, and which may contribute to a sense of role strain. We also consider the perceived efficacy of some common work-place programs and policies designed to help working parents. The resource and demand model described in Chapter 5 serves as the framework for our analysis in this chapter. According to this model, strain experienced by working parents can be understood as a transactional process reflecting an imbalance between the demands of their combined work and family roles and the resources available to cope with those demands. This perspective emphasizes the interactive relationship between family and work roles and allows for an assessment of role demands and resources in both domains.

Of importance is the balance between the magnitude of work and family responsibilities and the adequacy of social support and other potential resources. In particular, higher levels of role strain and work interference are apt to occur when family and work demands are relatively high and family and work resources are relatively low. Among the demands considered here are the ages and number of children, other family responsibilities, problems with child-care arrangements, hours worked, and work-place pressures. Potential resources include household income, job flexibility, and support from coworkers and supervisors. In addition, we examine the potential helpfulness to working parents of a variety of work-place policies and programs.

CHILD-CARE RESPONSIBILITIES

In our study of employees at the Lawrence Berkeley Laboratory, we found that 35 percent reported having responsibility for at least one child age 18 or younger, consistent with Census Bureau estimates that 37 percent of all employees in the U.S. have children under the age of 18 (Ferber et al., 1991). Sixteen percent had one or more children under the age of six, also the same as the national average for all workers. An additional 15 percent did not currently have children but expected to have a child within the next five years.

IMPACT OF CHILD-CARE RESPONSIBILITIES ON WORK AND FAMILY LIFE

Parenting Strain

The demands of attempting to balance two potentially competing jobs, raising children and paid work, frequently affect employees' physical and emotional well-being. As shown in Table 6-1, 75 percent of the working parents in this study reported experiencing some level of emotional strain as a result of their family-care responsibilities, with 18 percent reporting "quite a bit" or "a great deal" of emotional upset. Physical fatigue due to family responsibilities was reported by 83 percent of working parents, with 31 percent indicating "quite a bit" or "a great deal" of fatigue. Financial strain associated with family responsibilities was reported by 78 percent of the working parents, with 36 percent indicating "quite a bit" or "a great deal" of financial strain. Eighty-eight percent reported that their family responsibilities interfered with their personal free time, and 47 percent indicated "quite a bit" or "a great deal" of such interference.

TABLE 6-1 Impact of child-care responsibilities
(as a percentage of respondents with child-care responsibilities)
(n = 660)

Parenting Strain	
Interference with Free Time	88%
Physical Fatigue	83%
Financial Strain	78%
Emotional Upset	75%
Family Accommodations	
Accommodations in Social Life	82%
Interference with Spousal/Partner Relationship	76%
Work-place Accommodations	
Missed Part of a Work Day	77%
Missed an Entire Work Day	58%
Reduced Productivity	41%
Reduced Working Hours	28%
Turned Down Extra Work Opportunities	26%
Missed Training Opportunities or Meetings	23%
Didn't Get a Promotion	7%
Any of the Above	89%
Role Strain	
Too Much To Do	42%
Responsibilities Out of Balance	37%
Exhausted at Night	31%
Not Enough Time for Self	27%
Not Meeting Responsibilities	23%

Family Accommodations

Working parents often must rearrange their personal lives and social activities to accommodate their work and family responsibilities. In this study, 82 percent of working parents reported that their family-care responsibilities required accommodations in their social activities, with 41 percent reporting "quite a bit" or "a great deal" of interference. Seventy-six percent reported that their family responsibilities interfered with their relationship with their spouse or partner, with 30 percent indicating "quite a bit" or "a great deal" of interference. These findings are consistent with those of other studies documenting work "spillover" into leisure time and marital relationships.

Work-Place Accommodations

The demands of balancing work and family-care responsibilities can require working parents to make substantial accommodations in their work habits. In this study, 89 percent of the employees with children reported accommodating work to their family-care responsibilities in one way or another. Almost 60 percent reported missing at least one day of work in the past two months because of family responsibilities; 42 percent had been absent one or two days; 13 percent were absent three or four days; and 3 percent were absent five days or more. More than three-fourths of the respondents reported missing part of a normal work day because of family responsibilities; examples given included coming late to work, leaving early, being interrupted, or being too tired or upset to work effectively. The total amount of missed work in the past two months ranged from 0 to 96 hours, with 43 percent of respondents missing an average of 2 hours a month or less, 42 percent missing 3 to 9 hours a month, and 16 percent missing more than 10 hours a month.

Forty-one percent of the respondents indicated that they were less productive at work because of their family responsibilities. In addition, approximately one-fourth indicated that they had reduced the number of hours they worked, had turned down extra work opportunities such as overtime or special projects, or had missed training opportunities or meetings; and 7 percent had not received a promotion or merit increase because of their family-care responsibilities. Sixty-one percent of the respondents indicated that they had taken a personal leave from their job for family reasons, with 13 percent taking the leave without pay.

Role Strain

Incompatibility between work and family responsibilities can result in role strain. Role strain has been associated with reduced physical and mental well-being, including increased depression and decreased life satisfaction. Considerable variability exists, however, in the extent to which working parents experience conflict between their work and family responsibilities. Whereas many report considerable role strain, some experience little or no distress as a result of their work and family responsibilities, and there even is substantial evidence of positive psychological effects of employment for working mothers (Emlen & Koren, 1984; Barnett & Baruch, 1985; Barnett & Marshall, 1989; Waldron & Jacobs, 1989).

In this study, 42 percent of respondents agreed that, taking into consideration all of their work and family responsibilities, they had more to do than they could handle comfortably. Thirty-seven percent felt that they did not have a good balance between their work, family, and personal responsibilities; 31 percent indicated that they were exhausted when they went to bed at night; 27 percent said they did not have enough time for themselves; and 23 percent felt that they were not doing a good job of meeting their work, family, and personal responsibilities.

These personal and family impacts can be understood in the context of the demands imposed by employees' work and family responsibilities and the resources available in each of those domains.

CHARACTERISTICS, DEMANDS, AND RESOURCES OF WORKING PARENTS

Social and Demographic Characteristics of Employees with Children

In this section, we examine employee characteristics and their relationship to indicators of work and family strain. Employee characteristics examined include age, gender, race/ethnicity, job classification, health, and marital status. Table 6-2 displays frequency distributions of many of these characteristics for respondents with and without children. Table 6-3 displays the associations between employee characteristics and outcomes such as family and work accommodations, role strain, and other indicators of personal stress. In general, we found that higher levels of strain are experienced by working parents who are female, hold clerical and administrative support positions, and are in poorer health. Working parents who are younger and

TABLE 6-2 Characteristics of respondents with and without child-care responsibilities

	Employees with Children (n = 660)	Employees without Children (n = 1,228)
Age ***		
Under 30	5%	9%
30–39	41%	23%
40–49	45%	29%
50–59	9%	31%
60 and over	1%	8%
Gender		
Male	72%	69%
Female	28%	31%
Race/Ethnicity **		
White	71%	79%
African-American	8%	5%
Asian/Pacific Islander	15%	11%
Hispanic	5%	4%
American Indian	<1%	<1%
Job Category *		
Scientists and Engineers	41%	36%
Administrative Professional	25%	31%
Administrative Clerical	10%	11%
Technical	24%	22%

* p <.05
** p <.01
*** p <.001

TABLE 6-3 Bivariate associations

	Family Accomm.	Work Accomm.	Missed Work	Role Strain
Social and Demographic Characteristics				
Age	− 0.08*	− 0.13**	− 0.11**	− 0.07
Gender (female)	t = 2.11*	t = 3.42***	t = 0.86	t = 4.88***
Race/Ethnicity	F = 1.83	F = 4.82*	F = 2.38	F = 0.76
Marital Status (married)	t = − 0.94	t = − 1.67	t = − 1.35	t = − 0.38
Occupation	F = 2.34	F = 5.18**	F = 0.91	F = 7.37***
Health	− 0.09*	− 0.11**	− 0.04	− 0.13**
Family Demands				
Number of Children	0.12**	0.08	0.09*	0.06
Age of Youngest Child	− 0.27**	− 0.24**	− 0.21**	− 0.12**
Disabled Child	t = 0.88	t = 0.78	t = 1.57	t = 2.49*
Child-Care Problems	0.28**	0.28**	0.18**	0.24**
Adult-Care Responsibilities	t = 1.35	t = − 0.76	t = 1.93	t = 0.79
Work Demands				
Hours Worked	0.02	− 0.01	− 0.01	0.17**
Job Demands	0.27**	0.27**	0.14**	0.42**
Family Resources				
Income	0.06	0.17**	0.01	0.17**
Satisfactory Child Care	− 0.32**	− 0.19**	− 0.21**	− 0.33**
Work Resources				
Coworker Support	− 0.19**	− 0.09*	− 0.12**	− 0.19**
Job Control	− 0.12**	0.00	− 0.06	− 0.08
Job Flexibility	− 0.07	− 0.02	− 0.01	− 0.10*
Work-place Policies and Programs				
Adjusted Work Schedule	t = 1.59	t = 6.12***	t = 3.16**	t = 3.07**
Dependent Care Account	t = 1.20	t = 3.70***	t = 1.09	t = 3.49***
Parent Fair	t = 1.94	t = 2.76**	t = 2.41*	t = 2.93**
Child Care Guide	t = 3.06**	t = 3.96***	t = 3.25***	t = 4.93***
EAP Counselor	t = 1.97*	t = 2.39*	t = 2.21*	t = 2.61**

who are African-American or Hispanic tend to make greater accommodations but do not necessarily experience higher levels of role strain or emotional distress.

AGE

The median age of employees with children 0–18 years of age in this survey was 41 years, compared with 46 years for respondents without children. The average age of working parents in most other surveys has been between 35 and 40, consistent with the average age (about 37) of employees in the nonfederal U.S. work force.

In this study, younger employees experienced higher levels of family accommodations, work accommodations, and missed work because of their

TABLE 6-3 *Continued*

	Physical Strain	Financial Strain	Emotional Strain
Social and Demographic Characteristics			
Age	− 0.12**	− 0.16**	− 0.02
Gender (female)	t = 7.50***	t = 2.76**	t = 4.46***
Race/Ethnicity	F = 3.23*	F = 5.00**	F = 1.95
Marital Status (married)	t = − 1.42	t = − 3.75***	t = − 3.29***
Occupation	F = 6.68***	F = 10.38****	F = 5.99***
Health	− 0.14**	− 0.07	− 0.10*
Family Demands			
Number of Children	0.07	0.13**	0.02
Age of Youngest Child	− 0.30**	− 0.21**	− 0.04
Disabled Child	t = 1.62	t = 2.25*	t = 1.50
Child-Care Problems	0.26**	0.17**	0.16**
Adult-Care Responsibilities	t = 2.75**	t = 1.10	t = 3.52***
Work Demands			
Hours Worked	− 0.06	− 0.08	− 0.11**
Job Demands	0.23**	0.11**	0.24**
Family Resources			
Income	0.07	− 0.24**	0.00
Satisfactory Child Care	− 0.23**	− 0.31**	− 0.28**
Work Resources			
Coworker Support	− 0.15**	− 0.10*	− 0.25**
Job Control	− 0.14**	− 0.23**	− 0.16**
Job Flexibility	− 0.12**	− 0.23**	− 0.12**
Work-place Policies and Programs			
Adjusted Work Schedule	t = 2.65**	t = − 0.12	t = 1.26
Dependent Care Account	t = 2.59**	t = 0.69	t = 2.65**
Parent Fair	t = 2.81**	t = 0.82	t = 1.92
Child Care Guide	t = 3.85***	t = 3.84***	t = 2.53*
EAP Counselor	t = 1.37	t = 0.48	t = 2.48*

* p <.05
** p <.01
*** p <.001

child-care responsibilities. Younger employees also experienced higher levels of physical strain and financial strain. Employee age was not associated with levels of role strain or emotional strain.

GENDER

Among the working parents, 72 percent were male and 28 percent were female, approximately the same gender breakdown as for employees without children. In all, 37 percent of men and 30 percent of women responding to the survey had children, a non-significant difference. The gender composition of this particular work setting was decidedly more heavily male than the overall nonfederal U.S. work force, in which men represent approximately 53 percent and women 47 percent of all workers.

Female respondents reported higher levels of family accommodations than males. Working mothers also reported making more work accommodations because of their family responsibilities, including missing meetings and training opportunities, not receiving promotions and raises, taking unpaid family leave, and working less productively. Consistent with previous studies, higher levels of role strain were evident among female respondents. Additionally, the women in this study reported higher levels of physical strain, financial strain, and emotional strain than men. Men and women did not differ significantly in the total amount of time missed from work because of family responsibilities.

That women experience greater conflict between work and family responsibilities is a consistent finding in studies of working parents. Much of the difference between working mothers and fathers is likely attributable to the unequal division of child-care responsibilities between men and women, particularly when the children are small. In one study of 8,000 workers, for example, 79 percent of mothers and only 5 percent of fathers said that they took all or most of the responsibility for their family's child-care arrangements (Emlen, Koren & Yoakum, 1990). When male employees have similar family responsibilities as females, they are as likely as the females to experience high levels of work-family role strain and reduced levels of physical and emotional well-being (Googins & Burden, 1987). Such gender differences will be discussed further in Chapter 9.

RACE/ETHNICITY

Employees with children age 18 or under in this study were significantly more likely than other employees to be African-American, Hispanic, or Asian/Pacific. U.S. census data indicate that African-American and Hispanic women have slightly higher birth rates than white women: White women of childbearing age in the United States average about 2.0 births per woman, while African-American women average 2.4 and Hispanic women 2.97. Asian women have a slightly lower birth rate than whites, with 1.95 births per woman (Campbell, 1996). Single-parent families comprise 64 percent of all African-American families with children present, compared to 36 percent of Hispanic families and only 25 percent of white families (U.S. Bureau of the Census, 1996b).

Respondents to this survey did not differ by race or ethnicity with regard to parenting stress, family accommodations, amount of work missed, or role strain. Physical strain and financial strain were highest for African-American and Hispanic employees, perhaps reflecting the tendency of these two groups to have a greater number of children and fewer economic resources with which to purchase assistance. A number of studies have found that the stressors associated with raising young children may be particularly acute for ethnic minority families (e.g., Zambrana & Hurst, 1984). Fernandez (1986), for example, found that African-Americans were more likely than other people of color and much more likely than whites to report child-care problems and dissatisfaction with child-care arrangements.

JOB CLASSIFICATION

Employees with children were found to differ significantly from other employees by job category, in that they were more likely to hold technical and scientific positions and less likely to hold administrative positions. Scientists and administrators experienced the greatest amount of work accommodations and role strain, whereas technical personnel experienced the least amount. Clerical and administrative support staff reported the highest levels of physical, financial, and emotional strain associated with their family responsibilities, while scientists and technical personnel experienced the lowest levels. The four job categories did not differ with regard to child-care problems, family accommodations, or the amount of missed work.

It seems likely that scientists and administrators reported more work accommodations precisely because their jobs afforded them greater freedom to miss part of a work day, turn down extra work opportunities, miss meetings, or make other modifications in their work to handle their family-care responsibilities. Workers in professional and managerial positions are apt to have more control over when and how their work is done, allowing them the flexibility to reduce potential role conflict. They are also apt to have greater income available to purchase child care and other services to assist with family care. However, they may experience relatively high levels of role strain simply because of the nature of their work and the time demands of their jobs.

That clerical and administrative support staff reported the highest levels of physical, financial, and emotional strain is likely due to the fact that workers in these positions are more likely than other employees to be female, from racial or ethnic minority groups, and low income. As such, they are apt to have the greatest responsibility for parenting and other family duties, but also the fewest resources for handling those responsibilities, such as household income and control over their jobs. The impact of such differences by job type will be discussed further in Chapter 9.

HEALTH

When asked to rate their general health, 89 percent of employees with children responded "Excellent" or "Good." Ten percent reported their health as only "Fair," while fewer than 1 percent complained of poor health. Parents with poorer self-rated health tended to report more family accommodations, work accommodations, and greater role strain. Additionally, they experienced higher levels of physical strain and emotional strain than their peers who felt healthier. Employees' health ratings were not associated significantly with the amount of time they missed from work or with the levels of financial strain associated with their family responsibilities.

MARITAL STATUS

Eighty-six percent of respondents were currently married, with another 3 percent unmarried but living with a partner; 11 percent were divorced, widowed, or single. Married and unmarried parents did not differ significantly in reported levels of family accommodations, missed work, work accommodations, or role strain. However, unmarried parents did experience higher levels of financial and emotional strain.

These findings are consistent with a number of other studies, which have found that single parents do not generally experience greater role strain or absenteeism than other working parents. However, there is some evidence from other studies that single parents may have a more difficult time managing their combined work and family responsibilities. In one survey of 42 single and 304 married parent employees of a high-tech firm (Mulroy & Pitt-Catsouphes, 1994), single parents were more likely than married parents to report that their children's problems hindered their work effectiveness and that their work interfered with their ability to take care of their children's problems. They also reported more difficulty taking their children to health-care appointments and finding alternative child-care arrangements when necessary on days they were working. Single parents may have a particular need for child care during nonschool hours and days.

Family Demands

In this section, we examine family responsibilities that have the potential to place particularly heavy demands on a worker's time and energy, including caring for children who are younger, having a relatively large number of children, having a child with special needs, experiencing difficulties finding child care, and having responsibility for the care of other dependent family members. We found that employees who have young children and those who have difficulty finding child care make the greatest accommodations in their family and work lives and experience the highest levels of strain. Having more children, children with special needs, or adult-care responsibilities are also each associated with higher levels of certain types of accommodations and strain.

AGE OF CHILDREN

Four percent of the employees responding to this survey were caring for an infant, 7 percent had a toddler (age 1–2), 11 percent had a preschooler (age 3–5), 17 percent had a child in elementary school (age 6–12), and 32 percent had a teenager (age 13–18). Problems finding care were reported by the majority of respondents who had infants or toddlers, more than one-third of those with preschool children, and one-half of those with school-age children. Parents with children under the age of six experienced significantly more work accommodations and higher levels of role strain. In general, the younger the child the more the employee experienced problems with family accommodations, work accommodations, missed work, and role strain. Employees with younger children also experienced significantly higher levels of physical strain and financial strain.

NUMBER OF CHILDREN

Fifteen percent of the respondents to this study had responsibility for one child, 15 percent had two children, and 5 percent had three or more children. The number of children an employee had was significantly associated with the extent of family accommodations, the number of hours of work missed because of family responsibilities, and the level of financial strain. The number of children was not related significantly to work accommodations, role strain, or physical or emotional strain.

CHILDREN WITH DISABILITIES

Among respondents to this study, 8 percent of those with children (representing 3 percent of the total employee sample) were caring for a child with special needs. Problems finding care were reported by 95 percent of parents of children with physical, mental, or emotional disabilities. Parents of children with disabilities experienced significantly higher levels of role strain and financial strain than other parents. They did not differ significantly from other parents in levels of family accommodations, work accommodations, amount of missed work, or physical or emotional strain.

Most other studies have also found that parents of children with disabilities experience difficulty finding child care to accommodate their children's needs. In one survey of child-care supply in several cities (Kisker et al., 1989), only 4 out of 10 family day-care providers would accept children with special needs. Care for children with special needs may also be more costly, due to the safety and liability concerns of providers.

CHILD-CARE PROBLEMS

Child-care problems were reported by the vast majority of working parents in this study. Problems finding care were reported by 55 percent of respondents who had infants or toddlers and 37 percent of those with preschool children. Half of respondents with elementary school children reported problems finding care before or after school, and two-thirds reported problems during school vacations.

Two-thirds of respondents experienced problems finding temporary or emergency care, particularly when their child was ill. Sixty percent had difficulty finding child care that matched their work schedule, 44 percent had trouble finding care that was conveniently located, 39 percent experienced problems with the quality of care, and 31 percent had problems finding child care that was dependable. Child-care problems were particularly acute for parents of children with disabilities, as discussed above.

Two-thirds found the cost of child care to be a problem. Monthly child-care expenses ranged from under $200 to more than $1000, with a median of $335 per month. Eight percent of respondents with children were currently paying $1000 per month or more for child care. The cost of child care is apt to be particularly problematic for lower income families, for whom child-care expenses may consume as much as 20 percent of their household income (Emlen et al., 1990). Difficulty paying for child care is associated with higher levels of work-family conflict and greater absenteeism.

The total number of child-care problems was computed for each employee. Those who experienced the greatest number of problems were found to experience significantly higher levels of family accommodations, work accommodations, missed work, role strain, physical strain, financial strain, and emotional strain.

OTHER FAMILY RESPONSIBILITIES

Twenty-two percent of employees with children were also providing assistance to a disabled adult over the age of 18. These parents reported higher levels of physical strain and emotional strain than those who did not have adult-care responsibilities. Parents with adult-care responsibilities did not experience significantly higher levels of family accommodations, work hours missed, work accommodations, role strain, or financial strain than other working parents.

Family Resources

In this section, we examine the potential buffering effect on work-family strain of family resources such as household income and satisfactory child-care arrangements. We found that employees who had more satisfactory child care made fewer accommodations and experienced less strain. Household income level, on the other hand, was associated with greater workplace accommodations and higher levels of role strain.

INCOME

Fourteen percent of respondents had annual household incomes under $40,000, 27 percent had incomes between $40,000 and $59,999, 26 percent between $60,000 to $79,999, and 33 percent had household incomes of $80,000 or more. These incomes were somewhat higher than national averages, reflecting the fact that these employees worked for a high technology research center.

Employees in this study who had higher incomes experienced greater work accommodations and higher levels of role strain than those with lower incomes. There were no significant differences in family accommodations, number of work hours missed, or physical or emotional strain. They did, however, report less financial strain.

That higher income employees have more work accommodations may be attributed in part to the greater flexibility and personal control their jobs offer, making it more possible for them to arrive late, interrupt their work routines, or miss meetings for family reasons. Employees with higher household incomes are more likely to have a working spouse, contributing a second income and additional caregiving resources, but are also likely to report greater role strain.

SATISFACTION WITH CHILD-CARE ARRANGEMENTS

Satisfactory child-care arrangements can be a particularly important resource for working parents. The majority of respondents in this survey indicated satisfaction with their child-care arrangements: 69 percent indicated that they were "quite satisfied" or "extremely satisfied," while 26 percent were "a little satisfied" and 5 percent were "not at all satisfied."

In this study, employee satisfaction with child-care arrangements was significantly associated with lower levels of family accommodations, fewer hours of missed work, fewer work accommodations, lower levels of role strain, and lower levels of physical, financial, and emotional strain.

Other studies also have found that when care arrangements are dependable and of reasonable quality, employees may be absent less often, take less time off during the work day, and may be less distracted and more productive while at work. The *National Study of the Changing Work Force* (Galinsky et al., 1993), for example, found that employed parents who were satisfied with their child-care arrangements felt more able to be good parents, felt more successful in their home lives and their lives in general, and experienced less stress than employees with unsatisfactory child-care situations.

Work Demands

In this section we examine aspects of employees' work situations that may place particularly heavy demands on their overall time and energy, potentially contributing to role strain as they attempt to manage their work and parenting responsibilities. We found that employees with greater pressures at work made greater accommodations at work and at home and experienced greater strain. The number of hours worked was associated with higher levels of role strain, but not with the number of accommodations made.

HOURS WORKED

Among the working parents in this survey, more than half (53 percent) worked 40 hours per week, 5 percent worked less than 40 hours per week,

16 percent worked between 41 and 50 hours, and 26 percent worked more than 50 hours, generally consistent with national employment data (U. S. Bureau of the Census, 1996b). Employees who worked longer hours experienced higher levels of role strain, but not significantly more family or work accommodations, missed work, or physical or financial strain. The number of hours worked was inversely related to the amount of emotional strain the parents experienced, perhaps because parents who were the most burned-out emotionally as a result of their family responsibilities were less likely to have the psychological energy to be able to work extra hours at their jobs.

JOB DEMANDS

Forty-two percent of the respondents indicated that they did not have enough time to get their work done. Those who reported more demanding jobs had significantly more family accommodations and work accommodations, and they missed significantly more work. They also reported significantly higher levels of role strain, physical strain, financial strain, and emotional strain.

Jobs that place heavy demands on employees' time and energy appear to leave less time and energy available to handle family responsibilities. In a study by Piotrkowski (1979), for example, men with extremely stressful jobs were tense at home and tended to withdraw from family interaction. Voydanoff (1988) found that the work-role characteristics most strongly related to work and family conflict were the number of hours worked and workload pressure (i.e., having too much work to do; being required to work too fast or too hard).

Work Resources

In this section we examine the potential buffering effect of work-place resources, such as the ability to control the nature of one's work and receiving personal support from coworkers and supervisors. We found that employees who had more job control, more support from coworkers and supervisors, and more job flexibility experienced less role strain and also less personal strain. In addition, employees with more job control made fewer family accommodations, while those with more supportive coworkers and supervisors made fewer family and work accommodations.

JOB CONTROL

In this study, 67 percent of respondents agreed that they have a lot of freedom to decide how to do their work, and 63 percent indicated they have a lot to say about what happens on the job. Greater job control was associated with fewer family accommodations and less physical, financial, and emotional strain. There was no significant association between job control and work accommodations, missed work, or role strain. These findings suggest that employees with more control over their jobs may have an easier time managing their child-care responsibilities without disrupting either their work or personal lives.

WORK-PLACE SUPPORT

Seventy-three percent of the working parents in this survey agreed that their coworkers took a personal interest in them, and 77 percent agreed that their supervisors were concerned about their welfare. Employees with more supportive coworkers made fewer family accommodations, missed fewer hours of work, and experienced lower levels of role strain, physical strain, financial strain, and emotional strain, but they did not differ from other employees with regard to the number of work accommodations. Employees with more supportive supervisors had fewer family accommodations, fewer hours of work missed, fewer work accommodations, and lower levels of role strain. Having supervisory support was also associated with significantly lower levels of physical and emotional strain, but not with financial strain.

The *National Study of the Changing Work Force* (Galinsky et al., 1993) found that supportive work environments, besides being associated with employees' well-being, were positively correlated with job performance. Workers who had supportive supervisors, good relationships with coworkers, and work places that took into consideration family needs and responsibilities were more loyal to their employers, more willing to work hard to further their employers' interests, and more satisfied with their jobs than were their counterparts with less supportive supervisors, coworkers, and work environments. Moreover, employees who perceived their supervisors and coworkers as being supportive felt more commitment to high job performance than workers who perceived little or no support. There was also a strong association between having a supportive supervisor and taking more initiative on the job.

Having the support of coworkers and supervisors also seems to have a buffering effect on role strain. Fernandez (1986) found that work and family stress was significantly lower for employees who had a supportive supervisor. Having a supervisor who is understanding of employees' family responsibilities has been found to reduce the risk of physical and psychological health problems, including coronary disease among clerical workers (Haynes, Eaker & Feinlib, 1984; Galinsky & Hughes, 1987). In general, it seems that support from supervisors and coworkers can moderate or buffer the impact of job stress on a variety of physical symptoms, somatic complaints, and depression.

JOB FLEXIBILITY

Flexibility regarding when and where work is done may make it easier for employees to assure that children are cared for properly during working hours. In this study, 83 percent of working parents agreed that they could adjust their normal work schedule, 81 percent indicated that they could take time off during normal work hours for personal reasons, and 40 percent could do their work at home if necessary. A measure reflecting these three indicators of job flexibility was constructed. This composite measure was found to be associated with significantly lower levels of role strain, physical strain, financial strain, and emotional strain. It was not associated significantly with the amount of family or work accommodations or the hours of work missed, perhaps because employees with greater job flexibility have the ability to make accommodations in a variety of areas of life to more effectively manage their work and parenting responsibilities.

Policies and Programs Considered Helpful by Working Parents

A number of work-place policies and programs have been identified as potentially beneficial for working parents. Policies and programs examined here include flexible work schedules, the ability to work at home, family leave, part-time work, child-care information, counseling, Dependent Care Accounts, child-care centers, and referral to community child-care resources. The policies considered most helpful to these working parents were the ability to adjust work schedules, take family leave, or work at home. Work-place programs considered most beneficial included talking to an Employee Assistance Program (EAP) counselor, utilizing a Dependent Care Account, having a child-care center for young children, or vacation programs for school-age children. However, adjusting one's work schedule or utilizing programs such as a Dependent Care Account, Child Care Guide, Parent Information Fair, or EAP counselor were associated with a greater number of work-place and family accommodations and higher levels of role strain, suggesting that work-place resources such as these are especially apt to be utilized by those working parents who are the most stressed.

FLEXIBLE WORK SCHEDULES

The ability to modify the time and place in which work must be done may make it easier for working parents to adapt work and child-care responsibilities to one another. In this study, 83 percent of working parents indicated that they could adjust their normal work schedules to fit their family responsibilities, and three-fourths of these had actually done so. Of those who had adjusted their work schedules, 99 percent indicated that this was helpful, and almost three-quarters considered it "very helpful." Surprisingly, those employees who reported adjusting their work schedules to fit their family responsibilities experienced significantly higher levels of role strain than those who had not done so. They also reported a greater number of other work accommodations, including more time missed from work.

INFORMATION PROGRAMS

Information about community child-care resources is consistently cited as a major need of working parents. In this study, the vast majority of employees with child-care responsibilities reported problems finding child care, as described earlier in this chapter. In response to this need, 38 percent of those with children age 12 or under said they would use a resource information and referral program that provided help in locating child-care services near their own home, if such a program were available. Despite the potential benefits of resource and referral programs, only 8 percent of respondents in the *National Childcare Survey* (Hofferth, et al., 1991) said that their employers offered such services.

To fill this need for their employees, the human resources department at Lawrence Berkeley Laboratory published a Child Care Resource Guide containing information for working parents and held a Parent Information Fair so that employees could speak with representatives of community child-care providers. Nine percent of the respondents had utilized the Child Care Guide; 77 percent found the Guide to be helpful, and 11 percent found it to be "very helpful." Seven percent of the respondents indicated that they had attended the Parent Information Fair; 74 percent of those attending found the Fair to be helpful, and 12 percent found it "very helpful."

Significantly higher levels of role strain were experienced by those employees who utilized the Child Care Guide or attended the Parent Information Fair, compared with those who did not utilize these programs. Work accommodations were also higher for those who utilized the Guide or attended the Fair. More time was missed from work by parents who utilized the Guide or attended the Fair than by those who did not use the programs. Significantly greater family accommodations were associated with utilization of the Child Care Guide, but not with attending the Parent Information Fair.

COUNSELING PROGRAMS

Seven percent of the respondents had spoken to an EAP counselor regarding their family responsibilities; of these, 83 percent found the counseling to be helpful and 43 percent found it "very helpful." Apparently, personal advice and counseling may be more important to working parents than having general information about child care and child-rearing issues, whether in the form of guidebooks or fairs. Significantly higher levels of role strain, family accommodations, work accommodations, and a greater number of hours missed from work were experienced by parents who spoke with an EAP counselor, compared with those who did not do so.

FINANCIAL BENEFITS

Employees had access to a Dependent Care Account, whereby they could reserve part of their salary on a pre-tax basis to pay for child-care expenses. Sixteen percent of working parents utilized the Dependent Care Assistance Plan; 88 percent of these found it to be helpful and 51 percent "very helpful." Those who used the Plan experienced significantly higher levels of role strain and work accommodations than employees who did not make use of this option.

CHILD-CARE PROGRAMS

Respondents were asked to indicate whether there were any child-care programs they "would definitely use" if the programs could be offered at or near their work site and at a reasonable cost. The program that received the greatest endorsement was the development of a child-care center, with more than half of respondents with children age 12 or under indicating that they "would definitely use" such a center if it could be offered at a reasonable cost. Fifty-eight percent of those with children under age one would use an on-site infant-care center; 56 percent of those with children ages 1–2 would use a toddler-care center; 49 percent of those with children ages 3–5 would use a preschooler-care center; and 41 percent of those with children age 12 or under would use a temporary or emergency child-care center. When asked where they would prefer child care to be provided, 44 percent said "at or near home," 26 percent said "at or near work," 17 percent said "at or near the child's school," and the rest had no preference.

Center-based care is apt to be particularly important for employees who experience problems with existing child-care arrangements. The 1990 *National Childcare Survey* (Hofferth et al., 1991) and the 1975 *National Childcare Consumer Study* (UNCO, 1975) both found that the majority of parents seeking alternative child-care arrangements preferred center-based care over in-home providers. Yet there remains a shortage of quality child care, especially for infants, children with disabilities, children from low-income families, and children whose parents work nonstandard hours. As of 1988, only 2 percent of companies with ten or more employees offered employer-supported child care for their employees (Galinsky & Stein, 1990). By 1995, according to a Hewitt Associates survey, 9 percent of companies offered such programs.

Other programs desired were those that would address the "gap" in child care that occurs when regular arrangements are unavailable. In the *National Childcare Survey* (Hofferth, et al., 1991), 20 percent of respondents cited the child-care facility being closed or unavailable as a major cause of child-care failure. When parents of school-age children were asked about child-care arrangements during the previous summer, more than one-quarter indicated that they had no regular arrangements. In this survey, 62 percent of respondents with children ages 5–12 indicated that they would use school vacation programs, and 29 percent indicated that they would use after-school programs.

OTHER POLICIES AND PROGRAMS CONSIDERED
HELPFUL BY WORKING PARENTS

Respondents also identified a number of other policies, programs, and benefits that they considered useful in meeting their combined work and family responsibilities. The most frequently endorsed policies were the ability to take unpaid family leave (cited by 61 percent of respondents) or work at home (57 percent). Less likely to be considered helpful were workshops (cited by 26 percent of respondents), part-time work (cited by 23 percent), and support groups (15 percent).

SUMMARY

The findings reported in this chapter indicate that working parents are apt to experience higher levels of strain associated with their work and family responsibilities if they are female, hold clerical jobs, are in poorer health, have young children, have difficulty finding child care, and work long hours at high-pressure jobs. Strain is reduced when working parents have more satisfactory child-care arrangements, more control over the nature of their work, and receive more support from coworkers and supervisors. These findings indicate a synergy between employees' work and parenting responsibilities, whereby certain combinations of work-place demands, work-place support, family demands and family resources predict corresponding combinations of work-family strain and work and family accommodations.

Respondents identified a number of work-place policies and programs they considered helpful or potentially helpful in their efforts to manage their potentially competing work and child-care responsibilities: ability to adjust work schedules, take family leave, or work at home; child-care center for young children; vacation programs for school-age children; counseling; and a Dependent Care Account. Yet, at least for these working parents, actual utilization of such services as counseling, information and tax relief was not associated with lower levels of role strain and parental stress. Indeed, our findings suggest that working parents may not utilize such programs until they are already experiencing substantial amounts of strain at home and at work, and have already made sizable accommodations in their family relationships and work routines.

Employees with Adult-Care Responsibilities

FINDINGS

INTRODUCTION

Chapter 3 described the problems experienced by individuals who, in addition to their work responsibilities, provide assistance to a disabled adult family member or friend. We indicated that adult care is a growing phenomenon, fueled by dramatic increases in the number of older persons in the population coupled with renewed reliance on families as primary providers of care for chronically ill family members. Currently, as many as one in four workers are providing some kind of assistance to a disabled family member, and it is estimated that this number will grow to one in three by the middle of the next century.

Caring for someone with a disability can be a demanding and stressful responsibility, often requiring employees to make accommodations in their personal lives and work routines. Caregiving responsibilities can produce substantial amounts of stress, including physical and financial sacrifices and emotional strain. Work can be an added source of strain, or sometimes also a source of relief. Indeed, some working caregivers report that working brings them rewards that help to offset the potential strains of their adult-care responsibilities. Similarly, there may be potentially beneficial aspects of employees' personal lives that help them to manage the stresses of a demanding job.

In this chapter, we explore the experiences of employees who provide assistance to an elderly or disabled adult. We will examine their caregiving responsibilities, their work situations, and the accommodations they make to balance the various demands of family and work. A primary focus of our analysis will be an examination of the interactive relationship between family and work roles, including the ways in which role demands and resources in each arena combine, in accordance with the resource and demand model described in Chapter 5.

ADULT-CARE RESPONSIBILITIES

In our study of employees at Lawrence Berkeley Laboratory, we found that 22 percent of the survey respondents were providing assistance to at least one adult family member or friend who had a health problem or a disability. Seven percent were providing assistance to an adult under the age of 65, and 19 percent were providing assistance to at least one person age 65 or older. An additional 2 percent had provided care in the past five years but were no longer doing so, and 10 percent reported they were not currently providing care but might need to do so within the next five years. In all, more than a third of all respondents indicated that they either were currently involved in caring for an adult family member or friend, had done so during the past five years, or expected to do so within the next five years.

These prevalence rates are consistent with those of previous work-place surveys, which typically find between 20 and 25 percent of respondents providing assistance to adults with disabilities. A study of university employees, for example, found that approximately 20 percent of all employees were providing assistance to an adult family member or friend who had a health problem; 9 percent were helping someone age 18–64, and about 14 percent were helping an elderly person (Scharlach & Fredriksen, 1994).

IMPACT OF ADULT-CARE RESPONSIBILITIES ON WORK AND FAMILY LIFE

Caregiving Strain

Stress and strain are common experiences for persons caring for someone with an illness or disability. In this study, 87 percent of employees with adult-care responsibilities reported experiencing stress as a direct result of these responsibilities, with 30 percent reporting "quite a bit" or "a great deal" of stress. As shown in Table 7-1, 80 percent of respondents reported experiencing some level of emotional strain, with 23 percent reporting "quite a bit" or "a great deal" of emotional upset. Physical fatigue was reported by 73 percent of respondents, with 23 percent indicating "quite a bit" or "a great deal" of fatigue. Financial strain was reported by 62 percent of the respondents, with 23 percent indicating "quite a bit" or "a great deal" of financial strain. Eighty-five percent of the respondents reported that their caregiving responsibilities interfered with their personal free time, and 33 percent indicated "quite a bit" or "a great deal" of such interference.

Family Accommodations

Employees who are providing assistance to disabled adults often need to make accommodations in their personal and social lives in order to balance

TABLE 7-1 Impact of adult-care responsibilities
(as a percentage of respondents with adult-care responsibilities)
(n = 414)

Caregiving Strain	
Interference with Free Time	85%
Emotional Upset	80%
Physical Fatigue	73%
Financial Strain	62%
Family Accommodations	
Accommodations in Social Life	74%
Interference with Spousal Relationship	61%
Work-place Accommodations	
Missed Part of a Work Day	65%
Missed an Entire Work Day	45%
Reduced Productivity	36%
Reduced Working Hours	16%
Turned Down Extra Work Opportunities	15%
Missed Training Opportunities or Meetings	15%
Didn't Get a Promotion	5%
Any of the Above	80%
Role Strain	
Not Enough Time for Self	64%
Exhausted at Night	60%
Too Much to Do	55%
Responsibilities Out of Balance	36%
Not Meeting Responsibilities	23%

their work and family responsibilities most effectively. In this study, 74 percent of respondents reported that their adult-care responsibilities required accommodations in their social activities, with 29 percent reporting "quite a bit" or "a great deal" of interference. Sixty-one percent reported that their care responsibilities interfered with their relationship with their spouse or partner, with 21 percent indicating "quite a bit" or "a great deal" of interference.

Work-Place Accommodations

Caring for an ill or disabled adult can require employees to make substantial accommodations in how and when they do their jobs. In this study, 80 percent of the respondents reported making some kinds of work accommodations in response to their adult-care responsibilities. Some of the particular aspects of work performance and work behavior that were affected are summarized in Table 7-1. Forty-five percent of respondents reported having to be absent from work at least once in the past two months in order to provide family care. Thirty-one percent had been absent one or two days in the past two months, 10 percent were absent three or four days, and 5 percent were absent five days or more.

Sixty-five percent of these respondents reported having to miss part of a normal work day in the past two months. Examples included coming late to work, leaving early, being interrupted, or being too tired or upset to work effectively. Thirty-three percent reported experiencing such work disruptions once a month, 16 percent twice a month, 8 percent once a week, and 3 percent two times a week or more; 5 percent failed to provide an exact figure. The total amount of time missed from work in the past two months because of caregiving responsibilities ranged from 0 to more than 60 hours, with 16 percent of caregiving employees missing 1–4 hours a month on average, 19 percent missing 5–8 hours a month, 15 percent missing 9–16 hours a month, 9 percent missing 17–32 hours a month, and 3 percent missing an average of more than four full days of work a month.

Thirty-six percent of the respondents indicated that they were less productive at work because of their care responsibilities. Other work accommodations reported included reducing the number of hours they usually worked (16 percent), turning down extra work opportunities such as overtime or special projects (15 percent), missing training opportunities or meetings (15 percent), and not receiving a promotion or merit increase because of their adult-care responsibilities (5 percent). Fifty-five percent indicated that they had taken a personal leave from their job for family reasons. Of these, almost half used sick leave for this reason; 29 percent used vacation leave; 4 percent took a disability leave; 2 percent reduced their work week; and 8 percent took leave without pay.

Role Strain

Caregiving employees in this study often experienced a significant amount of role strain. Almost two-thirds of employees with adult-care responsibilities agreed that, taking into consideration all of their work and family responsibilities, they didn't have enough time for themselves; 60 percent indicated that they were exhausted when they went to bed at night; 55 percent said that they had more to do than they could handle comfortably; 36 percent felt that they did not have a good balance between their work, family, and personal responsibilities; and 23 percent felt that they were not doing a good job of meeting their work, family, and personal responsibilities.

CHARACTERISTICS, DEMANDS, AND RESOURCES OF EMPLOYED CAREGIVERS

Social and Demographic Characteristics of Employees with Adult-Care Responsibilities

The types of caregiving responsibilities employees have and the manner in which those responsibilities impact their personal and work lives are likely to be affected by a variety of social and demographic characteristics. In this section, we examine characteristics such as employees' age, gender, race/ethnicity, job classification, health, and marital status. Table 7-2 displays frequency distributions of these characteristics for respondents with and without adult-care responsibilities. In Table 7-3, we show the associations between these employee characteristics and outcomes, such as family and work accommodations, role strain, and other indicators of personal stress. In general, we found that higher levels of strain were experienced by care-giving employees who were younger, female, held clerical and administrative support positions, and were in poorer health.

AGE

Employees caring for dependent adults were slightly older than other employees, on average. The median age of employees with adult-care responsibilities was 46 years, compared to 43 years for those without adult-care responsibilities. More than one-third of employees with adult-care respon-

TABLE 7-2 Characteristics of respondents with and without adult-care responsibilities

	Employees with Adult Care (n = 414)	Employees without Adult Care (n = 1,474)
Age ***		
Under 30	2%	9%
30–39	24%	31%
40–49	39%	33%
50–59	29%	22%
60 and over	6%	5%
Gender ***		
Male	62%	72%
Female	38%	28%
Race/Ethnicity		
White	75%	76%
Asian/Pacific Islander	13%	12%
African-American	7%	6%
Hispanic	4%	5%
American Indian	<1%	<1%
Job Category *		
Scientists and Engineers	33%	39%
Technical	34%	27%
Administrative Professional	22%	23%
Administrative Clerical	11%	11%

* p <.05
** p <.01
*** p <.001

sibilities were age 50 or older. However, more than one-fourth of those caring for an elderly or disabled person were under the age of 40.

Younger employees experienced higher levels of family accommodations, work accommodations, role strain, physical strain, financial strain, and

TABLE 7-3 Bivariate associations

	Family Accomm.		Work Accomm.		Missed Work		Role Strain	
Social and Demographic Characteristics								
Age		−.10*		−.12*		−.10*		−.11*
Gender (female)	t =	1.79	t =	2.63**	t =	1.49	t =	4.20***
Race/Ethnicity	F =	0.59	F =	2.35	F =	1.97	F =	1.43
Marital Status (married)	t =	1.46	t =	.34	t =	.74	t =	.16
Occupation	F =	1.56	F =	0.28	F =	1.37	F =	3.75*
Health		−.14**		−.10*		−.03		−.18**
Family Demands								
Number of Care Recipients (CR)		.06		.05		−.02		.02
Hours of Assistance Given		.26**		.20**		.20**		.15**
Provides Personal Care	t =	4.27***	t =	1.35	t =	2.30*	t =	2.61**
Financial Assistance		.24**		.08		.14**		.16**
CR Behavior Problems	t =	4.65***	t =	3.30***	t =	2.76**	t =	3.28***
Age of Primary CR		−.12*		−.10*		−.11*		−.03
Relationship of CR to Caregiver (CG)	F =	2.58*	F =	2.66*	F =	4.37**	F =	2.08
CR Lives with CG	t =	2.16**	t =	−.35	t =	−1.34	t =	−.18
Problems Finding Care		.37**		.31**		.28**		.26**
Child-Care Responsibilities	t =	2.30*	t =	4.88***	t =	3.69***	t =	.30*
Work Demands								
Hours Worked		−.02		−.01		−.06		.05
Job Demands		.25**		.18**		.09		.41**
Family Resources								
Income		.02		.06		.01		.04
Help Received by CG		−.04		.04		.02		−.08
Paid Help Received by CR	t =	1.10	t =	3.68**	t =	1.77	t =	1.02
Any Help Received by CR	t =	.24	t =	.86	t =	−.24	t =	.60
Work Resources								
Coworker Support		−.17**		−.09		.00		−.13*
Job Control		−.16**		−.05		−.04		−.13**
Job Flexibility		−.14**		.01		.02		−.12*
Work-place Policies and Programs								
Adjusted Work Schedule	t =	3.20**	t =	6.35***	t =	3.14**	t =	2.71**
Dependent Care Account	t =	2.20*	t =	2.94**	t =	1.28	t =	0.52
Elder Care Fair	t =	2.12*	t =	2.89**	t =	3.06**	t =	3.21***
Elder Care Guide	t =	3.47***	t =	4.09***	t =	2.82**	t =	3.06**
EAP Counselor	t =	2.50*	t =	2.25*	t =	1.05	t =	1.81

Table 7-3 *Continued*

	Physical Strain	Financial Strain	Emotional Strain
Social and Demographic Characteristics			
Age	−.14**	−.15**	−.13**
Gender (female)	t = 3.33***	t = 1.35	t = 4.23***
Race/Ethnicity	F = 1.04	F = 3.97**	F = 0.46
Marital Status (married)	t = .22	t = −.82	t = −2.67**
Occupation	F = 3.95**	F = 5.91***	F = 6.16***
Health	−.19**	−.18**	−.18**
Family Demands			
Number of Care Recipients (CR)	.03	.00	−.03
Hours of Assistance Given	.31**	.20**	.18**
Provides Personal Care	t = 3.21***	t = 1.86	t = .67
Financial Assistance	.22**	.45**	.22**
CR Behavior Problems	t = 4.31***	t = .74	t = 4.79***
Age of Primary CR	−.15**	−.23**	−.12*
Relationship of CR to CG	F = 2.08	F = 5.07***	F = 2.13
CR Lives with CG	t = 1.85	t = 2.77**	t = −.73
Problems Finding Care	.33**	.23**	.29**
Child-Care Responsibilities	t = 6.57***	t = 6.53***	t = 1.09
Work Demands			
Hours Worked	−.08	−.07	−.11*
Job Demands	.19**	.08	.20**
Family Resources			
Income	−.04	−.18**	−.14**
Help Received by CG	−.04	−.07	−.02
Paid Help Received by CR	t = .45	t = −.60	t = 1.32
Any Help Received by CR	t = −.57	t = −1.73	t = −1.70
Work Resources			
Coworker Support	−.16**	−.15**	−.17**
Job Control	−.22**	−.20**	−.15**
Job Flexibility	−.15**	−.18**	−.19**
Work-place Policies and Procedures			
Adjusted Work Schedule	t = 4.61***	t = 2.68**	t = 1.06
Dependent Care Account	t = 4.15***	t = 3.14**	t = 0.49
Elder Care Fair	t = 2.77**	t = 0.10	t = 1.23
Elder Care Guide	t = 2.54*	t = 0.86	t = 3.95***
EAP Counselor	t = 2.29*	t = 1.10	t = 2.37*

* p <.05
** p <.01
*** p <.001

emotional strain. Younger employees also missed more work because of their family-care responsibilities.

GENDER

In this study, female employees were more likely than males to be providing assistance to an elderly or disabled adult and to be the person with primary caregiving responsibility, consistent with the findings of most previous studies of caregivers. Women are more likely than men to assume care responsibilities (Horowitz, 1985b; Stone et al., 1987; Fredriksen, 1995) because of sex-role expectations, limited alternative opportunities, and the greater likelihood of a male spouse needing assistance than a female spouse. When an elderly parent requires assistance, a daughter is most likely to become the primary caregiver, while sons assume a secondary role. Daughters also tend to provide greater amounts and more intense types of care (Starrells, Ingersoll-Dayton, Neal & Yamada, 1995).

In this study, female respondents reported significantly greater work accommodations and higher levels of role strain, emotional strain, and physical strain than male respondents. However, gender was not found to be associated significantly with hours of work missed, family accommodations, or financial strain. The influence of gender on work and family responsibilities is discussed further in Chapter 9.

RACE/ETHNICITY

The majority (75 percent) of respondents with adult-care responsibilities were white, 7 percent were African-American, 13 percent Asian, 4 percent Hispanic, and 1 percent American Indian. This breakdown was similar to that of the overall employee population in this study.

In this study, African-American respondents reported significantly greater financial strain than other ethnic groups. Respondents did not vary significantly by race or ethnicity with regard to family accommodations, work accommodations, role strain, or physical or emotional strain. As will be discussed in Chapter 9, previous studies have been inconclusive about the influence of race and ethnicity on caregiving. Some have found that African-American caregivers report lower levels of role strain and depression than whites, at least among those caring for demented elderly persons. Cook and Pickett (1987/1988), moreover, found that white parents of mentally ill adult children experienced caregiving as more of a burden than nonwhite caregivers in the same situation.

JOB CLASSIFICATION

Employees with adult-care responsibilities were somewhat more likely than other respondents to hold technical rather than administrative positions. Similarly, in a national survey, Anastas, Gibeau & Larsen (1990) found that service workers predominated among employed caregivers.

In this study, administrators and clerical staff experienced the highest levels of role strain, while scientists and technical personnel experienced the lowest. Clerical staff also experienced the highest levels of physical strain, financial strain, and emotional strain, with scientists and technical personnel experiencing the lowest levels. There were no significant differences based on job classification in levels of family or work accommodations or missed work.

MARITAL STATUS

Seventy-two percent of respondents with adult-care responsibilities were married and another 3 percent were not married but living with a partner. The remaining 25 percent were divorced, separated, widowed, or single. These findings are similar to those of Gorey, Rice and Brice (1992) who found that, averaging across 17 studies, 69 percent of employees with elder-care responsibilities were married.

In this study, unmarried respondents experienced significantly higher levels of emotional strain than those who were married. There were no significant differences by marital status on other measures of family or work accommodations, missed work, role strain, physical strain, or financial strain.

For some married caregivers, spouses may serve as an important source of physical and emotional support with caregiving tasks. A husband's instrumental assistance to his parent-in-law, for example, can help to relieve some of the physical burden on his wife, resulting in fewer health impacts for her (Franks & Stephens, 1996). There is little evidence, however, that spousal support can do much to relieve the psychological distress associated with caregiving, and in some instances marriage can make caregiving more problematic, particularly if the spouse is unemployed.

HEALTH

When asked to rate their health status, 90 percent of employees caring for dependent adults reported that their health was "excellent" or "good," while 9 percent said it was "fair," and 1 percent "poor." Caregivers who reported that their health was "fair" or "poor" experienced significantly greater family accommodations, work accommodations, and role strain, and higher levels of financial strain, physical strain, and emotional strain, but not greater amounts of work missed because of family responsibilities.

Some previous studies have found that caregivers who themselves are in poor health experience increased strain from the physical and emotional demands of their care responsibilities. Good health, on the other hand, can make caregiving less stressful. Grad and Sainsbury (1963), for example, found that when caregivers were healthy, their mentally ill care recipients were less problematic. Good health has also been found to be important in determining who will provide care; when a number of potential caregivers are available, health status will likely be an important factor in determining who will take on primary caregiving responsibility. Englehardt, Brubaker and Lutzer (1988) found that healthy caregivers of developmentally disabled adults were more likely than unhealthy caregivers to report being able to provide care. It also is likely that highly stressful caregiving situations may predispose at least some caregivers to health problems.

Caregiving Demands

Employees who have the most demanding caregiving responsibilities are likely to make the most accommodations in their work and family lives and experience the greatest distress. Potentially demanding aspects of caregiving situations include the types and amount of assistance provided, the extent of the care recipient's disability, the care recipient's age, the number of care recipients, the relationship of the caregiver to the care recipient, the residence of the care recipient, problems finding care, and the presence of other family-care responsibilities. In this study, we found high levels of role strain among those caregiving employees who provided large amounts of personal and financial assistance, cared for someone with behavior problems, had difficulties finding adequate care, or also had responsibility for a child. In addition, higher levels of family and work accommodations and certain types of strain were especially likely among those caring for a spouse, son or daughter, or someone else relatively young.

TYPES AND AMOUNT OF ASSISTANCE PROVIDED

Caring for a disabled adult can involve a range of tasks, including emotional support, transportation, housekeeping, personal care, and financial assistance. In this study, 10 percent of respondents reported providing assistance with personal care (feeding, bathing, toileting, dressing or grooming); 60 percent were providing household chores (cooking, laundry, housecleaning, or shopping); and 56 percent were arranging or coordinating outside help. In addition, 49 percent were providing transportation; 31 percent were helping obtain information about programs and services; and 74 percent were providing emotional reassurance. Forty-eight percent of respondents indicated that they were the primary person responsible for providing care for the dependent adult family member or friend.

Caregiving can be costly, both in terms of money and time. In this survey, financial assistance was provided by 85 percent of respondents with adult-care responsibilities. While 39 percent of respondents spent less than $100 per month on adult care, 21.5 percent spent $100–$249, 15 percent spent $250–$499, 7 percent spent $500–$999, and 3 percent spent at least $1000 a month. Greater amounts of financial assistance provided were associated with higher levels of family accommodations, missed work, role strain, physical strain, emotional strain, and financial strain, but not significantly greater work accommodations.

The total amount of help given per week ranged from 1 to more than 30 hours, with a median of 3.5 hours per week. About one-third of employees with adult-care responsibilities provided 1–2 hours of assistance per week, 30 percent provided 3–4 hours, 17 percent 5–9 hours, 12 percent 10–19 hours, 4 percent 20–29 hours, and 3 percent 30 hours or more each week (essentially a second full-time job). Respondents who provided more hours of assistance per week experienced significantly higher levels of family accommodations, work accommodations, missed work, and role strain, as well as greater physical, financial, and emotional strain.

Respondents whose adult-care responsibilities included the provision of personal care (e.g., feeding, bathing, toileting, dressing, or grooming) reported more family accommodations, missed work, role strain, and physical strain than those not providing such care. Respondents who provided personal care did not report significantly higher levels of work accommodations, financial strain, or emotional strain than other respondents.

EXTENT OF CARE RECIPIENT DISABILITY

Care recipients were reported to have a variety of major health conditions, including arthritis and other joint problems (19 percent), senile dementia (18 percent), psychological problems (12 percent), stroke or other neurological problems (11 percent), heart conditions (9 percent), and cancer (6 percent). Seventy-two percent of the care recipients were reported to have cognitive limitations or behavioral problems, including difficulties with memory or decision-making, agitation, or unsafe behaviors. Respondents caring for adults with behavioral problems reported more family accommodations, work accommodations, missed work, role strain, physical strain, and emotional strain than those caring for adults without behavioral problems, but not higher levels of financial strain.

CARE RECIPIENT AGE

Care recipients ranged in age from 19 to 95. Nineteen percent were under the age of 65, while 81 percent were age 65 or older. Respondents whose care recipients were younger reported more family accommodations, work accommodations, missed work, physical strain, financial strain, and emotional strain, but not higher levels of role strain. Respondents caring for a disabled adult under the age of 65 provided significantly more personal and financial assistance than those caring for individuals age 65 or older, and they experienced significantly higher levels of overall caregiving strain.

NUMBER OF CARE RECIPIENTS

Of those employees who were providing assistance to a dependent adult, 61 percent reported that they were caring for one person, 27 percent were caring for two persons, and 10 percent were caring for three or more persons. The number of care recipients was not significantly associated with measures of role strain, work or family accommodations, physical, financial, or emotional strain, or number of work hours missed.

RELATIONSHIP OF CAREGIVER TO CARE RECIPIENT

When respondents were asked to identify the one adult for whom they provided the most assistance, 74 percent indicated it was a parent or parent-in-law, 5 percent indicated a spouse or partner, 4 percent a son or daughter, 13 percent another relative, 3 percent a friend or relative, and 1 percent someone else.

Caregiver relationship was found to be significantly associated with the extent of family and work accommodations, number of work hours missed, and financial strain, but not levels of role strain, physical strain, or emotional strain. Respondents caring for a spouse or partner missed the most work, an average of 15.3 hours per month, whereas other respondents missed only 3.9 to 6.6 hours of work per month, on average. Those caring for friends or neighbors missed the least amount of work. Respondents caring for a son or daughter experienced the greatest amount of financial strain, followed by respondents caring for a spouse or partner. Those caring for friends or neighbors experienced the least amount of financial strain.

RESIDENCE OF CARE RECIPIENT

The majority of the adult-care recipients (60 percent) lived in their own home or apartment; 18 percent lived with the employee, 9 percent with another family member, and 12 percent lived in a group living situation such as a group home or nursing home. Employees who lived with the care recipient experienced more family accommodations and greater financial strain than those who did not live together. Living arrangement was not significantly associated with levels of work accommodations, number of work hours missed, role strain, or physical or emotional strain.

PROBLEMS FINDING CARE

Approximately 72 percent of respondents in this study reported that they had experienced problems obtaining information or assistance with their adult-care responsibilities. Respondents with adult-care responsibilities were especially likely to report problems understanding government programs such as Medicare or SSI (reported by 38 percent). In addition, 27 percent reported difficulty finding out about legal options, 27 percent had problems locating services in the community, 25 percent had problems finding trained and reliable care providers, 24 percent had difficulty getting cooperation from other family members, 22 percent didn't have enough money to pay for care, and 19 percent had problems associated with breakdowns in care arrangements.

Employees who reported more problems in these areas reported more family accommodations and work accommodations, and more hours of work missed. They also reported higher levels of role strain, physical strain, financial strain, and emotional strain.

OTHER FAMILY RESPONSIBILITIES

Having responsibility for more than one care recipient has also been found to impact caregiver stress. In this study, 28 percent of employees with adult-care responsibilities also had a child under the age of twelve, and 16 percent had a teenager. These findings are consistent with other studies, which typically have found that between one-quarter and one-half of caregivers for elderly persons also have children at home.

In this study, respondents who were caring for children in addition to a disabled adult reported greater family accommodations, work accommodations, missed work, role strain, physical strain, and financial strain, but not more emotional strain, than those without child care responsibilities. The impact of having multi-generational care responsibilities is discussed further in Chapter 8.

Family Resources

Previous research suggests that employed caregivers with fewer social and economic resources are apt to experience higher levels of caregiver strain. Lower levels of social and economic resources have repeatedly been found to be associated with increased vulnerability to stress and to related physical and mental health impacts (Voydanoff & Donnelley, 1989; Huff-Corzine, Corzine & Moore, 1991; Hausenstein & Boyd, 1994). In this study, lower income is associated with higher levels of financial and emotional strain.

INCOME

Sixteen percent of respondents with adult-care responsibilities had an annual household income between $20,000 and $39,999. Twenty-seven percent had an income between $40,000 and $59,999; 23.5 percent between $60,000 and $79,999; and 34 percent had incomes of $80,000 a year or higher. Respondents with lower household incomes experienced significantly higher levels of financial strain and emotional strain than those with higher incomes. Household income was not significantly associated with levels of work or family accommodations, hours of work missed, role strain, or physical strain.

ASSISTANCE WITH CAREGIVING

The informal support and assistance provided by friends and family members are hypothesized to serve as important resources in coping with caregiving responsibilities. Most disabled adults receive care from more than one person (Eustis & Fischer, 1992). In this study, 85 percent of respondents indicated that the person for whom they were caring also received assistance from other sources. Fifty-five percent of the caregivers receiving assistance were assisted by family members or friends, 33 percent were assisted by the respondent's own spouse or partner, and 17 percent by a paid provider of personal care or homemaking services. Only about half (51 percent) of the respondents reported receiving any information, guidance, financial assistance, or emotional support to assist them in handling their adult-care responsibilities, with 33 percent indicating that they received "a little help," 14 percent "quite a bit of help," and only 4 percent "a great deal of help."

Employees whose care recipients received assistance from paid care providers reported significantly higher levels of work accommodations than those without paid help; but receiving paid help was not related significantly to levels of family accommodations, hours of work missed, role strain, or financial, physical, or emotional strain. The amount of information, guidance, or other help that respondents in this study received with their adult-care responsibilities was not associated with the extent to which they experienced any of these care-related outcomes. It seems likely that those employees whose jobs allow them to make substantial accommodations in how and when they work are also more likely to have the resources and organizational skills to be able to access paid services in the community. That receiving assistance is not associated with lower levels of strain may be attributable to the likelihood that many caregivers do not seek assistance, whether in the form of information or paid care providers, unless their stress level already is relatively high.

Work Demands

Work-place demands have been identified as important factors in studies of employee stress and well-being. Jobs with heavy workload demands, particularly in the context of low decision latitude, have been found to be associated with a greater risk of job strain, mental distress, myocardial infarction, and cardiovascular disease. It seems likely, therefore, that work-place demands, including the number of hours worked and the amount of pressure on the job, may well impact employees' ability to manage their work and adult-care responsibilities. In this study, we found that employees with more demanding jobs tended to make more accommodations and experienced higher levels of most measures of work-family strain, whereas the number of hours actually worked was not generally associated with these outcomes.

NUMBER OF HOURS WORKED

Fifty-four percent of respondents worked 40 hours per week, 6 percent worked less than 40 hours per week, 31 percent worked between 41 and 50 hours, and 9 percent worked more than 50 hours. The number of hours worked was significantly associated with higher levels of emotional strain, but not with levels of family or work accommodations, work hours missed, role strain, or physical or financial strain.

JOB DEMANDS

Forty-one percent of respondents indicated that they did not have enough time to get their work done. Having a more demanding job, as measured by not having enough time to get work done, was associated with significantly higher levels of family accommodations, work accommodations, role strain, physical strain, and emotional strain, but not significantly more hours of work missed or greater amounts of financial strain.

Work Resources

Work resources that have been reported to have a "buffering" effect between work and family include control over working conditions and support from coworkers and supervisors. In this study, we found that employees who had more job control and work-place support experienced consistently lower levels of family accommodations and strain, but not work accommodations.

JOB CONTROL

The amount of control over the manner in which work is performed has been identified as a buffer against high levels of employee stress and a mediator of greater well-being. In this survey, 68 percent of respondents agreed that they have a lot of freedom to decide how to do their work, and 60 percent indicated they have a lot to say about what happens on the job. A measure reflecting these two indicators of job control was associated with significantly lower levels of family accommodations, role strain, physical strain, financial strain, and emotional strain. It was not associated significantly with the amount of work accommodations or the hours of work missed, perhaps because employees with a great deal of freedom on the job are more likely to be able to alter work routines to accommodate caregiving responsibilities. Moreover, employees with more control over their jobs may be able to compensate for time missed and may not even consider it as time lost from work.

WORK-PLACE SUPPORT

Having the support of coworkers and supervisors has been shown to have a direct buffering effect between job stressors and psychological strain. In this study, 73 percent of respondents agreed that their coworkers took a personal interest in them, and 77 percent agreed that their supervisor was concerned about their welfare. Support from coworkers was associated with significantly lower levels of family accommodations, role strain, physical strain, financial strain, and emotional strain. Support from supervisors was also associated with significantly lower levels of family accommodations, physical strain, financial strain, and emotional strain. Neither coworker nor supervisor support was significantly associated with amount of work accommodations or hours of work missed, perhaps in part because supportive supervisors are more likely to allow caregiving employees to take time from work and make other work accommodations when necessary.

Policies and Programs Considered Helpful by Employees with Adult-Care Responsibilities

In this section, we examine the helpfulness of a number of work-place policies and programs that have been identified as potentially beneficial for employees with adult-care responsibilities. Policies and programs examined here include flexible work schedules, the ability to work at home, family leave, part-time work, elder-care information, counseling, Dependent Care Accounts, referral to community adult-care resources, and long-term care insurance. The policies considered most helpful to these caregiving employees are the ability to adjust work schedules, take family leave, or work at home. The work-place programs considered most beneficial include utilizing a Dependent Care Account or talking to an EAP counselor. However, adjusting one's work schedule or utilizing programs such as a Dependent Care Account, Elder Care Guide, Elder Care Information Fair, or EAP counselor are associated with a greater number of work-place and family accommodations and higher levels of role strain, suggesting that these resources are apt to be utilized especially by those working caregivers who already are the most stressed.

FLEXIBLE WORK SCHEDULES

The ability to modify one's work routine can make it easier for employees who provide assistance to an elderly or disabled adult to more effectively manage their work and family responsibilities. In this study, 82 percent of employees with adult-care responsibilities could adjust their normal work schedules. Of the 46 percent who indicated that they already had adjusted their work schedules to fit their family responsibilities, 98 percent reported that this was helpful, and 75 percent found it "very helpful." However, they did experience significantly higher levels of family accommodations, role strain, physical strain, and financial strain than those who had not adjusted their work schedules. They also reported a greater number of other work accommodations and missed more work. These findings suggest that adjusting one's work schedule is just one of a myriad of family and work accommodations that employees may make in an effort to manage their adult-care responsibilities, and that accommodations such as changing one's work schedule may not occur until employees experience substantial amounts of strain.

The lack of adequate information about community resources is one of the greatest problems facing many employees who care for elderly or disabled persons. In this study, more than one-fourth of the respondents reported that they had experienced problems in locating community services, with similar numbers reporting problems finding trained and reliable care providers and finding out about legal options. Approximately one-half of the employees with adult-care responsibilities indicated that they would utilize help locating community services for a disabled or elderly adult, and 36 percent indicated that they would attend workshops or seminars on adult care and other work and family issues if such programs were offered.

In an effort to make information about community resources more available to employees, human resources staff at Lawrence Berkeley Laboratory sponsored an Elder Care Information Fair, which brought representatives of community elder-care programs to the work site. Eleven percent of employees with adult-care responsibilities reported attending the Elder Care Information Fair, which 85 percent of them found helpful and 22 percent found "very helpful." Those employees who attended the Fair reported making significantly more family accommodations and other work accommodations than other caregivers, and they missed more time from work because of family responsibilities. They also experienced significantly higher levels of role strain and physical strain, but did not differ significantly from other caregivers regarding levels of financial strain or emotional strain.

Lawrence Berkeley Laboratory also produced an Elder Care Resource Guide, which was utilized by only 10 percent of the respondents with adult-care responsibilities. Of those who used the Resource Guide, 75 percent found it helpful, but only 15 percent found it "very helpful." Those utilizing the Guide reported making significantly more family accommodations and other work accommodations, and missing more time from work than other caregivers, because of family responsibilities. They also experienced significantly higher levels of role strain, physical strain, and emotional strain, but did not differ significantly from other caregivers with regard to their level of financial strain.

An EAP counselor was available to speak with employees regarding their adult-care concerns. Eight percent of the respondents indicated that they had spoken to a counselor regarding their family responsibilities; of these, 89 percent found the counseling to be helpful and 61 percent found it "very helpful." Those who spoke with the counselor reported making significantly more family accommodations and other work accommodations than other caregivers, as well as experiencing significantly higher levels of physical strain and emotional strain. They did not differ significantly from other care-givers in time missed from work or levels of role strain or financial strain.

FINANCIAL BENEFITS

Employees had access to a Dependent Care Account, whereby they could reserve part of their salary on a pre-tax basis to pay for adult care. Only 9 percent of employees with adult-care responsibilities utilized the Dependent Care Assistance Plan and of these, 85 percent found it helpful and 53 percent found it "very helpful." Those who used the Plan reported making significantly more family accommodations and other work accommodations than caregivers who did not use it. They also experienced significantly higher levels of physical strain and financial strain, but did not differ significantly from other caregivers with regard to their levels of role strain, emotional strain, or time missed from work because of family responsibilities. To some extent, this may be due to the fact that participation in a Dependent Care Assistance Plan is limited to those individuals who care for someone in the employee's home, who are apt to be experiencing substantial physical and financial strain, and are more likely to need to make accommodations in their marital relationships and social activities.

Long-term care insurance is emerging as an important financial benefit for employees with disabled adult relatives because of its potential to offset the costs of providing care. Almost one-fourth of employees with adult-care responsibilities in this study indicated that having enough money to pay for care was a problem for them, and 54 percent said they would utilize long-term care insurance if it were available. Moreover, long-term care insurance offers assistance in understanding government programs such as Medicare or SSI, which was reported as a problem by more than one-third of the adult-care providers in this study.

OTHER WORK-PLACE POLICIES AND PROGRAMS

Respondents identified a number of other policies, programs, and benefits that they would consider helpful in meeting their adult-care responsibilities. The ability to take unpaid family leave without loss of benefits, cited by 57 percent of respondents, was the most frequently endorsed benefit, followed by the ability to work at home (47 percent). The ability to use sick leave or family leave to care for a domestic partner or friend, and the ability to use donated sick leave or vacation time each were endorsed by approximately one-third of respondents. Less likely to be considered helpful were support groups and part-time work, each endorsed by fewer than one-fourth of employees with adult-care responsibilities.

Those employees assisting adults under the age of 65 were especially likely to endorse nontraditional leave policies, such as the ability to utilize sick leave or unpaid family leave to care for persons not covered under federal and state family-leave laws. This reflects the fact that many of these employees are caring for partners, friends, or extended family for whom current work-place policies and benefits are not applicable. In fact, more than 50 percent of respondents caring for someone under the age of 65 had caregiving situations that did not qualify for coverage under the provisions of the federal Family and Medical Leave Act, which provides up to 12 weeks of unpaid leave without loss of benefits in order to care for an ill or disabled parent, child, or spouse.

SUMMARY

The findings reported in this chapter indicate that employees are especially likely to be impacted by their adult-care responsibilities when they are younger, female, in poorer health, hold clerical jobs, have more extensive caregiving responsibilities, have more demanding jobs with less control over the pace of work, and have difficulty finding help. These findings indicate a synergy between employees' work and caregiving responsibilities, whereby certain combinations of work demands, work-place support, family demands and family resources predict corresponding combinations of work-family strain and work and family accommodations.

Respondents identified a number of work-place policies and programs they considered helpful or potentially helpful in their efforts to manage competing work and adult-care responsibilities: family leave, work schedule adjustments, the ability to work at home, and employer-sponsored programs such as counseling, information about community adult-care services, Dependent Care Accounts, and long-term care insurance. Yet, at least for the employees with adult-care responsibilities in this study, actual utilization of personal and work-place resources such as counseling, information, financial relief, and hands-on assistance was not associated with lower levels of role strain and caregiving stress. Our findings suggest that employees may not turn to programs such as these until they are already experiencing substantial amounts of strain at home and at work and have already made significant accommodations in their family relationships and work routines.

· 8 ·

A FAMILY-CARE MODEL

INTRODUCTION

In the preceding chapters we examined the characteristics and experiences of employees providing child care (Chapter 6) and adult care (Chapter 7). In this chapter, we will explore the relationship between family care and work across all types of care, utilizing the integrative family care model described in Chapter 5. We will examine the impact of demands, resources, and personal characteristics on those providing family care, whether for children or adults. Such an analysis will allow us to identify those factors that are predictive of role strain and family and work accommodations for working caregivers in general, regardless of the specific type of care they provide.

In this chapter we also will examine variations among caregivers that reflect the type of care they provide: care only for children, care for ill and disabled adults, and multi-generational caregiving responsibilities (care for both children and adults). We will compare these three groups of caregivers with regard to strain, family and work accommodations, resources, demands, and social and demographic characteristics. In addition, we will explore the utilization rates and perceived helpfulness of a variety of workplace programs and benefits among employees with these differing types of care responsibilities.

FAMILY-CARE MODEL

As described in Chapter 5, the family-care model utilized here builds on transactional stress and role theory approaches to understanding the culmination of work and family responsibilities. In so doing, it enables us to examine the interplay between role demands and the availability of social resources in both work and family domains, while highlighting the particular factors that most directly affect the stress process. Based on this family-care model, role strain and family and work accommodations are examined in light of a variety of potential contributors: work and family role demands, work and family resources, and personal social and demographic characteristics.

Based on these family-care constructs, stepwise multiple regression models were developed to examine the predictors of role strain and family and work accommodations, as shown in Table 8-1. Background characteristics entered into the regression equations included the employee's age, gender, race, marital status, job classification, and health status, with dummy variables created for gender (female = 0, male = 1), race (non-white = 0, white = 1), marital status (not married or partnered = 0, married or partnered = 1), job classification (staff = 0, professional and managerial = 1), and health (poor/fine = 0, good/excellent = 1). Demands included number of care recipients, whether the care recipient was disabled, problems with care arrangements, hours worked, and level of work demand. Resources included income, level of assistance received with caregiving, support from coworkers, job flexibility, and job control.

TABLE 8-1 Hierarchical multiple regressions of role strain, family accommodations, and work accommodations
(Standardized Betas)

	Role Strain	Family Accommodations	Work Accommodations
Social and Demographic Characteristics			
Age	− .12***	− .13***	− .19***
Gender	− .16***	− .03	− .03
Race/Ethnicity	.07*	.12***	.13***
Marital Status	.05	.07*	− .01
Occupation	− .01	− .02	− .02
Health	− .10***	− .03	− .02
Adjusted R^2 (step 1)	*.07*	*.04*	*.06*
Family and Work Demands			
No. of Care Recipients (CR)	.01	.07*	.06
CR Disability Status	.05	.06*	.06*
Care Arrangement Problems	.16***	.27***	.26***
Hours Worked	.07*	− .01	− .05
Job Demands	.32***	.18***	.16***
Adjusted R^2 (step 2)	*.19*	*.16*	*.11*
Family and Work Resources			
Income	.08*	.03	.11**
Assistance	− .12***	− .02	.01
Coworker Support	− .10**	− .09**	− .04
Job Flexibility	.03	.07	.13**
Job Control	− .02	− .07	− .05
Adjusted R^2 (step 3)	*.02*	*.01*	*.02*
F =	23.8***	16.8***	14.6***
Total Adjusted R^2	*.28*	*.21*	*.19*

* $p < .05$
** $p < .01$
*** $p < .001$

The next sections provide an overview of the various factors that were found to contribute significantly to role strain and family and work accommodations, followed by in-depth discussions of the critical role of such factors (demands, resources, and personal characteristics) in integrating work and family responsibilities.

Role Strain

As discussed in Chapters 6 and 7, the integration of family care and work impacted the physical, financial, and emotional well-being of many of the employees in this study, contributing to a sense of role strain. Physical fatigue, financial strain, and emotional strain were each reported by approximately three-fourths of those with family-care responsibilities.

As shown in Table 8-1, role strain was significantly higher for employees who were younger, female, white, or in poor health. Work and family demand factors that contributed significantly to role strain included problems with care arrangements, number of hours worked each week, and high job demands. Resources that were associated with lower levels of role strain included assistance with caregiving, coworker support, and having less income.

Family Accommodations

As a result of their family-care responsibilities, three-fourths of the employees in this study reported experiencing at least some interference with their social activities; 70 percent reported experiencing interference with their relationship with their spouse or partner; and, 86 percent reported interference with their free time. Our family-care model revealed that family accommodations were significantly greater for employees who were younger, white, or married. Work and family demands that contributed significantly to the level of family accommodations included number of care recipients, disability status of those care recipients, problems with care arrangements, and high job demands. Support from coworkers was the only work or family resource found to contribute significantly to lower levels of family accommodations.

Work Accommodations

Because of their care responsibilities, employees missed as many as 96 hours of work each month; 10 percent of the employees missed more than 10 hours per month. Employees who made the most work accommodations were those who were younger or white. Work and family demands that contributed significantly to higher levels of work accommodations included the disability status of the care recipient, problems with care arrangements, and high job demands. Resources that contributed significantly to lower levels of work accommodations included having less income and less job flexibility.

Family and Work Demands

Work and family demands, as a set of variables, made the most significant contribution to role strain and to work and family accommodations, explaining between 11 percent and 19 percent of the total variance in each model. Problems with care arrangements and job demands were the most potent contributors to all three outcome measures. In addition, hours worked was associated with higher levels of role strain, and the disability status of the care recipient impacted both work and family accommodations. Not surprisingly, family accommodations were greater for employees with more care recipients.

PROBLEMS WITH CARE ARRANGEMENTS

Accessibility and availability of adequate care for dependents were found to be of critical importance in our family-care model. When care arrangements are dependable and of reasonable quality, employees experience less strain when combining work and family-care responsibilities. When care arrangements are inadequate, both care providers and care recipients may suffer the consequences: greater personal stress and inadequate care. Neal et al. (1993), for example, found that problems finding adequate care and dissatisfaction with care arrangements were significant predictors of difficulty combining work and family, as well as work disruptions, after controlling for a variety of family and work-place characteristics. For problems to be reduced, care arrangements must be of good quality (e.g., adequate ratio of staff to those receiving assistance), dependable (e.g., stability of care), accessible (e.g., moderate distance and travel time to care and cost of care as a percentage of household income), and available (e.g., sufficient supply in the community).

JOB DEMANDS AND HOURS WORKED

Work demands contributed significantly to role strain and work and family accommodations in this study, whereas number of hours worked contributed only to role strain. Apparently, it is the pressure experienced at work, more than simply time conflicts due to working long hours, that most strongly forces employees to make accommodations in their work and family responsibilities.

While "family friendly" policies such as increasing flexibility at the work place are often advanced as helpful in alleviating caregiving strain, the findings from this study suggest that initiatives to provide more employment flexibility while maintaining comparable or heavier work demands will do little to relieve the pressure employees experience. Thus, the concept of "family friendly" work place needs to be redefined to incorporate ways to address overall work demand. If we are to support workers in meeting their work and family responsibilities, the impact of demanding jobs and long work hours must be considered and ways must be found to encourage family members to spend more time, rather than less time, with those for whom they care.

DISABILITY

Employees caring for disabled care recipients experienced higher levels of work and family accommodations than did other caregiving employees. These findings are consistent with a number of earlier studies. The National Long Term Care Survey, for example, found that employees who were caring for elders with higher levels of impairment were more likely than other employees to experience accommodations such as unpaid leave, reduced work hours, and rearrangement of work schedules (Stone & Short, 1990). Those assisting family members with disabilities also tend to experience more difficulty in securing care arrangements and high-quality care.

Family and Work Resources

Although previous research has found that employed caregivers with more social and economic resources tend to experience lower levels of stress, in this study caregiving and employment resources had only a small impact on role strain, or on work and family accommodations, explaining only about 2 percent of the total variance in each model. The resources that contributed significantly to at least one of the three outcome factors were income, assistance received with caregiving, coworker support, and work-place flexibility.

INCOME

Income was a significant predictor of increased levels of role strain and work accommodations. The finding that employees with higher incomes reported higher occupational impacts likely reflects their ability to modify their work schedules and make other accommodations in their work activities to respond to their family-care responsibilities. Employees with greater financial resources are more able to afford to take time from work when necessary, and more likely to occupy jobs that allow the flexibility to do so.

ASSISTANCE RECEIVED WITH CAREGIVING

Receiving assistance with care responsibilities contributed to decreased role strain. Higher levels of social support have been found to decrease vulnerability to stress. In a previous study, Scharlach et al. (1991) found that higher levels of social support were associated with lower levels of interference between work and family-care responsibilities.

COWORKER SUPPORT

The extent of work-place support helped to reduce the levels of role strain and family accommodations, but not work-place accommodations. Social support from one's coworkers has been found to be associated with lower levels of conflict and stress in meeting multiple family and work responsibilities. In a study of employed mothers of preschool children, for example, Warren and Johnson (1995) found that supervisors' practices (e.g., supervisor flexibility) had a strong influence on the degree of work and family conflict experienced. And a supportive supervisor has sometimes been found to be more important than a supportive spouse in helping working women to manage their multiple role demands.

JOB FLEXIBILITY

Employees with greater job flexibility reported higher levels of work accommodations, which likely reflects their ability to modify their work schedules and activities to respond to their family-care responsibilities. While work-place flexibility is generally considered beneficial for employees with family-care responsibilities, these findings suggest that there may not be a simple, linear relationship between job flexibility and levels of role strain and work and family accommodations. Moreover, some policies, such as flex-time and telecommuting, may inadvertently lead to increased levels of family interference for some employees, given the potential for blurring the boundaries between work and family.

Sociodemographic Characteristics

Employees' personal social and demographic characteristics accounted for less than 7 percent of the total variance in each family-care model. The social and demographic characteristics that emerged as significant predictors of all three outcome variables in this study were employee age and race. In addition, employee gender and health status contributed significantly to role strain. Marital status contributed to family accommodations, probably because unmarried respondents were less likely to reside with a partner or other family members with whom accommodation might be required.

CAREGIVER AGE

In this study, younger caregivers experienced significantly higher levels of role strain and work and family accommodations, perhaps because their comparative youth makes their care responsibilities seem "off time" and different from the norms of their age peers. Consequently, these employees are apt to have access to fewer resources such as social and emotional support with which to buffer the stressors of caregiving; moreover, their financial resources may be more limited than those of older caregivers.

Younger caregivers tend to be assisting younger care recipients. Employees who care for ill and disabled adults who are younger (e.g., under the age of 65) have generally been found to report higher levels of strain as well as more work and family accommodations than do employees who care for older adults. Parents of young children, moreover, are more likely to report family and work conflict than are parents of older children. Klein (1986), for example, found that women with children under the age of six missed twice as many days of work as women with children aged 6–17.

CAREGIVER RACE/ETHNICITY

White employees experienced significantly higher levels of role strain and work and family accommodations than did employees from racial and ethnic minority groups. These racial and ethnic differences are particularly impressive, given that whites on average have less demanding caregiving situations, greater economic resources, and fewer problems with care arrangements than their minority counterparts. It seems likely that there are substantial cultural differences in family and work adaptations and methods of coping, as well as with regard to what constitutes role strain. It also is possible that white employees' greater likelihood of altering their work schedules to meet their care responsibilities may in part reflect the over-representation of minorities in occupations that do not allow high degrees of flexibility. These issues are discussed in greater detail in Chapter 9.

GENDER

Numerous studies of working parents and caregivers of adults have found that women are more likely than men to assume caregiving responsibilities, and they tend to experience greater conflict between work and family-care responsibilities. Regardless of their level of participation in the formal labor market, women tend to retain primary responsibility for the care of ill and disabled adults, contributing to consistently higher levels of strain. In this study, gender was a significant predictor of role strain, but was not significantly associated with the extent of work-place or family accommodations. These findings are discussed further in Chapter 9.

HEALTH

Caregivers who themselves were in poor health reported higher levels of role strain, suggesting the possibility that their preexisting health problems may be exacerbated by the additional physical and emotional demands of their caregiving responsibilities, resulting in a greater sense of physical and emotional exhaustion than experienced by other employees with similar family-care situations. Good health, it seems, may be a much needed personal resource when it comes to managing the potentially competing responsibilities of work and family care. Health status, moreover, is apt to be important in determining who will provide care, with primary caregiving responsibilities often being reserved for those family members who have the greatest physical and emotional capacity.

SUMMARY

The family-care model utilized in this study has enabled us to examine the factors that contribute most significantly to the personal and work impacts experienced by employees with family-care responsibilities. Work and family demands, as a set of variables, were found to make the greatest contribution to role strain and to work and family accommodations, far exceeding the influence of resources and background characteristics. Notable is the interplay among work and family variables, both of which made substantial contributions to the demand and resource domains in the family-care model. Demands at home affect one's job, just as demands at work affect one's home life. Clearly, any serious attempt to relieve role strain and/or enhance role performance needs to consider strategies for reducing excessive demands employees experience both at home and at work.

Particularly stressful were caregiving situations in which care arrangements were unreliable or otherwise problematic, and jobs that involved a great deal of time pressure. In both cases, employees are forced to expend extra time and effort just to fulfill their basic role responsibilities at home and at work, forcing them to make additional accommodations in their lives and adding to existing psychological and social stress. Neither the number of care recipients, their level of disability, the type of job one has, nor the number of hours one works seems to matter as much as whether those caregiving or work roles are excessively demanding and require unusual expenditures of energy. Apparently, it is not the type nor the number of roles, but the quality of those roles which has the greatest impact on personal and social well-being.

Employees who were younger and/or white also experienced particularly high levels of role strain and work and family accommodations. For older employees and those from minority racial and ethnic groups, caregiving is apt to be considered more normative, and their personal and cultural communities are more apt to have well-developed informal structures for offering social and emotional support. For younger employees and those who are white, family caregiving may be more likely seen as something that is atypical, and for which communities of care are less well-developed. Employees who are younger or white may also have had fewer previous direct family-care experiences, whether for siblings, parents, grandparents, or non-blood kin; consequently, they may have less personal and social wisdom on which to draw in responding to their current care situations than do their older and/or non-white counterparts. As we shall discuss further in Chapter 9, ethnic and racial communities seem to play an important role in providing personal and social support for employees attempting to manage the demands of work and family care.

In considering the efficacy of our family-care model, it should be noted that the resource variables included here had only a very modest influence on role strain or work or family accommodations. Apparently, the demanding nature of today's jobs and family situations exceeds the ability of simple external resources to protect employee well-being from role strain and other deleterious impacts. In a world of ever-greater demands on our time and energy, it seems obvious that resources alone won't be enough to reduce work-family stress. Instead, we need to consider ways to alleviate the excessive demands individuals experience, while simultaneously enhancing their capacity for mitigating the impact of those demands that are unavoidable in a productive and caring society.

TYPE OF FAMILY-CARE RESPONSIBILITIES

While the family-care model has been shown to be a useful metaphor for understanding the experiences of caregiving employees in general, it also is important to consider variations that evolve from the type of care that employees provide. It is to this issue that we now turn our attention. In particular, we examine differences among three groups of employees: those who care only for children, those who care only for ill or disabled adults, and those with multi-generational caregiving responsibilities (caring for both children and adults). In so doing, we compare the characteristics, needs, and experiences of employees providing differing types of family care across the life span.

Among the respondents in this study, 49 percent (n = 928) had child-care responsibilities or were providing assistance to an ill or disabled adult family member or friend. Of these, 27 percent (n = 514) had only child-care responsibilities, 14 percent (n = 267) had only adult-care responsibilities, and 8 percent (n = 147) had both child- and adult-care responsibilities.

Given that more families are delaying childbearing and the increase in life expectancy, the number of employees with combined child- and adult-care responsibilities is growing. It is estimated that approximately 1.8 million American women are caring for both children and an elderly relative, and that more than 50 percent of these women are employed (Older Women's League, 1989). Utilizing a probability sample, Spitze and Logan (1990) found that approximately 8 percent of women were actively employed and involved in both child and parent care.

Impact of Care Responsibilities by Type of Care

STRAIN

As shown in Table 8-2, levels of physical fatigue were highest among those employees with both child- and adult-care responsibilities and lowest among those with only adult-care responsibilities. Employees caring for children and those caring for both a child and adult reported significantly higher levels of financial strain than those providing only adult care. Those with adult-care responsibilities and those with child- and adult-care responsibilities

TABLE 8-2 Personal impacts, demands, and resources, by type of care (means and f-values)

	Child Care Only (n = 514)	Adult Care Only (n = 267)	Both Child and Adult Care (n = 147)	F-Value
Personal Impacts				
Role Strain**	2.67	2.55	2.72	4.48
Physical fatigue***	2.16	1.81	2.38	26.66
Financial strain***	2.22	1.71	2.32	32.07
Emotional upset***	1.91	2.10	2.17	8.20
Family Accommodations***	2.23	1.84	2.35	27.21
Work Accommodations***	2.63	1.69	2.49	25.12
Family and Work Demands				
No. of Care Recipients (CR)***	1.74	1.46	3.25	182.73
CR Disability Status***	.07	.69	.64	304.59
Care Arrangement Problem***	1.22	.98	2.19	41.54
Hours Worked	43.95	43.88	42.55	1.80
Job Demands	2.43	2.44	2.41	.09
Family and Work Resources				
Income	3.88	3.81	4.14	2.94
Caregiving Assistance***	2.16	1.81	2.86	146.98
Coworker Support***	2.04	1.98	2.28	7.12
Job Flexibility	2.20	2.25	2.17	.67
Job Control	2.24	2.22	2.42	3.20

* $p < .05$
** $p < .01$
*** $p < .001$

reported significantly higher levels of emotional strain than employees with only child-care responsibilities. Those with combined child- and adult-care responsibilities and those with only child-care responsibilities had the highest levels of role strain, followed by those with adult-care responsibilities.

In summary, while role strain and physical and financial strain were highest among those with child-care or combined child- and adult-care responsibilities, emotional strain was highest among employees with adult-care or combined child- and adult-care responsibilities. These findings likely reflect the differing types of care activities, demands, and resources associated with the various types of care responsibilities.

Research has fairly consistently demonstrated that parents of children, especially those with young children, are likely to experience relatively high levels of strain and financial difficulty. The care of young children tends to be particularly labor intensive and can be costly due to purchasing child care or the loss of a second income, while emotional strain is likely offset by the rewards of raising a family. The financial and physical strains of adult care may in some cases be reduced by the resources of the care recipient and other family members, while the emotional strain may remain high due to role ambiguity, lack of predictable care needs, and limited social support.

Employees who have both child- and adult-care responsibilities report consistently high levels of strain. It has been suggested that the "sandwich generation" may be at particular risk for negative consequences resulting from the increased demands of their dual roles. However, research that has examined the impact of multiple-care responsibilities is relatively limited and has produced mixed results. For example, in a study of employed care-givers of the elderly, Gibeau and Anastas (1989) found that having children in the home was positively associated with increased levels of conflict. Neal and her colleagues (1993) found that among working parents, those who also had adult caregiving responsibilities experienced higher levels of diffi-culty in combining their work and family lives. Other studies, however, have found that, among caregivers to the elderly, having children in the home had no effect or was associated with a positive effect on caregivers' well-being (Stull, Bowman & Smerglia, 1994; Loomis & Booth, 1995).

These disparate findings may in part reflect the relative balance of de-mands and resources, as well as the fact that multi-generational responsi-bilities may simultaneously result in both positive and negative effects. In a study of elder care, for example, Stoller and Pugliesi (1989) found that care-givers with combined child- and adult-care responsibilities reported higher levels of burden if they provided more hours of assistance, and lower lev-els if they received higher levels of support from family and friends. Fur-ther, they found that those with multiple-role responsibilities (more hours of elder care, employment, and involvement with nonfamily members) ex-perienced increased levels of burden as well as lower levels of psychologi-cal distress.

Although Stoller and Pugliesi (1989) did not assess the impact of multi-generational care responsibilities directly, it may be that such multiple-care responsibilities create more strain due to increased demands and a corre-sponding limited availability of time. The increase in well-being may be due to the satisfaction of involvement with additional family members and the potential for increased assistance and support. Stull, Bowman, and Smerglia (1991) found that among daughters caring for elderly parents, the presence of children in the home was associated with less depression and physical strain and higher levels of well-being. Almost two-thirds of the children in the sample were over the age of 18, so it is quite likely that they offered important assistance and support to mothers in carrying out family-care responsibilities.

FAMILY ACCOMMODATIONS

As a result of their family-care responsibilities, many of the employees in this study reported experiencing at least some interference with their per-sonal and social activities. Those with combined child and adult care and those with only child-care responsibilities reported making the most accommodations in their family lives. These findings are consistent with previous studies, which have found that the integration of work and family responsibilities among working parents is associated with marital tension and with decreased levels of and satisfaction with leisure time.

WORK-PLACE ACCOMMODATIONS

Employed caregivers in this study made a number of work accommodations, including altering schedules, taking time off without pay, and missing promotions. Those with only child-care responsibilities and those with both child care and adult care were significantly more likely than those with only adult-care responsibilities to make work-place accommodations such as these.

Neal et al. (1993) also found that child care only and child care in combination with other caregiving roles were associated with increased rates of absenteeism. In a comparison across single types of family care, she found that those caring for children experienced the highest rates of absenteeism, followed by those caring for both children and working-age adults, then by those caring for both children and elders. Fernandez (1986) attributed the high rates of absenteeism and work-place adjustments experienced by working parents to the intensive, ongoing care needs of young children.

When adult caregiving is defined broadly, as in this study, there is a wide spectrum of caregiving needs, and in some cases caregivers may be able to accommodate those needs during nonworking hours. Among those assisting an elderly family member, for example, caregiving has been found to impact employment for approximately 15 percent of the caregivers (McKinlay et al., 1995). Being the primary caregiver and caring for ill and disabled adults with unpredictable care needs and behavioral disturbances is associated with an increase in the caregiver's number of work-place accommodations.

Characteristics, Demands, and Resources by Type of Care

SOCIAL AND DEMOGRAPHIC CHARACTERISTICS

In this section we will compare the social and demographic characteristics of those providing the differing types of family care. As illustrated in Table 8-3, there were several significant differences in the social and demographic characteristics of the caregivers by type of care provided. For example, employees with child-care responsibilities, adult-care responsibilities, and both child- and adult-care responsibilities differed significantly by age, gender, race/ethnicity, job classification, and marital status, but not health status.

As one would expect, younger employees in this study tended to be most heavily involved with child-care responsibilities, middle-aged employees were most likely to have combined child- and adult-care responsi-

TABLE 8-3 Characteristics of the caregivers, by type of care
(percentages)

	Child Care Only (n = 514)	Adult Care Only (n = 267)	Both Child and Adult Care (n = 147)
*Age***			
under 30	5.5	1.8	1.2
30–39	43.6	20.3	29.4
40–49	42.6	30.4	53.2
50–59	8.1	39.7	11.9
60 and over	0.2	7.8	4.3
*Gender***			
Male	76.5	64.3	66.3
Female	23.5	35.7	33.3
*Race/Ethnicity**			
White	74.4	81.4	64.5
African-American	7.4	5.8	9.3
Asian/Pacific Islander	13.3	9.7	20.1
Hispanic	4.9	3.1	5.3
*Job Category***			
Scientists/Engineers	43.3	32.4	37.6
Technical	25.1	22.5	23.0
Admin. Professionals	22.9	35.8	28.2
Admin. Clerical	8.7	9.3	11.2
*Marital Status**			
Married/Partnered	89.2	66.8	90.0
Divorced/Separated	7.8	12.0	4.6
Widowed	0.8	0.5	0.7
Single	2.2	20.7	4.7
Health Status			
Excellent	38.7	44.3	38.5
Good	51.3	45.9	49.8
Fair	9.6	8.0	11.1
Poor	0.4	1.8	0.6

* p <.05
** p <.01
*** p <.001

bilities, and older employees were most heavily involved in providing adult care. Those caring for children were most apt to be in their thirties, those caring for an adult were most apt to be in their fifties, and those caring for both a child and an adult were most apt to be in their forties.

Yet contrary to some previous assumptions, adult care is not the only dependent care issue for older employees, and child care is not the only issue for younger employees. Ten percent of the employees with children were over the age of 50 and, of those, more than 5 percent had children 12 and younger and 21 percent had teenagers. Approximately 22 percent of those caring for adults were under the age of 40.

Women were over-represented among employees providing care for an adult or having both child-care and adult-care responsibilities. Cantor (1983) has described a preferential hierarchical patterning involved in caregiving, consisting of spouses (primarily wives), then daughters, sons, other relatives, and friends and neighbors respectively, providing the majority of care when possible. Those in clerical positions were also significantly more likely to be providing multi-generational care than those in other occupations. Fredriksen and Scharlach (1997) found that those in staff positions were more likely to be providing higher levels of care than those in professional or managerial positions.

While unmarried respondents were more likely to be providing care for an ill or disabled adult, the married respondents in this study were more likely to be providing both types of care at the same time. In some cases, it is likely that employees who choose to take on multiple-care responsibilities may be more advantaged than those who do not take on such responsibilities. For example, Loomis and Booth (1995) found that persons with stronger marriages were more likely to take on multi-generational care responsibilities than were those with weaker marriages.

African-American, Asian/Pacific Islander, and Hispanic respondents were more likely than whites to be providing care to children and to have combined child-care and adult-care responsibilities. African-American and Hispanic women have slightly higher birth rates than do white women. In addition, racial and ethnic minority caregivers are more likely to be providing adult care at a younger age and to be caring for younger care recipients, likely due to differing disability and life expectancy rates by race and ethnicity. Thus, increased fertility rates combined with providing adult care at an earlier point in one's life may increase the likelihood of multi-generational family-care responsibilities among racial and ethnic minorities.

FAMILY AND WORK DEMANDS

In this section we compare the demands on employees with differing types of family-care responsibilities, including the age, number, and disability level of those receiving care, and problems with care arrangements. In general, we found that those with child only and combined child- and adult-care responsibilities experienced the heaviest family demands; disability level of care recipient, on the other hand, was highest among those with adult-care responsibilities. Work demands, such as the number of hours worked and workload demand, were relatively consistent regardless of the type of care responsibilities.

Employees with only child-care responsibilities differed significantly from those with combined child- and adult-care responsibilities with regard to the children's age and the number of children. For example, 65 percent of employees with only child-care responsibilities had children age 5 or younger compared to 51 percent of those with combined child- and adult-care responsibilities. In addition, those with only child care were more likely than those with child- and adult-care responsibilities to be assisting more than one child.

When comparing those with only adult-care responsibilities and those with combined child- and adult-care responsibilities, significant differences were observed with regard to the number of adults assisted, as shown in Table 8-2. Those with combined child and adult care were most likely to be assisting more than one adult. As would be expected, those with combined adult- and child-care responsibilities were assisting more care recipients than those caring only for children or only for adults.

Reflecting the differing disability rates by age, caregivers assisting adults or both children and adults were significantly more likely than those caring for children to be assisting a disabled care recipient. Four percent of persons in this country under the age of 55 require assistance meeting personal needs because of mobility or health-related disabilities. Among persons 80 and older, approximately 34 percent need assistance due to a disability (U.S. Bureau of the Census, 1997b).

Those assisting both children and adults experienced the highest level of problems with care arrangements. In addition, those caring for children were more likely to experience problems with care arrangements than those caring for disabled adults. Working parents of young children have been found to be at high risk for stress resulting from problems in breakdown in care arrangements. Research has also shown that employees with combined child- and adult-care responsibilities generally experience high levels of stress and difficulties with care arrangements. Managing and coordinating multiple-care arrangements likely leaves these caregivers particularly vulnerable to difficulties associated with breakdowns.

FAMILY AND WORK RESOURCES

In this section we will examine the availability of family and work resources to buffer any potentially negative effects of multiple-role responsibilities among those providing differing types of care. We found that, overall, those providing care to both children and adults received the most assistance with their care responsibilities and experienced the highest level of support from coworkers. Those caring for children reported significantly higher levels of assistance and work support than did those caring for ill and disabled adults. We found no significant differences by type of care for many of the resource variables such as income, or flexibility or control at the work place.

Perhaps those with combined child- and adult-care responsibilities experienced higher levels of support and assistance as a result of the opportunities afforded them through having child-care responsibilities, as well as their level of need. It is likely that those with children received higher levels of assistance and support than those assisting ill and disabled adults, given the cultural context and the social value placed on raising a family and the opportunities provided for interaction with other parents. It has been suggested that caring for ill and disabled adult family members may be particularly isolating, and is a role for which there is limited recognition or social support. Brody (1985) has argued that as a society we have not yet developed clear role expectations or behavioral norms to support those with adult caregiving responsibilities.

Policies and Programs Considered Helpful by Type of Care

In this section, we examine the utilization and perceived helpfulness of workplace benefits and programs to those providing differing types of care. We found that those with combined child- and adult-care responsibilities endorsed the greatest number of programs and benefits compared to those providing a single type of family care. Among those with only child- or only adult-care responsibilities, the endorsement of programs and policies tended to reflect their differing needs and experiences.

As illustrated in Table 8-4, employees with caregiving responsibilities for children, adults, and both children and adults utilized many of the same types of leave programs and other benefits to meet their care responsibilities, although there were significant differences in relation to disability leave, sick leave, vacation leave, unpaid leave, dependent care account, flexible schedule, and use of an EAP counselor. For example, employees with both child- and adult-care responsibilities were significantly more likely than the other caregiver groups to use sick leave and vacation leave as well as the dependent care account, flexible work schedule, and an EAP counselor.

Among the benefits and programs endorsed by employees, significant differences by type of care provided were found with regard to seminars, support groups, long-term care insurance, job sharing, ability to work at home, ability to use donated sick leave, locating adult-care services, and child care at or near the work site. Overall, those with combined child- and adult-care responsibilities were most likely to endorse the vast majority of benefit options. While those with child-care responsibilities were more likely than those with adult-care responsibilities to endorse job sharing, ability to work at home, and the ability to use donated sick leave, employees with adult-care responsibilities were more likely to endorse long-term care insurance, support groups, and seminars.

As employers implement programs and benefits to assist employees with family-care responsibilities, their differing types of responsibilities and needs should be considered. Working parents, for example, are apt to find especially helpful programs and services designed to relieve physical strain, provide financial assistance, or reduce time constraints. Employees caring for disabled adults, on the other hand, are especially likely to benefit from

TABLE 8-4 Work-place policies, benefits, and programs utilized, endorsed as very helpful, and desired, by type of care
(percentages)

	Child Care Only (n = 514)	Adult Care Only (n = 267)	Both Adult and Child Care (n = 147)
Type of Leave Taken			
Disability***	9.2	1.0	8.1
Sick***	47.2	38.2	62.6
Vacation***	29.3	19.4	45.3
Leave, No Pay**	12.8	5.5	12.8
Benefits Utilized			
Dependent Care Account			
Utilization Rate**	13.6	.04	24.5
Very Helpful	49.9	.00	54.5
Work Schedule Adjustment			
Utilization Rate***	59.3	36.0	64.9
Very Helpful*	72.2	72.9	77.3
EAP Counselor			
Utilization Rate***	4.7	5.7	12.7
Very Helpful	37.1	69.5	53.6
Child Care Guide			
Utilization Rate	7.9	NA	13.4
Very Helpful	13.0	NA	6.0
Elder Care Guide			
Utilization Rate	NA	8.4	13.1
Very Helpful	NA	16.8	11.8
Parent Information Fair			
Utilization Rate	6.7	NA	11.9
Very Helpful	11.7	NA	13.2
Elder Care Fair			
Utilization Rate	NA	9.2	14.3
Very Helpful	NA	16.5	31.1
Benefits Desired			
Unpaid Family Leave	60.9	54.7	59.7
Work at Home***	56.3	39.5	61.0
Donated Sick Leave*	39.6	28.6	40.8
Domestic Partner Leave	37.6	35.0	36.1
Long-Term Care Insurance***	33.5	50.5	61.5
Job Share*	22.9	15.5	24.8
Seminars/Workshops***	22.7	34.8	39.1
Support Groups**	12.1	20.3	26.0
Locating Child Care	36.2	NA	28.1
Locating Adult Care*	NA	54.3	39.4
Child-Care Center**	55.7	NA	40.5

*p <.05
** p <.01
*** p <.001
NA = Not Applicable

long-term care insurance and programs and services that provide information and emotional support such as seminars, workshops, and support groups. Those with multi-generational care responsibilities often experience high demands and may be in need of multiple types of benefits. Across all types of care, employees may also need assistance in locating or developing adequate care for their children or disabled family members, as well as mechanisms for financing that care (e.g., long-term care insurance and dependent care accounts).

SUMMARY

In this chapter we examined the caregiving experiences of employees providing a range of family-care responsibilities. Utilizing a family-care model that can be applied across all types of care allows factors that are unique to a particular type of care, as well as those that are most salient across types of care, to emerge. We found that family and work demands have the major influence in determining the extent of family and work accommodations and role strain, far outweighing the contribution of personal and social characteristics and family and work resources. We also found that physical strain and financial strain were highest for working parents, especially those who also had adult-care responsibilities; whereas, emotional strain was highest for employees with adult-care responsibilities, especially those who also had child-care responsibilities.

As part of a comprehensive response to the needs of family-care providers, it will be important to tailor programs and services to those employees who are at greatest risk of experiencing detrimental consequences associated with their potentially competing work and family roles. The findings from this research suggest that particular attention be directed to those employees caring for children, those with more demanding work and family situations, and those experiencing problems with care arrangements. Especially at risk for role strain and occupational and familial impacts are employees who experience difficulty arranging care that is affordable, accessible, dependable, and of good quality; and those with especially demanding jobs.

A family-care model that can be applied across types of care has the potential to broaden and redefine relevant care needs, rather than relying on an arbitrary and restrictive age-based approach. Such a perspective encompasses family care of dependents across the life cycle, and is paramount for developing programs and policies responsive to the needs of employees with diverse family-care responsibilities. It identifies those factors (e.g., problems with care arrangements and work demands) that significantly impact family and work strain across all types of care. Potentially of interest to all caregivers, these issues are likely most amenable to forming intergenerational coalitions to advocate for addressing the needs of employees with family-care responsibilities.

While the development of such a framework is critical, caution must be exercised to ensure that the differences that do exist between generations are not obscured. For example, the needs of disabled dependent adults, compared to children, often involve more variations in problems, can be of longer duration, and may lead to advanced dependency rather than increased autonomy. Thus, it is important that discussions of family care be responsive to the diversity as well as the similarities of care needs across generations.

In the next chapter we will examine in greater depth the impact of structural characteristics (i.e., gender, race and ethnicity, and occupational role) on the demands, resources, and experiences of combining family-care and work responsibilities.

IMPACT OF GENDER, RACE/ETHNICITY, AND OCCUPATIONAL ROLE

INTRODUCTION

Demographic trends in this country show that women and racial and ethnic minorities are comprising an increasing portion of the American work force. Women accounted for at least two-thirds of the growth in the labor market in the past decade. In addition, there has been considerable growth in the participation of Hispanic, African-, and Asian Americans in the labor force. While whites remain the largest group in the formal labor market, the proportion of non-white workers increased from 20 percent in 1986 to 25 percent in 1996. By the year 2006, non-whites are expected to account for 27 percent of the labor force (Jacobs, 1998).

In combination with these shifts in labor-force participation rates, women, racial and ethnic minorities, and those in blue-collar and low-status occupational positions tend to have some of the highest rates of providing informal family care. Yet most work and family research has focused on the experiences of white caregivers employed in high-status positions, and has not adequately explored the experiences and needs of other diverse groups as they combine their family-care and employment responsibilities.

In this chapter we examine the important influences of gender, race and ethnicity, and occupational role on the integration of work and family-care responsibilities, drawing on the family-care model discussed in the last chapter.

GENDER

Women are increasingly combining employment with family-care responsibilities. Indeed, the greatest increase in labor-force participation rates has been among women in their prime child-bearing and child-rearing years. More than 75 percent of women between the ages of 20 and 44 are in the labor force (Sancier & Mapp, 1992).

146

Whether or not they participate in the formal labor market, women maintain the primary responsibility for the care of dependents of all ages, including children and ill and disabled adults. Existing research suggests that employment does not impact the acquisition of a caregiving role, although it may reduce the hours of care provided. Moreover, adult caregiving is becoming more common, with women born more recently more likely to become caregivers than were their mothers' generation (Moen et al., 1994).

Personal Impacts by Gender

As described in Chapter 8, hierarchical linear regression models were used to examine role strain, family accommodations, and work accommodations in terms of our family-care model. As shown in Table 8-1, gender entered significantly into the model for role strain, but not for family or work accommodations.

Given the relatively small, independent contribution of gender to role strain, it seems likely that the highly significant gender differences with regard to role strain and work accommodations illustrated in Table 9-1 are largely accounted for by other factors, such as family and work demands and resources. Previous research suggests that gender, per se, is likely not

TABLE 9-1 Personal impacts, demands, and resources, by gender
(means and standard deviations)

	Male (n = 633)	Female (n = 255)
Personal Impacts		
Role Strain***	2.48 (.62)	2.75 (.62)
Family Accommodations	2.00 (.78)	2.21 (.86)
Work Accommodations*	− .01 (.83)	.15 (.91)
Family and Work Demands		
No. of Care Recipients (CR)*	1.96 (1.14)	1.77 (1.09)
CR Disability Status*	1.13 (2.06)	1.32 (2.09)
Care Arrangement Problems*	1.27 (1.36)	1.46 (1.45)
Hours Worked ***	44.80 (7.36)	41.07 (8.18)
Job Demands***	2.38 (.82)	2.56 (.87)
Family and Work Resources		
Income**	3.99 (1.27)	3.70 (1.44)
Caregiving Assistance**	2.48 (.94)	2.24 (.96)
Coworker Support*	2.90 (.74)	3.04 (.78)
Job Flexibility*	2.82 (.66)	2.71 (.73)
Job Control**	2.80 (.79)	2.58 (.86)

* $p < .05$
** $p < .01$
*** $p < .001$

the most significant factor impacting the degree of inter-role conflict; rather it is the assignment of various role responsibilities, most often according to gender (Googins & Burden, 1987). Studies of dual-career families consistently demonstrate that when both spouses are employed, there is not a reassignment of household responsibilities, and women remain primarily responsible for family and household tasks (Gilbert, Holahan & Manning, 1981; Rexroat & Shehan, 1987; Hochschild, 1989; Gutek et al., 1991). Although men are providing more family care than they did two decades ago, women are still doing 50 percent more of the household work than are their male counterparts (Higgins, Duxbury & Lee, 1994).

Women also experience somewhat higher levels of role strain regardless of work and family demands and resources, due to sex-role socialization and societal structures, which support women's care of dependents. Such influences may promote gender differences in terms of emotional involvement, methods of interpretation, coping, and reporting of informal adult-care experiences. In addition, women may be more likely than men to interpret their caregiving experiences as a reflection of personal self-worth and to report feelings of ambivalence or inadequacy. Males, on the other hand, may be less likely to interpret or disclose feelings of distress in relation to employment and family care since it is less socially sanctioned.

It is interesting to note that women and men did not differ significantly with regard to levels of work or family accommodations associated with their family-care responsibilities, in our family-care model. Although men experience fewer caregiving demands and less caregiving stress, they are about as likely to make changes in their work lives to accommodate their caregiving activities. Moreover, like their female counterparts, men must also adjust to the concomitant changes in their family relationships, given the changing needs and demands that they and other family members face.

Family and Work Demands by Gender

There were significant differences between male and female employees in relation to the number of care recipients, disability status, problems with care arrangements, hours worked, and work demands, as illustrated in Table 9-1. Women tended to care for persons with higher levels of disability and experienced more problems with care arrangements.

Other studies also have documented a gender-based division of labor across all types of care. Working mothers, for example, are more likely than fathers to provide direct caregiving. In one study of 8,000 workers, 79 percent of the mothers and only 5 percent of the fathers said that they took all or most of the responsibility for their family's child-care arrangements (Emlen et al., 1990). Among men and women providing adult care, women tend to provide more hours of care and higher levels of assistance, especially for family members with high levels of cognitive and behavioral impairments—

those conditions most often associated with higher levels of strain and stress (Fredriksen, 1995).

Women in this study reported higher levels of work demand, although they were working fewer hours. Women are often employed in jobs with low status, significant time pressures, and repetitive work. Men, perhaps because they are less involved in the care of dependent family members, are able to work longer hours and experience less overall job demand.

Family and Work Resources by Gender

Female and male caregivers in this study differed significantly with regard to income, the amount of assistance they received with their caregiving responsibilities, coworker support, job flexibility, and job control. At home, employed women had lower household incomes and less caregiving assistance than did men. At the work place, women had less job flexibility and control, although they had higher levels of coworker support in relation to their family-care responsibilities.

Perhaps because caregiving and nurturing are culturally defined as primarily female roles, women are less likely to receive and perhaps are more reluctant to seek assistance with their family-care responsibilities. Men, on the other hand, report that female spouses or partners provide much of the assistance they receive with family-care responsibilities. And spousal social support and equity in the division of labor in the home has a small but significant mediating effect on work-family conflict and marital adjustment. In general, mothers' well-being and their marital satisfaction is increased when husbands share family work and assist with housework and child-care responsibilities.

In the U.S., 46 percent of female heads of household live in poverty compared with 7 percent of men (U.S. Bureau of the Census, 1994b). Regardless of their caregiver status, women compared to men tend to be employed in lower paying occupational positions (U.S. Bureau of the Census, 1997a), with lower status, less job flexibility, and less control on the job.

Men in this study reported receiving significantly less support from coworkers than did women. Likely reflecting gender roles, men are less likely than women to be viewed as family-care providers and may be less public about their work and family concerns. Although men may receive relatively limited support for their family-care responsibilities at the work place, informal social support at the work place has been found to influence the well-being of working fathers more than mothers.

Work-Place Policies and Programs by Gender

As shown in Table 9-2, women were more likely than men to have taken disability leave, sick leave, and leave with no pay in order to meet their

TABLE 9-2 Work-place policies, benefits, and programs utilized, endorsed as very helpful, and desired, by gender
(percentages)

	Male (n = 633)	Female (n = 225)
Type of Leave Taken		
Disability***	0.8	21.7
Sick*	46.1	54.2
Vacation	29.3	32.4
Leave, No Pay***	4.6	27.1
Benefits Utilized		
Dependent Care Account		
Utilization Rate	11.3	11.9
Very Helpful	49.3	52.9
Work Schedule Adjustment		
Utilization Rate	52.2	55.7
Very Helpful	71.8	78.1
EAP Counselor		
Utilization Rate***	3.5	13.1
Very Helpful	46.1	50.0
Child Care Guide		
Utilization Rate***	4.6	11.7
Very Helpful	11.2	9.7
Elder Care Guide		
Utilization Rate*	4.1	8.3
Very Helpful	15.4	20.8
Parent Information Fair		
Utilization Rate*	5.5	9.3
Very Helpful	15.2	18.5
Elder Care Fair		
Utilization Rate*	4.6	8.3
Very Helpful	17.2	27.3
Benefits Desired		
Unpaid Family Leave***	53.4	75.3
Work at Home***	48.3	64.6
Donated Sick Leave**	33.3	46.8
Domestic Partner Leave*	35.5	42.8
Long-Term Care Insurance*	41.7	49.0
Job Share***	16.1	35.7
Seminars/Workshops**	26.6	36.8
Support Groups***	12.8	28.6
Locating Child Care	26.4	28.6
Locating Adult Care	29.7	35.7
Child-Care Center*	38.2	45.2

* p <.05
** p <.01
*** p <.001

family-care responsibilities. Women were also more likely than men to utilize an EAP counselor, child-care guide book, elder-care guide book, and to attend a child information or elder care fair. The perceived helpfulness of the benefits utilized did not differ by gender.

Female employees were significantly more likely than males to endorse a number of work-place policies, programs, and benefits as potentially helpful in meeting their family-care responsibilities, including the following: unpaid family leave, ability to work at home, job sharing, seminars and workshops, support groups, leave to assist domestic partners, long-term care insurance, and a child-care center.

This research illustrates that women as compared with men have consistently higher utilization rates of family and work benefits such as unpaid leaves. Some have maintained that the utilization of work and family benefits can result in employment discrimination (Fierman, 1994; O'Connell, 1990) and increased economic inequalities between men and women (Scarr, 1998). It is interesting to note that, once benefits were utilized, there were no significant differences in terms of perceived helpfulness by gender in this study.

Implications

With the expanding number of women entering the labor market, the culmination of familial and work responsibilities will be particularly evident for women, since they are the primary providers of all types of family care. The predominance of females in the provision of informal family care likely reflects gender differences in domestic labor involvement and kinship relations, as well as cultural definitions of family caregiving and nurturing as primarily female roles. Although women who are combining family care and employment often experience role overload and excessive work hours, they report higher levels of satisfaction and well-being than do women not in the labor force.

The findings from this research indicate several significant differences by gender in relation to family and work demands and resources, personal life impacts, and benefits desired when combining employment and family-care responsibilities. In general, female caregivers had fewer resources, experienced higher levels of family care and work demand, and desired more work and family benefits. Women also reported slightly higher levels of role strain after controlling for social and demographic characteristics and family care and employment resources and demands. While these findings illustrate the importance of gender differences in the culmination of work and family-care responsibilities, they also underscore the importance of not ascribing to gender outcomes that are likely multi-causal in nature. The findings in this study suggest that the majority of gender differences in the integration of family care and work likely reflect differences in the gender distribution of demands and resources, rather than gender per se.

Although women are increasingly involved in the labor market, their earnings consistently lag behind men's, and the majority of women are in low-paying positions. Moreover, working women tend to experience fewer career advancements and lower salaries than do men in comparable positions. They also have higher turnover rates, most often because of a perceived lack of career advancement opportunities (Stroh et al., 1996).

Women's family responsibilities also are associated with a substantial reduction in monthly Social Security benefits. For example, the Social Security primary insurance amount for women who left their last job to care for others was reduced by approximately $127 in 1983; and benefits losses were more pronounced for low- to moderate-income women than for high-income women (Kingston & O'Grady-LeShane, 1993). Such findings raise important issues regarding the relationship of familial dependent care to women's decreased economic productivity and to structural economic inequalities.

If public policies and work-place initiatives are to be responsive to those in need, they must incorporate the social and economic implications of women's lives. In terms of an organizational response, women are the most likely constituent to exert pressure on an institution to respond to work and family issues; however, they also are most likely to be employed in low-prestige positions with limited power in the organization (Ingram & Simons, 1995). It is the number of female managers, not the number of women employed as a whole, that has been found to be significantly associated with the degree of a business's responsiveness to work and family issues (Ingram & Simons, 1995).

If, as a society, we are to value and promote the family care of dependents, comprehensive supports for family-care providers are needed. A gender-justice perspective in the analysis of work and family issues emphasizes the importance of "promot[ing] the capacity of both sexes to make life choices unhampered by limitations rooted in sexual stereotypes" (Osterbusch, Keigher, Miller & Linsk, 1987). Within such a framework, men and women must have equal access to paid work, and the distribution of family-care responsibilities needs to be considered as a means by which to lower overall family demands. In addition, work-place benefits, public policies, hiring practices and promotion standards need to be evaluated for gender bias and to eliminate sex discrimination and ensure pay equity.

Although the findings presented in this book demonstrate that women tend to be in a disadvantaged position relative to males in terms of work and family resources and demands, one also must consider some of the similarities that transcend gender. For example, many men in this study reported significant levels of strain and made numerous family and work accommodations to meet their dual role responsibilities. The literature on dual-career couples illustrates that combined work and family responsibilities do significantly impact men, albeit differently from women. For example, men tend to be less public about their work and family concerns, and are potentially stigmatized more than women if they utilize relevant work and family policies. As long as work and family are simply defined as women's issues, they will continue to be marginalized.

RACE AND ETHNICITY

Existing research has demonstrated that there are racial and ethnic differences in relation to filial norms, values and behaviors, service utilization, and social-support networks. Yet the provision and consequences of family care combined with employment among diverse ethnic and racial groups have rarely been examined.

To date most of the studies on work and family issues have primarily examined the experiences and needs of white middle-class families and have only controlled for race statistically. Yet African-American, Asian, and Hispanic-American families tend to be larger than non-Hispanic white families. In addition, a study of employees caring for ill and disabled adults, compared to noncaregiving employees, found that caregivers were significantly more likely to be African or Hispanic-American, and were less likely to be White (Fredriksen, 1993b).

The limited number of studies that have specifically addressed racial and ethnic differences in family care have generally compared African-Americans with whites. The research reported here moves beyond a comparison of two racial and ethnic groups to examine the differences and similarities among African-American, Asian, Hispanic, and white employees with family-care responsibilities.

Personal Impacts by Race/Ethnicity

As discussed in Chapter 8, hierarchical linear regressions utilizing our family-care model revealed a significant effect of race/ethnicity on role strain, as well as on family and work accommodations. The highest levels of role strain were reported by white employees; the highest levels of family accommodations by white and Hispanic employees; and, the highest work accommodations by white and African-American employees, as illustrated in Table 9-3. Although a significant predictor in the family-care model, it is important to note that the magnitude of the contribution of the race/ethnicity variable is relatively small.

Although limited, existing research indicates that racial and ethnic minority parents as well as caregivers of adults experience both strain and positive consequences as a result of combining employment and family-care responsibilities. Some studies have demonstrated racial variations in levels of burden, role strain, and depression, while other studies have found no significant effect of race or ethnicity.

Racial and ethnic differences may reflect cultural variations in interpretation, expectation, and/or methods of coping when providing informal family care combined with employment responsibilities (Gibson, 1982; Mui, 1992). For example, that African-American employees report lower levels of role strain and family accommodation than do whites may reflect the long history of African-American women combining employment and family care roles (Gibson, 1982). African-Americans have also been found to score higher

TABLE 9-3 Personal impacts, demands, and resources, by race/ethnicity
(means and F-values)

	White $(n = 642)$	African-American $(n = 59)$	Asian $(n = 111)$	Hispanic $(n = 45)$	F-Value
Personal Impacts					
Role Strain	2.58	2.47	2.51	2.48	1.02
Family Accommodations	2.17	1.97	1.96	2.15	2.76
Work Accommodations*	.08	.09	− .24	− .06	4.90
Family and Work Demands					
No. of Care Recipients (CR)	1.87	1.77	2.07	2.04	1.44
CR Disability Status	1.22	.95	1.05	1.03	.60
Care Arrangement Problems	1.25	1.41	1.48	1.57	1.56
Hours Worked	43.99	42.26	43.85	41.69	1.99
Job Demands	2.45	2.37	2.30	2.37	1.15
Family and Work Resources					
Income***	4.04	2.89	3.76	3.58	15.87
Caregiving Assistance	2.44	2.24	2.41	2.35	.89
Coworker Support	2.97	3.01	2.78	2.78	2.56
Job Flexibility**	2.79	2.65	2.96	2.54	5.03
Job Control***	2.81	2.31	2.70	2.36	10.09

* $p < .05$
** $p < .01$
*** $p < .001$

than whites on self-efficacy in relation to adult caregiving (Haley et al., 1996), and it has been suggested that they may have increased levels of resilience based in part on their inner resources and positive attitudes (Young & Kahana, 1995). The experience of African- and Hispanic-Americans, in particular, may offer important insights about the role of psychological and cultural resources in the successful integration of employment and family care.

Family and Work Demands by Race/Ethnicity

In this study, there were no significant differences in family or work demands, by race or ethnicity, as shown in Table 9-3. Although some studies have found that African-American caregivers were providing more extensive levels of assistance to more severely impaired care recipients than were white caregivers, studies of family care among employed persons have found few racial or ethnic differences. An earlier study of university employees, for example, found few significant differences in caregiving demands among white, Hispanic and African-American employees, although care recipients of white employees had significantly higher levels of ADL/IADL impairment and cognitive and behavioral limitations than those cared for by Asians (Fredriksen, 1993b). Similarly, Lechner (1993) found that African-American and white employees providing parent care reported very similar levels of caregiving demands. It may be that racial and ethnic differences in demands are less common among employed persons due to some of the leveling that may occur among caregivers whose situations allow them to maintain a full-time job and who benefit from the various formal and informal supports available at the work place.

Family and Work Resources by Race/Ethnicity

There were several significant racial and ethnic differences with regard to income, job flexibility, and job control. White employees reported the highest levels of income, followed by Asians, Hispanics, and African-Americans, respectively. Whites and Asians reported the highest levels of job control and flexibility, followed by Hispanics and African-Americans. There were no significant differences in assistance received with family-care responsibilities and levels of coworker support.

The income differentials in this study follow the trends by race and ethnicity in the U.S. population: African-Americans and Hispanics are much more likely to be living below the poverty level than non-Hispanic whites and Asians. For example, in 1992, 29.3 percent of Hispanics were living in poverty compared with 9.6 percent of the non-Hispanic whites; and in 1993, approximately one-third of African-Americans were living in poverty (U.S. Bureau of the Census, 1995a). Asians and Pacific Islanders have comparable family incomes and educational attainment levels to whites.

The disparity in income among the groups of caregivers in this study raises several important issues regarding access to and need for formal support services. Lack of economic resources has been found to be a significant barrier to accessing formal support services. Existing community-based services need to be examined and modified, as necessary, to ensure that those with limited financial resources have equitable access to culturally appropriate family support services.

It has been suggested that the demands of family care experienced by racial and ethnic minority caregivers may be offset by higher levels of social support. However, in this study, as in a number of others, no overall differences in social support were found between African-Americans and whites with adult-care responsibilities. There is some reason to believe, however, that the types of informal support networks may vary somewhat among various racial and ethnic groups. One study, for example, found that while the total size of the informal caregiving network did not differ among African- and white Americans, African-Americans were more likely to be assisted by nonimmediate family members (Burton et al., 1995). Similarly,

Fredriksen (1995) found that African-, Asian-, and Hispanic-American care-givers were more likely to provide assistance to a family member other than immediate family.

That white and Asian-American employees reported significantly higher levels of job control and flexibility than did African-Americans and Hispanics likely reflects the fact that whites and Asians in this study were more likely than other groups to be employed as scientists, engineers, and administrative professionals.

Benefits Utilized and Desired by Race/Ethnicity

There were no significant differences by race/ethnicity in terms of benefits utilized, with the exception of disability leave. Hispanics were more than twice as likely and African-American caregivers were nearly twice as likely as whites and Asians to use disability leave to meet their family-care responsibilities, as shown in Table 9-4.

There were several significant differences by race/ethnicity in the extent to which the caregivers found available benefits to be helpful, particularly with regard to the perceived helpfulness of dependent care accounts, work schedule adjustment, and the parent information fair. While white and Asian-Americans were most likely to find the dependent care account and work schedule adjustment very helpful, African-Americans were by far the most likely to rate the parent information fair as helpful.

In terms of benefits desired by respondents, there were significant differences by race and ethnicity regarding the desirability of domestic partner leave, long-term care insurance, support groups, and help locating adult-care services. Racial and ethnic minority caregivers, particularly African-Americans, were more likely than whites to desire leave for a domestic partner and long-term care insurance. In addition, African-American care-givers were nearly twice as likely as whites to desire support groups. Whites, on the other hand, were most likely to express the desire for help locating adult-care services.

In several previous studies, African-, Hispanic-, and Asian-American caregivers have been found to be more likely than whites to provide direct, hands-on care. For example, providing personal care and emotional support have been cited as the most frequent problems encountered by Hispanic family caregivers. This may explain why racial and ethnic minority employees are especially likely to endorse support groups to alleviate some of the physical and emotional demands of caregiving and long-term care insurance to reduce its financial impact. White employees, who are less likely to be providing hands-on care and more likely to be providing indirect care and coordinating services, may benefit more from resource and referral services that can help them in their efforts to locate adult care.

That racial and ethnic minority employees with family-care responsi-

TABLE 9-4 Work-place policies, benefits, and programs utilized, endorsed as very helpful, and desired, by race/ethnicity
(percentages)

	White (n = 642)	African-American (n = 59)	Asian (n = 111)	Hispanic (n = 45)
Type of Leave Taken				
Disability*	6.1	12.0	6.5	15.6
Sick	48.5	42.2	50.5	53.6
Vacation	29.5	24.9	38.4	30.3
Leave, no Pay	11.5	10.5	8.3	15.6
Benefits Utilized				
Dependent Care Account				
Utilization Rate	12.0	5.8	12.9	4.7
Very Helpful***	53.5	0.0	58.9	33.3
Work Schedule Adjustment				
Utilization Rate	55.1	48.8	46.8	46.7
Very Helpful***	75.5	60.2	73.2	66.8
EAP Counselor				
Utilization Rate	6.7	10.7	2.7	4.2
Very Helpful	51.5	54.9	50.0	0.0
Child Care Guide				
Utilization Rate	6.5	11.0	4.5	8.3
Very Helpful	9.5	22.2	15.9	0.0
Elder Care Guide				
Utilization Rate	5.6	9.4	2.8	2.1
Very Helpful	15.8	35.6	23.3	0.0
Parent Information				
Utilization Rate	7.4	5.6	3.6	2.3
Very Helpful*	14.3	60.5	0.0	0.0
Elder Care Fair				
Utilization Rate	6.2	5.6	4.5	0.0
Very Helpful	21.6	50.0	18.9	0.0
Benefits Desired				
Unpaid Family Leave	59.4	64.3	59.2	53.7
Work at Home	52.9	55.3	50.6	46.6
Donated Sick leave	36.7	45.6	28.3	47.1
Domestic Partner Leave*	34.8	54.0	41.7	35.2
Long-Term Care Insurance*	41.1	53.5	52.9	52.2
Job Share	23.1	17.4	15.7	21.0
Seminars/Workshops	29.2	36.2	27.9	34.6
Support Groups*	15.6	31.3	19.2	16.3
Locating Child Care	25.9	30.0	26.4	39.0
Locating Adult Care*	34.4	28.3	21.0	22.9
Child-Care Center	39.0	45.8	39.9	51.4

* p <.05
** p <.01
*** p <.001

bilities are more likely than whites to endorse domestic partnership benefits reflects their greater likelihood of providing assistance to family members other than immediate family. Yet to date most employment-based programs and public policies have been constructed only for those caregivers who provide support to children, parents, and other immediate family members, in essence producing an inherent cultural bias. More programs and policies are needed that provide support to extended networks of family and friends, those often requiring assistance by racial and ethnic minority caregivers.

Implications

Employees with family-care responsibilities differed by race and ethnicity with regard to the resources available to assist in the provision of care. In general, African-American and Hispanic family caregivers had fewer economic and work-place resources than did whites and Asians. Race/ethnicity was a predictor of role strain and family and work accommodations in our family care model, with whites generally reporting higher levels than African- and Hispanic-Americans. These differences likely reflect cultural differences in interpretation and ways of coping when integrating work and family-care roles.

As work-place benefits are developed and implemented to meet the needs of employed caregivers, it is imperative that there be consideration of the applicability and differential impact of particular benefits and programs, given the differing experiences and availability of resources among various racial and ethnic caregivers. For example, it is likely that resource and referral services will most likely benefit white caregivers, while increased social support and financial assistance will more likely benefit African-American and Hispanic employees.

The majority of previous research on caregiving employees has primarily examined the experiences of white caregivers or has controlled for race statistically. Yet this study illustrates that familial caregiving impacts different racial and ethnic groups in similar as well as diverse ways. It is imperative that in future research, samples include diverse racial and ethnic caregivers and that the experiences and needs of these caregivers be fully explored. Additional attention also should be given to racial and ethnic variations as they are impacted by gender, filial norms, the role of kinship support networks, and methods of interpretation and coping with dual role responsibilities.

Although this study has demonstrated that racial minorities tend to be disadvantaged relative to whites in terms of resources, other aspects of intergroup and intragroup variability must also be considered. For example, on several characteristics, Asians were more similar to whites than were African- or Hispanic-Americans. Such findings likely reflect the effects of differing occupational roles. Future research also needs to examine the extent of intragroup variations within each racial and ethnic group, given that the number of subjects in this study did not allow for such an analysis. Asian and Pacific Islanders, in particular, include heterogeneous groups, which differ considerably in terms of language, culture, immigration patterns, and various social and demographic factors.

OCCUPATIONAL ROLE

There has been limited attention to how occupational role and work-place characteristics impact the needs and experiences of employees with family-care responsibilities. To date the majority of work and family research has examined the experiences and needs of middle-class men and women in professional and managerial positions. Yet the majority of workers in the U.S., particularly those who have child-care or adult-care responsibilities, are employed in working-class or blue- or pink-collar positions.

Previous research on work and well-being provides ample evidence of the salutary effects of such work-place factors as worker autonomy, job flexibility, and support from coworkers and supervisors, and the potentially deleterious effects of high job demands; however, only limited research has examined how occupational role impacts the integration of work and family responsibilities.

This section of the chapter will examine how occupational role affects work and family outcomes, and the demands and resources that contribute to those outcomes, among employees with family-care responsibilities. We will examine the experiences of employees with four different job classifications: scientists/engineers, administrative professionals, administrative clerical staff, and technical personnel.

Personal Impacts by Occupational Role

Hierarchical linear regressions utilizing our family-care model revealed no significant effect of job classification on role strain, nor on family or work accommodations, as shown in Table 8-1. These findings suggest that bivariate differences in role strain by job classification (see Table 9-5) are most likely a function of background characteristics, resources, and demands. Indeed, the highest levels of role strain are reported by administrative professionals, who have the greatest job demands, and clerical staff, who have the fewest family and work resources, as we will see.

Family and Work Demands by Occupational Role

Scientists and administrators reported the highest job demands and worked the longest hours, compared with technical personal and clerical staff. In ear-

TABLE 9-5 Personal impacts, demands, and resources, by occupation
(means and F-values)

	Scientist/ Engineer (n = 355)	Administrative Professionals (n = 156)	Administrative Clerical (n = 95)	Technical (n = 236)	F-Value
Personal Impacts					
Role Strain**	2.59	2.69	2.63	2.43	6.23
Family Accommodations	2.17	2.17	2.18	2.10	.39
Work Accommodations	.16	.19	.29	.11	.41
Family and Work Demands					
No. of Care Recipients (CR)	1.90	1.81	1.75	2.04	2.13
CR Disability Status	.29	.40	.38	.39	3.02
Care Arrangement Problems	1.28	1.41	1.43	1.32	.51
Hours Worked***	46.83	44.66	38.77	41.15	46.67
Job Demands***	2.50	2.70	2.41	2.20	11.51
Family and Work Resources					
Income***	4.60	4.13	2.83	3.26	94.07
Caregiving Assistance***	2.58	2.19	2.37	2.40	6.01
Coworker Support	2.92	3.01	3.00	2.89	.91
Job Flexibility ***	3.08	2.76	2.52	2.53	42.50
Job Control***	3.11	2.73	2.24	2.43	53.85

* p <.05
** p <.01
*** p <.001

lier studies, job demand overload and increased number of hours worked have been found to be positively associated with the extent of work and family conflict, and with stress and strain levels, in general.

Although the needs of the care recipients in this study were similar for staff, technical personnel, academics, and administrators, other studies suggest that family-care demands can differ by job classification. For example, one study found that staff members provided more hours of assistance than academics and administrators, and they were more likely to be providing direct, hands-on care, even though the two groups did not differ with regard to the care recipient's level of disability, whether the employee lived with the care recipient, or whether she or he was the primary caregiver (Fredriksen & Scharlach, 1997).

A study by Duxbury and Higgins (1994) sheds light on the differences between employees in professional/managerial and clerical jobs. They studied two sets of couples: "dual career" couples, in which both members held managerial or professional positions and had high scores on a measure of work involvement; and "dual earner" couples in which both members held clerical, administrative, or production positions and had low work involvement. They found that, although members of dual career couples spent more time at work and had greater work demands than dual earner couples, they did not generally experience higher levels of work-family interference, role overload, or personal stress. Dual career women, for example, apparently compensated for their higher work demands by reducing the amount of time they spent on household chores, resulting in approximately the same over- all amount of time spent on work and family responsibilities as the dual earner women.

Family and Work Resources by Occupational Role

There were significant occupational differences with regard to income, as- sistance with caregiving, job flexibility, and job control. Clerical staff gener- ally reported the fewest resources with which to meet their family and work responsibilities.

Decreased job autonomy, limited control at the work place, and inflexi- ble work schedules have all been found to be associated with greater con- flict between employment and familial care responsibilities. Furthermore, previous research suggests the potential salutary effect of job flexibility and control on employee well-being.

For employees with family-care responsibilities, work-place characteris- tics such as flexibility and support can enhance the ability to manage po- tentially competing work and family responsibilities in a manner that does not create undue personal strain. Such work-place characteristics likely pro- vide more options for meeting family-care responsibilities, and may affect the type of work adjustments that employees are able to make, as well as what is even interpreted as work interference. For example, employees who have a great deal of job flexibility may be able to take time off during the work day to meet their care responsibilities and compensate for the time lost, while employees with less control over how their jobs are performed may be unable to prevent interference between their work and family roles.

Previous research suggests that employed caregivers with fewer social and economic resources tend to experience higher levels of caregiver strain. Lower levels of social and economic resources have repeatedly been found to be associated with increased vulnerability to stress, and to related phys- ical and mental health impacts (Voydanoff & Donnelley, 1989; Rocha, 1994).

Benefits Utilized and Desired by Occupational Role

As shown in Table 9-6, clerical staff members were more likely than the other employee groups to take disability leave and unpaid leave to meet their fam- ily care responsibilities. Scientists were the most likely to use dependent care accounts and work schedule adjustments, followed by administrative pro-

TABLE 9-6 Work-place policies, benefits, and programs utilized, endorsed, as very helpful, and desired, by occupation
(percentages)

	Scientist/ Engineer (n = 355)	Administrative Professionals (n = 156)	Administrative Clerical (n = 95)	Technical (n = 236)
Type of Leave Taken				
Disability***	3.4	11.7	19.1	4.5
Sick	46.7	48.0	48.3	51.2
Vacation	30.3	33.9	25.9	30.7
Leave, No Pay***	6.2	12.3	25.9	12.5
Benefits Utilized				
Dependent Care Account				
Utilization Rate*	15.0	11.9	8.5	7.3
Very Helpful	47.7	50.7	49.3	60.8
Work Schedule Adjustment				
Utilization Rate*	60.0	50.1	46.6	48.1
Very Helpful	75.6	68.7	71.9	73.2
EAP Counselor				
Utilization Rate***	3.1	14.7	11.1	4.5
Very Helpful	47.1	40.9	71.8	45.6
Child Care Guide				
Utilization Rate	7.6	7.1	12.0	3.7
Very Helpful	12.0	16.0	9.0	0
Elder Care Guide				
Utilization Rate*	4.1	9.8	5.5	2.8
Very Helpful	13.7	12.8	48.8	27.3
Parent Information Fair				
Utilization Rate	5.9	7.3	10.7	5.1
Very Helpful	0	39.2	17.9	24.5
Elder Care Fair				
Utilization Rate	4.0	8.0	8.9	3.2
Very Helpful	18.5	42.2	24.6	12.7
Benefits Desired				
Unpaid Family Leave	59.7	58.0	68.5	57.4
Work at Home***	55.2	64.4	61.8	40.5
Donated Sick Leave***	30.8	36.6	54.2	41.5
Domestic Partner Leave	36.5	33.5	46.3	39.2
Long-Term Insurance	42.5	42.7	50.5	42.5
Job Share**	21.0	25.0	33.0	16.0
Seminars/Workshops**	24.1	39.1	39.7	30.2
Support Groups***	11.9	20.9	32.8	18.1
Locating Child Care	30.7	22.5	29.3	26.7
Locating Adult Care	28.9	39.3	30.1	31.8
Child-Care Center	42.5	38.1	46.4	36.3

* $p < .05$
** $p < .01$
*** $p < .001$

fessionals. Administrative professionals were the most likely to see an EAP counselor or use the elder care guide. There were no significant differences between groups in perceived helpfulness of the various utilized benefits.

Clerical personnel tend to have less discretion over their work schedules and less access to work-place policies and benefits designed to help employees manage their family responsibilities. Moreover, clerical workers and other lower-income employees experience more frequent breakdowns in child-care arrangements, while paying a disproportionately greater share of their income for child care (Galinsky & Stein, 1990; Hofferth et al., 1991), making it more likely that they would take an unpaid leave of absence if necessary.

Persons in staff positions were significantly more likely than scientists, professional administrators, or technical personnel to endorse the following work-place policies as desired: donated sick leave, job sharing, seminars and workshops, and support groups. Professional administrators, followed by staff, were more likely than the other groups to endorse the ability to work at home as a desired benefit.

In examining the policies and programs employees with family-care responsibilities endorsed as being of greatest potential benefit, some important differences between staff and the other employee groups emerged. Policies that provided greater job flexibility or time off from work were endorsed more frequently by staff than by academics and administrators. These differences most likely reflect differences in work-place characteristics, caregiving tasks, social and economic resources, and access to existing support services and benefits.

Staff members, because of limited economic resources and cultural and gender-role norms, are particularly likely to be providing direct assistance to a disabled family member or friend. What they most need is the flexibility to alter the patterning of their work to be able to provide that care, whether by rearranging their work schedule, taking a leave of absence, working at home, or sharing a job. Scientists and administrators, on the other hand, are more likely to have the resources to pay for service provision but need help finding suitable service providers. They place a high priority on dependent care accounts, to reduce the out-of-pocket expenses associated with purchasing services.

Implications

A number of work-place factors and occupational characteristics (e.g., work overload, high levels of occupational stress, poor relationships between supervisors and coworkers, low job rewards, conflicting work demands, underutilization of abilities, and lack of participation in decision-making) have been found to be associated with such outcomes as employee illness and mortality.

Similarly, the research findings reported here demonstrate that work-family role strain is apt to be highest among clerical and administrative staff, those employees with the least flexibility and control at the work place. The majority of these differences, however, likely reflect sociodemographic characteristics and the relative balance between family demands and resources, since occupation did not enter significantly into the regression models. Staff positions are relatively low-paying and largely occupied by women and racial and ethnic minorities.

Some of the differences among the occupational groups also likely reflect differences in the provision of care. Earlier studies of adult care, for example, have found that staff members provided more hours of assistance and were more likely to be providing direct, hands-on care than academics and administrators; whereas, academics and administrators were more likely to be providing indirect care (e.g., coordinating services) and significantly higher levels of financial assistance, reflecting their increased ability to pay other persons to provide whatever direct or specialty care was needed (Fredriksen & Scharlach, 1997). Similarly, Secret and Green (1998) found that working mothers in professional and managerial positions were likely to have greater financial resources to purchase high-quality care or assistance and better positioned to coordinate care rather than provide high levels of direct care.

These findings are consistent with Archbold's (1983) earlier research differentiating care managers, who help to identify resources and manage care but do not provide direct assistance, from care providers, who provide direct assistance. Archbold attributed this to care managers' tendency to have higher status jobs, higher incomes, and more job flexibility than care providers. Fredriksen and Scharlach (1997) likewise found that more economically advantaged employees, to the extent that they are able to buffer themselves against some of the time, energy, and resource demands of dependent care, were significantly less likely to believe that they would have to quit work to provide care to a disabled loved one.

As employers develop dependent-care policies and programs, it is important that they give particular attention to the needs of staff and similar occupational groups. Yet access to employee benefits is often related to such factors as seniority and occupational status, with those in higher status positions getting a disproportionate share of benefits and wages. Moreover, the types of assistance most needed by staff are more likely to require the implementation of policies and procedures that make the entire work organization more flexible and adaptable to dual work and family responsibilities.

The findings in this study also raise a classification issue in this type of research. In some cases the U.S. Department of Labor's Bureau of Labor Statistics combines technical and clerical assistance to form one category: administrative support. However, in this analysis the technical personnel more closely resembled the administrative professionals. Other studies as well (e.g., Mutschler, 1994) have found more similarities (such as educational attainment level) between technical personnel and administrative professionals than between clerical and technical employees.

SUMMARY

Although women and racial and ethnic minorities represent the greatest number of new entrants into the work force, the majority of them are entering with low-paying employment positions, with limited flexibility and restricted opportunities for advancement. And the responsibility for family care has generally remained with the family, with women, racial and ethnic minorities, and those in low-status occupational positions providing the majority of care.

This chapter examined differences among employees with family-care responsibilities based on their gender, race/ethnicity, and occupation. The findings suggest that women experienced higher levels of role strain than their male counterparts, as well as higher demands and fewer resources at home and at work. Whites experienced higher levels of role strain and family and work accommodations than persons from other racial and ethnic groups, in spite of higher levels of resources. Occupational groups did not differ with regard to work-family impacts, when examined in a multivariate family-care model; whereas, scientists and administrators reported the most demanding jobs, clerical staff had the fewest work and family resources.

After controlling for background characteristics and work and family demands and resources, the contributions of these structural characteristics to personal impacts were relatively small. It seems likely that much of the difference in role strain and work and family accommodations that has been attributed to gender and occupational role may be a function of background factors and differences in work and family demands and resources. Racial and ethnic variations, by comparison, seem to be exacerbated when subjected to a multivariate analysis. The higher levels of personal impact experienced by white caregivers in spite of their comparatively higher levels of resources when compared with their African-American and Hispanic counterparts, likely reflect differences in interpretation, socialization, and methods of coping when integrating work and family responsibilities. These findings underscore the importance of increasing research attention to the needs and experiences of diverse groups of employees with family-care responsibilities, yet not ascribing all differences to gender, race, and occupational status, when they are in fact multi-causal in nature.

The findings presented in this chapter likely reflect the intersection between social and economic vulnerability and gender, race and ethnicity, and occupational status. In almost every domain assessed, females, staff personnel, and racial and ethnic minorities had lower levels of personal, family, and work resources with which to offset the potential stresses of caregiving responsibilities. Lower levels of social and economic resources have repeatedly been found to be associated with increased vulnerability to stress and its related physical and mental health impacts.

Historically, access to employee benefits has related to such factors as seniority and occupational status, with those in higher-status positions getting a disproportionate share of wages and benefits. Yet the majority of women and racial and ethnic minority workers in the U.S. are concentrated in low-paying positions. Combining work and family care has been historically, and is still today, often most difficult for poor women. These employed family-care providers are often unable to purchase formal services because of economic constraints, and may work long hours with rigid schedules and high demands. Thus, the very groups most in need of assistance may be least able to access it.

As we enter the twenty-first century, work-place and public policies need to reflect the changing structure and diverse nature of our society. Community-based and work-place programs need to be assessed with regard to potential institutional barriers, which may make it more difficult for employees with high care demands but low resources to have equitable access to support services. Work-place benefits and employment practices, as well public policies, need to be examined and modified, as necessary, to ensure that they are culturally sensitive and provide equitable access to persons regardless of gender, race and ethnicity, and occupational status.

In the next chapter we will review and evaluate a variety of work-place programs, benefits, and policies that have been designed to assist employees with family-care responsibilities.

PART FOUR

Family-Care Programs and Policies

· 10 ·

EMPLOYER-SPONSORED
WORK/FAMILY POLICIES
AND PROGRAMS

INTRODUCTION

In the preceding chapters, we examined how the magnitude of work and family demands and the adequacy of social support impact stress and work and family interference among employees with family-care responsibilities. We will now explore how the work place and the public sector have responded to the needs of these employees as they attempt to balance their work and family-care responsibilities. We will examine employer-based initiatives in this chapter and government policies and programs in Chapter 11.

The past ten years have seen tremendous growth in the quantity and quality of work-place policies and programs designed to assist employees with their family responsibilities. In 1991 there were approximately 3,500 companies with family-oriented benefits—only a small fraction of the 17 million companies in the United States (Gonyea & Googins, 1992). By 1996, 86 percent of major U. S. employers offered some kind of child-care assistance, up 30 percent since 1991; and 30 percent offered elder-care assistance, up 130 percent since 1991 (Hewitt Associates, 1997). One of the main factors driving increased interest in work/family programs is the changing composition of the paid work force and the desire of companies to maintain a competitive edge by attracting and retaining the best pool of workers. Ultimately, employers hope that by addressing workers' family concerns they can improve employee productivity and thereby positively impact the corporate bottom line.

This chapter examines a number of common employer-sponsored initiatives designed to assist employees with their family-care responsibilities. Included are paid leave policies, "flexible" (i.e., nontraditional) work arrangements, informational programs and materials, counseling and referral programs, direct-care services, and financial assistance. We also review labor union involvement in the development of policies and programs for working families. This chapter examines critically the extent to which em-

169

ployer work and family initiatives are actually reaching those employees who need them most, and whether the American work place is indeed becoming truly "family friendly."

LEAVE POLICIES

Leave policies are especially important when workers must take a period of time away from work to tend to family issues, such as caring for a newborn child or helping a family member who is ill. In our study, family leave was the single most frequently endorsed work-place policy, with more than half of all employees with child-care or adult-care responsibilities indicating that they would use it if it was available to them. In this chapter we will examine employer-sponsored paid family leaves. Unpaid leave available under the Family and Medical Leave Act (FMLA) of 1993 will be discussed in the next chapter on public policies.

Current status. Paid leave policies enable workers to care for dependents without having to worry about lost income from staying at home. Yet for the vast majority of workers, family leaves are unpaid. Data from the 1995 *Bureau of Labor Statistics Employee Benefits Survey* found that only 2 percent of employees in medium and large size companies have access to paid family leaves (U.S. Bureau of Labor Statistics, 1997). This number has remained largely unchanged for the past decade (Ferber et al., 1991). The United States is one of only six countries in the world that does not have a national policy mandating paid maternity leave, according to a 1998 United Nations survey of 152 countries (Olson, 1998). Spalter-Roth and Hartmann (1990) estimated the cost of public assistance due to mothers quitting their jobs because of lack of access to maternity leave to be about $108 million a year. When paid maternity leave is available, new mothers are more likely to take longer leaves, and they are less likely to need to give up their jobs.

Many employees are able to achieve the equivalent of a paid family leave through a combination of accrued sick and vacation time. Some flexible leave policies explicitly give workers "family/personal" leave time to accommodate various living situations. According to the U.S. Chamber of Commerce (1988), 95 percent of employers provide some paid vacation and 92 percent provide an average of 10 paid holidays a year. Sick leave of 10 to 15 days per year per worker is available from about 80 percent of employers (Wyatt Company, 1988). In large firms with over 100 employees, approximately 14.1 million employees have access to paid sick leave. Yet only 29 percent of these employees can officially use their sick leave to care for elderly relatives or sick children. Moreover, only 72 percent of working mothers have sick leave available to them at all, and only 31 percent had access to sick leave during the entire five year period from 1985 to 1990 (Heymann et al., 1996). Employees whose children are chronically ill are even less likely to be able to take sick leave than other employees: 36 percent of employed mothers of children with chronic health conditions had no sick leave available to them at any time during the five year period from 1985 to 1990 (Heymann et al., 1996). There are no legal requirements for employers to provide sick leave or vacation time. However, those choosing to voluntarily provide leave benefits must follow state and federal regulations.

Paid time off, like other employee benefits, differs by size of company, industry type, public versus private sector, and white- versus blue-collar occupations. Sick leave is a benefit for 97 percent of workers in public-sector jobs, but only for 68 percent of workers in medium and large private-sector companies. Paid sick leave is available to 93 percent of professional workers but only to 44 percent of production workers (Ferber et al., 1991), and to 77 percent of white parents but only 69 percent of nonwhite parents (Heymann et al., 1996). Only 20 percent of working mothers with incomes below the poverty line have at least one week of paid sick leave, compared with almost 50 percent of mothers with higher incomes (Heymann et al., 1996).

FLEXIBLE WORK ARRANGEMENTS

Part-Time Work

Part-time work (less than 35 hours per week) offers flexibility for workers who have family responsibilities or need to be close to dependents at home. It also can be helpful for workers who are either re-entering the labor force or changing from full-time paid employment to full-time family responsibilities. In this study, part-time work was endorsed by less than one-fourth of working parents and less than one-fifth of employees with adult-care responsibilities.

Current status. A survey by the U.S. Government Accounting Office (GAO) in 1994 found that 43 percent of companies with over 100 employees offered part-time employment with partial or full benefits. Approximately 12 percent of large firms offered job-sharing, whereby two or more workers can split the work and often the benefits of one full time job (U.S. GAO, 1992a). A study by Christensen (1989) of 500 employers each with more than 100 employees found that 90 percent of them had at least some regular part-time workers, and nearly 20 percent allowed job sharing. The availability of part-time employment varies according to the type of work. While only 13.7 percent of California's private-sector employers have job-sharing programs, 34 percent of that state's public employers offer job sharing to their employees. Employers with larger work forces are more likely to provide job sharing than those with fewer workers (DeLapp & Lawhorn, 1991). Part-time work is currently most readily available in the clerical and service sectors, in which wages are relatively low. However, part-time work is increasingly available in industries in which independent practice is the norm (Lawlor, 1995).

Partly as a result of the secular shift to a contingent work force, part-time work represents an increasing percentage of the total number of jobs. However, most of this growth has been involuntary; for example, as workers are released from full-time positions to permanent part-time positions. Although part-time work can offer a great deal of flexibility, part-time workers typically receive lower pay and fewer benefits. Hourly wages earned by part-time employees have been found to be 40 percent lower on average than those received by full-time employees. Approximately 84 percent of part-time workers have no health insurance through their jobs, and 20 percent are the heads of households that are below the poverty line (Levitan & Conway, 1988). Moreover, because part-time work is most often held by women and others in low-skill positions, there are concerns that it may exacerbate inequities in wages and employment opportunities.

Relatively little research is available on the costs and benefits to employers of part-time work, and existing studies have been inconclusive. Some studies show that there are savings due to the lower wages, lower or nonexistent benefits, and decreased absenteeism associated with part-time work (Nollen, 1982; U.S. Bureau of National Affairs, 1989a). Others have found increased costs in administration, training, and management for supervisors of part-time workers (Ferber et al., 1991). Some advocates have proposed the idea of temporary part-time employment, whereby full-time employees may change their work schedule to part-time to accommodate specific family-care needs, and then return to full-time work.

Flexible Schedules

Work and family tensions often arise because workers cannot accommodate family needs if they must follow a "set" work schedule. Although "flex-time" conveys the image of workers being able to vary their starting and ending times each day as needed, most "flexible schedules" actually involve a set schedule that workers can determine within certain parameters. Examples of flex-time include: (1) "fixed flex-time," in which workers begin work at a predetermined time each day (typically, between 6 AM and 10 AM) and then leave work 8 or 9 hours later, at a predetermined time (typically, between 3 PM and 7 PM); (2) a "compressed work week," in which workers are given the option of working 40 hours in less than five days; and (3) "gliding time," in which workers can adjust their work hours as needed.

Flexible scheduling is the benefit most often cited by employees as what they need in order to manage conflicting work and family responsibilities (Gallup Organization, 1980; Shinn, Wong, Simko & Ortiz-Torres, 1989). In our study, where flex-time was available as a company policy, 60 percent of working parents and 46 percent of employees caring for a disabled adult actually altered their work schedules to accommodate their family responsibilities. Virtually all of those who did so found this to be helpful, and about three-fourths considered it "very helpful."

Current status. U.S. employers started experimenting with flexible work schedules in the 1960s. By 1989, 13 percent of full-time and 43 percent of part-time employees were on some sort of flexible schedule (U.S. Bureau of Labor Statistics, 1989). The numbers have been steadily increasing; in 1993, 28 percent of all large firms offered flex-time (choosing the arrival/departure times), and 20 percent offered compressed work schedules. A GAO study found that federal, state, and municipal governments with the largest work forces were particularly likely to offer flexible scheduling options (U.S. GAO, 1994b). The 1998 Business Work-Life Study found that 68 percent of companies with 100 or more employees allow employees periodically to change starting and quitting times, and 24 percent allow employees to make these changes on a daily basis (Galinsky & Bond, 1998). Private-sector employers are more likely to provide this benefit than public-sector employers, possibly due to the additional hours usually required by private companies. Service industries are more likely to offer flex-time to their employees than are manufacturing companies (DeLapp & Lawhorn, 1991).

Evidence of the personal and family benefits of flex-time is mixed. Studies have found, for example, that flexible schedules only decrease absenteeism and tardiness by very slight amounts, if at all (McGuire & Liro, 1987). However, flexible schedules have been shown to result in increases in job satisfaction and morale, which come at little cost to employers (Golembiewski & Proehl, 1980; Harrick, Vanek, & Michlitsch, 1986; Nollen, 1989; U.S. Bureau of National Affairs, 1989b). Harrick et al. (1986) showed that employees using flex-time took less leave time and reported higher satisfaction with their work schedules than other employees.

The salutary benefits of flex-time are most apparent when employees have a great deal of flexibility with their work schedules, including the ability to change their beginning and ending times frequently if they need to. The more commonly available form of "flex-time"—the ability to vary work schedules only within limited parameters and with only occasional modifications—may not be associated with any such salutary effects (Zedeck & Mosier, 1990). In our study, the ability to adjust one's work schedule, take time off during the work day for personal reasons, and work at home were associated with lower levels of role strain and fewer family accommodations. However, those employees who actually utilized flex-time because of their family responsibilities tended to be those experiencing significantly higher levels of role strain and work accommodations than those who worked normal schedules.

Alternative Work Locations

Alternative work locations allow workers to work away from the main office, including at home or in satellite offices. Working at or closer to home has the potential to help workers better accommodate work and family responsibilities. Workers may be less stressed and more productive knowing that they are close to their family members in case an emergency arises. "Neighborhood Offices" that are closer to home than the central office also provide an alternative to having to commute (sometimes a long distance) to the main office. In this study, 57 percent of working parents and 47 percent of employees caring for a disabled adult indicated that they would do some of their work at home if able to do so.

Current status. Alternative work locations (such as home) have had a long history, but are much more common today than in the past. In 1995, only about 2 percent of employees in medium- and large-size firms were offered the option of flexible work places (U.S. Bureau of Labor Statistics, 1997). However, with the rapid growth of computer technology and electronic communications, home-based work is experiencing new growth. The 1998 Business Work-Life Study, for example, found that 55 percent of companies with 100 or more employees allowed employees to work at home occasionally, and 33 percent allowed employees to work at home or off-site on a regular basis (Galinsky & Bond, 1998).

Employees who work in flexible locations tend to fall into two categories: low-skilled workers and high-level professionals. At the low-skilled end, home-based work has traditionally been piece work, typically performed by immigrants and other low-wage workers who may be barred from the primary labor force because of limited English skills or discrimination. They typically earn low wages and have no benefits. Violations of minimum wage laws are not uncommon, and exploitation of child labor often occurs (Boris & Daniels, 1989).

At the other end of the spectrum are high-level professionals, for whom home-based work is possible through advanced technology. For many such workers, their homes can become "virtual offices," saving employers substantial overhead costs required to maintain actual office space. External work locations also help employers to save employee parking costs and comply with federal and state clean air standards. In addition, there is some evidence that workers who telecommute may be more productive than their on-site counterparts (Ferber et al., 1991, p. 130).

Despite its advantages, home-based work can lead to inefficient communication with management, isolation from coworkers, and reduced chances for promotion. Moreover, home-based work typically requires employees to provide and maintain supplies and equipment traditionally provided by employers, including computers, telephones, office furniture, and supplies. Home-based work also may leave workers at risk for occupational injuries, for which they typically are not covered under existing Workers' Compensation laws and for which employers may be unwilling to take fiscal responsibility.

Home-based work and satellite work locations seem to offer lots of flexibility, particularly for employees who have intermittent care responsibilities. However, it seems painfully obvious that working at home and caring for a family member who requires constant attention may be incompatible, at least if one hopes to perform both activities adequately. Indeed, there is some evidence that working at home can exacerbate role conflict by removing the physical barriers between work and family settings (Shamir & Salomon, 1985). Moreover, particularly for low-skilled workers, there is a substantial risk of exploitation. Thus, even though alternative work locations are typically promoted as a perquisite for employees, the evidence suggests that in many cases they may benefit employers far more than workers.

INFORMATIONAL PROGRAMS AND MATERIALS

In an effort to help their employees better manage their family responsibilities, many employers make available a variety of informational materials and programs. Informational materials typically include Dependent Care Guides, brochures, newsletters, fact sheets, and other written communications designed to give employees the information they need to better understand and respond to various aspects of their dependent-care responsibilities. Lawrence Berkeley Laboratory, for example, had a Child Care Guide, which was used by 9 percent of the working parents in our survey, and an Elder Care Guide, which was used by 11 percent of employees with elder-care responsibilities. Informational programs include lectures, workshops, seminars, fairs, and other presentations by family-care experts. Eight percent of working parents in our survey had attended a Parent Information Fair, while 12 percent of employees with adult-care responsibilities had attended a Caregiver Fair.

Current status. In 1994, information on caring for an impaired elder was offered by 7 percent of United States employers, with another 6 percent considering doing so. Approximately 13 percent of employers offered seminars or other informational programs on parenting. Five percent offered seminars on elder care, and 7 percent were considering doing so. Only about 2 percent of employers offered parenting fairs or caregiving fairs, and another 4 percent were considering doing so (U.S. GAO, 1994a). Informational materials and programs are apt to be more available to employees who work for larger employers. A GAO study found that federal, state, and municipal governments with the largest work forces were particularly likely to offer information about elder care (U.S. General Accounting Office, 1994b).

Information for parents and other family-care providers is increasingly available through electronic sources such as web sites, discussion groups, and other on-line services. Dependent Care Connection (1997), for example, has established a web site that includes a national directory of work and family consultants, free subscriptions to electronic mailing lists on work and family issues, and on-line forums covering topics such as adoption, child care, elder care, financial planning, and work/life balance. Some employers have developed their own work and family internet sites and electronic discussion groups that allow employees with children or adult-care responsibilities to discuss common concerns and share information and resources.

Informational materials and programs are a relatively inexpensive way for employers to educate a large number of employees about parenting strategies and dependent-care resources. However, some have argued that informational materials and programs, while potentially enhancing employee knowledge, may have little impact on their actual ability to manage their family-care situations (Montgomery & Borgatta, 1989). Indeed, while about three-fourths of working parents in our study found the company's Child Care Resource Guide and Parent Information Fair to be helpful, fewer than 12 percent found these to be "very helpful." Similarly, three-fourths of the employees with adult-care responsibilities found the Elder Care Guide to be helpful, but only 15 percent found it "very helpful." More highly regarded was the Elder Care Fair, which 85 percent found to be helpful and 22 percent found "very helpful."

REFERRAL AND
COUNSELING PROGRAMS

Resource and Referral

Decent quality child care and long-term care services are hard to find. In our study, employees who experienced difficulty finding adequate, dependable care had to make the most accommodations in their work and family activities and experienced the highest levels of role strain. Resource and referral (R & R) programs (also called counseling and referral, information and referral, care consultation, etc.) represent one possible mechanism for alleviating this problem.

R & R programs provide information on available community resources, information to help employees locate and select from existing dependent-care providers, and may also provide counseling or consultation to help employees more effectively manage their family-care situations. In this study, 38 percent of employees with children age 12 or under said they would use a program that provided help in locating child-care services near their own home. Approximately one-half of those with adult-care responsibilities indicated that they would use a program that helped them locate community services for an ill, disabled, or elderly adult.

Current status. Resource and referral services were offered by fewer than 10 percent of employers in 1989 (U.S. Bureau of Labor Statistics, 1989). Among employers today with at least 100 employees, however, more than one-third offer R & R for child care and 24 percent offer R & R for elder care (Hewitt Associates, 1997; Galinsky & Bond, 1998).

Resource and referral programs may be provided in-house, or employers may choose to contract with an outside consulting agency or community organization. In 1992, there were approximately 600 child-care R & R agencies in the United States (National Association of Child Care Resource and Referral Agencies, 1992). Among employees who have access to child-care resource and referral programs, about 11 percent actually use them. Among those with access to elder-care programs, about 6 percent use them (Galinsky et al., 1993). A 1994 survey by Work-Family Directions, a resource/referral company that has been contracted by many large employers, showed that 66 percent of employees who used its services reported that the availability and convenience of a toll-free information number reduced stress. Three-fourths of employers who contracted with this agency said that it helped their company keep valuable employees, and 82 percent found that the program helped them anticipate future needs and prevent problems (*Is Your Work/life C & R Earning Its Keep?* 1995). Marriot Corporation, which provides its employees both child- and elder-care R & R, in 1995 reported a 400 percent return on its investment in a toll-free counseling helpline for its employees (Marriott Considers Employee Problems, 1995).

Resource and referral may be especially useful for employees who are willing and able to purchase child-care or adult-care services, and somewhat less useful for those who either cannot afford to pay someone else to provide care or whose culture or family values locate responsibility for dependent care with the family rather than outsiders. R & R provided by a national vendor is apt to be especially helpful for employees who are providing assistance to someone who lives at a distance, which is often the case for elder care.

By offering R & R programs, employers can attempt to reduce the workplace impact of employees' family responsibilities without incurring the fixed costs associated with providing a direct service such as child care or adult day care. However, the benefit to employees of R & R programs is limited to some extent by the quantity and quality of the actual services available. In addition, some employers are concerned about the potential liability associated with providing dependent-care information and referrals to employees, particularly if that information were to prove inaccurate or inappropriate or if a dependent child or adult were to suffer abuse or neglect by a referred provider. Employers attempt to protect themselves against potential legal liability through "hold harmless" clauses in their contracts with R & R providers and by assuring that employees are given multiple referrals from which to choose, whenever possible.

Employees with particularly difficult dependent-care situations (i.e., those situations most likely to result in significant work disruptions) are apt to require more than simply a list of referrals. Employees caring for a child with special needs or an adult with serious disabilities may need substantial assistance in sorting out the care recipient's needs and capabilities, their own capabilities and limitations, the capacity of their existing social network, activities for enhancing their own caregiving ability, opportunities for expanding and reinforcing external resources, strategies for coping and adapting, and planning and preparations for future changes. Also needed by employees with complex care situations is a comprehensive in-person assessment of the elderly or disabled dependent, as well as ongoing assistance in developing, coordinating, and monitoring an appropriate care plan. These assessment and care-management services are seldom available through employer-sponsored resource and referral programs.

Counseling

Consultation and counseling regarding family-care concerns are often provided by a company's Employee Assistance Program (EAP), either in-house or through a contract with an outside vendor. Talking to a counselor can help employees better understand and resolve conflicts related to their efforts to manage their work and family responsibilities. Counseling can help to reduce the psychological impact of family dependent care, thereby yielding positive benefits for both employees and employers.

In this study, 7 percent of employees with children had spoken to an Employee Assistance Counselor about their parenting responsibilities; of these, 83 percent found the counseling to be helpful and 43 percent found it "very helpful." Eight percent of employees with adult-care responsibilities indicated that they had spoken to an Employee Assistance Counselor; of these, 89 percent found the counseling to be helpful and 61 percent found it "very helpful."

Current status. Employee assistance programs are increasingly common. The 1995 *Bureau of Labor Statistics Employee Benefits Survey* found that EAPs were available to 58 percent of full-time workers in private companies with 100 or more employees (U.S. Bureau of Labor Statistics, 1997). Among large employers, 84 percent offer EAPs (Hewitt Associates, 1997). About 6 percent of workers actually see an EAP counselor each year (Galinsky, Friedman & Hernandez, 1991).

There are two EAP models, in-house and external. Hewitt Associates' 1996 survey of 1,050 large employers found that 80 percent of those with an EAP program contracted with an external provider, 14 percent used an internal program only, and 6 percent used a combination (Hewitt Associates, 1997). Internal EAPs have a slightly higher cost per employee ($26.59) than the external EAPs ($21.47), although the difference may be associated with greater service provision (French, Zakin, Bray & Hartwell, 1997).

Employee Assistance Programs were developed initially to address alcohol problems, but have grown to address other potential causes of work disruption or employee stress. Family problems have replaced drug and alcohol issues as the most frequent reason for using EAP services (Parkinson, 1995). Some have questioned, however, whether EAPs are best suited to assist employees with family-care concerns. Particular concern has been raised about whether EAP counselors generally have sufficient knowledge and training, particularly with regard to the needs of elderly and disabled adults and their caregivers. One study of 180 EAP coordinators (Brice & Gorey, 1989) found that the majority of respondents reported little knowledge of the basic disorders of aging. As Dana Friedman, then at The Conference Board, has noted, "The EAP program [counselor] may know as little as the employee" (Friedman, 1986, p. 48). A related problem is that EAP counselors may see employees' difficulty managing work and family responsibilities as personal problems, fostering stigma toward EAP services.

A few companies with EAP programs have conducted rigorous analyses of the costs and benefits of such programs. In the federal sector, the U.S. Postal Service reported an annual saving of $2 million as a result of its EAP. A survey of members of the Work-Family Roundtable found that 68 percent said their EAP improved their morale, 62 percent said it raised their productivity, 59 percent said it decreased absenteeism, and 55 percent said it lowered health costs (Parkinson, 1995). Most research concerning EAPs, however, has been focused on substance abuse, with little attention to the EAP's expanding role in helping employees with family issues. Measurements of success, such as reduced absenteeism and tardiness, focus almost exclusively on the individual, ignoring families or overarching business issues.

Support Groups

Peer support groups provide an opportunity for employees with similar family-care situations to share concerns, discuss common problems, exchange useful information, and receive emotional support. Support groups offered at work during the lunch hour can provide relief from the emotional strains of family caregiving, without requiring an additional time commitment from the employee or the need to find additional child care. After-work "drop in" groups have been found to be attractive to some senior-level managers who are not available at lunch time (Edinberg, 1987). In this study, 22 percent of employees with adult-care responsibilities indicated they would attend support groups if they were available, as compared with 15 percent of those with child-care responsibilities.

Current status. The U.S. General Accounting Office (1994a) estimates that of 23 million Americans who work for medium to large companies, 2.5 million have access to caregiver support groups through their employers. The Families and Work Institute (Galinsky et al., 1991) found that only 5 percent of the companies they surveyed offered work/family support groups.

Caregiver support groups provide participants an opportunity to share information and resources, receive assistance with problem-solving, and explore new coping and care-management strategies (Hartford & Parsons, 1982). Participants typically report increased use of community resources and improvements in their ability to solve caregiving problems (Barusch & Spaid, 1991; Labrecque, Peak & Toseland, 1992). However, substantial reductions in caregiving stress or work disruptions have not consistently been found among participants in most caregiver support groups (Haley, 1989;

Toseland & Rossiter, 1989). Indeed, support groups seem to be inferior to individual counseling for reducing caregiving strain and improving psychological well-being (Toseland, Rossiter, Peak & Smith, 1990). Lowering levels of distress may not be as important to some caregivers as improving their effectiveness as care providers and obtaining needed social support (Glosser & Wexler, 1985; Haley, Brown, & Levine, 1987).

DIRECT PROVISION OF SERVICES

Child Day Care

In our study, more than half of working parents with infants or toddlers and more than one-third of those with preschool children reported problems with child-care arrangements. Moreover, such problems were a major contributor to role strain and to the need to make accommodations in the work place and at home. Given the difficulty employees often experience in attempting to find decent quality, conveniently located care for their dependents during work hours, some employers have seen on-site care as the best solution to employees' family-care problems.

Working parents in this study were particularly likely to endorse the need for a child-care center at or near their work site; more than two-thirds of employees with children age 12 or under indicated they "would definitely use" such a center if it were offered at a reasonable cost. The younger the age of their children, the more likely employees were to say they would use such a center. There was a particular need for child care for children with disabilities and vacation programs for school-age children.

Current status. In 1984, there were 415 employer-supported child-care centers in the country (Burud, Aschbacher & McCroskey, 1984); in 1989, there were 1,077 on-site or near-site child-care centers (U.S. Bureau of Labor Statistics, 1989); and by 1995, there were close to 1,700. Although this was a dramatic increase, still only 9 percent of companies with 100 or more employees provide on-site or near-site child care (Galinsky & Bond, 1998). Moreover, private companies are not expanding child-care and elder-care centers as rapidly as government and public-sector employers.

Studies of the effects of company-provided child care on absenteeism, job performance, and employee satisfaction have produced conflicting results. Some have found that parents who had access to and used company child care had lower rates of absenteeism and turnover than other parents (Youngblood & Chambers-Cook, 1984; Ransom & Burud, 1986). Friedman (1989a), in a review of 17 studies of employer-provided child care, found slight reductions in turnover rates but no evidence of a direct effect of company child care on employee productivity. A study of the Catherine McAuley Health Center in Ann Arbor, Michigan, however, showed no significant differences in turnover rates between working parents who used the center and those who did not. Nor were there significant differences in job satisfaction levels, loyalty to the work place, or stress levels stemming from work and family conflicts.

One advantage of employer-supported child care is that corporate underwriting can often result in higher quality care than is typically available in the community. But there appears to be a delicate balance between benefits, costs, and the varying needs of employees. In the past, some companies (such as AT&T) have actually closed on-site child-care centers. For AT&T, the cost of operating the program was believed to be greater than the benefits it was providing for their workers (National Research Council, 1990). In some cases, employees themselves have taken over the management of child-care centers that employers were no longer able or willing to support. When employees of Apple Computer learned that Apple would no longer subsidize its innovative child care center, the parents quickly raised the money necessary to keep the center open. The center continues to be supported by user fees and contributions raised by the employees themselves.

Instead of operating "full-time" care centers, some employers have chosen the alternative of targeting services to particular needs. For example, there is a particular need for child-care centers for employed parents who work nonstandard shifts. An example is a 24-hour center near San Francisco International airport, which was developed by a consortium of employers and public agencies to meet the needs of airline employees. Other employers have helped to develop or subsidize summer programs or after-school programs for children of employees.

Adult Day Care

Just as child-care centers can provide for the needs of young children during their parents' work day, adult day-care centers can provide care for adults while their caregivers are at work. Among the types of adult day care currently available are social day care, adult day health care, and dementia care. Social day care typically provides social interaction and psychosocial support for individuals who otherwise would be alone during the day but who do not necessarily have significant physical impairments. Adult day health care typically provides nursing care, rehabilitation therapy, case management, and social interaction for individuals who might otherwise require residential care. Dementia care centers typically provide supportive care and supervised activities for individuals with moderate levels of impairment due to Alzheimer's disease or other progressive dementias.

Current status. Some employers have experimented with care programs that provide care for both children and elders. In 1990, Stride-Rite became the first U.S. corporation to open an employer-sponsored intergenerational care center. In 1993, the center had 55 children and 30 elders enrolled, each attending a minimum of two days per week, six hours per day. It included children from 15 months to 6 years and elders aged 60 and older. Fee scales for the elder program included: full pay at an employee discounted rate (the center also serves the community); full state-subsidized care for low-income elders; and full company-subsidized care for low-income families who do not qualify for state funding. However, elder participants must be able to care for their own personal needs with minimal assistance (Laabs, 1993), limiting participation of those seniors who have the greatest need for adult day care.

It is clear that many more adult day-care centers are needed. According to one estimate, the United States needs 10,000 adult day-care centers, over three times as many as are available currently (Gunby, 1993). However, employers have had serious concerns regarding their role in meeting this need. One issue is the large capital investment required for the benefit of a relatively small number of employees. Other issues are space, transportation, and legal liability. One option for employer-sponsored care centers is to support the development of adequate community-based adult-care resources, and to provide the information and financial assistance that employees and their disabled family members require to avail themselves of those resources. The 1998 Business Work-Life Study found, however, that only 5 percent of employers with 100 or more employees provided financial support to local elder-care programs.

Sick or Emergency Child Care

A substantial amount of worker absenteeism is directly related to a parent (usually a mother) taking time off to care for a sick child. In one study, 27 percent of all absenteeism was due to family issues such as caring for an ill child (*Commerce Clearing House Unscheduled Absence Survey*, 1995). According to the American Medical Association, children are typically sick from six to ten times a year, for a period of three to nine days each incident (Seitel, 1997). Working parents must make difficult decisions when their children become ill, influenced by such factors as the severity of the illness, advantages and disadvantages of available options, job flexibility, and the availability of paid leave.

In a *Working Mother* magazine survey of 1,706 women (Moskowitz, 1996), 70 percent reported that having a sick child created the worst possible conflict between job and family responsibilities. Work-place needs assessments have shown that 33 percent of mothers had a sick child under age 12 in the previous month. Fifty-one percent of these women missed work to care for the child; 49 percent went to work but worried about the child (Johnson, 1995). In this study, two-thirds of working parents reported problems finding care when a child was ill, and 41 percent of parents with a child age 12 or under indicated that they definitely would use temporary or emergency care facilities if they were available.

Current status. Sick-child care is receiving increasing attention. Hewitt Associates' 1996 survey of 1,050 major employers found that 11 percent offered some type of sick or emergency child-care program (Hewitt Associates, 1997). By comparison, a 1991 survey of Fortune 1000 corporations found that only 4 percent of the companies offered sick-child care benefits (Galinsky et al., 1991). A 1990 study found that only 0.5 percent of private California firms employing at least 10 workers and 1.5 percent of public California employers provided benefits relating to sick-child care (DeLapp & Lawhorn, 1991). Among firms with at least 100 employees, only about 5 percent offer sick or emergency child care (Galinsky & Bond, 1998).

Sick-child benefits can include sick-child care centers, in-home health care, or paid time off to care for an ill child. For example, First Union Corporation offers 12 sick-child days per year for employees' to care for their own children. Honeywell began a sick-child care pilot program in 1990, which included in-hospital or at-home service for children aged 6 to 15 years. The program charged an at-home fee of $11 an hour for a home-health aide or $20 an hour for a practical nurse. There was a four-hour minimum and $2 charge for each additional child, to a maximum of three children. Johnson & Johnson has a 100 percent subsidized on-site sick-child care program, and employees can take sick-child care days as needed. Finally, Dupont links employees to backup and emergency dependent care and subsidizes 80 percent of the cost.

There is some evidence that sick-child care can be extremely cost effective. An organization that spends $50 a day to reserve a space in a sick-child center can save $100 a day or more if that sick-child care enables an employee to avoid being absent from work (Zedeck & Mosier, 1990). Honeywell and 3M estimate that they have saved from $1 to $3 per hour by paying from 50 percent to 100 percent of employees' sick-child care costs (Family Friendly Programs, 1990). Honeywell determined that it saved $45,000 over and above the cost of the programs in the first nine months of operation (Johnson, 1995).

Employees consistently express interest in sick-child care programs such as in-hospital or at-home sick-child care. Yet in 1989, when several Get Well Centers were established in Kansas City, Missouri, few parents would bring their children to them. Similarly, Transamerica Life Companies closed down a sick-care center at a nearby medical center due to low utilization (Ruben, 1991). One reason for low utilization may be cost. Unless it is company subsidized, a day at a sick care facility adds from $35 to $50 per day to regular child care costs. In-home care can exceed $100 per day.

Finally, there is concern among many medical and child-development professionals that sick-child care programs may create a society that values economic productivity over childrearing. Critics Marian Blum and Edward Zigler warn that "corporate-sponsored child care programs may ultimately prove to be more coercive than liberating" (Ruben, 1991, p.100). As one Atlanta mother of two children observed, "Maybe what we really need are more options to be at home when our kids are sick. In the conflict between work and a sick child, should work win out?" (Ruben, 1991, p. 102).

Home Care

One-fourth of employees caring for an elderly or disabled adult in our study reported problems finding trained and reliable care providers. Nearly 20 percent reported problems associated with breakdowns in care arrangements. Moreover, such problems were associated with higher levels of role strain, as well as greater work and family accommodations.

Employers can help employees with adult-care responsibilities by helping them to arrange and/or pay for in-home nursing or home-chore services. In-home nursing includes a range of personal care and therapeutic services provided by nurses, home-health aides, or rehabilitation therapists. Home-chore services include assistance with household activities such as housecleaning, meal preparation, laundry, and shopping. Use of these services is increasing dramatically with the growing number of elderly and disabled Americans and because patients are being released from hospitals sooner and with more follow-up care requirements. In the seven years from 1982 to 1989 alone, the percentage of persons with disabilities relying entirely on paid home-health providers increased from 5.5 to 9 percent (Buchanan & Alston, 1997). These services can be expensive, accounting for the vast majority of current increases in Medicare expenditures. The average national Medicaid payment for skilled nursing in 1995 was $68.16 per visit, and the average national payment for home-health aides was $35.64 per visit (Buchanan & Alston, 1997).

Current status. Recognizing their employees' needs for assistance with dependent care, a few companies are subsidizing the costs of home care. For example, Travelers is part of a consortium of employers that trains family-care workers in addition to sharing the cost of three days of in-home care for family emergencies. Other examples are IBM and Motorola, members of American Business Collaboration, who fund a case-management service that offers one home assessment visit to an elderly relative of an employee and produces a written report of the assessment (Shellenbarger, 1993). However, only a few employers assist directly with home care. More commonly, employers assist employees in obtaining these services through their information and referral programs, or by helping employees pay for services through Dependent Care Assistance Plans or long-term care insurance.

Maternity Care

A growing number of employers now offer programs designed to assist new mothers. Champion International, for example, provides a maternity package for their female employees that includes a prenatal health program, a maternity risk assessment, case management conducted by an obstetric/gynecology nurse, educational resources, and pediatric visits until age five years. Champion's health insurance pays for birth, prenatal vitamins, prenatal care, and pediatric visits. An internal study found that cost-savings resulting from this program included a 16.7 percent decrease in the number of days new mothers were spending in the hospital and a significant decrease in the C-section rate (Jacobson, Kolarek & Newton, 1996).

CIGNA, a Philadelphia-based insurance company with a 70 percent female labor force, provides a public health program for its employees including a prenatal program called "Healthy Babies." "Healthy Babies" gives working mothers-to-be relevant educational materials. CIGNA's 1994 study claimed a $2 million savings that year due to less complicated pregnancies, fewer premature births, and healthier birth outcomes (Jacobson et al., 1996).

FINANCIAL ASSISTANCE

Family-care responsibilities can be a significant economic burden, with some employees spending $1,000 or more a month for child care or to assist a disabled family member or friend. In our survey, more than three-fourths of working parents and about 60 percent of those with adult-care responsibilities reported experiencing some degree of financial strain associated with family care. Employer-sponsored efforts to relieve some of this financial strain include health benefits, long-term care insurance, Dependent Care Assistance Plans, adoption assistance, and flexible benefit policies.

Some have argued that the greatest contribution employers could make to the welfare of workers' families would be to increase salaries. Better salaries would enable employees to work fewer hours, choose between paying for excellent child care or caring for children themselves at least on a part-time basis, and increase the chances of better health for them and their families, which in turn would result in decreased need for family or medical leaves. Indeed, women continue to earn approximately two-thirds of men's salaries, as they have for more than 40 years; yet, combining work inside and outside the home, women are working about six hours longer per week than they did 40 years ago (Mason, 1992).

Health Insurance

Health insurance is perhaps the most important component of employee benefit packages, critical not only for workers but for their dependents. In our study, employees who were in poorer health experienced significantly higher levels of role strain and other deleterious impacts associated with their care responsibilities. However, many smaller firms do not provide health insurance because they must pay higher premiums than large firms

(U.S. Small Business Administration, 1987). Until 1995, health insurance represented the most rapidly increasing cost of benefit packages.

Current status. Today, approximately 31 million Americans have no health insurance. And of the 31 million, 80 percent are either employed or are dependents of workers (Belous, 1989). Indeed, almost 25 percent of the U.S. work force are employed by companies that do not offer group health insurance to employees' family members (Mukherjee, 1997). Included in the group without insurance are 12 million children. Moreover, the percentage of children under 18 without health insurance rose 25 percent between 1989 and 1995.

Employers and employees both know that health care is crucial, and it is difficult and very expensive for workers to purchase health insurance plans that are not part of a job benefit package. Until recently, employers were facing premium increases of 20 percent each year. With the advent of managed care, employers have been able to stem the increasing costs of health-insurance benefits, often by reducing health-care options and increasing contributions by workers. The cost of health insurance to employees has been rising rapidly, with the cost of family coverage increasing more than 60 percent between 1989 and 1995. Small businesses have been particularly quick to eliminate health-care benefits for employees' families, leaving employees to pay out of pocket for health insurance or else drop coverage for family members. As with almost all other benefits, health insurance is more likely to be available to employees in professional, white-collar, full-time work.

Long-term Care Insurance

Long-term care insurance can help to offset the costs of providing care to a disabled adult. Almost one-fourth of the employees with adult-care responsibilities in this study indicated that having enough money to pay for care was a significant problem for them. Moreover, long-term care insurance can provide assistance in understanding government programs such as Medicare or SSI, which was reported as a problem by more than one-third of the adult-care providers in this study. More than half of the employees caring for a disabled adult indicated that they would definitely use long-term care insurance if it were available through work.

Current status. The private long-term care insurance market has been growing dramatically in recent years. Approximately 5 percent of employees work for employers who offer long-term care insurance covering either spouse, parents, or parents-in-law (U.S. General Accounting Office, 1995b). Among 1,050 major employers surveyed in 1996 by Hewitt Associates, 7.5 percent offered long- term care insurance to their employees. By 1998, 9 percent of companies with at least 100 employees offered long-term care insurance for employees' family members, and 14 percent were considering doing so

(Galinsky & Bond, 1998). By comparison, none of the California employers surveyed in the 1990 *California Family Benefits Study* offered any type of long-term care insurance to their employees (DeLapp & Lawhorn, 1991).

Private long-term care insurance still covers only a small proportion of the costs incurred by disabled adults and their caregivers. A 1995 GAO report, for example, found that only about 0.2 percent of all long-term care costs are paid by private long-term care insurance (U.S. General Accounting Office, 1995b). By comparison, private insurance accounts for more than 15 percent of all expenditures for acute-care services for elderly persons (Health Insurance Association of America, 1997).

Long-term care insurance is expected to become more available to employed persons as a result of tax clarifications included in the Health Insurance Portability and Accountability Act of 1996. Employers are now able to deduct the administrative costs of setting up long-term care insurance plans for their employees, as well as any contributions they make toward employees' premiums. Employee premiums and benefits are tax deductible to the same extent as other health care expenses (Health Insurance Association of America, 1997).

Dependent-Care Assistance Plans

A Dependent Care Assistance Program (DCAP), or Dependent Care Reimbursement Account, allows employees to reduce the amount that they spend out-of-pocket for the care of a dependent family member. The most common type of DCAP involves salary reduction, whereby an employee agrees to have up to $5,000 ($2,500 for married individuals filing separately) of his or her salary set aside in pretax dollars for future dependent-care expenses. The employer may also make tax-free contributions or transfers from profit-sharing funds to the employee's DCAP account as long as the total amount does not exceed the $5,000 limit. The employee estimates the dependent-care expenses he or she will incur while at work and a fund is set aside for that amount. As the employee incurs care costs, he or she submits receipts for reimbursement.

Both the employee and the employer benefit from tax savings. The employee's taxable income is reduced by the amount deposited in the DCAP account, and the employer does not pay payroll taxes on the amount contributed. Additionally, any contributions made by the employer to an employee's DCAP account may qualify as a deductible business expense (New York Business Group on Health, 1986). Employers do incur any costs associated with administering a DCAP, but these typically are exceeded by savings in payroll and other taxes (Meeker & Campbell, 1986).

At Lawrence Berkeley Laboratory, 16 percent of working parents utilized the DCAP; of these, 88 percent found it to be helpful and 51 percent "very helpful." Only 9 percent of employees with adult-care responsibilities utilized the DCAP, 85 percent finding it to be helpful and 53 percent finding it "very helpful."

Current status. The Bureau of Labor Statistics' 1995 *Employee Benefits Survey* found that 38 percent of workers for work sites with at least 100 employees had reimbursement accounts available to them, most of which allowed employees to set aside pretax dollars for child care expenses (U.S. Bureau of Labor Statistics, 1997). The proportion of employees with access to dependent care reimbursement accounts ranges from 11 percent for employees of small private companies to 47 percent for public employees (Wiatrowski, 1995). In its 1996 survey, Hewitt Associates reported that 83 percent of the 1,050 large employers they surveyed offered DCAPs for employees with children (Hewitt Associates, 1997). First Hawaiian's ShareCare program, for example, matches employees' pretax deposits to a dependent care account on a dollar-for-dollar basis, up to $200 each month. Qualifying dependents are children claimed on the employee's federal tax return or an employee's spouse or parent who is unable to take care of herself or himself (With First Hawaiian, 1993).

However, DCAPs have not been heavily utilized by employees. According to Hay Huggins, 5 percent participated in the DCAPs offered by the employers they surveyed (as cited in Fingerman, 1997). For example, at Aetna Life & Casualty (named as one of the "Four Friendliest Companies" by Galinsky, et al., and included in the "100 best companies for working mothers" by *Working Mother* magazine), only 1,485 of 30,000 employees participate in pretax set-asides (Galinsky et al., 1991; Moskowitz, 1996).

That DCAPs are not more popular among employees with family-care responsibilities may be due in part to relatively restrictive IRS regulations. Eligible expenses must be substantiated with invoices or receipts bearing the care provider's legal name, place of business, and social security number or tax ID number, a problem for employees who can only find or afford care providers who are willing to earn below minimum wage in exchange for not having their earnings reported to the IRS. It is estimated that 50 to 70 percent of child-care providers do not report their earnings to the IRS (Adolph, 1988). DCAPs are of limited usefulness for employees caring for a disabled adult, because IRS regulations require that the dependent must spend at least eight hours a day in the employee's home, be unable to care for himself or herself, and must be financially dependent on the employee. Many employees also do not participate because they fear losing some or all of the money they deposit in the DCAP account, since the pretax set-asides must be spent by the end of the year and overages are forfeited to the employer. DCAPs are of greatest benefit to those employees who have the financial means to afford to set aside part of their salary, pay for their child care, and wait for reimbursement.

Adoption Assistance

Employers are increasingly including adoption assistance as a work and family benefit, based on the realization that adopting a child can consume substantial time and energy and can interfere with job performance. Employers who offer adoption-assistance programs typically offer to cover a percentage of the costs of adopting a child, including adoption agency fees, legal costs, and maternity costs for the birth mother. Employers may also offer paid leave, in addition to the twelve weeks of unpaid leave mandated under the FMLA.

Current status. The Bureau of Labor Statistics' 1995 *Employee Benefits Survey* found that 11 percent of workers in work sites with at least 100 employees had access to some kind of adoption assistance (U.S. Bureau of Labor Statistics, 1997). Among large employers, about 23 percent provide some sort of adoption assistance other than paid leave (Hewitt Associates, 1997). This is up from 16 percent in 1991 (Galinsky et al., 1991).

The average adoption costs parents $9,000, while the average aid from companies with adoption assistance is $2,000. For example, IBM's adoption-assistance program, which was established in 1973, reimburses employees for up to 80 percent of the adoption cost, up to a maximum of $2,500 for one adoption (U.S. GAO, 1992a; Galinsky et al., 1993). Employers find that in comparison to maternity leave, adoption-assistance programs are far less expensive. For example, in 1990, Wendy's Restaurants helped 20 employees adopt 21 children, which cost the company a total of $70,000. During the same year, Wendy's spent over $7.5 million on maternity benefits (National Adoption Center Press Release as cited in Fingerman, 1997).

Flexible Benefits

Some employers offer their employees the option of selecting the specific set of benefits that best suits their needs, since these needs vary between types of caregivers (with or without children, for example). Employees are typically guaranteed some basic level of health-care coverage and certain other basic benefits, and then are given the option of selecting from a range of possible additional benefits up to a certain limit. Benefits available through such "cafeteria" plans might include dental care, vision care, life insurance, legal services, dependent care resource and referral, dependent care pretax spending accounts, and even van pools.

Current status. A 1995 survey by the Bureau of Labor Statistics found that approximately 12 percent of employees in large- and medium-size firms had access to some sort of flexible benefit plan, up from 9 percent in 1989 (U.S. Bureau of Labor Statistics, 1997).

Flexible benefits are especially favorable for dual-income households with children, in which flexible benefits can prevent duplication of benefits for dependents. In 1990, the *National Report on Work and Family* found that 73 percent of employees contacted in a random survey of 21,000 workers favored flexible benefit accounts, even when accompanied by a reduction in benefits. However, flexible benefits occur mainly in large, professional, administrative firms (Wyatt Company, 1988). Smaller firms are apt to have more difficulty with the extra administrative costs associated with such a program.

Domestic Partner Benefits

Given the changing composition of the family, an increasing number of employers are extending employee benefits to domestic partners. The U.S. Census Bureau estimates that 8.4 million people are in relationships that constitute domestic partnerships, in that they are partners but are not married or not legally permitted to wed (Laabs, 1998). The types of benefits available to domestic partners range tremendously and may include health and dental care, family leave, sick leave, bereavement leave, or pension benefits, similar to those provided to married employees.

Domestic partnership benefits are a step toward addressing the issue of equity in benefits for employees living in nontraditional families. Most employers offering domestic partner benefits desire to insure fair and equitable access, as well as strengthen their image as innovative leaders in all aspects of business. Other employers are reluctant to offer such benefits out of fear it could create controversy and adverse public opinion. In this study, unpaid family leave or sick leave to care for domestic partners was endorsed by 37 percent of working parents and by 35 percent of employees with adult-care responsibilities.

Current status. In one survey conducted by the Society for Human Resource Management, 2 percent of the companies surveyed extended health benefits to domestic partners (Savasta, 1997). A Buck Consultants' Welfare Benefit Survey of approximately 1,000 employers found that 6 percent of the survey participants were offering domestic partnership coverage and 29 percent were considering doing so in the future (Tax Management, 1998). Most companies that have instituted domestic partnership benefits have found the cost to be much lower than expected. It generally costs an employer between 1 and 2 percent in terms of cost implications to offer domestic-partnership benefits, depending on the size of the company. Covering a domestic partner is typically less expensive than covering a spouse (Savasta, 1997).

Levi-Strauss, Microsoft, Disney, Xerox, IBM, and Bank of America are among the more than 300 companies that have extended benefits to domestic partners. Nationally, more than 40 city and state governments offer domestic partner benefit coverage (Flynn, 1998). Further, both the cities of San Francisco and Seattle passed ordinances prohibiting the cities from doing business with companies that do not provide domestic partnership benefits equivalent to those they make available to married spouses.

In 1996, the state of Hawaii passed a law requiring employers to provide family health coverage to domestic partners of employees if a couple is registered with the state as a "reciprocal beneficiary." According to Hawaiian law, domestic partners are treated as family members for such purposes as state family leave and Workers' Compensation. At the federal level, the Domestic Partnership Benefits and Obligations Act, which would extend federal benefits to domestic partners, has also been debated.

Definitions of domestic partnerships are widespread across industries. Generally, domestic partnership requirements include a committed relationship of two unrelated individuals, shared responsibilities for one another's welfare and financial obligations, cohabitation, and not being currently married or registered as another's domestic partner. In addition, many companies require that employees sign an affidavit or certification that requirements such as these are met. While some extend coverage to both opposite and same-sex couples, others provide coverage only to same-sex couples (since they legally cannot marry). Interestingly, approximately two-thirds of domestic partner benefit recipients are heterosexual (Savasta, 1997; Laabs, 1998), perhaps because gay and lesbian employees may be more reluctant to reveal their sexual orientation at the work place.

In 1996, the Internal Revenue Service issued a private letter stating that employees who receive employer-provided health insurance for an adult companion to whom they are not married must pay income taxes on the benefits unless the person is a dependent of the employee. If one of the parties is a dependent (the two parties live together for the entire tax year and the person receives more than half of his or her support from the employee), then domestic partnership benefits are not a taxable event for the employee, and the employer is able to treat the expense as a pretax contribution to a health-insurance program (Flynn, 1998).

Flexible benefit plans that include extra amounts of money or credits for coverage of a domestic partner (who is not a legal dependent) must also be treated as taxable income. Under Internal Revenue Code section 125, health-care flexible spending account benefits cannot be provided to domestic partners if the plan is to qualify for the tax sanctions afforded to flexible benefit plans (Savasta, 1997). While the position of the U.S. Department of Labor is that employers can provide leaves for employees to care for domestic partners, the FMLA does not officially sanction it. Another controversial area is retirement-plan benefits, because the tax code does not recognize domestic partners as qualified beneficiaries (Flynn, 1998).

LABOR UNION POLICIES AND PROGRAMS FOR WORKING FAMILIES

Labor unions have traditionally fought, at least indirectly, for work and family benefits for their members. By bargaining for higher wages, health-care benefits, paid vacation, sick time, and shorter hours, and through their support for education, child labor laws, Social Security, the minimum wage, and job security, labor unions have attempted to improve the lives of workers and their families. Union status has a greater effect on benefit levels than on wages. Indeed, unionized companies typically pay 25 percent more on benefits than non-union work places, and union workers receive about 8 percent more in benefits than their non-union counterparts.

As far back as 1959, the AFL-CIO promoted a program that included equal pay for comparable work, maternity leave, and child care. During the following thirty years, the program progressed to include protection from sexual harassment and gender discrimination, and support for family leave (as opposed to just maternity leave). In 1971, the AFL-CIO supported laws that would make child care available to every working family. Yet family issues and policies have not generally been a top priority of the U.S. labor movement. Until the late 1980s and 1990s, work and family topics did not form an explicit part of labor-management discussion or union contracts (U.S. Department of Labor, 1992; Cowell, 1993).

LABOR CONTRACTS

Specific work and family provisions in recent labor contracts fall into three major categories: (1) standard work and family issues—family and medical leaves, child care, elder care, and EAPs (employee assistance programs); (2) less common work and family issues—flexible schedules, personal and sick leaves, personal and floating holidays, vacations in aggregates of less than one day, and excused absences; and (3) areas indirectly related to work and family concerns—family financial planning, group insurance programs, mortgage allowances, employee discounts, and school tuition allowances (U.S. Department of Labor, 1992).

A study by the Bureau of Labor Management Relations and Cooperative Programs examining 452 union contracts taking effect July 1, 1990 or later found that slightly over 50 percent of the contracts contained at least one explicit work and family program or policy (U.S. Department of Labor, 1992). These contracts, which covered 2,818,900 workers or 76 percent of the total workers studied, included the following work and family provisions: 72 percent guaranteed maternity leaves, 15 percent had parental leaves, 12 percent included adoption leaves, 11 percent contained child-care access, 36 percent provided family illness leaves, 11 percent had Employee Assistance Programs, and 4 percent provided for elder-care resources (U.S. Department of Labor, 1992).

Both the CWA (Communication Workers of America) and the IBEW (International Brotherhood of Electrical Workers) Local 2213 negotiated a child- and elder-care fund for the duration of their contract with N.Y.N.E.X. The fund pays for part of employees' child- and elder-care costs and will count as untaxed benefits (CWA, 1995). AFSCME (American Federation of State, County and Municipal Employees) has successfully bargained for more than 70 on-site child-care centers. The UAW (United Auto Workers) negotiated for and developed a long-term care program for disabled retired UAW employees, their spouses, and other dependents in Ohio. The plan covers home care, adult day care, and nursing-home care, as well as providing an information and referral service (UAW, 1995). AFSCME has won a 70 percent wage replacement parental leave policy for its State of Ohio employees (Paid Leave, 1995).

LABOR RESOLUTIONS

Individual unions, as well as the AFL-CIO collectively, have taken strong positions on a variety of labor policy concerns. A significant number of them have focused on work and family topics. SEIU (Service Employees International Union), for example, issued a resolution in 1992 supporting a work and family policy that would encompass greater funding and higher standards for child care, family and medical leave, and a minimum benefit level for part-time employees. In the domain of child care, SEIU has advocated strong standards in the areas of health and safety, staff training, and staff-to-child ratios. Additionally, they support increased funding for Child Care and Development Block Grants, child care for AFDC mothers, and Head Start. Concerning elder care, SEIU advocates expanded social-service programs for seniors. They support existing government programs such as the Earned Income Tax Credit, Dependent Care Tax Credits, and Dependent Care Assistance. Although SEIU does not envision a major change in the near future, their ultimate goal is a dependent-care program that provides universal access to child and elder care for all U.S. workers.

AFSCME issued a 1990 resolution in favor of employers providing leaves for elder care, the right to use sick leave for elder caregiving, personal leaves, on-site day-care centers for elders, flexible work schedules and job-sharing policies, information and referrals to adult day-care centers, home-care services, nursing homes, and stress-management counseling for employees, with a focus on elder care. The resolution stated that its eventual objective was a federal program for long-term care. AFSCME's resolution further called for a federal child-care law that would provide resources to pay for safe, quality child care, increases in Head Start and Child Care Food Program revenues, and establishment of on-site child- and elder-care programs (Putting Families First, 1992).

BARRIERS TO DEVELOPING "FAMILY-FRIENDLY" WORK PLACES

Variations in Employee Access to Work-Place Policies and Programs

Although a number of employer-supported work and family programs have been developed, concerns have been raised regarding barriers to their use and substantial inequities in workers' ability to access them. Benefit types and amounts vary by industry, size of work place, union status, nature of work, and whether work is constant or seasonal. Companies with fewer than 100 employees are significantly less likely than larger firms with over 100 employees to offer benefits such as retirement, health insurance, life insurance, disability insurance, or paid time off (U.S. Bureau of Labor Statistics, 1985; U.S. Chamber of Commerce, 1988; Wyatt Company, 1988; Ferber et al., 1991). Companies that encounter competition in their industries provide fewer benefits for their employees than those with more control over their product. For example, textile workers receive significantly fewer benefits than most other workers, while metal industry workers have access to more valuable benefits than average (U.S. Chamber of Commerce, 1988). Similarly, family-friendly benefits are much more generous in the finance, real estate, and insurance industries than in the wholesale and retail trades (Galinsky & Bond, 1998).

Companies facing more competition for labor, on the other hand, may develop more enticing work and family policies and benefits, in an effort to attract the best new workers. IBM, for example, used to have a corporate commitment to being the "employer of first choice" and to retaining employees once they were hired. These corporate values translated into an innovative and comprehensive work and family policy. In the 1990s, the competitive economic environment resulting from the globalization and decentralization of the computer industry led to downsizing and reduced commitment to long-term investment in employees, not surprisingly resulting in a somewhat reduced emphasis on traditional work and family programs at IBM and many other major employers.

Other factors that seem to affect a company's generosity with family-friendly benefits are the proportion of top executive positions filled by women and minorities, the percentage of employees who are women, the percentage of salaried (versus hourly) employees, and the percentage of unionized employees. Indeed, companies with women in at least half of their top executive positions are six times more likely than companies with no top female executives to offer child care, and twice as likely to offer dependent care assistance plans or elder-care resource and referral programs (Galinsky & Bond, 1998).

Some employers give preference to certain groups of employees for eligibility or access to employer-sponsored work and family benefits or programs. Access is often related to such factors as seniority and occupational status, with those in higher-status positions getting a disproportionate share of benefits and wages (Fredriksen, 1995b). Better-paid, more highly educated workers are more likely to have access to health insurance, pensions, dependent-care plans, and flexible work schedules. Moreover, professional and technical personnel are twice as likely as service workers to have access to family-related programs such as child care, elder care, dependent care reimbursement accounts, or paid parental leave.

Equity issues are also of concern to many employers, particularly in light of actual and feared backlash from "under-benefited" employee groups such as single adults without dependent children. Such concerns have led to the emergence of "work-life" programs to replace "work/family" programs. These work-life programs are based on the principle that all employees need and deserve to have a reasonable balance between their jobs and their personal lives. Such programs continue to be based on the assumption that work is the priority and that "balance" is needed so that employees can return to work as rested and productive as possible. Yet from a societal perspective, we must consider society's need for family stability and the care of its dependent members. Work-life balance programs argue for cafeteria plans, whereby a set pool of resources (whether economic or in terms of time off from work) will be sufficient for all employees. Yet employees have differing care situations, and the needs for work and family benefits change over time, across the life cycle. The needs of parents with disabled children can be particularly demanding, and may be unremitting throughout the employee's work life.

Work-Place Culture

Perhaps one of the most fundamental obstacles to a "family-friendly" work place is corporate culture. There is the persistent myth that the worlds of work and family can and should be separate, and that interaction between the two should be treated as an anomaly rather than the norm. In a context of reduced job security and limited commitment of employer to employee or vice versa, employers may resist development of family-friendly policies because of concern about creating a culture of entitlement, in which employees become too dependent on employers to meet their personal needs (Bankert & Lobel, 1997).

Most companies continue to regard work and family issues in terms of accommodation to or by individual employees, rather than as part of a company's overall organizational approach to doing business. Framing family concerns as an individual issue, companies simply superimpose work and family policies and programs on the traditional work culture, thereby giving employees conflicting messages regarding the legitimacy of utilizing such programs. The existence of such programs projects the image that a company is interested in the well-being of its employees; however, when traditional values of long hours and "face time" as signs of employee dedication remain unchanged, it is not surprising when employees perceive that a company's true commitment is to productivity over employee well-being, let alone the well-being of employees' families. In this climate, it is no wonder that employees may be reluctant to utilize existing work and family programs or may receive little benefit when they do (Gonyea, 1997).

Indeed, even when family-friendly policies and programs are "on the books," only a minority of employees actually use them. Employees express concern about being perceived by their supervisors and/or coworkers as unable to handle their "personal problems" or allowing those problems to affect their jobs, or being stigmatized as "needing help." A study conducted at one large company revealed that 52 percent of employees believed that taking advantage of the company's established policies offering time off could endanger their jobs or careers (Galinsky, 1992). The Families and Work Institute's report for the U.S. Labor Department's Glass Ceiling Commission found that women who used family-friendly programs were thought to be "less serious about their jobs than people who [didn't] use them." Many also felt resented by their peers for taking time off. Attitudes of supervisors and managers compound the problem. A survey of 100 work and family managers, for example, found that 40 percent felt that supervisors do not have a good understanding of employees' work and family issues; and only 11 percent believed that supervisors greatly respect employees' needs to balance work and family (Bankert & Lobel, 1997).

THE "FAMILY-FRIENDLY" WORK PLACE

Consistent with previous studies of working parents and employed caregivers, the benefits and programs most frequently endorsed by respondents in our study reflected broad work-place policies that transcend particular employee care responsibilities or family situations. Flexible work schedules, family leave, and the ability to work at home were all endorsed by at least 44 percent of the respondents. These findings indicate the importance of an organizational climate in which employees have the options to meet their family and work responsibilities in the way that is best for their employer, their families, and themselves (Galinsky et al., 1991). Job flexibility needs to be accompanied by support from coworkers and supervisors. More than 10 percent of large companies now offer training to managers and supervisors regarding work and family issues (Galinsky, 1992).

Some experts have advocated redefining "family-friendliness" in considerably broader terms than simply the presence of a few specialized work and family policies or programs. True "family-friendliness" might be defined in terms of a company's real commitment to and support for the overall well-being of its employees, their families, and the society at large. Family-friendliness, moreover, must pervade the company's corporate culture and be a key element of its business strategy, rather than just another employee benefit or human resources program under the control of a select group of managers or human resources staff. Ultimately, family-friendliness would be observed in the company's participation in the larger community and in its efforts as a corporate citizen to promote a society that supports the well-being of its families.

The Families and Work Institute has created a "Family Friendly Index," which indicates a company's development toward a family-friendly corporate culture by comparing the company's policies and procedures with benchmark standards (Galinsky et al., 1991). The Index examines the level of corporate development in seven areas: flexible work arrangements, leaves, financial assistance, corporate giving/community service, dependent-care services, management change, and work and family stress management. Each of these areas is scored using six criteria: impact, coverage, institutionalization, commitment, level of effort, and innovativeness.

Utilizing the Family Friendly Index, the Families and Work Institute has identified three stages of development toward corporate family-friendliness. One-third of the largest companies in 30 industries were found to not even have reached the first of these three stages (Galinsky, 1992). Companies at this Pre-Stage I level have few policies to address work and family issues, and managers are barely aware of employees' family concerns or are actively resistant to those concerns. Companies at Stage I, by comparison, have several work and family policies, typically focusing on child care (e.g., subsidized child care and/or DCAP payroll deductions). However, work and family concerns are primarily perceived as an issue only for female employees, and there is no overall approach to work and family issues. In 1992, 46 percent of companies were found to be at Stage I.

Companies at Stage II, representing 19 percent of companies studied by the Families and Work Institute, have an integrated approach to meeting employees' work and family needs (Galinsky, 1992), usually including a formal process of reviewing and redesigning personnel policies to be more family-friendly under the auspices of senior management (Friedman & Galinsky, 1991). Companies at Stage II provide greater time flexibility specifically to reduce employee work and family strain, enabling employees to negotiate arrangements such as flex-time, compressed work weeks, and alternative work locations. In addition, these companies are likely to offer benefits such as permanent part-time positions, job-sharing, longer and more flexible leave policies with part-time return provisions, company-authorized days off for sick family members, and pooled time off (Friedman & Galinsky, 1991).

Companies at Stage III are focused not just on offering specific programs but on altering the entire corporate culture to make it more family-friendly. Companies at this stage give attention to interventions in the larger community designed to enhance the infrastructure for supporting families and improving the quality of family life. Johnson & Johnson, for example, in 1989 changed its company credo to include the following statement: "We must be mindful of ways to help our employees fulfill their family responsibilities" (Bankert, Googins & Bradley, 1996, p. 49). Levi Strauss, in its corporate mission and aspiration statement, vows a "commitment to balanced personal and professional lives" (Vogel, 1992, p.4). Only 2 percent of companies have reached Stage III.

Boston University's Work and Family Roundtable has also proposed a reconceptualization of "family-friendliness" that moves beyond the traditional focus on isolated work and family programs and policies to embrace a company's external relations and its overall business strategy. This expanded vision opens the possibility for corporate support of families to be manifested in partnerships with community organizations, legislative advocacy, changes in corporate culture, and collaborative efforts to develop private- and public-sector solutions to social issues. Taken together, these domains represent the components of a comprehensive work and family program designed to meet the needs of employees, their families, and society. They reflect the reality that the well-being of a company is integrally linked to the well-being of its employees and the community at large. True "family-friendliness" requires action in each domain, and the value shift associated with such action.

The Work and Family Roundtable identified four "Principles of Excellence" to guide employers in their efforts to create work environments that maximize both organizational and individual effectiveness (Bankert & Lobel, 1997):

1. The employer recognizes the strategic value of addressing work and personal life issues, as evidenced by a company's sensitivity to employees' personal and family needs and its willingness to make a long-term investment in responding to work and personal life issues.

2. The work environment supports individual work and personal life effectiveness, as evidenced by meaningful work/personal life programs and policies and a corporate culture that supports a healthy balance between personal and work responsibilities.

3. The management of work and personal life effectiveness is a shared responsibility between employer and employee, as evidenced by real empowerment and mutual accountability of managers and employees in achieving personal and work objectives.

4. The employer develops relationships to enhance external work and personal life resources, as evidenced by corporate participation in partnerships to strengthen community resources for employees and other community members.

The private sector, in partnership with workers, families, communal agencies, and the public sector, can be instrumental in developing a community-based infrastructure that supports family care. Indeed, approximately 10 percent of companies with at least 100 employees are already involved in some kind of contribution to local community organizations or government agencies to improve community services for people with dependent-care responsibilities.

The most extensive employer-sponsored effort to support community infrastructure development to date is the American Business Collaboration for Quality Dependent Care (ABCQDC). In 1992, 11 lead corporations established ABCQDC to raise money to build and expand child- and eldercare facilities across the nation. From 1992 through 1994, the ABCQDC invested more than $27 million in 45 communities in 25 states and the District of Columbia. In September 1995, ABCQDC's 21 lead corporations targeted 56 communities where their employees lived and worked, and agreed to invest $100 million over six years. By 1997, more than 350 projects had been funded (Bankert & Lobel, 1997).

The primary objective of the Collaboration is to enhance the quantity and quality of community child-care and elder-care resources. This cross-industry consortium facilitates regional partnerships, whereby companies combine resources and contribute funds to promote the development of local community-based programs. The Collaboration typically provides initial start-up costs only; ongoing programmatic expenses must be met by user fees and other sources of income. In exchange for their participation, employers have priority access to certain of the services that are developed.

SUMMARY

The new demographics of the work force are creating pressure for employers to accommodate work and family needs. Employers have implemented work and family programs in hopes of relieving worker stress, as well as to give companies a competitive edge in recruitment and retention of employees, thereby cutting costs associated with locating, hiring, and training new employees. Indeed, some employers see work/family programs as a relatively inexpensive way to preserve employee loyalty at a time when considerably more expensive benefits such as health-care coverage and salary increases are being reduced.

Although work and family programs are presumed to reduce family-related barriers to employee productivity, including absenteeism, tardiness, work interruptions, distractions, and fatigue, there have been relatively few evaluative studies of the impact of such programs and benefits. Among existing studies, the findings have been mixed. In some cases, specific workplace benefits have been associated with small or moderate improvements in employees' well-being and job performance; in others, no differences have been found in stress, work performance, absenteeism, or turnover rates.

At a time of retrenchment from public spending, the involvement of the corporate sector in providing family-care benefits seems promising. As this chapter has illustrated, business has an essential role to play in improving the lives of workers and their families. Business can assist employees to locate and pay for family-care services, provide employees with the job flexibility they need to be able to utilize those services, develop programs that meet their workers' needs for specific services, create an organizational climate that sees the well-being of employees and their families as a key component of corporate business planning and goal-setting, and support the development of needed family-care services, such as child-care and adult-care services, in the community.

But business cannot single-handedly solve work and family conflicts. First of all, work-place supports are not available to the vast majority of working Americans, since most work for small companies with relatively few family-care benefits. In addition, having family-care benefits primarily available through the corporate sector has the potential to create a two-tiered system of benefits—one service system for the corporate sector and another for those dependent on public subsidies or programs. Thus, the private sector needs to form a partnership with workers, families, communal agencies, and the public sector in developing a community-based infrastructure that supports family care.

· 11 ·

WORK AND FAMILY
PUBLIC POLICIES

INTRODUCTION

The previous chapter examined programs and benefits at the work place that have been developed to assist employees in integrating their work and family lives. Yet difficulties managing work and family-care responsibilities are due in part to the lack of adequate community-based resources for children and chronically ill and disabled adults. Historically, different constituencies in the U.S. have advocated for various work and family policies and programs, ranging from child care in the 1960s to an emphasis on alternative work schedules in the mid- to late 1970s, to parental and family leave in the 1980s and early 1990s. More recently, there have been public policy debates in relation to health care, long-term care, and welfare reform, and renewed efforts to improve the quality and accessibility of publicly-funded child care.

The various constituencies in the work and family debate have had differing and sometimes conflicting agendas. We've also seen the insurgency of conservative counter-advocacy groups, seeking to limit the expansion of family-care public policies. To date, the U.S. has developed a fragmented array of services rather than a comprehensive family-care policy or integrated community-based infrastructure to support family care and employment. This fragmented approach is indicative of several basic value dilemmas inherent in American society, one of which is an ambivalence regarding private versus public responsibility in providing assistance to families and their dependents.

In the majority of advanced industrialized nations, social policies incorporate more extensive universal family supports than in the U.S. In Europe today, the current work and family discussion centers around the reconciliation of work and family responsibilities, "a process of seeking accommodations between the needs and interests of employers, employees, and those for whom they care" (Lewis & Lewis, 1996). Kamerman (1989) maintains that European family-care policies are much more extensive in part because of the different structures of government and their aligned responsibilities, the differing goals and strategies of various interest groups, and more favorable opinions toward taxation.

The purpose of this chapter is to examine current U.S. public policies and initiatives to assist employees with family-care responsibilities such as family leave, child care, and long-term care, and to review some of the public policy supports that exist internationally. We will conclude by exploring possible components of a family-sensitive public policy framework necessary to build a community-based infrastructure that supports family care.

FAMILY LEAVE

Family leave policies can assist employees in caring for a newborn child or helping a family member who is seriously ill. The guaranteed availability of a job can make a difference in a female employee's ability to re-enter the work force after childbirth or family illness. One study found that the most important predictor of whether a female employee returned to work after having a baby was whether her employer offered maternity leave with a job guarantee included (National Council of Jewish Women, 1987).

In our study, family leave was the single most frequently endorsed workplace policy; 61percent of working parents and 57 percent of employees with adult-care responsibilities endorsed unpaid family leave.

Current status. Under the Family and Medical Leave Act (FMLA) of 1993, employers with more than 50 employees are required to allow at least 12 weeks of unpaid leave during a 12-month period for employees to care for ill family members or new children or to attend to personal illness. Employers must continue to provide health-care coverage during leaves and restore employees to their jobs or equivalent positions on their return. Furthermore, employers must post notices of the Act's requirements and keep records of their compliance.

Implementation of Family Leave

The Families and Work Institute found that only 54 percent of working mothers were aware of state parental leave laws. A nationwide BNA study found that more than half of all Americans knew little or nothing about the FMLA (U.S. Bureau of National Affairs, 1994). Studies of employers' responses to federal and state family leave laws have found inconsistent implementation. A 1993 study of 300 mostly California businesses by the University of California and William Mercer, Inc., found that 40 percent of employers surveyed were not in compliance with at least one of the FMLA's four basic provisions (12 weeks of leave, continuation of health benefits, job guarantees, and notification of employees' rights), and 6 percent were not in compliance with any of these provisions.

Compliance rates were significantly lower for small firms, those with a lower proportion of female employees, and those with more limited labor representation (Scharlach & Stanger, 1994). By 1998, however, fully 90 percent of employers with at least 100 workers offered at least 12 weeks of maternity or paternity leave (Galinsky & Bond, 1998). The failure of some employers to comply with these laws has been attributed to a variety of factors, including administrative difficulties linked to mandated leave, ambiguities in the FMLA legislation, supervisor resistance, and a lack of oversight by regulatory agencies.

Utilization of Family Leave

When family leave is available, employee utilization has been low. In the University of California-Mercer study, two-thirds of employers surveyed reported that fewer than 1 percent of their employees had taken leave under California's family leave law, while only 7 percent reported utilization rates of more than 2 percent. This finding was consistent across industry types, employer size, proportion of women employees, and presence of unions (Scharlach & Stanger, 1994). In another survey conducted by Hewitt Associates, 55 percent of employers with a family leave policy indicated that less than 1 percent of their employees per year took leaves (Hewitt Associates, 1993).

Employee income is an important factor in determining length of leave taken. The 1990 National Child Care Survey found that low-income workers were less likely to take leave, to have paid leaves, or to keep their health coverage during leaves (Hofferth et al., 1991). The Families & Work Institute study of four states with parental leave laws found that women with household incomes of less than $10,000 averaged 9.5 weeks of leave after childbirth, and 21 percent took less than the recommended 6 weeks off after giving birth. In contrast, women with incomes above $60,000 took an average of 13.8 weeks, and only 7 percent took less than 6 weeks (Bond, Galinsky, Lord, Staines & Brown, 1991).

Many employees are unable to avail themselves of the leave to which they are entitled because they cannot afford the loss of income during the leave period. Only a small percentage of families can afford to give up an income for 12 weeks. A survey by "9 to 5" found that 19 percent of new mothers returned to work less than six weeks after giving birth because they could not afford any more unpaid leave (Labor Project for Working Families, 1994). Moreover, women in low-income jobs have access to the fewest employer family benefits and are much less likely than other employees to be aware of family leave laws.

Rates of leave-taking tend not to be altered substantially by the passage of leave laws. Maternity leave patterns, for example, did not change after passage of leave laws in the four states studied by the Families and Work Institute. There was a small but significant increase in the percentage of fathers taking paternity leave (from 19 to 22 percent); but the mean paternity leave was only one week, and the majority of fathers used paid vacation time to avoid income loss (Bond et al., 1991).

The only major changes associated with passage of leave laws found in the Families and Work Institute study were among low-income women in Rhode Island, where Temporary Disability Insurance (TDI) provides wage replacement to women on maternity leave. The proportion of Rhode Island women with household incomes below $20,000 taking less than 6 weeks of leave after childbirth fell to zero percent after enactment of family leave laws, compared to 19 percent in three other states where TDI is not required. Low-income women in Rhode Island also took longer leaves than low-income women in the other three states (Bond et al., 1991).

Discrimination by supervisors also affects employee leave-taking rates. The Equal Employment Opportunity Commission (EEOC) reports a yearly average of 3,400 charges of employer discrimination related to maternity (Ferber et al., 1991). One survey of 5,000 women found that more than 4 percent reported losing their jobs because of pregnancy (O'Connell, 1990). Employees may also fear more subtle repercussions such as barriers to promotion, less desirable assignments, or loss of other perquisites. A majority of panelists from the Conference Board's Work-Family Research and Advisory Panel (representing companies with commitments to work-family issues) felt that both men and women were justified in worrying about damage to their careers when taking family leaves (The Conference Board, 1994). Given employers' tendency to spread a leave-taker's work among other workers rather than hiring temporary replacement workers, employees taking leave may also fear resentment from their coworkers (Marra & Linder, 1992; NEWFA Survey: Family and Medical Leave Act, 1993).

Impact of Family Leave

Studies of mandated family leave have focused primarily on work-place outcomes such as cost, productivity levels, and absenteeism. These studies have generally found that mandated leave has not had a substantial impact on employer costs or work-place functioning. The University of California-Mercer study, for example, found that more than half of the employers surveyed reported insignificant administrative costs associated with complying with California's family leave law, and only 7 percent reported moderate to major costs (Scharlach & Stanger, 1994). The only negative effects reported involved problems in supervisor and coworker relationships.

Similarly, the Families and Work Institute study of the impact of maternity leave laws in four states found that only 9 percent of employers surveyed reported that the state laws were difficult to implement (Bond et al., 1991). Most employers reported no increase in costs associated with complying with the leave statutes, and only a few reported significant costs. This is not surprising since there has been low utilization of leaves and most leaves are *unpaid*, so that employee leave-taking may actually result in a reduction in employer salary costs.

Although family leave is an important step in providing flexibility and assistance for employed caregivers and in minimizing the institutionalization of seriously ill adults (Pearlman & Crown, 1992), it is limited by many of the same drawbacks as corporate-sponsored family-care services. Since it is contingent on steady, full-time employment in a rather large business (more than 50 persons), it is evident that most working families will not be covered. Since the vast majority of dependent-care statutes are written to provide uncompensated leave, they require adequate resources in order to utilize them. In addition, because of the preponderance of women taking family leaves, they have the potential to further increase gender inequality and exacerbate wage, income, and benefit differentials between men and women.

International Family Leave Policies

Family leave policies of most developed countries differ from those in the U.S. in that the majority of them mandate paid maternity leave, the amount of leave time is longer than 12 weeks, and the leave policies cover all workers rather than just those employed by firms with 50 or more employees. A review of parental leave policies in 16 European countries and Canada found that those countries mandated an average of 68 weeks of leave per child, of which 33 weeks were paid (Ruhm & Teague, 1993). In the majority of European countries, maternity leave begins two to six weeks before the birth of the child (Kamerman, 1991), and adequate infant care to provide the child with "a good start in life" is assured through paid, job-protected leave.

Sweden, for example, offers 270 days of parental leave to share between the two parents at 90 percent of full-time pay, 90 additional days at a flat rate set by the employer, and another 18 months of unpaid leave. Like the U.S., Sweden's leave policy guarantees a job of the same or equivalent position. Augmenting these benefits is the availability of 90 days of leave a year to care for a sick child under the age of 10, at 90 percent of full-time salary up to 60 days a year, and 2 paid days a year to visit a child's school (Stoiber, 1989). Parents can also reduce working hours from 8 to 6 hours a day with a pro-rated salary until a child is eight (Galinsky, 1989). In 1987, 25 percent of Swedish fathers took some leave following the birth of their children, beyond the two weeks that are available at the time of childbirth (Kamerman, 1991). Fathers utilized the parental leave an average of 47 days, less than a quarter of the time that mothers took for leave. To balance the participation of both parents in parental leave, Sweden has instituted quotas for leave to be taken by fathers, that cannot be traded with the mother (Mahon, 1997). In most EEC countries, employers and workers pay indirectly toward the costs of leave programs through contributions to social insurance, unemployment insurance programs, or parental employment funds.

CHILD CARE

Child care is often identified as the most pressing need of families with children. In our study, we found that problems with child care were reported by the vast majority of working parents. Parents that experienced the greatest number of child-care problems experienced significantly higher levels of family accommodations, work accommodations, missed work, role strain, and physical, financial, and emotional strain.

Many employees in our study reported difficulty in finding high-quality care that is dependable, conveniently located, and affordable. Adequate care for infants, very young children, children with special needs, or sick children remains especially difficult to secure. In addition, parents who work weekend or irregular hours often experience difficulty finding suitable child care, an issue particularly problematic for low-income parents. The availability of before- and after-school programs is also of concern, given that a significant percentage of school-age children with working parents do not have any adult supervision before or after school.

Current status. In 1994 there were more than 10 million preschool age children whose mothers were working and in need of child-care assistance (Casper, 1997). The types of child care utilized by working parents have changed dramatically over the last several decades. While care by relatives is still the single most used type of care, the use of group child care has steadily increased. In 1993, approximately one in three children of preschool age received care in an organized child-care facility (day care, nursery school, or preschool).

The child-care system in the U.S. is complex and fragmented, incorporating involvement of the public and private sectors, as well as the family. Provision of care is a mixture of nonregulated private arrangements, regulated private programs, private programs receiving public subsidies, public programs, and the corporate-sponsored programs discussed in the previous chapter.

Unlike most industrialized nations, the U.S. does not have a comprehensive, integrated government-sponsored child-care system or policy. Overall, child care in the U.S. today is neither universal nor means tested; rather, it is contingent upon availability of resources. Although the rise in the cost of child care has been relatively modest (Hofferth et al., 1991), the overall proportion of public funding has actually decreased, leaving parents increasingly responsible for the cost of care (Zigler & Finn- Stevenson, 1995).

The role of the public sector in ensuring the availability, affordability, and quality of out-of-home care has been limited, with child care remaining primarily a private rather than public responsibility. Although there are numerous federal and state programs and subsidies that provide some support for child care, families continue to finance the vast majority of the costs of care, and few benefit from child-care subsidies or public child-care programs. The major federal programs that currently support child care include the Child and Dependent Care Tax Credit (a nonrefundable tax credit for taxpayers who are working or seeking employment), Head Start, Title XX Social Services Block Grant, the Child Care Food Program, and the Child Care Development Block Grant. In response to the overall decline of federal funding for child care, several states have also created their own state-level tax allowances, subsidies, and programs.

In 1999, President Clinton proposed a five-year, $18 billion child-care initiative. The major components of this proposal include $7.5 billion to expand the Child Care and Development Block Grant, extending child-care subsidizes; $5 billion in tax credits under the Child and Dependent Care Tax Credit; and $600 million to provide after-school and summer-school programs for latchkey kids (The National Report on Work & Family, 1999).

Child and Dependent Care Tax Credit

With a political emphasis on privatization, tax allowances have become one of the primary means of federal involvement in child care. One of the single largest sources of federal assistance for child care in this country is the child-care tax credit available to working parents, which in 1996 accounted for approximately 60 percent of all federal spending on child care (Leibowitz, 1996). In 1997, the Child and Dependent Care Tax Credit amounted to approximately $2.8 billion in potential tax revenue (U.S. House of Representatives, 1998).

The Child and Dependent Care Tax Credit allows working taxpayers a credit on their tax liability for expenses incurred caring for a child or a disabled household member (U.S. Internal Revenue Service, 1997). The credit may be claimed by a taxpayer who maintains a household that includes one or more qualifying individuals (a dependent under the age of 13 or a physically or mentally incapacitated dependent or spouse). The taxpayer must have earned income, and have incurred all deductible care expenses due to meeting employment responsibilities. The maximum tax credit is up to 30 percent of the taxpayer's allowable expenses for dependent care ($2,400 for one recipient and $4,800 for two or more). The percentage used to calculate the credit depends on the taxpayer's adjusted gross income. In the event an employer provided dependent-care benefits, the maximum allowable expenses must be reduced accordingly.

Almost six million households took the child-care tax credit in 1991 (Gentry & Hagy, 1996), and it was primarily utilized by those with family incomes between $20,000 and $50,000 (Goodman, 1995). The tax credit does not reach families at the bottom 10 percent of the income distribution because it is nonrefundable (Gentry & Hagy, 1996). The majority of impoverished families have low or no tax liabilities and may not be able to afford the out-of-pocket care expenses for dependents; thus, such tax credits are likely not beneficial to them. This raises important equity issues. In general, the Dependent and Child Care Tax Credit has provided a disproportionate share of benefits to persons from middle- and upper-income groups. In 1988, only one-quarter of the child-care tax credits went to families in the lower half of the income distribution (Robins, 1988).

Several states have implemented tax credits or deductions similar to those available through the federal government. In addition, a few states developed tax credits for families with a stay-home parent. For example, in 1990, California implemented a personal state income tax credit of up to $1,000, based on family income, for a parent who stays at home with a child younger than 13 months. Minnesota created a tax credit of up to $720 for low- and moderate-income married couples with a parent at home and children under 6 years of age (Groginsky & McConnell, 1998). Other federal and state tax credit proposals for child care recently introduced include: increasing the already existing tax credits for child-care expenses; developing additional tax credits for stay-at-home parents; implementing tax incentives aimed at improving the quality of child care; and developing tax incentives to encourage businesses to provide child-care services to employees.

Tax credits, a form of public-sector subsidy of private-sector provision, have both benefits and disadvantages. One of the primary benefits of tax allowances is the flexibility and choice they provide to the consumer. Tax credits, in particular, have the advantage of providing uniform and administrative efficiency. However, given the stringent regulations and eligibility requirements, many working families are not eligible, and tax credits tend to disproportionately benefit upper-income groups.

Head Start

Although the majority of child care in this country is funded privately, there are limited public programs and subsidizes available for low-income families. The largest is Head Start, an early childhood education program, which is often characterized as a child-care program. The Head Start program aims to provide comprehensive health, educational, nutritional, and social services to economically disadvantaged preschoolers and young children. The program also provides education and support for parents, seeking to advance the economic and social well-being of the participating families.

Since 1965, Head Start has served more than 16 million children. In 1997, nearly $4 billion dollars were appropriated to the Head Start program (U.S. House of Representatives, 1998). Currently nearly 800,000 children are enrolled in 1,600 programs, with children with disabilities constituting 13 percent of the total enrollment. At least 90 percent of the children participating in the programs must be from families with income levels at or below the poverty level or receiving benefits from the Temporary Assistance for Needy Families programs.

Research demonstrates positive outcomes among Head Start children. Compared to children not participating in Head Start, children enrolled in the program receive higher scores in early literacy and verbal skills; there is a high level of parental participation in school activities and support of children's learning at home; and there are long-term positive effects on academic achievement and reduction in grade repetition (U.S. Senate, 1998). Although Head Start generally operates as a part-time, part-year program, efforts are being made to better link it with other all-day care providers to address the needs of full-time working parents.

Social Services Block Grant/ The Child & Adult Care Food Program

While Title XX of the Social Services Block Grant of the Social Security Act was once the largest source of federal dollars for child-care subsidizes, its share of federal assistance for child care has declined. The Omnibus Budget Reconciliation Act of 1989 originally authorized $2.8 billion annually for the program, which Congress reduced to $2.38 billion in 1996. The Act authorizes grants to fund "appropriate" social services at the state level and, typically, the majority of states spend some portion of their grants on child-care services. In 1995, states spent approximately 14 percent of their Title XX funds on child care (U.S. House of Representatives, 1998). The Child and Adult Care Food Program (CACFP) also provides federal subsidizes for meals in licensed nonresidential child-care centers and family and group day-care homes. In 1996, the program cost approximately $1.5 billion, with an average of 2.4 million children (the majority between the ages of 3 and 6) in attendance in subsidized centers.

Child Care and Development Block Grant

The Child Care and Development Block Grant program provides a large portion of public subsidies for child care. A national network of child-care systems to serve low-income families was originally proposed under the Act for Better Child Care (ABC); however, the Act was vetoed and the Child Care and Development Block Grant program was eventually adopted in 1990, with coverage far more limited than initially proposed. The Child Care and Development Block Grant program was originally authorized for five years, with yearly allocation levels ranging from over $700 million to over $900 million (U.S. House of Representatives, Committee on Ways and Means, 1994), with appropriated funds being distributed to states.

Welfare Reform

Sweeping welfare-reform legislation was passed in 1996, with the objective of having families on welfare, including those with very young children, seek and maintain employment. In the majority of welfare-to-work programs, mothers on welfare with children over the age of three are expected to be employed; some of the programs mandate that mothers begin work within 6 to 12 weeks after the birth of a child.

Prior to the welfare-reform movement, the Aid to Families with Dependent Children (AFDC) program provided support to women and children living in poverty. For example, $19.9 billion was distributed to approximately 4.6 million families with 8.7 million children (U.S. General Accounting Office, 1998). The Personal Responsibility and Work Opportunity Reconciliation Act of 1996 (P.L. 104–193) replaced AFDC with the Temporary Assistance for Needy Families (TANF) block grants, providing states with federal funds to assist families in poverty, at a cost of approximately $16 billion annually. Under TANF, states are required to insure that at least 25 percent of the adults receiving assistance are working or are involved in work-related activities. By the year 2002, states are required to have at least 50 percent of recipients working. If states do not meet these federal requirements they may incur financial penalties (U.S. General Accounting Office, 1998). These legislative changes shifted responsibility for the support of low-income children and their families from the federal government to state and local governments. States now have the ability to implement these programs within general program requirements, most likely leading to variations in benefits and less accountability across states.

The Child Care and Development Block Grant (CCDBG) was amended as part of the Personal Responsibility and Work Opportunity Reconciliation Act of 1996. Congress merged the CCDBG with three other existing programs—AFDC/Job Opportunities and Basic Skills Training program (JOBS); Transitional Child Care; and At-Risk Child Care. The stated goals of these changes are to provide states with increased flexibility to develop child-care programs to support poor families, develop an integrated child-care system rather than relying on multiple, separate programs, and to provide funds to improve the quality and supply of child-care services.

Between 1997 and 2002, it is estimated that the program will provide approximately $20 billion for child care, to assist both welfare families and nonwelfare poor families. In 1997, the CCDBG provided approximately $2.4 billion in mandatory and discretionary funds to states for child care (U.S. House of Representatives, 1998). States are required to use at least 70 percent of their total entitlement funds for child-care services for families who are trying to become independent of TANF through work-related activities. Children eligible for services are those whose family income does not exceed 85 percent of the state median. A portion of the funds are also to be used to improve the overall quality and availability of child care.

Several experts have argued that welfare-to-work programs are futile unless they provide affordable, safe, and dependable child care for low-income families. In the development of such programs, however, there is a constant tension between insuring availability, maintaining low costs, and providing quality care. Several government initiatives exist to increase the supply of providers, but without an understanding of how such expansion might impact the overall quality of care. Currently, of the states reviewed by the federal government, the majority report that the supply of available child care is sufficient to meet existing needs of working welfare families. However, the programs are unable to fund child care for all eligible families, especially the nonwelfare working poor, even though they meet federal eligibility requirements and might benefit from such support (U.S. General Accounting Office, 1998). Moreover, there is evidence that some states are actually diverting funds previously used to provide child care for the working poor to fund child care for welfare families (Blank, 1997).

It has been estimated that funds set aside for child care under the existing legislation are inadequate to meet the future needs generated by the stringent welfare-to-work requirements (Polakow, 1997). It is unlikely that current supply can meet future child-care needs given the likely increase in welfare recipients seeking employment as mandated by the new welfare reforms. Although some states are providing differential reimbursement rates to programs that meet national accreditation standards or to those that provide care during nontraditional hours, little is known about the safety or quality of care currently being used in welfare-reform programs. In part because of the mandated participation rates of the welfare-to-work programs and the priority to ensure families economic self-sufficiency rather than providing enriched care, it is likely that much of the child care offered to families as part of the welfare-to-work programs will not be of high quality.

Quality of Care

There is substantial evidence that high-quality child-care programs that provide enriched curricula can benefit the development of children (Zigler & Finn-Stevenson, 1995), particularly children from disadvantaged homes (Ramey & Ramey, 1992). Generally, the majority of research has found that the overall quality of child care is related to such factors as the ratio of children to caregiver, the number of children, the rate of staff turnover, staff training (Hayes, et al., 1990; Helburn, Culkin, Morris, et al., 1995), the stability of care (Philips, 1987), and parent involvement (Zigler & Muenchow, 1992). Among both parents and child-care providers, the components that were most often identified as constituting quality care included insuring safety of the child, effective communication between provider and parent, and an attentive relationship between the child and the provider (Galinsky, Howes, Kontos & Shinn, 1994).

The availability of high-quality child care is a serious problem in this country—a problem likely to be further exacerbated by the recent welfare-reform measures. One national study rated more than half of the child-care centers it assessed as poor quality (Whitebook, Howes & Phillips, 1990). Another study of family day-care centers and care by relatives found that the majority of children received adequate care (56 percent), with 35 percent receiving care rated as inadequate or potentially harmful to the child. Only 9 percent of children were receiving care rated as good quality and growth enhancing (Zigler & Finn-Stevenson, 1995). In a fairly recent study, only 14 percent of child-care centers were found to be providing quality care (Helburn et al., 1995).

While states are increasingly implementing licensing codes to maintain basic minimal standards of care, many child-care settings are not covered under existing regulations, there is a great deal of variation in the application of the standards, and no consistent federal standards have been applied. In 1990, it was estimated that approximately 40 percent of child-care settings were exempt from regulation (Blank, 1997). Yet there is evidence to suggest that licensed providers rate higher on quality of care (Belsky, 1984). Day-care providers that voluntarily met federal standards were found to provide higher-quality child care than centers that did not meet such standards (Whitebook et al., 1990).

In an analysis of the cost of care, Clifford and Russel (1989) calculated that high-quality care costs approximately 79 percent more than low-quality care. Using standards set by the National Association of the Education of Young Children, they based their calculations on relatively high teacher and assistant teacher salaries, a low child-staff ratio, and a modest fund for teacher training and development. In general, child-care workers are poorly paid and have high turnover rates. In 1994, the average pay for a child-care worker was $6.83 per hour (Goodman, 1995). In one recent study, it was found that the wage received by a teacher was more closely related to quality than other structural variables in center-based child-care settings (Scarr, Eisenberg & Deater-Deckard, 1994).

Several demonstration projects have been instituted to increase the quality of child care in a variety of settings, and the findings seem promising when adequate resources are available (Dombro, 1995; Howes, Smith & Galinsky, 1995). Several of these projects have demonstrated that provider training results in significant increases in the quality of care. For example, in one study of family-care providers, quality of care was increased through professional development of providers, education of parents, implementation of accreditation standards, and the creation of local provider associations and networks (Dombro, 1995). Providers tend to receive higher-quality scores if they are committed to their work and the children for whom they provide care; seek educational opportunities; plan their educational activities; provide regulated care; and maintain slightly lower adult-to-child ratios (Galinsky et al., 1994). In 1992 in Florida, legislation was enacted that decreased teacher-to-child ratios and increased training requirements for staff. Evaluation of the new requirements found improvement in the intellectual and emotional development of children, the sensitivity and responsiveness of teachers, and the overall quality of the programs (Howes et al., 1995).

International Child-Care
Policies and Programs

In Europe there is growing recognition of the need to provide very young children with an opportunity for development and socialization with peers as well as adults. Yet in many European countries toddler care is evolving with mixed approaches and an adequacy of supply similar to that of the U.S. As women return to work following parental leave, quality care is often not available. In response to such problems, some European countries have extended their leave policies, provided cash benefits to parents who remain at home to care for their children, and expanded the availability of early child care in the community.

Denmark has the most extensive child-care system serving children under the age of three. Child care is a guaranteed entitlement funded by the Ministry of Social Affairs, and the country has instituted a comprehensive subsidized public day-care system that is decentralized and administered by local municipalities, offering both professional center-based care and paraprofessional care provided in homes (Kamerman & Kahn, 1995a). The day-care system serves children from infancy to six years of age, with the majority of children entering after one year of age (Polakow, 1997). Program philosophy generally focuses on psychological and social development, with child-initiated activities in a relatively unstructured environment. Although the demand for such child care tends to exceed supply, the quality of care in these programs is high, based on staff-child ratios, small group sizes, and implementation of regulatory standards.

In most European countries, preschool, beginning at age 2 to 3½ through compulsory school age, is largely universal and has become relatively standard, regardless of parents' employment status. Voluntary and free of charge, preschool programs are generally as accessible and available as primary school. Enrollment in these programs is very high, with the vast majority of young children participating. Such programs aim to enhance the child's development through education and socialization, as well as provide care for working parents. The majority of these programs are regulated under educational auspices.

The availability, structure, and auspices of preschool education vary. France and Belgium, for example, have the most extensive preschool programs in the world (Kamerman, 1991). In France, the curriculum is based on an educational model, publicly financed, and operates as a unit of the French educational system. In Sweden, although preschool for children under the age of seven is available, there is a fee for attending, and the child-care programs are administrated under social-welfare auspices rather than the educational system.

In Europe, the discussion of family child-rearing supports extends beyond child care for working parents. A comprehensive and integrated system of family-care support services is emerging that includes income supplements, maternal and child health care, child day care, and early child-hood education. For example, most European countries have family al-lowance benefits, an income supplement to assist families with the cost of raising children. Although there are differences in how such allowances are paid and how revenues are generated, the goal of the programs is to assist families financially, especially low-income families, in addressing the needs of children.

LONG-TERM CARE

Long-term care services include health, personal care, and social services delivered over a sustained period of time to persons who have limited ca-pacity for self-care. Long-term care services are needed by the frail and dis-abled elderly and by adults and children with physical disabilities, serious mental-health problems, developmental disabilities, and terminal or chronic conditions such as cancer, heart disease, arthritis, HIV, dementia, stroke, and diabetes. A mix of long-term care services has been developed to assist dis-abled persons, including nursing home care, community-based residential facilities, home health and homemaker services, respite care, support groups, and day centers.

In our study, nearly three-quarters of the employees assisting disabled adult family members reported experiencing problems obtaining informa-tion and assistance with care responsibilities. More than a quarter of these employees reported specific problems finding trained and reliable care providers, locating services in the community, and understanding govern-ment programs that fund services. In addition, more than 20 percent did not have enough money to pay for services. Employees who reported more prob-lems in these areas experienced higher levels of work and family accom-modations and strain.

Current status. In the U.S. population, two in five persons 45 years of age and older report some experience with long-term care needs among family members. Although the majority of persons in need of long-term care ser-vices are 65 years and older, 40 percent are working-age adults and 2 per-cent are children (American Association of Retired Persons, 1995). It is estimated that in the year 2000, nearly 14 million Americans are in need of some form of long-term care assistance (U.S. Senate, 1996). Of these, 10 mil-lion need home or community-based care.

The long-term care system in the U.S. is complex, incorporating famil-ial, state, and federal involvement. The funding streams for long-term care in this country come from a variety of sources. While families and those us-ing long-term care privately fund a substantial portion of the costs, more than 100 federal programs provide some support for long-term care services. Several major federal programs finance the majority of care, including Med-icaid, Medicare, the Older Americans Act, the Rehabilitation Act, and Social

Services Block Grants. In addition, many programs exist that are funded by the general revenues of individual states.

As costs for long-term care services escalate, they continue to absorb a large proportion of the federal budget. It is estimated that formal long-term care services in this country now exceed $100 billion per year (U. S. Senate, 1998), with Medicaid paying approximately 44 percent of the costs, Medicare 16 percent, and individuals and their families paying approximately 33 percent. Medicaid is now the largest public payer for long-term care services. In 1995, $28.5 billion of Medicaid funding was spent for long-term care services, and $22.7 billion was paid for by Medicare. Of Medicaid expenditures in 1993, states spent $19.0 billion and the federal government spent $24.7 billion (U.S. General Accounting Office, 1995a). In addition, in 1993, the Older Americans Act financed $0.8 billion and the Rehabilitation Act financed $0.1 billion for long-term care services (U.S. General Accounting Office, 1995a). The cost of long-term care services is expected to rise substantially during the next several decades, primarily due to the aging of the population. It is estimated that inflation-adjusted expenditures for long-term care for the elderly will increase by 2.6 percent per year between years 2000 and 2040 (Hagen, 1999). Long-term care expenditures are estimated to reach $207 billion in 2020 and $346 billion by 2040.

One study estimated that approximately 70 percent of the population receiving community and/or institutional long-term care services rely on their private resources to pay for care (Spillman & Kemper, 1995), paying more than one-third of the overall costs out-of-pocket (U.S. GAO, 1995a). The Department of Health and Human Services estimates that the value of long-term care assistance provided by family members and friends ranges from $45 to $94 billion per year (Hagen, 1999).

In response to the rising costs, several presidential and congressional proposals have been advanced in recent years. Such proposals have ranged from revamping the Medicaid and Medicare systems to replacing Medicaid with a social insurance program, modifying Medicare to increase cost-sharing requirements for high-income beneficiaries, increasing the use of managed care, promoting the growth and availability of long-term care insurance, and increasing tax credits. Deficit politics, the complexity of financing and delivery of health and long-term care services, and congressional fragmentation, however, have all resulted in making health and long-term care reform difficult.

To date, the U.S. does not have an integrated government-sponsored long-term care system or policy, and a comprehensive federal long-term care proposal has never been enacted, generally due to controversy regarding potential economic costs. The delivery of long-term care services is fragmented and varies considerably state by state. Disabled persons may be cared for through private arrangements, private and publicly subsidized institutional and community-based programs, or corporate-sponsored programs as outlined in the previous chapter. Currently, publicly supported long-term care assistance is most often provided through institutional care, community-based care, cash allowances, and tax credits.

Institutional-based Long-Term Care

Approximately 2.0 million persons, generally those with severe disabilities, live in nursing homes (U.S. General Accounting Office, 1995a); approximately 90 percent of nursing home residents are 65 or older (Lair, 1992). Yet only about 5 percent of the elderly population live in nursing homes at any one time (Roy & Russell, 1992). It is estimated that more than 40 percent of persons turning 65 in 1990 will use a nursing home at some time before their death, with approximately 9 percent residing there for five or more years.

The majority of public long-term care dollars in this country are paid for nursing home care rather than home or community-based care. Of the federal expenditures for long-term care in 1993, 70 percent was paid for institutional care (U.S. General Accounting Office, 1995a), with Medicaid financing the majority of care. In 1994, 65 percent of the Medicaid budget was for institutional-based care (U.S. House of Representatives, 1996).

The cost of long-term care often creates serious financial consequences for the disabled and their families. The average annual cost for nursing home care is $40,000 (Scanlon, 1998), approximately half of which is paid for by care recipients or their families and half by federal and state governments (U.S. General Accounting Office, 1994a). This often results in the impoverishment of the disabled and negatively impacts retirement income security. In 1994, Medicaid financed part of the care for about two-thirds of nursing home residents, although more than one-quarter of Medicaid nursing home residents were initially admitted as private payers (Scanlon, 1998).

Because of rising costs and a desire to maintain disabled persons in the least restrictive setting possible, several measures have been implemented to limit institutional care. Several states have begun utilizing Certificate of Need programs, and have instituted screening and preauthorization procedures to limit nursing home admissions and costs. Likely due to the disparities in public versus private reimbursement rates, those on Medicaid are less likely to be admitted to a nursing home than those paying privately (Reschovsky, 1996). Increasing Medicaid reimbursements, as well as relaxing the regulations that limit available beds, would be required to increase access to nursing homes for Medicaid patients. As initiatives are implemented to curb the rising costs of nursing homes, they further shift the burden of care of the ill and disabled to community-based or informal supports.

Home and Community-Based Long-Term Care

More than 10 million Americans of all ages need some type of long-term care assistance to live in their homes or in another community-based setting. Yet less than one-third of noninstitutional long-term care is publicly subsidized. Of the total 1995 Medicaid budget, for example, only 8.2 percent covered home-care services (U.S. House of Representatives, 1998).

The Omnibus Budget Reconciliation Act (OBRA) of 1981 provided for state Medicaid waivers for community and home-based services for the indigent disabled at high risk of institutionalization. OBRA allowed states to provide home and community-based services to functionally disabled Medicaid beneficiaries, with the provision that the federal matching not exceed 50 percent of what it would have cost to provide nursing facility care. Medicaid financing for home and community-based waivers increased substantially at an average of 33 percent per year between 1987 and 1996, costing $5.8 billion in 1996 (Scanlon, 1998). All states have now received Medicaid waivers for community-based and home services, with more than 200 waiver programs serving more than 250,000 persons (Scanlon, 1998). Few of the waiver programs, however, are available on a statewide basis (U.S. Senate Special Committee on Aging, 1992).

Medicare has become the largest public payer for home-care services, generally providing skilled nursing and therapy services, although increasingly it is covering services that meet long-term care needs (Scanlon, 1998). Medicare home-health services have experienced significant growth, increasing from $2.3 billion in 1989 to $9.5 billion in 1993 (U.S. General Accounting Office, 1995b). The number of persons under Medicare receiving home-health care and the number of visits per patient has more than doubled between 1989 and 1996 (Scanlon, 1998). The Balanced Budget Act of 1997, however, instituted a new prospective payment system (effective in 1999) that may reduce the number of services financed by Medicare.

In 1992 there were approximately 14,000 home-care agencies in the U.S. (National Association for Home Care, 1993). The number of paraprofessionals providing home-care services are estimated to total between 300,000–500,000 (Feldman, Sapienza & Kane, 1990). Yet research has shown that nearly three-quarters of the disabled elderly reside in areas where there are inadequate levels of home health, homemaker services, and community-based care (Palley and Oktay, 1983). Reimbursement issues and labor supply considerations further exacerbate the problem of limited availability of agency-based home-care services or non-affiliated homemaker providers.

In general, home-care workers tend to be untrained and low paid, without employment benefits. The vast majority of home-care workers are women and racial/ethnic minorities with low educational levels, many of whom are living at the poverty level (Feldman, et al., 1990). Not surprisingly, such positions tend to experience high rates of turnover. Among home health aides, the rates of turnover have in some cases been found to exceed 60 percent annually.

The provision of direct services such as home care are often the preferred method of governmental assistance among caregivers, yet there is an inadequate supply of such services. Also problematic is that while public provision of such services allows for regulation and monitoring of the quality of care, it also has the potential to reduce flexibility and choice among consumers.

Tax Credits

With the political emphasis on privatization over the last decade, tax allowances are often a preferred form to address the increasing need for long-term care assistance. In 1999, President Clinton proposed a $6 billion Family Caregiver Initiative designed to assist families in the long-term care of family members with disabilities. This innovative initiative included (1) tax credits for caregiving families; (2) an information campaign about long-term care financing options; (3) the development of "one-stop-shops" that offer respite care, information and referral, counseling, support groups, and caregiver training; and (4) the availability of group long-term care insurance for all federal employees, retirees, and their families.

The core component of the proposal is the $1,000 tax credit designed to assist families by offsetting some of the direct costs (such as day health or home health visits) or indirect costs (such as unpaid leave) of providing long-term care assistance. Financed through revenues resulting from the balanced budget, the tax credit is expected to cost $5.5 billion over five years, and will be available to approximately 2 million Americans (Goldstein, 1999). The tax credit as proposed is relatively easy to administer and will require only that people document the level of disability rather than submitting bills from services. The tax credit, however, is nonrefundable and is not accessible to the majority of low-income Americans who pay little or no income taxes. Caregivers of ill and disabled adults can also utilize the federal Child and Dependent Care Tax credit, but due to the eligibility requirements most do not qualify.

Increasingly, states (e.g., Arizona, Idaho, Iowa, Oregon) have implemented tax credits for the care of dependent family members, although each state varies considerably in allowance specifications and eligibility requirements. In a comparison study of Idaho's and Arizona's tax incentive programs, Hendrickson, Jewitt, Emerson, and Seck (1988) found considerable variations in design and related outcomes. Idaho's program was designed primarily to encourage caregiving assistance with activities of daily living, whereas Arizona's main objective was to stimulate greater financial assistance by informal caregivers. Findings from this study indicate that both programs seemed to encourage greater levels of care and involvement among informal family caregivers.

Tax credit proposals are notable in their potential for bringing long-term care issues to the attention of the American public and increasing awareness of potential long-term care solutions for family caregivers. But they are apt to be of little use if long-term care services are not available or easily accessible. Since the majority of impoverished families have low or no tax liabilities and may not be able to afford the out-of-pocket care expenses for dependents, nonrefundable tax credits are likely not beneficial to them. In addition, only 1.5 percent of family caregivers cite tax credits as their preferred method of obtaining governmental support for caregiving (Horowitz and Shindleman, 1983).

Cash Allowances

A few programs provide cash allowances to disabled persons that may be used to purchase service from an agency or to provide compensation to family members or friends for their caregiving activities. Robert Wood Johnson Foundation, for example, is sponsoring an innovative Cash and Counseling Initiative that provides disabled persons with a monthly cash allowance and counseling, to help consumers obtain information as well as select and arrange long-term care assistance (Cohen, 1998).

Linsk, Keigher, and Osterbusch (1988) found in a national survey that 70 percent of the states permit some form of payment for family caregivers of persons needing long-term care assistance. The majority of such publicly funded grants in the U.S. tend to be restrictive and most often only provided to at-risk, low-income families, with compensation generally at the minimum-wage level. As currently administered, few caregivers or care recipients are eligible for cash payment programs, with the exception of disabled veterans, who are eligible for a subsidy from the Veteran's Administration Aid and Attendance program to compensate familial caregivers. Some state Mental Retardation and Developmental Disability agencies provide direct cash payments to families and reimbursement or direct payments to service providers; however, such support has been limited to only 2.5 percent of all federal and state mental retardation and developmental disability expenditures (U.S. Senate, 1994).

Among economic support options, monthly support payments are often a preferred type of governmental assistance (Cohen, 1998). In a demonstration project that assessed the impact of receiving monthly payments totaling approximately $2,000 per year, caregivers of elderly persons who received such compensation reported an increase in their ability to cope and to provide care; but the subsidies did not reduce the rates of institutionalization of care recipients (Whitfield & Krompholz, 1981).

Direct cash payments are generally need-based and provide assistance to low-income families caring for a disabled family member. However, the majority of such programs are poorly funded, gap-filling measures, which differ significantly by jurisdiction. In most cases, payments are available only when a family member is at high risk of institutionalization and both the caregiver and care recipient are impoverished. As such programs have been applied, cash payments are most feasible for nonworking caregivers whose skills in the marketplace would be paid at or near minimum wage. Thus, they are generally of limited benefit to employed caregivers and their disabled family members. Purchasing services also assumes the availability of services, yet in the vast majority of areas there is an inadequate supply of long-term care support services. Accessing services places the responsibility for obtaining, supervising, and evaluating informal care on the care recipient or family members. In either case, service quality will likely be dependent upon the level of knowledge and expertise of service consumers.

Long-term Care Insurance

In recent years, several congressional and presidential proposals have been advanced to increase the availability and attractiveness of private long-term care insurance. During the last decade, there has been substantial growth in the long-term care insurance market. While in 1986, approximately 30 insurers were selling long-term care insurance, by 1995 more than 125 insurers were offering such policies (U.S. House of Representatives, 1998). However, only a very small proportion of persons have long-term care insurance coverage, likely due to limited knowledge about the insurance or the risk of needing long-term care and the relatively high cost of such policies. Among the elderly, only about 5 percent have long-term care insurance. In 1995, private long-term care insurance covered less than 1 percent of total long-term care expenditures (Scanlon, 1998).

Because of their high costs, it is likely that long-term care policies are not affordable to the majority of disabled and elderly persons. It has been estimated that only 10 to 20 percent of the elderly can afford such policies (Scanlon, 1998). In 1995, policies that paid $100 per day for nursing home care and $50 for home-health care cost an average $1,881 in premiums if purchased at the age of 65 and $5,889 if purchased at the age of 79. There is also concern over consumer protection and adequacy of coverage issues. In response to such concerns the National Association of Insurance Commissioners (NAIC) developed the Long-Term Care Insurance Model Act and regulations for long-term insurance products. By 1997, all of the states had implemented laws and regulations covering long-term care insurance, and nearly 40 states had adopted half or more of the NAIC recommendations.

The Health Insurance Portability and Accountability Act of 1996 amended the tax code so that private long-term care insurance policies and long-term care expenses are treated in a way similar to health insurance policies and expenses. The primary changes are that (1) amounts received under a qualified long-term care insurance plan are considered as medical expenses and excluded from gross income; (2) contributions of an employer to the cost of qualified long-term care insurance premiums are excluded from the gross income of the employee and are exempt from tax (within certain dollar limits); (3) out-of-pocket long-term expenses including premiums are allowed as itemized deductions (to the extent that they and other medical expenses exceed 7.5 percent of the adjusted gross income); and (4) self-employed individuals are able to include the premium costs of long-term insurance in determining the allowable deduction for health insurance premiums (U.S. House of Representatives Committee on Ways and Means, 1998). The Act requires that policies meet the requirements of the NAIC Long-Term Care Insurance Model Act to be tax deductible.

One goal of President Clinton's 1999 Family Caregiver Initiative is to increase the availability of long-term care insurance to all federal employees, retirees, and their families. As the nation's largest employer, it is hoped that federal involvement in the long-term care insurance market will encourage the private sector to develop more options and choices for disabled individuals and their families. The federal government will also initiate a campaign to educate Medicare recipients about long-term care issues and insurance options.

Several states have been experimenting with new long-term care insurance models. One option being tested is the purchase of long-term care insurance according to the level of assets one wants to protect. For persons purchasing such policies, states extend the protection of Medicaid without requiring them to deplete their assets as normally required (generally $2,000 for a single individual). Insured persons are then able to retain assets at the level that corresponds to their private insurance pay-outs, while being covered by Medicaid for the care needed after their private policies are no longer providing coverage (U.S. House of Representatives, 1998).

An innovative model of public-private long-term care financing has been implemented by the Robert Wood Johnson Partnership Program, which provides individuals with various incentives to purchase long-term care insurance (Cohen, 1998). The partnership program in New York, which has been the most successful of various models implemented, protects all assets after insurance benefits are exhausted. By 1995, approximately 10,000 people had purchased long-term care insurance through the Partnership program. It is hoped that increasing tax deductibility, adding new configurations of long-term care insurance policies, and enhancing public and private partnerships will accelerate the growth of the long-term care insurance market, resulting in a reduction of public expenditures.

Quality of Care

The current emphasis in the long-term care arena is cost, not quality control. The vast majority of long-term care initiatives are aimed at reducing spending through increasing private contributions, reforming the delivery system to provide care more efficiently (such as increasing the role of managed care and integrating acute and long-term care), and implementing cost-cutting measures (such as reducing the supply of nursing home beds and Medicaid reimbursement rates).

Quality of long-term care has been defined as "the degree to which health and social services for individuals and populations increase the likelihood of desired health and social outcomes and are consistent with current professional knowledge" (Institute of Medicine, 1996, p.12). Overall quality has been noted to be the weakest aspect of the current long-term care system (Kodner, 1996). Serious problems in the quality of nursing home care (Kodner, 1996) and community-based services (Oktay, Steinwachs, Mamon, Bone, & Fahey, 1992) have been reported.

As a private industry that relies heavily on public funds, nursing home care is now relatively heavily monitored and regulated, given the potential for exploitation of physically and mentally vulnerable residents. Yet until the passage of the 1987 Omnibus Budget Reconciliation Act (OBRA) there existed substantial interstate variation in the types and levels of standards applied in nursing home care. The discussion of quality assessment in nursing home care generally incorporates issues in relation to structure, process, and outcomes. Kane (1998) suggests that an "accountable innovation" approach is needed, which compares actual results with those expected if comparable cases were treated under similar or better circumstances. Such an outcomes framework can be applied in a variety of long-term care settings, incorporating functional and quality of life measures across domains, while controlling for various client characteristics.

To curb the rising costs of institution-based long-term care, several measures have shifted the burden to community-based services and informal supports. Although public subsidization of community-based assistance is not an inexpensive solution, it does provide important options. In an evaluation of comprehensive case-management services, for example, it was found that such services did not reduce overall costs, but did improve access to home care, reduce unmet needs, and improve life satisfaction among care recipients and their caregivers (Kemper, 1988). Case-management services had a positive impact on client satisfaction, both directly and through the use of in-home care (Rabiner, Mutran & Stearns, 1995). Thus, community-based services offer an important means to assist families and to allow seriously ill or disabled persons to live in the community as independently as possible.

Yet at the federal level, a comprehensive long-term care quality assurance program has not been developed for community- and home-based care, although some states have developed their own quality control programs. Kane (1995, p. 9) maintains that "federal and state government have continuing responsibilities for establishing and enforcing a minimum definition of quality and fostering the conditions under which programs can be innovative, respond to consumer preferences, and encouraged to exceed minimum standards." One study found that board and care facilities in states that had implemented extensive regulations for long-term care had quality indicators much higher than states that were less regulated (Institute of Medicine, 1996). However, common structural measures such as credentials and minimum levels of training have not been found to be consistently related to higher levels of quality.

A federal committee established to assess the quality of long-term care services determined that to achieve high-quality home and community-based services will require sound regulatory requirements, reasonable monitoring of performance and quality, and internal programs that encourage ongoing assessment and evaluation to promote continuous quality improvement (Institute of Medicine, 1996).

International Long-term Care Policies

Long-term care services in European countries are generally guaranteed in the form of public sponsorship of professional support services. In the majority of countries there is a strong preference toward noninstitutional care and community-based services for the chronically disabled and seriously ill, although historically many of the countries initially adopted social insurance schemes that were heavily biased toward medicalization and institutional care (Coleman, 1995).

Local governments are assuming increased responsibility for long-term care services. In the Nordic countries, for example, long-term care has developed into a uniform, public, decentralized system, with responsibility at the local level. In many countries, such as Denmark and Sweden, each municipality sets its own priorities and establishes its own long-term care programs. However, in Germany, long-term care services have become standard benefits under its national health insurance program (U.S. General Accounting Office, 1994c).

In a comparison of ten developed countries with high life expectancy, Iceland, Denmark, and the Netherlands were found to have the highest rates of nursing home care among the elderly, while Japan, Italy, and France had the lowest rates (Ribbe, Ljunggren, Steel & Topinkova, 1997). There was considerable variation by country in the definition of nursing home care, level of regulation, function of care, and eligibility criteria for admission. Countries also differed in the degree of support services offered within a nursing home care setting. In some countries, such the Netherlands, highly developed rehabilitation programs are part of nursing home care, resulting in high rates of patient discharge. Others countries, such as Denmark and the United Kingdom, have very limited rehabilitation services and longer patient stays.

Financing systems for nursing home care also vary considerably by country. In France, for example, nursing home care is means-tested or requires a co-payment or private payer (as in the U.S.). Other countries, such as Denmark and Sweden, rely on tax revenues by state and municipality, to finance nursing home care for all citizens.

In many European countries, especially the Scandinavian countries, institutional care is being actively discouraged. Many countries are promoting home and community-based care through expanding community services, designing new types of housing, and providing comprehensive community-based services. Home-care assistance is becoming more readily available. In Sweden, for example, home help is available "around-the-clock"—days, evenings, and weekends. While home nursing care is free of charge, a sliding-scale fee is charged for homemaker and home help services. The services are paid for through user fees, local taxes, and the central government. Seventeen percent of Swedes age 65 and older receive home-care assistance. In Denmark, the "Aging Package" was implemented to encourage independence, autonomy, and self-care, freeze the building of new nursing homes, and provide permanent home health care free of charge.

Several European countries are experimenting with emerging types of service allocation and delivery, and more often than in the past they are emphasizing individual needs and the increased use of case management. In Great Britain, for example, there is increased experimentation with an open market of services, combined with case management of long-term care services. In the Netherlands, there is also an increased use of case management, with an emphasis on advocacy and the brokerage of services. There is also an increased privatization of community-based long-term care services. In the United Kingdom, private-sector home care increased from 2 percent in 1992 to 32 percent in 1996 (Harrington & Pollock, 1998).

Several public-policy initiatives exist to insure the economic security of the disabled and their informal caregivers. In Germany, disabled persons have a choice either to receive services that are arranged by a case manager or to receive a monthly cash allowance of approximately half the cost of the formal services. More than 80 percent of eligible persons choose the monthly cash allowance (Cohen, 1998). In both Sweden and Denmark, caregivers assisting ill and disabled family members can be released from employment to meet their caregiving responsibilities, and are provided a wage for caregiving equivalent to the cost of a trained professional (Evers, 1995). In Sweden, employed caregivers can receive a maximum of thirty days of paid leave to care for an elderly parent or spouse, and their salary is paid through the social insurance system. In Germany, informal caregivers receive pension entitlements.

There have been increased efforts to recognize the contribution of informal caregivers in meeting the long-term care needs of the ill and disabled. In Great Britain, such efforts include the development of the Carers National Association to provide support to informal caregivers and to advocate on their behalf, and respite services such as "sitting services" to ensure caregivers a break from their caregiving responsibilities.

High rates of inflation, unemployment, public debt, and budget deficits have, however, resulted in reductions in social benefits in European countries. In several countries, there is an increased emphasis on individual responsibility and privatization of services. There have been reductions in long-term care support services available through the government, and decentralization of the finance and delivery of long-term care services. In addition, there is a shift in emphasis from direct support services for care recipients and informal caregivers to indirect support (such as financial assistance). There is also a trend to place a greater emphasis on informal care, increasingly supporting the role of caregivers.

A FAMILY-SENSITIVE POLICY AGENDA

The breakdown of traditional communities of family care is a major contributor to individual and societal conflicts regarding work and family responsibilities. Yet the United States, unlike most other developed countries, has not been able to develop a comprehensive family-care policy and integrated community-based infrastructure to augment or replace traditional supports for family care. Our system of public income transfers, including social insurance (unemployment and social security) and welfare benefits (income-tested cash transfers), does not provide an adequate safety net for American families.

A tiered system has developed in this country, in which there are federal subsidies for low-income families and tax deductions for dependent-care expenses that primarily benefit upper-income families. It is questionable whether this system serves any of these groups well. In this section, we will discuss several potential components—family leave, child care, and long-term care—of a family-sensitive public policy framework that we consider essential if we are to develop an adequate community-based infrastructure to support family care.

Family Leave

Family leave was endorsed by the vast majority of respondents in this study as being the policy most apt to help them manage their work and family responsibilities. Toward a family sensitive public policy agenda, it is therefore particularly important to consider expanding mandated federal family leave. The majority of U.S. workers are not covered by the FMLA (Family Medical and Leave Act), which excludes individuals whose work sites have fewer than 50 employees, who work less than 1,250 hours a year, or who have been at their current jobs less than 12 months. Yet these workers have no less need for family leave than those who meet the criteria. As a first step, coverage could be expanded to include all work sites with 10 or more employees, with an eventual goal of universal coverage. Tax incentives could be developed to reduce any undue impact on small employers at risk of incurring excessive costs as a result of family leave. Expanding coverage to employees who work less than full-time could be achieved by mandating leave proportional to the time an employee works.

The greatest barrier to employee utilization of family leave is the fact that it is usually unpaid. Lower-income families especially tend to take the shortest leaves, and often take no leave at all. Yet as the Rhode Island example demonstrates, when leave is accompanied by wage replacement, lower-income women significantly increase the amount of maternity leave they take (Bond et al., 1991). Many large employers offer some form of wage replacement for employees taking family leaves. All Fortune 1,000 companies provide women on maternity leave with partial wage replacement under company short-term disability insurance plans. However, paid disability leaves are available to only 25 percent of workers in companies with fewer than 100 employees (Families & Work Institute, 1993). Furthermore, paid maternity disability leave is limited by law to the period of actual disability (i.e., the weeks surrounding childbirth), not including the postnatal period for the purpose of parent-child bonding. In five states (California, Hawaii, New Jersey, New York, and Rhode Island), temporary disability insurance (TDI) provides partial wage replacement during pregnancy and childbirth, both defined as disabilities.

As a first step, TDI could be expanded to cover workers in all 50 states. As noted by the Families and Work Institute (1993), national or statewide TDI could be operated as a true social insurance program, with premiums based on established risks calculated from actuarial data from existing state TDI plans. The plans could be administered by the state or federal government to avoid the negative consequences sometimes associated with private insurance: high percentage of administrative costs, profit incentive pitting insurers against claimants, and refusals to insure pre-existing conditions. Once TDI is available in all states, unemployment compensation programs could expand to cover leaves for new babies, parenting, or personal or family illness. The program could be covered by payroll taxes or financed indirectly as in other industrialized countries.

As leave laws are expanded, it is important to consider the economic implications of such policies. Policies that support absences from the work place can have serious economic consequences, particularly for women who may lose continuity from the work force, promotions, and wage increases. Research has documented that women's early as well as late life family caregiving is associated with a substantial reduction in Social Security benefits, and benefit losses are more pronounced for low- and moderate-income women than for high-income women (Kingston & O'Grady-LeShane, 1993). Toward equalization of earnings, a number of reforms have been advanced, such as earning sharing (redistributing the earnings between spouses), credits provided for years of caregiving, and allowing drop-out years from the calculation of benefits.

Child Care

Problems with child-care arrangements emerged as a major predictor of role strain and work and family accommodations for the working parents in this study. More than two-thirds of parents with children under age 13 endorsed the need for child care. Child-care services in this country remain inadequate, despite the fact that child care is now a necessity for the vast majority of American families. Many existing child-care services do not even meet health and safety standards, let alone provide sufficient stimulation for children's optimal development. With this in mind, President Clinton has described child care as America's next great frontier, stating that no parent should have to choose between work and family.

Although the U.S. has not developed a comprehensive or coordinated system of child-care services, it has long been argued that government has the responsibility to ensure that child care is affordable for all working families, and that it is regulated both for safety and for opportunities for children to develop emotionally, socially, and intellectually. The Panel on Child Care Policy has advanced that child-care services in the U.S. should ensure quality of care, improve accessibility across diverse families, and insure affordability for low- and moderate-income families (Hayes et al., 1990).

To ensure quality of care as well as equity, several leading experts support separating child care from welfare and providing universal availability of high-quality care. Kamerman and Kahn (1997), for example, define universal child care as "child care for all whose parents wish them to participate, either free or with income-related fees; but not limited to the poor and not involving two systems of child care delivery, one for the welfare poor and a second for the middle class." They advocate the development of a child-care system with both infant and toddler programs that is universal, developmental, and voluntary, and serves both the working and welfare poor and the middle class. Such a system could incorporate income-related fees with "wrap-around" services that would provide high-quality care during the full work day.

Zigler and Finn-Stevenson (1995) have identified several critical elements necessary for the development of an effective child-care system in the U.S. "First, the system must provide universal access to quality child care by subsidizing middle and lower income families with a sliding scale parental fee system, in addition to providing direct subsidies through federal, state, and/or local funding. Second, child care must promote the optimal development of children and should focus on all domains of development, including physical, social, emotional, and cognitive development. Third, child care must be predicated on a partnership between parents and providers. The fourth guiding principle . . . calls for recognition and support of child care providers through training, the provision of benefits, and pay upgrades. Fifth, . . . any child care policy must ensure a flexible system that is adjustable to the needs of families and available to families on a voluntary basis. Finally, we must build a stable, reliable, good quality child care system that is integrated with the political economic structure of the society and tied to recognized and easily accessible societal institutions" (pp. 222–223).

It has been suggested that in order to develop an integrated and comprehensive child-care system, child-care programs should be developed and implemented within the already existing educational system. Kentucky's Education Reform Act of 1990, for example, created needed child care and social services for families that were available through the public school system. Child-care centers were funded in all schools in which at least 20 percent of the students were eligible for free-lunch programs.

The largest proportion of federal funds for child care is available through the Dependent Care Tax Credit. Yet the credit is not available to those with incomes below tax level or those who use informal family day care, again most likely low-income families. Only about 3 percent of the child and dependent care tax credit goes to the poorest 30 percent of American families. To maintain equity and insure that low-income families can also benefit from tax initiatives, it is important that tax credits be made refundable. Under refundable tax credit programs, persons with no tax obligations are eligible to receive money back from the government. Credit could be paid out as reimbursement for child-care expenditures.

However, even a comprehensive child-care policy combined with refundable tax credits will not sufficiently address the needs of American families trying to combine family care and employment responsibilities, especially among the working poor. The poverty rate among children in this country is alarming. Children under three years of age are the poorest, with more than one-quarter living in families below the poverty line. In 1992, the poverty rate of children was almost 22 percent, 1.7 times higher than that of elderly persons (U.S. House of Representatives, 1994). Yet in 1990, the per capita welfare spending for children was one-eleventh of that for the elderly (U.S. House of Representatives, 1993). To provide a safety net for American families and to raise the income level of poor families, reforms of the minimum wage, child support payments, child care, and health care have all been suggested.

Perhaps one of the most effective mechanisms for assisting poor working families is to increase the minimum wage. It has been suggested that the minimum wage should represent at least 50 percent of the average industrial wage, with built in cost of living adjustments. Recent increases in the minimum wage have not been sufficient to keep minimum wage earners out of poverty. To support working families, it is imperative that the minimum wage be raised to the extent necessary to insure that a full-time earner, working all year at minimum wage level, can obtain income above the poverty line.

Long-term Care

Given the existing fragmentation and uneven availability of long-term care services in this country, a cohesive and comprehensive policy framework is needed that addresses issues of equity and access and supports home and community-based care. A comprehensive, long-term care system should include such elements as personal care, homemaker and chore services, congregate and home delivered meals, adult day care, rehabilitative care, assisted transportation, home health care, supportive services for caregivers, assisted living, and nursing home care. The primary goal of such a system should be to promote the independence of the chronically disabled in as least restrictive a setting as possible, and with sufficient flexibility to address diverse individual needs, preferences, and a continuum of care as individuals change over time.

A publicly funded home and community-based long-term care system has been proposed; however, it should be noted that such a program is apt to result in only small reductions in the amount of care provided by informal caregivers or in overall long-term care costs, although some experts maintain that those costs could be reduced substantially if home-care services were more carefully targeted. It has been estimated that comprehensive, subsidized home and community-based care might enable about 15 percent of nursing home residents to receive appropriately lower levels of care (Spector, Reschovsky & Cohen, 1996).

It is unlikely that significant, new, public long-term care policies will be initiated in the United States without a major shift in health-care policy. In the absence of a universal health-delivery system for primary care or a universal health insurance program, more than 30 million Americans have no health insurance at all; moreover, more than three-quarters of the uninsured are either employed or dependents of workers (Belous, 1989). Because of limited access to health care, many families are exposed to health risks that have both immediate and long-term implications. The U.S. ranks among the lowest of all developed nations in maternal health and infant mortality (Martin, 1997). Yet a comprehensive national health-care policy has never been enacted, generally due to strong disagreements among interest groups over economic costs, the most effective service delivery and allocation systems, and the appropriate relationship between public and private sponsorship and control.

Torres-Gil (1992) has suggested reforming the long-term care system and public benefits structures through a three-stage approach. In the initial (incremental) stage, Supplemental Security Income (SSI) and Disability Insurance (DI) would be enhanced through targeting low-income recipients, eliminating earnings limitation tests, and using waivers for home care. In the second (transitional) stage, a comprehensive home-care system for the frail elderly and disabled young would be adopted, and the eligibility age for age-restrictive services would be raised. The third (fundamental) stage would feature more comprehensive change, including the enactment of a universal health-care system and the implementation of multi-generational (rather than age-restricted) policies.

Without major structural reforms in health-care financing and delivery, it will be difficult to develop a coordinated, comprehensive, integrated long-term care system that is responsive to the diverse needs of individuals with disabilities.

SUMMARY

Difficulties managing work and dependent-care responsibilities are due in large part to the lack of adequate community resources for children, elders, and others who have traditionally depended on families for assistance. Whether because of the growth of a consumer-driven economy that demands increased individual productivity or because of the emergence of an ethic of individual responsibility that takes precedence over mutual concern, communities do not typically have the ability to provide the supports necessary for families to fulfill their work, family, and personal responsibilities without making significant accommodations in each of these areas.

Recently we have seen a dramatic shift in the premises of several major public policies. Coined the "devolution revolution," there is a current trend to shift responsibility for social protection from the federal government to state and local governments (Nathan, 1995, as cited in Kamerman, 1996). In addition, there has been a significant reduction in many publicly supported benefits. It is estimated that by the year 2002, benefit levels for poor children and their families will be approximately 25 percent less than in 1995 (Ellwood & Gold, 1995).

Although the majority of families with dependents need child-care or long-term care assistance, these have generally been regarded as individual responsibilities. As this review has demonstrated, there are only limited public policy initiatives available to assist family caregivers and their dependents. The existing array of service options, from indirect public subsidies to direct service programs, is fragmented and inconsistent. Moreover, the current mix of policy and service initiatives raises questions regarding provision of and access to family support services. This fragmented approach is indicative of several basic value dilemmas inherent in American society: (1) the appropriate role of states, communities, businesses, and families in assisting dependent individuals; (2) the tension between publicly funded service provision and market economy service development; and (3) the appropriate level of federal, state, or local governmental involvement in assisting children, working-age adults, the elderly, families, and the employed. All of these issues reflect a basic ambivalence regarding private versus public responsibility for the welfare of our families.

A comprehensive and coordinated public policy framework—including expanding family leave policies and income support programs and developing more comprehensive child-care and long-term care systems—is necessary in order to develop a community based infrastructure that supports family care. To increase equity and accessibility, it is important that such policies integrate a multi-generational approach rather than continuing to rely on age-based restrictions. In the development of such a public response, a partnership among workers, families, employers, communal agencies, and the public sector is essential.

PART FIVE

Work and Family: Entering the Twenty-First Century

· 12 ·

RESEARCH DIRECTIONS

INTRODUCTION

Existing research models, including the resource and demand model utilized in this book, have provided useful information on how work and family responsibilities affect individuals and their work places. However, as noted in Chapter 8, these models typically do not explain the majority of variance in outcomes, such as role strain and work and family accommodations. Our findings suggest that there may well be other relevant factors or perspectives that have not received sufficient attention in existing theoretical and empirical models. Of particular interest are personal, interpersonal, and community resources that may help employees to manage more effectively the demands of their work and family situations.

In this chapter, we look first at the effectiveness and limitations of existing work and family program evaluation approaches and possible strategies for improvement. We then turn to the importance of broadening the scope of future research to reflect the diversity of individuals combining work and family and to provide a more comprehensive understanding of how individuals integrate their multiple role responsibilities. We will discuss the importance of attending to the personal characteristics of working caregivers, as well as enlarging the unit of analysis to include families, work groups, and societal variations. The final section focuses on emerging issues in work and family research, including the implications of evolving changes in the nature of work, the structure of families, gender roles, and the societal context within which work and family reside.

RESEARCH ON THE
EFFECTIVENESS OF WORK AND
FAMILY PROGRAMS AND POLICIES

Existing research has done a far better job of documenting deleterious work-place impacts associated with family-care responsibilities than with demonstrating the effectiveness of programs or policies designed to alleviate them. Evidence that work-place impacts exist is often interpreted to mean that interventions will reduce or even eliminate them. For example, estimates that employees' elder-care responsibilities result in approximately $2,500 of lost productivity per employee each year (Scharlach et al., 1991) have been utilized repeatedly to suggest that work-site interventions can automatically save employers hundreds of dollars per year for each caregiving employee.

As discussed in Chapter 10, while some work-place programs and policies appear to improve workers' job performance or reduce the strain of balancing work and family roles, others seem to have no or sometimes negative effects. Existing research on the effectiveness of intervention programs has been hampered by a variety of limitations, including the tendency of employers to implement programs that do not adequately reflect employee needs or are not adequately targeted to vulnerable employees. Other problems include: the failure to evaluate programs; methodological problems that limit the adequacy of program evaluations; and a focus on limited outcomes. We will examine such limitations and potential strategies for resolving them in future research.

Program Targeting

Intervention programs are typically implemented without an adequate assessment of employee needs or a clear understanding of the explicit processes by which change is hypothesized to occur. Sophisticated research designs are needed that can identify when, why, and for whom combining family care and paid work results in various outcomes. Process models can enable interventions to be targeted more accurately and be sufficiently intensive to produce measurable outcomes. In the absence of adequate models, it is not surprising that programs frequently do not produce their intended results and that evaluations fail to detect those results that are produced.

The combination of external circumstances and individual traits is what determines each employee's risk for negative outcomes at home or at work. Two individuals, both with similar dependent-care responsibilities, may have very diverse needs because of differences in their support networks, their personalities and expectations, and the needs of those for whom they are caring. In evaluating interventions, researchers should ask not simply whether programs work, but which programs work best under what conditions and for whom.

The importance of targeting research designs to reflect employee needs is illustrated by Zarit's 1990 re-analysis of data from a caregiver support group intervention. Whereas no overall effect of support was found when all treated caregivers were examined, a positive effect was found when the analysis was limited only to those who had entered the program with high baseline levels of caregiving strain. There are numerous examples of programs that, while well-intentioned, have had limited utilization or effectiveness, as noted in Chapter 10. As we have seen, what employees want is often not consistent with what employers offer. Considerably more information is needed regarding factors that determine when, or whether, employees will utilize programs and policies that are offered. Such analyses would ideally incorporate longitudinal designs that track employee service utilization from the time a child is born or a family member becomes ill.

Particularly needed are studies that examine work and family issues within the context of a company's overall organizational culture. As noted by Gonyea and Googins (1992), an organizational culture approach enables researchers and program developers to consider corporate norms and beliefs regarding employee family responsibilities, their attitudes toward changing societal factors and the impact on corporate well-being, and the role of key decision-makers in setting and implementing company work and family policies.

Lack of Program Evaluation

Most employers who implement work and family programs do not complete a formal evaluation to determine whether the programs are having a positive impact on their employees or on their company overall. For some companies, the programs have not been in effect long enough to study their impact; for others, the research is considered too costly, complex, and time-consuming.

Companies that do evaluate their work and family programs are typically concerned only with whether workers are satisfied, rather than with whether the programs actually impact absenteeism, job performance, or other outcomes. The ease of measuring perceived satisfaction, compared with the complexity of more rigorous examination of objective outcome measures, is a primary reason for this. It also seems that some employers are motivated by the need to *appear* responsive to workers' family needs, rather than by an expectation that programs will have measurable effects in other areas such as job performance. Some employers feel that they have "done enough" by implementing a program that satisfies employees. Subjective anecdotal reports provide a "human face" that may be more understandable by corporate audiences as an indication of programmatic success, than are rigorous objective measures. The lack of proven "bottom line" benefits, however, may make existing programs less defensible and the introduction of new programs less likely, in times of budgetary reductions.

Methodological Limitations

Substantial improvements are needed in the methodological sophistication of evaluation research on work and family programs and policies. Most existing evaluations have significant methodological limitations, typically associated with the use of nonexperimental, cross-sectional designs. Other common problems include the use of nonrepresentative samples and inappropriate comparison groups, the failure to collect pre-intervention data, and the lack of longitudinal designs.

Generalizing from existing work and family research has been hampered by reliance on nonrepresentative groups, particularly employees who work for large and heavily benefited employers. It is difficult to generalize about a particular policy when studies are limited to certain industries or specific companies.

Evaluations often compare outcomes for employees who utilize specific programs with those who do not. Such evaluations fail to account for the strong selection bias inherent in program utilization, which may mask any potential benefits of participation. Employees who have particularly stressful care situations, for example, are more likely to seek out family-related work-place programs. As we found in this study, this can result in the finding that employees who utilize such programs have higher levels of role strain and work interference than other employees. Controlled interventions that enable random assignment of employees to treatment and control conditions are needed. At a minimum, comparing employees providing care to those who have children or disabled relatives but are not providing care would be a better choice than comparing them to employees in general. Whenever possible, longitudinal research designs should be employed that enable statistical control of pre-intervention levels of relevant outcome variables.

A similar problem arises in evaluations that examine work-place outcomes at work sites with and without specific work and family programs. Work sites have substantial covarying differences, including management style and corporate culture, which contribute to the initial decision to implement specific programs. Work sites selected for comparison should be as similar as possible on relevant factors, and efforts should be made to control for features that might covary with the provision of family-friendly benefits.

Related difficulties occur when employers implement more than one program simultaneously, making it difficult to ascertain the effects of one or the other. To the extent possible, efforts should be made to disentangle the effects of separate programs, preferably by phasing in programs over an extended period of time and utilizing time-series methods to observe changes in outcomes of interest. Underlying changes in corporate culture or personnel that may have contributed to the introduction of new programs should be identified, and may have a greater overall impact on work and family outcomes than individual programs themselves.

Outcomes Investigated

Existing interventions have focused on eliminating or mitigating disjunctions between work and family domains, virtually ignoring potential benefits to individuals or society of integrating paid work and family-care roles. Investigations of strategies for enhancing the interface between paid work and family care could lead to significantly different interventions, with the potential to positively impact outcomes such as coping strategies at work and at home, effectiveness as a parent or caregiver, stress management techniques, and peer support.

Another important area for further investigation is the possibility that work and family policies may exacerbate existing gender inequities. If women are expected to take maternity leave when men are not taking comparable paternity leave, or are working part-time while men are working longer hours, they are likely to have lower incomes and may have more limited career advancements than men with comparable human capital. While this may reflect individual choice, it is important to note that such decisions are often constrained by social and economic realities. Many family benefits may be formally offered to all employees, but corporate cultures may make it very difficult for men to take advantage of such benefits. The benefits may be viewed as being designed only for women, reinforcing the status quo of women providing more care and earning less. In addition, families may be less able to afford the income loss if men utilize unpaid family-related benefits, since they typically earn more than women.

Work and family intervention research has been limited by its reliance on employer-sponsored programs, which typically reflect employer rather than family interests. In this context, family interference with work is typically seen as the problem, and interventions are designed with the ultimate goal of removing barriers to worker productivity. Reflecting a somewhat anachronistic perspective of the work place, self-reported absenteeism, tardiness, and time off during the work day are most commonly utilized as measures of work interference. Less often, self-reports of job commitment, morale, and job turnover are assessed. An examination of the impact of interventions on other entities such as families, communities, and society might conceivably find salutary benefits that transcend the limited realm of worker productivity, as well as unintended or undesirable secondary effects.

Research is needed to determine whether some work and family programs reinforce the ethic that work should take precedence over family. For example, the provision of sick child care may support the notion that it is more important for employees to be at work when their children are sick than to be at home caring for them. The long hours offered by many on- and off-site child-care providers can have a similar effect, potentially making it more difficult for employees to justify taking time from work or refusing to work overtime to be with their families. Elder-care resource and referral programs have been praised for their ability to help employees find nursing home care for their parents without interrupting their jobs. While such programs may create positive outcomes for employers and even for employees, their effects on children, parents, and communities should also be examined.

A related issue is whether the increase in family-friendly personnel policies may actually result in caregivers providing fewer hours of personal care

(Starrells et al., 1995), perhaps because they are able to access alternative community-based sources of assistance and can thereby reduce the amount and level of care they themselves provide. From a compensation perspective, some have argued that work-place supports can actually lead employees to place less value on family responsibilities.

BROADENING THE SCOPE
OF FUTURE RESEARCH

We now turn to the importance of broadening the scope of theoretical and empirical inquiry to reflect the diversity of individuals and their circumstances and to provide a more comprehensive understanding of how individuals integrate their work and family roles. Future research designs need to attend to the personal characteristics of working caregivers and utilize a longitudinal, life-course approach. We also consider the importance of enlarging the unit of analysis to include families, work groups, interactions across multiple domains, and societal variations.

Workers and Caregivers
as Unique Individuals

Our resource and demand model emphasizes the transactional nature of work and family roles and their associated social contexts. However, this and other models of work and family processes include only limited attention to the nature of the individual worker as a person, including such factors as human agency, personality, the potential for role enhancement, and the importance of subjective experience.

HUMAN AGENCY

Much of existing research treats workers as relatively passive respondents to the demands of their work and family situations. Employees might be better understood as constructive actors, attempting to adapt to potentially competing situations by selecting those actions and reactions that best meet their needs across the various domains in which they function. These include the need for mastery, intimacy, and effectiveness. Successfully meeting these needs, whether in one or in a variety of domains, is apt to be associated with greater personal well-being and life satisfaction. Considerably more research is needed regarding the coping strategies employees select as they attempt to minimize potential conflict and maximize potential benefits at home and at work.

We need to understand better the specific types of modifications employees make at home, at work, and in their personal and social lives, and the ways in which those accommodations differ for employed and nonemployed individuals. Little is known, for example, about how employees make up for the time lost when they need to miss work because of family demands or how they ensure that their dependents are cared for when they work overtime. Nor is much known about the conditions under which employees will terminate work to care for a child or assist an elderly relative, or how those conditions differ from the ones that lead caregivers to abandon their primary caregiving roles. Research is needed to identify which coping strategies are most adaptive for specific work and family situations, and the personal factors, behaviors, and resources that mediate such decision-making processes.

PERSONALITY

Personality research suggests that enduring psychological characteristics could have a substantial influence on how an individual responds to multiple role demands. Characteristics such as an individual's energy level, achievement orientation, extraversion, emotional stability, and conscientiousness are likely candidates for investigation. Personality characteristics might help explain why one individual experiences a specific combination of employment, caregiving, and support structures as overly stressful, while another finds it demanding but not overwhelming. In this regard, personality characteristics remain a potential resource which, at least to date, remain largely unresearched.

ROLE ENHANCEMENT

Much of the research on work and family has focused on the negative aspects of their interaction, with limited effort to investigate the potentially constructive aspects of combining work and family and how multiple role responsibilities may contribute to individual well-being. Most existing research has tacitly adopted a role-strain perspective, assuming family responsibilities, work responsibilities, and their interface to be inherently stressful. An alternative approach is a role-enhancement perspective, wherein multiple roles have the potential to enhance psychological well-being by providing opportunities for social integration, a sense of mastery, personal and social recognition, and fulfillment of disparate psychological and social needs. In fact, both role-strain and role-enhancement perspectives appear to have some support. Research to date supports the notion that multiple roles hold both risks and rewards.

Certainly, rapid social and economic changes contribute to personal and societal dislocation and stress, arguing for investigations of potential problems with changing work and family arrangements. Moreover, the negative results of combining work and family may seem more salient or apparent than the positive results, leading to a greater research focus on the negative. However, it seems that much existing work and family research is motivated in part by political agendas, either supporting "traditional family values" or greater social change. Negative outcomes and dire projections are more useful for advocacy purposes than are discussions of potential benefits. But whatever the explanation, there is a clear need for new research designs that consider both positive and negative outcomes of work and family integration, including the potential rewards and benefits of various combinations of work and family roles for men, women, children, the disabled, and society.

SUBJECTIVE EXPERIENCE

More extensive qualitative research on the subjective experience of family care can contribute substantially to our understanding of how individuals perceive and give meaning to their work and family situations. Of particular importance is research that examines how individuals and families themselves define and conceptualize the provision of assistance to family members. Kline and Cowan (1988), for example, note that paid labor, housework, and providing family care are all forms of "work," and most important is the manner in which these different domains and activities are perceived, by actors as well as by observers.

Questions that would benefit from further qualitative research include the following:

- Under what conditions and for whom is providing assistance to a family member considered a "burden" as opposed to a "blessing?"
- How do individuals define the term "caregiver" and under what conditions do individuals consider themselves, and one another, "caregivers"?
- To what extent are family-care outcomes affected by attitudes about the provision of care, including the prominence of caregiving roles, the meaning they provide, and the extent to which they are perceived as under one's personal control?

Existing work and family research tends to view individuals who have family-care responsibilities only as "care providers," rather than as participants in complex, multi-faceted relationships that have meaning and relevance in the lives of the participants that far exceed simple notions of services given and received. Although interactions among caregivers and care recipients may at times seem unidirectional, those involved may actually experience the relationships as mutually beneficial. Parents derive substantial personal and psychological benefits from parenting, even when children require a great deal of time and care.

There is ample evidence, moreover, that caring for elderly or disabled family members is not one-sided, and that the persons being helped are far more than simply passive care recipients. Most older adults are heavily involved in providing assistance to younger family members, as well as receiving it. Indeed, until about the age of 85, the average older person gives more practical and financial assistance to younger family members than he or she receives (Morgan, Schuster & Butler, 1991). For caregivers who are employed, elderly or disabled relatives may provide the child care or house-keeping that makes it possible for them to work outside the home. As Sally Gallagher (1994) notes in her book, *Older People Giving Care: Helping Family and Community*, much of this assistance is virtually unnoticed because it is an inherent part of family life. Moreover, ageist and handicapping stereotypes may blind us from seeing the important contributions made by elderly and disabled individuals. Qualitative research is needed to penetrate societal stereotypes and enhance our understanding of the subjective meanings of work and family care, for employees and care recipients alike.

Diversity in Individuals and Circumstances

As discussed in Chapter 9, we found substantial differences among employees in this study based on their gender, race, ethnicity, and occupational role. Women experienced higher levels of role strain than men, attributable in large part to the comparatively greater demands made on them at home and at work and the fewer resources available to them with which to meet those demands. Whites experienced especially high levels of role strain, even though they had the benefit of more resources than their African-American and Hispanic counterparts. These findings underscore the importance of increasing research attention to the needs and experiences of diverse groups of employees, including the cultural, societal, and personal factors that enable them to withstand demanding work and family situations without undue negative repercussions.

Theoretical models need to be examined in terms of their relevance for diverse groups. Fredriksen (1993b) found that a family-care model based on a stress and coping perspective explained considerably less variance in role strain and other caregiver outcomes for non-white caregivers than it did for white caregivers. It is likely that a model that defines caregiver outcomes primarily in terms of strain, and looks to "objective" demands of the care-giving situation as primary predictors, may not adequately represent the nature of the caregiving experience for many ethnic and racial minority groups. In developing more relevant family-care models, additional attention needs to be given to the influence of culturally mediated factors such as variations in filial norms and behaviors, interpretation, socialization, kinship support networks, and styles of coping.

One variable that has been overemphasized in research on adult dependent care has been age. Most of the research has focused on care of the elderly, with comparatively little attention to persons caring for younger adults. To some extent, this reflects the fact that the likelihood of chronic illness and disability increase with age. Yet the absolute number of persons living in the community who have activity limitations due to health conditions is almost the same for persons under the age of 65 as for persons age 65 or older. As our findings indicate, caregivers for persons under the age of 65 are apt to experience at least as much strain as caregivers for elderly persons. For most research purposes, the type and extent of care-recipient disability may be more appropriate selection criteria than age, although in some cases neither age nor disability may be as critical as other aspects of the caregiver's situation (such as the caregiver's health or competing responsibilities). Given present knowledge, care-recipient age should be treated as any other factor to be evaluated in terms of its potential contribution to various relevant outcomes. Gerontologists, program planners, and policy makers may well find "adult care" a considerably more useful (and less ageist) term than "elder care."

Workers, caregivers, and care recipients vary along a number of other dimensions that have not been taken into account adequately in existing models. The needs of working versus nonworking parents and caregivers, the perspectives of small versus large businesses, and the perspectives of "nontraditional" families, such as gay and lesbian parents, are especially in need of further study.

A Longitudinal, Life-Course Approach

Most work and family research conducted to date has been cross-sectional. As noted throughout this book, individuals' family responsibilities and their relationships to work shift as they traverse the life course. Only longitudinal designs can capture these changes, particularly in light of the disjunctions often associated with women's work patterns; and only life-course research can fully examine causal relationships, place family care and work responsibilities within the context of other life-cycle events, and explore how they ebb and flow over time. Life-course research allows investigators to explore the importance of contextual issues such as the following:

- How do culture-based variations in expectations and gender roles affect the likelihood, timing, nature, and duration of women's and men's caregiving experiences?

- How does family context, especially in light of variations in family forms (e.g., step-families) and family system characteristics and dynamics, affect the likelihood and nature of care provided?

- What are the ripple effects of combined work and family responsibilities on other family members, family relationships, and social networks?

- How do earlier experiences giving and receiving care affect later caregiving choices, behaviors, and attitudes? For example, what is the impact on later family caregiving of being abused as a child?

- Similarly, how does a parent's experience as a care provider for young children affect subsequent adult or elder care attitudes and responsibilities?

Looked at historically, who provides care as an adult may have more to do with the availability of alternative sources of care than with personal choice. For example, women born earlier in this century were less likely to have parents and other family members living for prolonged periods of time with disabilities than were women born later, and they had more siblings and neighbors to provide assistance. Consequently, they were less likely to become caregivers and provided care for shorter time periods than later cohorts (Robison et al., 1995). Despite increased labor-force participation, later cohorts of women are more likely to become caregivers of adults, largely because of a reduction in the number of siblings and fewer alternatives. Women who work more years are especially likely to become caregivers. Perhaps the economic necessity that caused them to work also prevented them from being able to pay for others to provide care in their stead. And it is possible that those who have the psychological, physical, and social resources to work have the necessary resources to assume family-care roles.

ENLARGING THE UNIT OF ANALYSIS

The majority of work and family research has taken place at the individual level. The advantage of studies at the individual level is that outcomes are frequently easy to measure and there is high internal validity, with the outcome and causal variables at similar levels of measurement. Unfortunately, many inputs and outcomes in the area of work and family are not at the individual level. For instance, while individuals may experience stress that can be measured physiologically or with surveys, the family as a whole may experience distress that results in divorce or dysfunction. Similarly, the effects on the work place have typically been measured in terms of the behavior of individual employees. Yet a work unit may be more or less functional, productive, or effective depending on the interplay among its members, each of whom is attempting to integrate work and personal responsibilities. Fernandez (1990), for example, found that 40 percent of employees reported being negatively impacted by dependent-care problems experienced by their coworkers.

NEED FULFILLMENT ACROSS DOMAINS

It has been argued that "work" takes place both in organizations and families, and what is relevant is the structure and meaning given to work across domains. This approach suggests that work and its impacts should be examined from multiple perspectives—individual, marital, familial, and work place. From the person-in-environment fit perspective, research needs to examine: (1) which combinations of work place, family, and individual conditions are associated with salutary outcomes, such as individual psychological well-being, marital satisfaction, effective family functioning, children's social competence, and functional independence in disabled family members; and (2) how individuals and groups meet their needs across various domains. Potentially fruitful areas of research include the implications of meeting affiliative needs in the work place (e.g., through emotional and social support from coworkers), meeting mastery needs at home (e.g., through feelings of self-efficacy in parenting or dependent care), or meeting a large proportion of one's needs in a single domain to the potential neglect of other areas. Hochschild (1997) has documented the situation of some women for whom work settings have come to provide more rewards than those available at home and who, therefore, spend increasing amounts of time at work and less time at home.

CROSS-NATIONAL RESEARCH

Work and family outcomes are apt to be more salient when measuring aggregate societal benefits and costs than when measuring individual stress levels. In addition to being highly interdependent, work and family systems are embedded in cultural features and social institutions that vary substantially across countries. These factors should be included in any attempt to understand or model work-family processes. Exploration of societal customs and practices is especially important for the United States, which differs substantially from other developed countries in its lack of formal acknowledgment—within institutional structures, laws, and cultural norms—of the needs of families, children, and the disabled.

Wilensky (1990) created a family policy index to highlight the innovativeness and expansiveness of a country's family policies. Included in this index are three policy clusters: (1) the length of paid and unpaid parental leave; (2) the availability and accessibility of public day care; and (3) the flexibility of retirement options. Wilensky found that a country's score on the family policy index was directly related to the percentage of the population aged 65 and older, the percentage of women in the work force, the power of leftist political forces, and the extent of democratic corporatism (reflected in a centralized policy-making structure). The United States scored in the lower third of the countries examined.

Cross-national research can add to our knowledge in a variety of ways. Because of the scarcity of large-scale interventions in the United States, analysis of quantitative international data comparing interventions across countries is one way to assess the outcomes of work and family policies. Ruhm and Teague (1997), for example, compared parental leave policies in 15 European countries and found that longer leaves—from 9 months to a year—were associated with increased female labor-force participation, while leaves of shorter duration were associated with decreased participation and income.

Qualitative studies of variations among cultures provide important insight regarding attitudes toward family care and work, role expectations, and potential support structures, such as extended families and domestic help. Such studies can help to reveal the outcomes of ongoing changes taking place in domains not typically studied in the United States. There is some evidence that international variations in family policies and individual practices reflect psychological and social factors such as the perceived role of the state, whether family is seen as an individual or collective responsibility, ideologies of families and childhood, including the social construction of the ideal mother, and whether there is a belief in equality, especially between the sexes (Lewis, 1997).

Cross-national research can help address conceptual issues regarding the very nature of work and family in modern society. As we discussed in Chapter 4, a number of macro-level theories have been advanced to understand the relationship between work and family, including Marxist, feminist, resource dependence, and institutional theories. From the Marxist perspective, changes in the nature of family life can best be understood as responses to capitalism and its inherent power structure. Feminist theorists, on the other hand, emphasize how women's roles at home and in the work place are intertwined. They focus on the effects of patriarchy, both in the work place and in the family, and the constraining and oppressive nature of institutionalized gender roles for women. From a political economic perspective, resource-based theories postulate that actors will behave according to the nature of their exchange relationships, while institutional theory emphasizes that organizations are permeable and, therefore, strongly influenced by their environments. Cross-national research provides a useful mechanism for examining the accuracy of predictions stemming from these various viewpoints.

EMERGING ISSUES

Work and family are dynamic constructs, evolving over time in response to the changing social, political, and economic context. There are a number of emerging issues that have the potential to alter substantially the relationship between work and family. These include changes in the nature of work, the structure of families, gender roles, and the societal context of family care and work.

Current work and family models do not typically recognize the increasingly contingent, entrepreneurial nature of the work force. It is not yet known whether workers will find it easier to manage their family responsibilities because of the potentially greater flexibility inherent in these new employment arrangements, or whether it will be more difficult because paid work will likely require more coordination and management in the future than in the past, when jobs were more stable. To some extent, the answer may depend on whether workers are choosing these new arrangements or are being forced to adopt them. There is some evidence that high-performance work places, marked by increased employee commitment and accountability, can exacerbate conflict between work and family responsibilities (Appelbaum & Berg, 1997). Workfare—work in exchange for public income support—is an especially timely and important aspect of the work and family juncture that requires further analysis as these public policies are being implemented.

Families are changing as well. Given the growing diversity of parenting and family-care arrangements, including care by single parents, gay and lesbian parents, grandparents, and other "nontraditional" families, researchers need to examine the adequacy of conceptual models. It is an empirical question whether the interface between work and family is experienced the same way by individuals in diverse family contexts, and whether interventions that are effective with one group will prove to be equally effective with another.

It is important to examine changes in the salience of gender roles, as well as the increasing ethnic and racial diversity and economic stratification in our society, as critical variables in work and family research. Certain employee groups, such as those from non-white racial and ethnic backgrounds or those with low occupational status, have not been adequately studied. Much of the research evaluating nonwork-place family interventions, by contrast, has focused on poor or at-risk families, including children obtaining child care through Head Start or disabled elders receiving Medicaid. Research on work and family programs needs to be more representative of the diversity of employees and the range of their family situations and experiences.

The changing nature of men's and women's gender roles has important implications for the integration of work and family responsibilities. Men's labor-force participation rates have decreased slightly in the last few years, mostly due to earlier retirement, whereas women's participation has leveled off, but does not appear to be declining. With more women working and more older men out of the work force, questions arise regarding traditional gender roles. Will men come to value family and other relational aspects of their lives more highly? Will nonworking, healthy older men begin to provide more care for grandchildren or disabled adults than they have in the past? The shifting nature of gender roles provides an opportunity to explore further the acquisition and integration of family care and work roles.

Finally, there is a need for increased attention to the societal context in which work and family reside. In a society in which individual responsibility is prized, the provision of family care is often considered an "individual choice" rather than a community or societal function. In this context, the recent semantic change from "work and family" to "work/life" seems especially notable. Researchers interested in the efficacy of potential solutions to the difficulties of work and family integration need to consider relevant social, political, and economic contexts within which we live. This transitional period offers an exciting opportunity to examine work and family impacts associated with changes in the larger society, as well as in the nature of work and families.

SUMMARY

In this chapter, we have examined methodological and conceptual issues relevant to the future of work and family research. Strategies necessary to improve the development and evaluation of work and family programs include specifying program outcomes, targeting programs to reflect the needs of those employees who are most vulnerable, and moving beyond simple measures of user satisfaction as proxies for intervention effects. There is a need for substantial improvements in the methodology of evaluation research on work and family programs and policies, including more sophisticated research designs, appropriate comparison groups, longitudinal studies, and representative samples. As we expand the scope of family and work inquiry, future research needs to attend to the limitations of individual-level analysis, the importance of recognizing diversity among individuals and their circumstances, and the need to enlarge the focus of analysis to incorporate families, work groups, communities, and societies.

In this book we have argued that considerably greater attention be given to factors that put workers at risk for deleterious personal and family outcomes. Our research suggests that vulnerability may be greatest for employees with particularly demanding work and family responsibilities in the context of inadequate resources such as health, social support at work and at home, or availability of reliable care providers. Further identification of factors contributing to personal and familial vulnerability versus well-being will require moving beyond existing models of individuals' work and family roles. Several theoretical approaches not yet adequately explored in existing work and family research, such as institutional, feminist, and cross-national approaches, provide an opportunity to explore the integration of work and family within a social, political, and economic context.

Societal forces are the context for work and family roles. The evolving nature of work, family structure, gender roles, and the social, political, and economic contexts within which work and family reside serve as critical issues for future research developments. Consideration of factors such as these can enable researchers and practitioners to understand better the forces that have resulted in and continue to affect the interrelationship between work and family. In the next, concluding chapter we will discuss directions necessary to strengthen our personal and societal commitments to family and work as we enter the twenty-first century.

· 13 ·

CONCLUSION

Family and work are central to the lives of most Americans. Yet the process of integrating the demands of our families and our jobs remains a source of stress and continual accommodation for many of us. Moreover, the societal balance between work and family is apt to change dramatically as a result of ongoing transformations in the age and ethnic structure of the population, the composition of the family, and the nature of work. As these social and demographic changes are occurring in American society, it is an opportunity to reflect on and publicly reconsider the relative balance between family and work responsibilities.

The research described in this book demonstrates the significance of both family care and work roles, and the paramount importance of understanding the characteristics of both. Our findings suggest that, despite tremendous social and communal changes and substantial demands on their time and energy, workers continue to have extensive family-care responsibilities. These family responsibilities are quite diverse, differing by types of generational care, by family composition, and by care arrangements.

Family and work constitute a reciprocal dynamic relationship, impacted by demands and available resources in both domains. Overall, however, demands far exceed resources in their salience for role strain and other employee and family outcomes. Women, employees from racial and ethnic minority groups, and those with lower occupational status are especially likely to experience greater demands at home and at work, yet they have fewer resources. To date, existing work-place and community programs and policies have not done an adequate job of responding to the diverse needs of working families. Indeed, it frequently seems that these programs are attempting to meet differing and sometimes conflicting goals, reflecting the diverging needs of families and business in this country.

In this concluding chapter we will explore ways to respond effectively to the increasing demands in our lives and achieve a relative balance between family and work responsibilities. We question what is an appropriate balance and what constitutes compatibility between these two life domains.

248

What are we trying to achieve, who is to benefit, and what are the costs? Under what conditions is a partnership feasible between families, business, and the community? What is the role of each in addressing the critical juncture between work and family as we enter the twenty-first century?

THE NATURE OF FAMILY-CARE RESPONSIBILITIES

As the findings in this book reflect, many working Americans have extensive family-care responsibilities, including caring for children, ill and chronically disabled working-age adults, and the frail elderly. One-third of employees in the study reported here had child-care responsibilities, and nearly one-fourth were providing assistance to an ill or disabled adult family member or friend. In all, about half of all employees surveyed had some kind of ongoing family-care responsibility.

Our commitment to care remains high; it is the context of family care that is changing. Work and family issues are in part an outgrowth of the shifting economy and the changes in traditional communities and neighborhoods, rather than solely an individual and family problem. The changes in our communities are themselves due to economic, societal, and cultural pressures, rather than just individual choice. To maintain a viable standard of living, it is increasingly necessary for families to have a second income or even to hold multiple jobs. As more family members are working, more children are receiving out-of-home care. In the U.S. today, more than 10 million children under the age of five need care while their parents are working, with increasing numbers receiving nonfamilial care at younger ages (Casper, 1996). In addition, as a result of changing labor-force participation rates and geographic mobility, the care of the frail elderly and the chronically ill is increasingly occurring at a distance.

Type of Care

Family-care responsibilities are becoming more diverse, because of differing generational responsibilities and differing care relationships and arrangements. We often treat work and family issues as static, but to capture the full range, extent, and changing nature of employees' family-care and work-related responsibilities, they need to be considered across the life span. Care responsibilities change as we move though time and across generations. Moreover, the configuration between work and family responsibilities is not a one-time career decision; it evolves continuously, across life-cycle stages throughout one's family and working life.

In this study, we found substantial differences in the impact of combining work and family roles, depending on the specific type of family-care responsibilities. In general, employees who were caring for children as well as elderly or disabled adults experienced the greatest demands on their time and energy, but also had high levels of work and family resources. We found that physical strain and financial strain were highest for working parents, especially those who also had adult-care responsibilities; whereas emotional strain was highest for employees with adult-care responsibilities, especially those who also had child-care responsibilities.

Similarities and differences among employees with diverse family-care responsibilities have not been adequately reflected in efforts to support workers and their families. Nor do existing programs and policies address the variety of family structures and the important role that persons other than immediate biological family members often play in the provision of care. Programs and policies need to reflect and respond to this diversity and recognize the importance of a range of family-care providers.

Gender, Race/Ethnicity, and Occupational Role

Reducing strain between work and family roles requires that families find ways to reduce demands and more equitably distribute family-care responsibilities—both in the provision of care and in securing and maintaining formal care arrangements. Yet the division of responsibility for family care remains highly gendered, despite the fact that most women are in the paid work force. Although men are providing significantly more family care than they did two decades ago, women are still doing 50 percent more of the household work (Higgins et al., 1994), reflecting power differentials as well as "women's reluctance to give up family work and men's resistance to take it on" (Thompson & Walker, 1989).

In this study, we found that female employees experienced both higher demands and fewer resources when combining family care and employment than did their male counterparts. Women also reported slightly higher levels of role strain after controlling for social and demographic characteristics and family care and employment resources and demands. Yet although 'work and family' is generally coined as a women's issue, it also significantly impacted the lives of the men in our study, frequently resulting in difficulties combining work and family-care responsibilities. Moreover, men are less likely to be public about their work and family concerns and seem to be stigmatized more than women if they utilize relevant work and family policies at the work site.

While it is important to understand the differences between women and men in relation to work and family, it is important that such an analysis does not simply perpetuate stereotypes, mask the similarities that may actually exist, or ultimately narrow our interpretation and response to work and family issues. As long as work and family balance is defined solely as a women's issue, it will continue to be marginalized. Furthermore, we cannot achieve balance unless men take more responsibility for family care. As long as there is a gendered division of family care in the home, there cannot be gender equality in the work place.

Like women, racial and ethnic minorities and those in low-status occupations all tend to provide the most family care with more limited resources at home and at work. Likely reflecting the intersection between social and economic vulnerability and gender, race and ethnicity, and occupational status, clerical staff, women and minority employees in this study tended to have fewer economic resources with which to offset the demands of family care. Lower levels of social and economic resources have consistently been linked to increased vulnerability to stress and health problems.

Likely reflecting differences in interpretation, socialization, and methods of coping when integrating work and family responsibilities, gender and race/ethnicity were significant but relatively small contributors to role strain after controlling for background characteristics, demands, and resources. These findings illustrate that difficulties in combining work and family care responsibilities are largely a function of differences in work and family demands and resources, rather than personal structural characteristics. These findings underscore the importance of increasing research attention to the needs and experiences of diverse groups of employees with family-care responsibilities, while maintaining an awareness that differences by gender, race, and occupational status are likely multi-causal in nature.

As we strive toward equality at the work place, the division of responsibility for caring has not changed, and we have not redistributed family-care demands. While we cannot achieve equality without full participation in all spheres of life, including family care, employment, and public governance, our formal systems of care are not being transformed to meet the demands and needs of caring. Unless we begin to discuss publicly and consider the significant role and value of family care, there will be a high personal cost among employees with the primary care of family members, the care received by dependents may be inadequate, and equality will likely remain elusive.

A FAMILY-CARE MODEL

The literature on the interface of work and family roles and the research on family caregiving have evolved quite independently, each from separate traditions with differing underlying assumptions. The work and family literature emphasizes conflict between work and family, with the primary emphasis on work. The caregiving literature highlights the demands inherent in caring for an elderly adult family member, primarily focusing on the experience of the caregiver and the provision of care. In this book, we presented a family-care model to integrate and synthesize key components of these two, sometimes discrepant conceptual and empirical traditions.

The family-care model utilized here was based on transactional stress and role theory approaches to understanding the culmination of work and family responsibilities. This combination enabled us to examine the interplay between role demands and the availability of social resources in both work and family domains, while highlighting the particular factors that most directly affected the stress process. Among the factors we identified as most likely to place employees at risk of experiencing detrimental consequences associated with their work and family roles were child care, demanding work and family situations, and problems with care arrangements. Especially at risk for role strain and occupational and familial impacts are employees who experience difficulty arranging care that is affordable, accessible, dependable, and of good quality, and those with especially demanding jobs.

THE INTERPLAY OF
FAMILY CARE AND WORK

Family care and work responsibilities have a reciprocal and synergistic impact on one another. Many of the conditions that make family care more stressful, such as caring for someone who has heavy care needs, also impact job satisfaction and performance. At the same time, many conditions that contribute to job strain, such as heavy job demands, make it more difficult for employees to manage their family-care responsibilities. Work and family can impact one another in positive ways as well. Satisfaction at home can help to lessen the impact of problems on the job, and good experiences at work can positively affect family life.

Positive and negative effects arising from work and family responsibilities can and do occur simultaneously. For example, working mothers often report high levels of strain but also higher levels of income, satisfaction, and social support than nonworking mothers. Caregivers of ill and disabled adults often report high levels of stress along with positive consequences gained from their work and family-care responsibilities. Given that combining family care and work responsibilities can result in such diversity of experience, it is important to understand under what conditions positive consequences might be maximized and strain minimized.

The degree of satisfaction or conflict experienced by employees with family-care responsibilities is not about the simple fact of being employed or about the occupancy of dual roles or the overall number of such roles. Rather it reflects the quality of people's experiences. The findings from this book suggest that people's experiences are impacted by the relative balance between demands and resources; high demands combined with low resources tend to lead to conflict and distress. A healthy balance will most likely be achieved by creating optimal conditions in which demands are offset by the rewards gained from effectively managing both work and family responsibilities.

Although substantial lip service is given to the goal of creating this balance, it is unlikely that it will be realized given the underlying values that define the relationship between work and family in American society. Given such robust American values as individual self-determination, the work ethic, and free enterprise in the pursuit of capital accumulation, there remains tremendous ambivalence regarding appropriate responsibility for the care of dependent family members and the relationship between work and family. Moreover, home and family boundaries seem to be more permeable than work boundaries, leaving personal time and family life especially vulnerable to interference from work.

Most Americans, both women and men, rate their families as of first importance in their lives (Chilman, 1979, 1993). Yet families seem to be receiving less of our energy and time. For example, the Carnegie Council on Adolescent Development found that children spend significantly less time with adults than they did a few decades ago. Among employees caring for disabled adults, employment generally takes precedence over the provision of care. While caregiving responsibilities typically occupy a relatively small percentage of an employee's working years, women who are both caregivers and workers are more likely to discontinue active caregiving than to leave their jobs (Moen et al., 1994). This is not surprising, given the financial benefits and social significance of being employed and the lack of societal recognition for family caregiving.

Family and Work Demands

The greatest barrier to employees' ability to balance their work and family-care responsibilities is the increasingly demanding nature of the two roles. In this study, family care and work demands were by far the most significant predictor of problems integrating work and family, across all types of care. We found that family and work demands had the major influence in determining the extent of family and work accommodations and role strain, far outweighing the contribution of personal and social characteristics and family and work resources.

Employees today are experiencing increased work-place demands, and many report that these demands are increasingly impacting their family lives. As the work place and family care are changing, we must consider the extent to which workers can keep pace with increased demands. Resources alone won't likely reduce strain or difficulty in integrating roles. To date, most family-friendly policies have served to increase employees' availability for work, without attending to the overall issue of work demands versus family needs. Such policies and programs will likely be ineffective.

FAMILY DEMANDS

In the research discussed in this book, the family demands that most significantly impacted employees were problems with care arrangements and the disability levels of those receiving care. The critical importance of accessibility and availability of adequate care for dependent family members is an issue that cuts across all types of family care. When care arrangements are dependable and of reasonable quality, employees tend to experience less strain with dual role responsibilities. When care arrangements are inadequate, caregivers are more likely to experience greater personal stress and care recipients are more likely to suffer from poor quality care. Caring for a disabled child or adult can further increase the level and unpredictability of caregiving needs, exacerbating family members' difficulties in securing adequate care arrangements.

WORK-PLACE DEMANDS

Work demands were a major predictor of role strain and work and family accommodations for employees in our study. There is ample evidence that work is becoming more demanding as a result of tremendous changes in the nature of work and a growing contingent work force. Employees today are likely to have greater demands and responsibilities and less job security than in previous decades. In her book *The Overworked American*, Juliet Schor (1991) estimated that Americans now work, on average, one month a year more than they did 30 years ago, at least in part because they are earning less in terms of real wages and also to demonstrate their commitment to the work place in an era of decreased job security.

The corporate American work place still tends to define contribution and commitment primarily through visibility and presence. The assumption is that to succeed at the work place, individuals must be present at work, work long hours, and be continuously committed to work as a top priority. "Face time" rather than productivity is the key measure of job commitment, even though hourly work productivity is higher when hours are shorter (Schor, 1991). Moreover, technological advances provide increased opportunity for extending work hours and locations, enabling work to encroach further into employees' family lives.

Traditionally, businesses have responded to work and family issues from a paternalistic stance, as a form of corporate welfare. Thus, the response of business to work and family issues has focused on individual accommodations rather than structural change within the organization. While "family-friendly" policies such as increasing flexibility at the work place are often advanced as helpful in alleviating caregiving strain, the findings reported here suggest that work demands contribute more strongly to difficulties combining work and family-care responsibilities. Initiatives to provide more employment flexibility while maintaining comparable or heavier work demands will likely do little to relieve the pressure to meet those demands. Furthermore, the blurring of boundaries currently occurring will likely benefit the work place more than families, since boundaries at home tend to be more permeable than boundaries at work.

The "Family-Friendly" Work Place:
Myth or Promise?

Some have questioned whether it is really in the best interest of individual businesses to be truly "family friendly," if that means doing what is necessary to help employees and their families. Employer work and family initiatives are typically predicated on the idea of increasing employee work time and productivity, rather than improving the quality of employees' lives, the lives of their families, or the society in which employees live and in which the company conducts business. Lambert (1993) has argued that "family friendly" is a misnomer, since most work and family policies and programs are actually "work supports," designed to ensure that work takes precedence over employees' family lives. Information and referral services, for example, are primarily designed to help employees meet family needs so that they can be more involved in work and more productive on the job. As *Fortune* magazine intimated in its cover story on March 17, 1997, "Families are no longer a big plus for a corporation; they are a big problem. An albatross" (Morris, 1997).

Indeed, there is growing evidence that employees' personal lives are suffering considerably more than their work lives as a result of work-family conflict. A 1994 Massachusetts Mutual Life Insurance public opinion survey on *Commitment and American Society* found that nearly half of respondents felt torn between their jobs and their family commitments, while only 20 percent said they were having problems fulfilling their work commitments (Bankert et al., 1996). In a 1992 study by Boston University's Center on Work and Family, 56 percent of employees at a large computer company said that they "always" or "most of the time" wished for more time with their families, up from 46 percent in 1985 (Bankert et al., 1996). Despite the increased complexity and challenges of family life in America, it is work that seems to be garnering more and more of our time and attention, to the possible detriment of our families.

These problems get to the heart of the purpose of work and family programs. While there is clearly a need for increased awareness of and solutions to the work and family pressures experienced by today's workers and caregivers, some of the solutions most promoted may benefit the work place at the expense of family or societal well-being. Lotte Bailyn makes this point in her fable at the beginning of her chapter "The Impact of Corporate Culture on Work-Family Integration" (1997). She describes a company that formerly employed only short people. This creates a problem, since the door to the company was built for short people so the tall people couldn't get in. The solution the company arrives at is to offer classes on how to stoop down and fit through the door, and to train its managers to be understanding in case the difficult entrance makes the tall people a little late. This parable suggests the need to consider whether some of the work and family programs offered by employers may be providing stopgap help to employees while avoiding or perhaps even exacerbating some of the underlying structural problems inherent in the way work places operate.

A PARTNERSHIP BETWEEN FAMILIES, BUSINESS, AND THE COMMUNITY

Society now is faced with the challenge of identifying and supporting strategies that have the potential to yield productive workers, produce healthy children, support well-functioning families, and enhance individual well-being. These goals can be accomplished only by understanding the conditions that result in satisfying work and family life, and through the cooperation of families, employers, and communities in the context of social values, practices, and policies that aim toward "family and work compatibility."

As we enter the twenty-first century, we must ask ourselves how we can best integrate and increase the compatibility between work and family roles. We prefer the concept of compatibility over "family-friendly work place," because it more clearly illustrates the contribution of both families and businesses in addressing work and family issues. Rather than maintaining the rather paternalistic stance that a family-friendly work place can single-handedly address work and family issues, a compatibility perspective recognizes that the goals and needs of these two domains can be both complementary and incompatible. For example, children provide families with a sense of continuity, as well as providing businesses with the next generation of workers. On the other hand, businesses increasingly want employees to be flexible to meet occupational demands, while family-care responsibilities tend to decrease that flexibility.

In our search for compatibility, we need to recognize that skills and knowledge learned in one domain can be transferred to the other, thereby benefiting both roles. Toward a relative balance between family care and work, we need to consider more fully how to distribute family-care demands. As a society, it will be necessary to consider the needs of employees, families, and businesses in relation to the larger community. Given the rewards associated with family care, ways need to be found to enable family members to spend more time, not less, with those for whom they care. And given the link between family welfare and the welfare of communities, all will benefit from investing in the economic security of those providing care.

Business' Role in Balancing Work and Family

Business has an important stake in work and family issues. The interrelationship between work and family has implications for the economic viability of the larger society, as well as for business and families. Work loss associated with marital distress, for example, has been estimated to cost businesses $6.8 billion per year (Forthofer et al., 1996). Moreover, the ability of families to provide adequate care and socialization for young children has significant implications for preparing the next generation of qualified employees.

Given current and future changes in the labor force, companies will increasingly need to compete for employees. If family-sensitive personnel policies can increase the attractiveness of an employer and assist in the retention of productive employees, they will be contributing to the corporate bottom line. Employees who have access to family-responsive policies tend to report higher levels of organizational commitment and decreased likelihood of terminating employment. Research suggests that the benefits of such policies extend beyond those who use them. Family-friendly policies symbolize an organizational-level concern for employees, which creates and promotes positive attachment to the organization.

At a time of retrenchment in public spending, the involvement of the corporate sector in providing extensive family-care benefits is particularly important. Yet having family-care benefits available through the work place may create a two-tiered system of benefits: one service system for those tied to the corporate sector and another for those dependent on public subsidies or programs. Linking family-care benefits to employment also raises other serious equity and access issues. For example, the provision of services becomes dependent on such factors as the type and size of business, the unionization of particular industries, and the overall health of the local economy. Access to employee benefits, moreover, is related to such factors as seniority and occupational status, with those in the higher-status positions getting a disportionate share of the benefits and wages. While family caregivers are primarily women, the majority of female workers are concentrated in low-paying positions, and persons with the lowest incomes are at highest risk of having to terminate employment to meet their family-care responsibilities. Given that more women, racial and ethnic minorities, and persons from lower socioeconomic classes are unemployed or working in part-time, low-paying positions with lower status, they are the least likely to be served by such work-place initiatives.

Yet it is clear that business has an essential role in creating conditions necessary to increase the compatibility between work and family. Employers can do several things: (1) assist employees to locate and pay for needed family-care services; (2) provide employees with the job flexibility they need to be able to utilize those services and to provide care in the way that best meets their unique circumstances and the needs of their families; (3) create an organizational climate that views the well-being of employees and their families as a key component of corporate business planning and goal-setting; (4) and assist in the development of a community-based infrastructure that offers adequate child-care and adult-care services.

If business is to support workers in meeting their work and family responsibilities, organizations must see work-family compatibility as a legitimate issue, with the support of management at all levels and recognition of the role of organizational culture as central to work and family solutions. Adoption of a life-cycle approach would assist business in recognizing that employees' family situations change over time and that they should restructure work paths to include approaches other than a strictly chronological-age approach. The impact of long work hours and demanding jobs must be considered, with a shift from "face time" to "productive" work time. Further, it would benefit business to recognize that employees' skills developed through family and personal interests may actually assist them in reaching their organizational goals.

The Community

The community is an important, yet largely neglected stakeholder in the work and family debate. Whether because most family members are now employed away from the home or because of differing geographic mobility among age groups, the breakdown of traditional neighborhoods, the growth of a consumer-driven economy that demands increased individual productivity, or the predominance of an ethic of individual responsibility over mutual concern, communities no longer provide the supports that families need as they attempt to respond effectively to the work, family, and personal demands with which they are faced.

A public response is needed to support families as they provide care for dependent family members. A comprehensive family-sensitive public policy framework, toward a community-based infrastructure that supports family care, will necessitate expanding family-leave policies and developing more comprehensive child-care and long-term care services. Such policies won't be effective, however, unless they appeal across racial and class lines. To reduce problems in securing and maintaining care assistance, a public policy response must attend to the quality, dependability, accessibility, and availability of care. Furthermore, to increase equity and accessibility, it is important that such policies integrate a multi-generational approach rather than continuing to base access on age.

The establishment of a family-sensitive public policy agenda will not be easy. There are no inexpensive solutions to insuring high-quality care of dependents. Yet we are already paying high costs for not adequately investing in our families. For industrialized nations, the U.S. has among the highest rates of infant mortality, divorce, crime, and drug and alcohol addiction, problems that are related in large part to the lack of adequate support for families and communities.

As we enter the twenty-first century, public policies need to reflect the changing structure and diverse nature of our society. Consideration should be given to expanding the definition of "immediate family." Presently, most work and family programs and benefits extend only to an employee's spouse, child, or parent. Yet workers often have care responsibilities for other relatives or loved ones, including nonmarried partners, siblings, in-laws, grandparents, grandchildren, and other extended family members. As families become more diverse, it is important to define family more broadly and encompass the full range of care responsibilities. In this study, more than 50 percent of respondents caring for someone under the age of 65 had caregiving situations that did not fit the definition of "family" utilized in current federal and state family-leave policies.

Community-based and work-place programs need to be evaluated with regard to their ability to cross institutional barriers—to ensure that employees with high care demands and low resources have equitable access to support services. Public policies need to be modified, as necessary, to ensure that they are culturally sensitive and provide equitable access to persons regardless of age, gender, race and ethnicity, sexual orientation, and occupational status.

NEXT STEPS

We are living at a time when the pace of life seems to be escalating, technological linkages are expanding, and time is a shrinking commodity. Yet as a society we must strengthen our families and invest in the development of qualified and competent workers. We must find ways to share our time and energies more successfully among our families, our jobs, and our communities.

In response to the many work and family challenges raised in this book, as a first step we advocate for further development of community-based consortiums to facilitate regional partnerships between employees, businesses, communities, and governments. Among the many potentially competing issues facing such consortiums, most critical is the need to enhance the quantity and quality of community-based care. Investment of adequate resources is necessary to develop an infrastructure that provides comprehensive high-quality, safe, and dependable child-care and adult-care services. It is imperative that such partnerships work together to ensure that communal and societal structures provide access to employment, with full-time pay to raise a family above the poverty level. The development and expansion of community-based consortiums can provide an important opportunity to promote public dialogue on the many critical family and work issues facing us today.

If we are to invest in our children and foster a caring approach to those in the community who are chronically disabled, we must develop mechanisms and institutions that promote compatibility between family care and employment responsibilities. As we do so, it is essential that we differentiate between efforts that are adaptations to existing structures, norms, and cultures and efforts to change these norms. Ultimately, the most effective efforts may well be those directed at changing social norms and structures to enhance the mutual well-being of individuals, families, work organizations, and society as a whole.

Through examining the richness and diversity of people's lives, we will likely come to understand more fully multiple ways to effectively integrate work and family roles. If indeed it takes a village to raise a child, and if the health of a society is measured by the way it treats the old and the young, it is critical that we continue to explore innovative ways to reinvest in our families and our communities. By working together to develop a more equitable partnership among families, employers, and communities we may produce a society in which work and family serve to support and enhance one another in ways as yet undiscovered. This is the challenge we face as we enter the twenty-first century.

Appendix

WORK AND FAMILY SURVEY

This questionnaire concerns work and family responsibilities of Laboratory employees. Please answer the questions on this page and return the survey, even if you do not currently have child care, elder care, or adult dependent care responsibilities. *ALL OF YOUR RESPONSES WILL BE KEPT STRICTLY CONFIDENTIAL.*

1. Do you currently have children for whom you have child care responsibilities?

Check all that apply:

* 1.___ YES, I currently have children 12 or under for whom I have child care responsibilities.
* 2.___ YES, I currently have children 13-18 for whom I have child care responsibilities.
   3.___ NO, I do not currently have children for whom I have child care responsibilities, but I expect to have children within the next five years.
   4.___ NO, I do not currently have children for whom I have child care responsibilities, and I do not expect to have children within the next five years.

2. Do you currently assist an adult family member or friend who has a physical or mental health problem, a disability, or is elderly? (Examples of assistance: offering emotional support, providing or arranging for housekeeping or personal care, monitoring the health of an elderly person who lives at a distance, assisting with financial matters, etc.)

Check all that apply:

* 1.___ YES, I currently assist someone age 65 or older.
* 2.___ YES, I currently assist someone age 18-64 who has a health problem or a disability.
   3.___ NO, I do not currently provide assistance, but I have done so within the past five years.
   4.___ NO, I do not currently provide assistance, but I may need to do so within the next five years.
   5.___ NO, I do not currently provide assistance, and I do not anticipate needing to do so within the next five years.

*

> **If you answered "YES" to question #1 OR question #2,**
> **PLEASE GO ON TO THE NEXT PAGE.**

> If you answered "NO" to both questions (you do not have children for whom you have child care responsibilities and you do not provide assistance to an adult family member or friend), stop here and return the survey. Please fold and staple the entire questionnaire so the address on the back is visible.

Please answer the following questions if you have children for whom you have child care responsibilities OR if you provide assistance to an adult family member or friend.

3. The following are a number of ways that an employer might help employees with their family responsibilities. Please check those benefits, policies or programs that you would be likely to use if they were available.

1.___ Workshops or seminars on child care, adult care, or other work/family issues

2.___ Support groups for employees with child care or adult care responsibilities

3.___ Child care center at or near the Laboratory

4.___ Help locating quality child care services near your home

5.___ Help locating services for an ill, disabled, or elderly adult in the community where he or she lives

6.___ Long term care insurance to cover family members

7.___ Part-time work or job sharing

8.___ Ability to do some of your work at home

9.___ Ability to take an unpaid family leave without loss of benefits, for child care or to care for an ill family member

10.___ Ability to use sick leave or unpaid family leave to care for a domestic partner or friend or his/her children

11.___ Ability to use sick leave or vacation time donated by colleagues or co-workers

---

If you have children for whom you have child care responsibilities, please GO ON TO THE NEXT PAGE.

If you provide assistance to an adult family member or friend, BUT you do not have children for whom you have child care responsibilities, please SKIP TO PAGE 6.

PART II: YOUR CHILDREN

4. How many children do you have for whom you have child care responsibilities?
   _____(number of children)

5. What are the <u>ages</u> of these children? (Please begin with your <u>youngest</u> child.)

   Child #1 (youngest) _____   Child #2 _____   Child #3 _____   Child #4 _____   Child #5 _____

6. Do any of your children have special needs (for example, physical, mental, or emotional disability)?

   1.___   No
   2.___   Yes (please describe)_____

For questions 7 and 8, please list your children in the same order as in question 5. (For example, "Child #1" refers to your <u>youngest</u> child, "Child #2" refers to your next oldest, and so forth).

7. For each child, please check the type of child care you <u>currently</u> use most often while you are working. If any child is usually cared for in more than one arrangement, check <u>only</u> the <u>one</u> option used for the <u>most</u> hours.

	Child #1	Child #2	Child #3	Child #4	Child #5
1. Relative in your home or theirs	—	—	—	—	—
2. Other care giver in your home	—	—	—	—	—
3. Other care giver in his or her home (family day care)	—	—	—	—	—
4. Center based care (including preschool, before and after school programs)	—	—	—	—	—
5. Extended day program at school	—	—	—	—	—
6. Child at home alone before or after school	—	—	—	—	—
7. Other (please describe)_____	—	—	—	—	—

8. For each child, please mark where you would <u>prefer</u> that care be located.
   (check only <u>one</u> option per child)

	Child #1	Child #2	Child #3	Child #4	Child #5
1. At or near work	—	—	—	—	—
2. At or near home	—	—	—	—	—
3. At or near child's school	—	—	—	—	—
4. At or near spouse's work	—	—	—	—	—
5. No preference	—	—	—	—	—
6. Other (please describe)_____	—	—	—	—	—

9. What is the average total amount you pay <u>per month</u> for child care for <u>all</u> your children while you work? (Include preschool, before and after school programs, care during school vacations and summer, overtime, emergencies, etc.) *(check <u>one</u>)*

   1.___   under $200

   2.___ $200-399

   3.___ $400-599

   4.___ $600-799

   5.___ $800-999

   6.___ $1000 or more

10. Overall, how satisfied are you with your current child care arrangements? *(check <u>one</u>)*

   1.___   Not at all satisfied

   2.___   A little satisfied

   3.___   Quite satisfied

   4.___   Extremely satisfied

11. Here are some common problem areas for working parents who need or use child care. Have you had problems in any of these areas in the past <u>three</u> years? *(Circle the appropriate response for each problem area.)*

	No Problem	Moderate Problem	Major Problem
1. Cost of care	1	2	3
2. Convenience of location	1	2	3
3. Schedule to match work	1	2	3
4. Quality of care	1	2	3
5. Dependability of care	1	2	3
6. Finding care for a sick child	1	2	3
7. Finding temporary/emergency care	1	2	3
8. Finding care for child under 2 years	1	2	3
9. Finding care for child 2 to 5 years	1	2	3
10. Finding before or after school care	1	2	3
11. Finding care during school vacations and summer	1	2	3
12. Finding care for children with special needs	1	2	3
13. Other (please describe)_____	1	2	3

12. Overall, how much stress do you experience as a result of problems with child care arrangements? *(check <u>one</u>)*

   1.___   None at all

   2.___   A little

   3.___   Quite a bit

   4.___   A great deal

13. If some of the following programs could be offered at or near the Laboratory and at a reasonable cost, which programs would you definitely use? *(check all that apply)*

1.___ Infant care center (under age 1)

2.___ Toddler care center (ages 1-2)

3.___ Preschooler care center (ages 3-5)

4.___ After school program (ages 5-12)

5.___ School vacation programs (ages 5-12)

6.___ Temporary/emergency child care (ages 0-12)

7.___ None of the above

8.___ Other (please describe) _____

14. What is the earliest time you usually require child care? _____ a.m.

15. What is the latest time you usually require child care? _____ p.m.

> If you provide assistance to an **adult** family member or friend who has a health problem or disability or is elderly, please GO ON TO THE NEXT PAGE.

> If you do **not** provide assistance to an **adult** family member or friend, please SKIP TO PAGE 9.

PART III: YOUR ADULT CARE RESPONSIBILITIES

16. How many adults <u>age 18 to 64</u> do you currently assist because they have a health problem or a disability?

    _____ (number of persons)

17. How many persons <u>age 65 or older</u> do you currently assist?

    _____ (number of persons)

18. Which of the following kinds of assistance do you provide to one or more of the persons listed in questions 16 and 17? *(check all that apply)*

    1.___ Cooking, laundry, house cleaning, or shopping

    2.___ Home maintenance or repairs

    3.___ Transportation

    4.___ Feeding, bathing, toileting, dressing or grooming

    5.___ Administering medications

    6.___ Managing the person's financial affairs

    7.___ Direct financial support

    8.___ Providing emotional reassurance

    9.___ Arranging or coordinating outside help in person or by telephone

    10.___ Monitoring assistance and services provided by others

    11.___ Finding out about government programs or community services

    12.___ **Do not provide assistance with any of the above**

19. Overall, approximately how many hours do you spend helping these person(s) <u>in a typical week</u>? *(check one)*

    1.___ None

    2.___ Less than 2 hours

    3.___ 3-4 hours

    4.___ 5-9 hours

    5.___ 10-19 hours

    6.___ 20-29 hours

    7.___ 30 or more hours

20. Overall, approximately how much money do you spend helping these person(s) <u>in a typical month</u>? *(check one)*

    1.___ None

    2.___ Less than $100

    3.___ $100-$249

    4.___ $250-$499

    5.___ $500-$999

    6.___ $1000 or more

21. Overall, how much help with your adult care responsibilities do you receive (including information, guidance, financial assistance, emotional support, etc.)? *(check one)*

   1.___ None at all
   2.___ A little
   3.___ Quite a bit
   4.___ A great deal

22. Have you experienced difficulty with any of the following since you began providing assistance? *(check all that apply)*

   1.___ Finding trained and reliable care providers
   2.___ Finding services in the person's own community
   3.___ Having enough money to pay for care
   4.___ Understanding government programs such as Medicare or SSI
   5.___ Finding out about legal options
   6.___ Getting cooperation and assistance from other family members
   7.___ Dealing with a breakdown in care arrangements
   8.___ **None of the above**

23. Overall, how much stress do you currently experience as a result of your adult care responsibilities? *(check one)*

   1.___ None at all
   2.___ A little
   3.___ Quite a bit
   4.___ A great deal

Please provide the following information about the ONE adult (18-64 or 65 or older) for whom you currently provide the most assistance because of a health problem or a disability.

24. How is the person related to you? *(check one)*

   1.___ Spouse/partner
   2.___ Parent or Parent-in-law
   3.___ Son or daughter (over age 18)
   4.___ Other relative
   5.___ Friend or neighbor
   6.___ Other (please specify): _____

25. What is the person's gender?   1.___ Male 2.___ Female

26. Approximately how old is the person? _____ years of age

27. Are you the primary person responsible for this person's care or well-being? *(check one)*

   1.___ Yes   2.___ No

28. What is the person's current marital/relationship status? *(check <u>one</u>)*

    1.___ Married, or living with partner

    2.___ Divorced or Separated

    3.___ Widowed

    4.___ Single

29. What is the person's <u>primary</u> living arrangement? *(check <u>one</u>)*

    1.___ Lives with you

    2.___ Lives in own home or apartment

    3.___ Lives with family member or care provider

    4.___ Lives in boarding home, group home, or nursing home

    5.___ Other (please specify): _____

30. Where does the person live <u>most of the time</u>? *(check <u>one</u>)*

    1.___ In the Bay Area

    2.___ Elsewhere in California

    3.___ Elsewhere in the United States

    4.___ Outside of the United States

31. In addition to yourself, who else provides assistance on a regular basis? *(check <u>all</u> that apply)*

    1.___ Your spouse or partner

    2.___ Other family members, friends or neighbors

    3.___ Someone paid to provide care

    4.___ **You are the only provider of assistance**

32. What major physical or mental health conditions does the person have?

    1._____ , 2._____ , 3._____

33. During the past month, has the person ever: *(check <u>all</u> that apply)*

    1.___ Had difficulty making common sense decisions

    2.___ Forgotten things he or she had just heard

    3.___ Become very agitated, upset, or depressed

    4.___ Behaved in ways that were unsafe or embarrassing

    5.___ Refused to cooperate with care providers

    6.___ **None of the above**

Please go on to the next page - - ->

PART IV: FOR EMPLOYEES WITH CHILD CARE <u>OR</u> ADULT CARE RESPONSIBILITIES

Now we would like to know a little bit about how care responsibilities can affect work. All responses in this survey will be kept completely confidential.

34. Please check the category that best describes your job at Lawrence Berkeley Laboratory: *(check <u>one</u>)*

   1.___ Scientist or Engineer (including Divisional and Post-Doctoral Fellows)

   2.___ Administrative Professional (including Managers)

   3.___ Administrative Clerical

   4.___ Technical exempt

   5.___ Technical non-exempt

35. In a typical week, how many hours do you usually work? _____ hours

36. Sometimes family responsibilities (child care and/or adult care) can affect a person's work. Has your work ever been affected in any of the following ways <u>because of your child care or adult care responsibilities</u>? *(check <u>all</u> that apply)*

   1.___ Missed part of a normal work day (for example, started later or stopped earlier than usual)

   2.___ Missed an entire day of work

   3.___ Was less productive than usual because of adult or child care responsibilities

   4.___ Turned down extra work opportunities (for example, overtime or special projects)

   5.___ Had to miss a training opportunity or meeting

   6.___ Reduced the number of hours usually worked

   7.___ Didn't receive a promotion or merit increase

   8.___ **None of the above**

37. All in all, how much do your family responsibilities interfere with your work? *(check <u>one</u>)*

   1.___ Not at all

   2.___ A little bit

   3.___ Quite a bit

   4.___ A great deal

38. In the <u>last two months</u> approximately how many <u>days of work</u> did you miss because of your child care or adult care responsibilities? *(check <u>one</u>)*

   1.___ None

   2.___ Less than 2 days

   3.___ 3-4 days

   4.___ 5-9 days

   5.___ 10 or more days

39. In the <u>last two months,</u> <u>how often</u> did you miss <u>part</u> of a normal work day because of your child care or adult care responsibilities (for example, because you started late, stopped early, were interrupted, or were too tired or upset to work effectively)? *(check one)*

    1.___   Never

    2.___   Once a month or so

    3.___   Twice a month or so

    4.___   Once a week or so

    5.___   Two or three times a week

    6.___   Every day

40. Taking into consideration all of the times <u>in the last two months</u> when you missed <u>part</u> of a normal work day or your work was disrupted by your child care or adult care responsibilities, approximately how many <u>total hours</u> of productive work do you think you might have missed? *(check one)*

    1.___   None

    2.___   Less than 2 hours

    3.___   3-4 hours

    4.___   5-9 hours

    5.___   10-19 hours

    6.___   20-39 hours

    7.___   40 hours or more

41. Some aspects of a person's job or career might affect their ability to care for children or help an adult family member or friend. To what extent would you agree that the following characteristics are true of your job? *(circle one number for each statement)*

	Strongly Agree	Agree	Disagree	Strongly Disagree
1. I can adjust my normal work schedule	1	2	3	4
2. I can take time off during normal work hours for personal reasons	1	2	3	4
3. If necessary, I can do my work at home	1	2	3	4
4. I have a lot of freedom to decide how to do my work	1	2	3	4
5. I have a lot to say about what happens on my job	1	2	3	4
6. I have enough time to get my work done	1	2	3	4
7. The people I work with take a personal interest in me	1	2	3	4
8. My supervisor is concerned about my welfare	1	2	3	4

42. Lawrence Berkeley Laboratory offers a number of paid and unpaid leave programs that may be helpful with your family responsibilities. Have you <u>ever</u> taken a family-related leave from your work at LBL (for example, maternity, paternity, parenting, or to care for an ill family member)?

   1.___ Yes

   2.___ No -- > **(please SKIP to question 44)**

43. What type(s) of leave did you take? *(check <u>all</u> that apply)*

   1.___ Disability leave

   2.___ Sick leave

   3.___ Vacation leave

   4.___ Leave without pay

   5.___ Reduced work week

   6.___ Other (please describe)_____

44. Taking into account <u>all</u> of your work, personal and family responsibilities (including the care of adults and/or minor children), to what extent would you agree with the following statements? *(circle <u>one</u> number for <u>each</u> statement)*

	Strongly Agree	Agree	Disagree	Strongly Disagree
1. I have more to do than I can handle comfortably	1	2	3	4
2. I don't have enough time for myself	1	2	3	4
3. I am exhausted when I go to bed at night	1	2	3	4
4. I have a good balance between my work, family and personal responsibilities	1	2	3	4
5. I am doing a good job of meeting my work, family and personal responsibilities	1	2	3	4

45. How much of the following, if any, do you currently experience <u>as a result of your family care responsibilities</u> (including the care of adults and/or minor children)? *(circle <u>one</u> number for <u>each</u> problem area)*

	None At All	A Little	Quite A Bit	A Great Deal
1. Physical fatigue	1	2	3	4
2. Financial strain	1	2	3	4
3. Emotional upset	1	2	3	4
4. Interference with free time	1	2	3	4
5. Interference with social activities	1	2	3	4
6. Interference with spouse/partner relationships	1	2	3	4

46. Lawrence Berkeley Laboratory offers a number of employee benefits, policies and programs that may be helpful with your family responsibilities. For each of the following, please indicate whether you have ever used it to help with your family responsibilities. For each option that you have used, please also indicate how helpful it was by circling the appropriate response.

		USED?			HOW HELPFUL?		
		No	Yes		Very	Somewhat	Not At All
1.	Put part of your salary into a Dep Care account (pre-tax reimbursement plan)	1	2	→	1	2	3
2.	Adjusted your work schedule to fit your care responsibilities (flex time)	1	2	→	1	2	3
3.	Attended a Parent Information Fair	1	2	→	1	2	3
4.	Attended an Elder Care Information Fair	1	2	→	1	2	3
5.	Met with an EAP counselor	1	2	→	1	2	3
6.	Used the LBL Childcare Resource Guide	1	2	→	1	2	3
7.	Used the LBL Eldercare Resource Guide	1	2	→	1	2	3
8.	Other (please specify):_____	1	2	→	1	2	3

PART V: BACKGROUND INFORMATION

47. What is your gender? *(check one)* 1.___ Male 2.___ Female

48. Your marital/relationship status: *(check one)*

1.___ Married   --> Is your spouse employed by LBL? 1.___ Yes 2.___ No
2.___ Not married, living with partner
3.___ Divorced or separated
4.___ Widowed
5.___ Single

49. Your ethnicity/race: *(check one)*

1.___ White (not of Hispanic origin)
2.___ Black/African American (not of Hispanic origin)
3.___ Asian/Pacific Islander
4.___ Hispanic
5.___ American Indian or Alaskan Native
6.___ Other (please specify): _____

50. In what city or town do you live? _____

51. What is your age? *(check one)*

1.___	Less than 30	4.___	50-59
2.___	30-39	5.___	60-69
3.___	40-49	6.___	70 or older

52. Compared to other people your own age, would you say your health in general is: *(check one)*

   1.___ Excellent

   2.___ Good

   3.___ Fair

   4.___ Poor

53. What is your approximate total household income per year, before taxes? *(check one)*

   1.___ Less than $20,000

   2.___ $20,000 - $39,999

   3.___ $40,000 - $59,999

   4.___ $60,000 - $79,999

   5.___ $80,000 - $99,999

   6.___ $100,000 or more

54. How many persons live on this total household income? _____ persons

55. Would you care to provide any other comments regarding what the Laboratory should consider to help employees meet their work and family responsibilities?

_____

_____

_____

_____

_____

_____

_____

_____

_____

_____

THANK YOU VERY MUCH.

Bibliography

Abel, E. K. (1986). Adult daughters and care for the elderly. *Feminist Studies.* 12:479–497.

Abel, E. K. & Nelson, M. K. (eds.) (1990). *Circles of care: Work and identity in women's lives.* New York: State University of New York Press.

Adams, G. A., King, L. A. & King, D. W. (1996). Relationships of job and family involvement, family social support, and work-family conflict with job and life satisfaction. *Journal of Applied Psychology.* 81:411–420.

Adolph, B. (1988). *The employer's guide to child care.* New York: Praeger

American Association of Retired Persons. (1995). *Long Term Care.* Washington, D.C.: AARP.

American Association of Retired Persons & The Travelers Foundation (AARP/ Travelers). (1988). *A national survey of caregivers.* Washington, D.C.: Opinion Research Corporation.

American Cancer Society. (1979). *Report on the social, economic, and psychological needs of cancer patients in California: Major findings and implications: A review and analysis.* San Francisco: American Cancer Society, California Division.

Anastas, J., Gibeau, J. & Larson, P. (1990). Working families and eldercare: A national perspective in an aging America. *Social Work.* 35:405–411.

Anastas, J. W., Gibeau, J. L. & Larson, P. J. (1987). *Breadwinners and caregivers: Supporting workers who care for elderly family members.* Final report submitted by the National Association of Area Agencies on Aging to the Administration on Aging, Grant #90AM158. Washington, DC.

Aneshensel, C. S., Pearlin, L. I., Mullan, J. T., Zarit, S. H. & Whitlatch, C. J. (1995). *Profiles in caregiving: The unexpected career.* New York: Academic Press.

Ansello, E. F. & Eustis, N .N. (1992). A common stake? Investigating the emerging "intersection" of aging and disabilities. *Generations.* 16(1):5–8.

Appelbaum, E. & Berg, P. (1997, January). *Balancing work and family.* Paper presented at the annual IRRA meetings, New Orleans, LA.

Archbold, P. G. (1983). The impact of parent-caring on women. *Family Relations.* 32:39–45.

Bagnato, S., Kontos, S. & Neisworth, J. (1987). Integrated day care as special education: Profiles of programs and children. *Topics in Early Childhood Education.* 7:29–47.

Bailyn, L. (1997). The impact of corporate culture on work-family integration. In Parasuraman, S. & J. H. Greenhaus, (eds.). *Integrating work and family: Challenges and choices for a changing world.* (pp. 209–219). Westport, CT: Quorum Books.

Bankert, E. C., Googins, B. & Bradley K. (1996). Family-friendly—says who? *Across the Board.* 33(7):45–49.

Bankert, E. C. & Lobel, S. A. (1997). Visioning the future. In S. Parasuraman & J. H. Greenhaus, (eds.). *Integrating work and family.* (pp. 177–191). Westport, CT: Quorum Books.

Barling, J. (1990). *Employment, stress and family functioning.* Chichester, England: John Wiley & Sons Ltd.

Barnes, R. F., Raskind, M. A., Scott, M. & Murphy, C. (1981). Problems of families caring for Alzheimer's patients: Use of a support group. *Journal of the American Geriatrics Society.* 29:80–85.

Barnett, R. C. (1994). Home-to-work spillover revisited: A study of full-time employed women in dual-earner couples. *Journal of Marriage and Family.* 56:647–656.

Barnett, R. & Baruch, G. (1985). Women's involvement in multiple roles and psychological distress. *Journal of Personality and Social Psychology.* 49:135–145.

Barnett, R. & Baruch, G. (1987). Social roles, gender and psychological distress. In R. Barrett, L. Biener & G. K. Baruch, (eds.). *Gender and stress.* (pp. 122–143). New York: Free Press.

Barnett, R. & Marshall, N. (1989). *Multiple roles, spillover effects and psychological distress.* Wellesley, MA: Wellesley College.

Barnett, R.C., Marshall, N.L. & Pleck, J.H. (1992). Men's multiple roles and their relationship to men's psychological distress. *Journal of Marriage and the Family.* 54:358–367.

Barr, J. (1990). Employee caregivers for dependent elders. Unpublished manuscript. Available from the New York Business Group on Health, 622 Third Avenue, New York, NY 10017-6763.

Barusch, A. S. & Spaid, W. M. (1991). Reducing caregiver burden through short-term training: Evaluation findings from a caregiver support project. *Journal of Gerontological Social Work.* 17:(1/2):7–33.

Bates, F. L. & Harvey, C. C. (1975). *The structure of social systems.* New York: Gardner Press.

Belous, R. S. (1989). *The contingent economy: The growth of the temporary part-time and contingent workforce.* Washington, D.C.: National Planning Association.

Belsky, J. (1984). The determinants of parenting: A process model. *Child Development.* 55:83–96.

———. (1988). The "effects" of infant day care reconsidered (Special Issue). *Early Childhood Research Quarterly.* 3:235–272.

———. (1992). Consequences of child care for children's development: A deconstructionist view. In A. Booth, (ed.). *Child care in the 1990s: Trends and consequences.* (pp. 83–94). Hillsdale, NJ: Lawrence Erlbaum.

Berk, H. J. & Berk, M. L. (1982). A survey of day care centers and their services for handicapped children. *Child Care Quarterly.* 11:(3):211–214.

Bernstein, H. (1984). An Alzheimer family support group project. *Journal of Jewish Communal Service.* 61:160–168.

Betz, C., Unger, O., Frager, B., Test, L. & Smith, C. (1990, May-June). A survey of self-help groups in California for parents of children with chronic conditions. *Pediatric Nursing.* 16:293–296.

Biegel, D. E., Sales, E. & Schulz, R. (1991). *Family caregiving in chronic illness.* Newbury Park, CA: Sage.

Biernat, M. & Wortman, C. (1991). Sharing of home responsibilities between professionally employed women and their husbands. *Journal of Personality & Social Psychology.* 60:844–860.

Black, M. M., Cohn, J. F., Smull, M. W. & Crites, L. S. (1995). Individual and family factors associated with risk of institutionalization of mentally retarded adults. *American Journal of Mental Deficiency.* 90:271–276.

Blank, H. (1997). Child care in the context of welfare "reform". In Kamerman, S.B. & A.J. Kahn, (eds.) *Child care in the context of welfare "reform."* New York: Columbia University School of Social Work.

Blau, D. & Robins, D. (1989). Fertility, Employment, and Child Care Costs. *Demography.* 26:287–99.

Boaz, R. F. & Muller, C. F. (1992). Paid work and unpaid help by caregivers of the disabled and frail elders. *Medical Care.* 30:149–158.

Bohen, H. & Viveros-Long, A. (1981). *Balancing jobs and family life: Do flexible schedules help?* Philadelphia: Temple University Press.

Bolger, N., DeLongis, A., Kessler, R. & Wethington, E. (1989). The contagion of stress across multiple roles. *Journal of Marriage and the Family.* 51:175–183.

Bond, J. T., Galinsky, E., Lord, M., Staines, G. L. & Brown, K. R. (1991). *Beyond the parental leave debate: The impact of laws in four states.* New York: Families and Work Institute.

Bonilla, C. (1989). *Determinants of employee absenteeism.* Washington, D.C.: National Chamber Foundation.

Boris, E. & Daniels, C., (eds.). (1989). *Homework: Historical and contemporary perspectives on paid labor at home.* Chicago: University of Illinois Press.

Bose, C. E., Feldberg, R. & Sokoloff, N. J. (1987). *Hidden aspects of women's work.* New York: Praeger.

Breslau, N., Salkever, D. & Staruch, K. (1982). Women's labor force activity and responsibilities for disabled dependents: A study of families with disabled children. *Journal of Health and Social Behavior.* 23:169–183.

Brice, G. C. & Gorey, K. M. (1989, November) *EAP coordinators self-reported competence to handle care problems.* Paper presented at the annual meeting of Gerontological Society of America, Minneapolis, MN.

Brody, E. M. (1985). Parent care as a normative family stress. *The Gerontologist.* 25:19–29.

———. (1990). *Women in the middle: Their parent-care years.* New York: Springer.

———. (1995). Prospects for family caregiving: Response to change, continuity, and diversity. In Kane, R.A. & J.D. Penrod, (eds.). *Family caregiving in an aging society: Policy perspectives.* (pp. 15–28). Thousand Oaks, CA: Sage Publications.

Brody, E. M., Kleban, M. H., Johnsen, P. T., Hoffman, C. & Schoonover, C. B. (1987). Work status and parent care: A comparison of four groups of women. *The Gerontologist.* 27:201–208.

Brody, E. M., Litvin, S. J., Hoffman, C. & Kleban, M. H. (1992). Differential effects of daughter's marital status on their parent care experiences. *The Gerontologist,* 32:58–67.

Brody, E. M. & Schoonover, C. B. (1986). Patterns of parent-care when adult children work and when they do not. *The Gerontologist.* 26:372–381.

Brown, B. W. & McCormick, T. (1988). Family coping following traumatic head injury: An exploratory analysis with recommendations for treatment. *Family Relations.* 37:12–16.

Buchanan, R. J. & Alston, R. J. (1997). Medicaid policies and home health care provisions for persons with disabilities. *Journal of Rehabilitation.* 63(3):20–34.

Burden, D. & Googins, B. (1987). *Balancing Job and Homelife Study: Managing and Family Stress in Corporation.* Boston: Boston University School of Social Work.

Burke, R. J. (1986). Occupational and life stress and the family: Conceptual frameworks and research findings. *International Review of Applied Psychology.* 35:347–369.

———. (1988). Some antecedents and consequences of work-family conflict. *Journal of Social Behavior and Personality*, 3:287–302.

———. (1994). Stressful events, work-family conflict, coping, psychological burnout, and well-being among police officers. *Psychological Reports*. 75:787–800.

Burke, R., Weir, T. & Duwors, R., Jr. (1980). Work demands on administrators and spouse well-being. *Human Relations*. 33:253–278.

Burley, K. A. (1995). Family variables as mediators of the relationship between work-family conflict and marital adjustment among dual-career men and women. *Journal of Social Psychology*. 135:483–497.

Burton, L., Kasper, J., Shore, A., Cagney, K., LaVeist, T., Cubbin, C. & German, P. (1995). The structure of informal care: Are there differences by race? *The Gerontologist*. 35(6):744–752.

Burud, S. L., Aschbacher, P. R. & McCroskey, J. (1984). *Employer supported child care: Investing in human resources*. National Employer Supported Child Care Project. Dover, MA: Auburn House.

Butler, J., McManis, M. & Newcheck, P. (1986). Issues in the financing of care for chronically ill children and their families. *Topics in Early Childhood Special Education*. 5(4):58–69.

Campbell, A., Converse, P. E. & Rodgers, W. L. (1976). *The quality of American life*. New York: Russell Sage Foundation.

Campbell, P. R. (1996). *Population projections for states by age, sex, race and Hispanic origin: 1995–2025*. U.S. Bureau of the Census, Population Division, PPL–47.

Cannon, W. B. (1932). *The wisdom of the body*, (2nd ed.). New York: Norton.

Cantor, M. H. (1979a). Neighbors and friends: An overlooked resource in the informal support system. *Research on Aging*. 1:434–463.

———. (1979b). The informal support system of New York's inner city elderly: Is ethnicity a factor? In Gelfand, D. & A. Kutzik, (eds.). *Ethnicity and aging*. New York: Springer.

———. (1983). Strain among caregivers: A study of experience in the United States. *The Gerontologist*. 23:597–604.

Cantor, M. H. & Little, V. (1985). Aging and social care. In Binstock, R.H. & E. Shanas, (eds.). *Handbook of aging and the social sciences*, (2nd ed.) (pp. 745–781). New York: Van Nostrand-Reinhold.

Carpenter, E. (1980, December). Children's health care and the changing role of women. *Medical Care*. 18:1208–1218.

Casper, L. M. (1996). Who is minding our preschoolers. (U.S. Bureau of the Census, *Current Population Reports*. P70–53). Washington, D.C.: U.S. Government Printing Office.

———. (1997). Who's minding our preschoolers? (Fall 1994 Update. U.S. Bureau of the Census, *Current Population Reports, Series P70–62*). Washington, D.C.: U.S. Government Printing Office

Cattan, P. (1991, October). Child-care problems: An obstacle to work. *Monthly Labor Review*. 114(10):3–9.

Champoux, J. E. (1978). Perceptions of work and nonwork: A reexamination of the compensatory and spillover models. *Sociology of Work and Occupations*. 5:402–422.

Chilman, C. (1979). Parent satisfaction-dissatisfactions and their correlates. *Social Service Review*. 53:195–213.

———. (1993). Parental employment and child care trends: Some critical issues and suggested policies. *Social Work*. 38:(4), 451–460.

Chi-Ching, U. (1995). The effects of career salience and life-cycle variables on perceptions of work-family interfaces. *Human Relations*. 48:265–284.

Chiriboga, D. A., Weiler, P. G. & Nielsen, K. (1988/89). The stress of caregivers. *The Journal of Applied Social Sciences*. 13:118–141.

Chodorow, N. J. (1978). *The reproduction of mothering: Psychoanalysis and the sociology of gender*. Berkeley: University of California Press.

Chow, E. N. & Berheide, C. W. (1988). The interdependence of family and work: A framework for family life education, policy and practice. *Family Relations* 37:23–28.

Christensen, K. (1989). *Flexible staffing and scheduling in U.S. corporations* (Research Bulletin No. 240). New York: The Conference Board.

Clark, M. S. & Mills, J. (1979). Interpersonal attraction in exchange and communal relationships. *Journal of Personality and Social Psychology*. 37:12–24.

Clarke-Stewart, A. (1992). Consequences of child care for children's development. In Booth, A. (ed.). *Child care in the 1990s: Trends and consequences* (pp. 63–82). Hillsdale, NJ: Lawrence Erlbaum.

Clifford, R. M. & Russell, S. D. (1989). Financing programs for preschool-aged children. *Theory into Practice*. 28:19–27.

Cohen, M. A. (1998). Emerging trends in the finance and delivery of long-term care: Public and private opportunities and challenges. *The Gerontologist*. 38(1):80–89

Coleman, B. J. (1995). European models of long-term care in the home and community. *International Journal of Health Services*. 25(3):455–474.

Commerce Clearing House (1995, May 24). Unscheduled absence survey. *Human Resources Management Ideas & Trends in Personnel*, 3.

Cook, J. A. & Pickett, S. A. (1987–1988, Fall/Winter). Feelings of burden and criticalness among parents residing with chronically (mentally) ill offspring. *The Journal of Applied Social Sciences*. 12:79–107.

Coverman, S. (1989). Role overloads, role conflict, and stress: Addressing consequences of multiple role demands. *Social Forces*. 67:965–982.

Cowell, S. (1993). Family policy: A union approach. In Cobble, D.S. (ed.). *Women and unions: Forging a partnership* (pp. 115–128). Ithaca, NY: ILR Press, School of Industrial and Labor Relations, Cornell University.

Crimmins E. M., Saito, Y. & Reynolds, S. L. (1997). Further evidence on recent trends in the prevalence and incidence of disability among older Americans from two sources: The LSOA and the NHIS. *Journal of Gerontology*. 52B:S59–S71.

Crosby, F. J. (ed.). (1987). *Spouse, parent, worker: On gender and multiple roles*. New Haven, CT: Yale University Press.

Crouter, A., Huston, T. & Robbins, E. (1983). *Bringing work home: Psychological spillover from work to family*. Paper presented at the Theory and Method Workshop preceding the annual meeting of the National Council on Family Relations, St. Paul, MN.

Crouter, A. & Perry-Jenkins, M. (1986). Working it out: Effects of work on parents and children. In Yogman, M. W. & T. B. Brazelton, (eds.). *In support of families* (pp. 93–108). Cambridge, MA: Harvard University Press.

Crowley, A. (1990). Integrating handicapped and chronically ill children into day care centers. *Pediatric Nursing*. 16(1):39–44.

CWA child and elder care fund/NYNEX. (1995, Winter). *Labor News for Working Families*. III(1).

Dawson, D. & Cain, V. (1990, October). Child care arrangements: Health of our nation's children, United States, 1988. *Advanced Data*. 1:1–12.

Deimling, G. T. & Bass, D. M. (1986). Symptoms of mental impairment among elderly adults and their effects of family caregivers. *Journal of Gerontology*. 41:778–784.

Deiner, P. L. (1992). Family day care and children with disabilities. In Peters, D. L. & A. R. Pence, (eds.). *Family day care: Current research for informed public policy*. New York: Teachers College Press.

DeLapp, L. & Lawhorn, S. (1991). *Family benefits in the California workplace: The California family policy and benefits study*. Assembly Office of Research, State of California Sacramento, CA.

Dependent Care Connection. (1997). *DCC Making work/life resources accessible*. [online] internet web site: <http://www.dcclifecare.com>.

Dhooper, S. S. (1983). Family coping with the crisis of heart attack. *Social Work in Health Care*. 9:15–30.

Dizard, J. E. & Gadlin, H. (1990). *The minimal family*. Amherst, MA: University of Massachusetts Press.

Dombro, A. L. (1995). *Child care aware: A guide to promoting professional development in family child care*. New York: Families and Work Institute.

Doty, P. (1986). Family care of the elderly: The role of public policy. *The Milbank Quarterly*. 64:34–75.

Doty, P., Liu, K. & Wiener, J. (1985). An overview of long-term care. *Health Care Financing Review*. 6:69–78.

Doyle, A. (1976, October). Incident of illness in early group and family day-care. *Pediatrics*. 58:607–613.

Drury, D. & Almand, S. (1990). *Contingent staffing arrangements in small and large firms, Report no. PB9*. Prepared by Berkeley Planning Associates for the U.S. Small Business Administration, Office of Advocacy. Springfield, VA: National Technical Information Service.

Dubin, R. (1976). Work in modern society. In Dubin R. (Ed.), *Handbook of work, organization, and society*. Chicago: Rand-McNally.

DuPont Co. (1989, January 5). *DuPont Corporate News*. Wilmington, DE: Dupont External Affairs Dept.

Durkheim, E. (1947). *Division of labor in society*. (Simpson, G., trans.). Glencoe, IL: Free Press.

Duxbury, L. & Higgins, C. (1994). Interference between work and family: A status report on dual-career and dual-earner mothers and fathers. *Employee Assistance Quarterly*. 9:(3/4):55–80.

Duxbury, L., Higgins, C. & Lee, C. (1994). Work-family conflict. *Journal of Family Issues*. 15:449–466.

Eckenrode, J. & Gore, S. (eds). (1990). *Stress between work and family*. New York: Plenum Press.

Edinberg, M. A. (1987). Eldercare support programs. In Creedon, M.A. (ed.). *Issues for an aging America*. Bridgeport, CT: University of Bridgeport, Center for the Study of Aging.

Elder, G. J. (1992). Lives and social change. In Heinz, W.R. (ed.). *Theoretical advances in life course research*. (Vol. 1). Weinhelm: Deutscher Studien Verlag.

Ell, K. & Northen, H. (1990). *Families and health care: Psychosocial practice*. New York: Aldine de Gruyter.

Elliot, G. R. & Eisdorfer, C. (1982). *Stress and human health*. New York: Springer.

Ellwood, D.A. & Gold, S. (1995). *Children and the balanced budget amendment*. Albany, NY: Center for the Study of the States.

Emlen, A. C. (1991, May) *Rural child care policy: Does Oregon have one? 1991 legislative discussion paper* (Legislative Discussion Series). Corvallis, OR: Rural Policy Research Group, Oregon State University, Oregon Economic Development Dept.

Emlen, A. & Koren, P. (1984). *Hard to find and difficult to manage: The effects of child care on the workplace.* Portland, Oregon: Regional Institute for Human Services.

Emlen, A. & Koren, P. (1988, March). *New findings on the affordability issue.* Paper presented at symposium of the Conference Board on Workplace Research on the Family, Boston University School of Social Work, Boston.

Emlen, A., Koren, P. & Yoakum, P. (1990). *1990 dependent care survey: 15 employers of Lane County, Oregon.* Portland, OR: Arthur Emlen, and Portland State University, Regional Research Institute for Human Services.

Engelhardt, J. L., Brubaker, T. H. & Lutzer, V. D. (1988). Older caregivers of adults with mental retardation: Service utilization. *Mental Retardation.* 26:191–195.

Ettelbrick, P. (1993). Who is a parent? *New York Law School Journal of Human Rights.* 10:513–553.

Eustis, N. N. & Fischer, L. R. (1992). Common needs, different solutions? *Generations.* 16:17–22.

Evers, A. (1995). The future of elderly care in Europe: Limits and aspirations. In Scharf, T. & G.C. Wenger, (eds.). *International perspectives on community care for older people.* Brookfield, Vermont: Ashgate Publishing Company.

Famighetti, R. (1998). *The world almanac and book of facts 1998.* Mahwah, New Jersey: World Almanac Books.

Families and Work Institute. (1993). *Parental leave benefits for American workers.* Unpublished report. New York: Families and Work Institute.

Family Friendly Programs. (1990, December). *Work & Family Trend Report.* 1–2.

Farber, B. (1959). Effects of a severely mentally retarded child on family integration. *Monographs of the Society for Research in Child Development* 24:Serial #71.

Feldman, P. H., Sapienza, A. & Kane, N. (1990). *Who cares for them: Workers in the home care industry.* New York: Greenwood Press.

Ferber, M., O'Farrell, B. & Allen, L., (eds.). (1991). *Work and family: Policies for a changing work force.* Washington, D.C.: National Academy Press.

Fernandez, J. (1986). *Child care and corporate productivity: Resolving family/work conflicts.* Lexington, MA: Lexington Books.

Fernandez, J. P. (1990). *The politics and reality of family care in corporate America.* Lexington, MA: Lexington Books.

Fewell, R. R. (1986). Child care and the handicapped child. In Gunzenhauser, N. & B. Caldwell, (eds.), *Group care for young children: Considerations for child care and health professionals, public policy makers, and parents* (pp. 35–47). Somerville, NJ: Johnson & Johnson.

Fierman, J. (1994). Are companies less family friendly? *Fortune.* 129:64–67.

Fingerman, J. (ed.). (1997). *Work & family: A retrospective.* Minnetonka, MN: Work & Family Connection, Inc.

Fleishman, J. A. & Fogel, B. (1994). Coping and depressive symptoms among people with AIDS. *Health Psychology.* 13(2):156–169.

Flynn, G. (1998). Make your company's domestic-partner benefits foolproof. *Workforce.* 77(2):95–96.

Forthofer, M. S. Markman, H. J., Cox, M., Stanley, S. & Kessler, R. C. (1996). Associations between marital distress and work loss in a national sample. *Journal of Marriage and the Family.* 58:597–605.

Fortune Magazine & John Hancock Financial Services. (1989). *Corporate and employee response to caring for the elderly.* Unpublished report (available from Fortune Magazine, Rockefeller Center, New York, NY 10020).

Franks, M. M. & Stephens, M. P. (1996). Social support in the context of caregiving: Husbands' provision of support to wives involved in parent care. *Journal of Gerontology.* 51B:43–52.

Fredman, L., Daly, M. P. & Lazur, A. M. (1995). Burden among White and Black caregivers to elderly adults. *Journal of Gerontology.* 50B(2):S110–S118.

Fredriksen, K. I. (1993a). *The provision of informal adult care: The impact of family and employment role responsibilities.* PhD. diss. University of California, Berkeley.

Fredriksen, K. I. (1993b). *The impact of adult care and work role responsibilities among African American, Asian, Hispanic, and White caregivers.* Paper presented at the 46th Annual Scientific Meeting of the Gerontology Society of America, New Orleans, LA.

Fredriksen, K. I. (1995). Gender differences in employment and the informal care of adults. *Journal of Women & Aging.* 8(2):35–53.

Fredriksen, K. I. (1995b). Informal caregiving: Current trends in public policy and service provision. *Journal of Clinical Geropsychology.* 2:37–50.

Fredriksen, K. I. & Scharlach, A. E. (1996, March). *Employee family care responsibilities.* Paper presented at the 42nd Annual Meeting of the American Society on Aging, Anaheim, CA.

Fredriksen, K. I. & Scharlach, A. E. (1997). Caregiving and employment: The impact of workplace characteristics on role strain. *Journal of Gerontological Social Work.* 28(4):3–22.

French, M. T., Zarkin, G. A., Bray, J. W. & Hartwell, T. D. (1997). Costs of employee assistance programs: Findings from a national survey. *American Journal of Health Promotion.* 11:219–222.

Friedman, D. E. (1989a). A life cycle approach to family benefits and policies. *Perspectives (No. 19).* New York: The Conference Board.

Friedman, D. E. (1989b). Impact of child care on the bottom line. In *Investing in people: A strategy to address America's Workforce Crisis.* Commission on Workforce Quality and Labor Market Efficiency, U.S. Department of Labor. Washington, D.C.: U.S. Government Printing Office.

Friedman, D.E. & Galinsky, E. (1991). *Work and family trends.* New York: Families and Work Institute.

Friss, L. R. & Whitlatch, C. J. (1991). Who's taking care? A statewide study of family caregivers. *American Journal of Alzheimer's Care and Related Disorders and Research.* 6:16–26.

Friss, L. R., Whitlatch, C. J. & Yale, R. (1990). *Who's taking care?* San Francisco: Family Survival Project.

Frone, M. R., Russell, M. & Cooper, M. L. (1992a). Antecedents and outcomes of work-family conflict: Testing a model of the work-family interface. *Journal of Applied Psychology.* 77(1):65–78.

Frone, M. R., Russell, M. & Cooper, M. L. (1992b). Prevalence of work-family conflict: Are work and family boundaries asymmetrically permeable? *Journal of Organizational Behavior.* 13:723–729.

Fujiura, G. T., Garza, J. & Braddock, D. (1989). *National survey of family support services in developmental disabilities* (Mimeo). Chicago: University of Illinois-Chicago.

Galinsky, E. (1988, March). *Child care and productivity*. Paper presented at the Child Care Action Campaign Conference on Child Care and the Bottom Line, New York.

Galinsky, E. (1989). *The implementation of flexible time leave policies: Observations from European employers*. Paper prepared for the Panel on Employer Policies and Working Families. Washington, D.C.: National Research Council.

Galinsky, E. (1992). Work and family: 1992. *Family Resource Coalition Report*. 11(2):2, 3, 21.

Galinsky, E. & Bond, J. (1998). *The business work-life study: A sourcebook*. New York: Families and Work Institute.

Galinsky, E., Bond, J. & Friedman, D. (1993). *The changing workforce: Highlights of the National study*. New York: Families and Work Institute.

Galinsky, E., Bond, J. & Friedman, D. (1996). The role of employers in addressing the needs of employed parents. *Journal of Social Issues*. 52:111–136.

Galinsky, E., Friedman, D. E. & Hernandez, C. A. (1991). *The Corporate reference guide to work-family programs*. New York: Families and Work Institute.

Galinsky, E., Howes, C., Kontos, S. & Shinn, M. (1994). *The Study of Children in Family Child Care and Relative Care*. New York: Families and Work Institute.

Galinsky, E. & Hughes, D. (1987). *The Fortune magazine child care study*. Paper presented at the annual convention of the American Psychological Association, New York.

Galinsky, E. & Stein, P. J. (1990). The impact of human resource policies on employees. *Journal of Family Issues*. 11(4):368–383.

Gallagher, S. (1994). *Older people giving care: Helping family and community*. Westport, CT: Auburn House.

Gallup Organization (1980). *American families—1980*. Princeton, NJ: Gallop Organization.

Gatz, M., Bengtson, V. L. & Blum, M. J. (1990). Caregiving families. In Birren, J. E. & K. W. Schaie, (eds.). *Handbook of the psychology of aging*. San Diego, CA: Academic Press.

Gentry, W. M. & Hagy, A. P. (1996). The distributional effects of the tax treatment of child care expenses. In Feldstein, M. & J.M. Poterba, (eds.). *Empirical foundations of household taxation*. Chicago, IL: University of Chicago Press.

George, L. K. (1993). Sociological perspectives on life transitions. *Annual Review of Sociology*. 19:353–373.

George, L. K. & Gwyther, L. P. (1986). Caregiver well-being: A multidimensional examination of family caregivers of demented adults. *The Gerontologist*. 26:253–259.

Gibeau, J. L. & Anastas, J. W. (1989). Breadwinners and caregivers: Interviews with working women. *Journal of Gerontological Social Work*. 14:19–40.

Gibeau, J. L., Anastas, J. W. & Larson, P. J. (1987). Breadwinners, caregivers, and employers: New alliances in an aging America. *Employee Benefits Journal*. 12:6–10.

Gibson, R. C. (1982). Blacks at middle and later life: Resources and coping. *The Annual of the American Academy of Political and Social Science*. 464:79–90.

Giele, J. Z., Mutschler, P. H. & Orodenker, S. Z. (1987). *Stress and burdens of caregiving for the frail elderly*. Working paper #36. Waltham, MA: Brandeis University.

Gilbert, L. A., Holahan, C. K. & Manning, L. (1981). Coping with conflict between professional and maternal roles. *Family Relations*. 30:419–426.

Gilligan, C. (1982). *In a different voice: Psychological theory and women's development*. Cambridge, MA: Harvard University Press.

Glosser, G. & Wexler, D. (1985). Participants' evaluation of educational/support groups for families of patients with Alzheimer's disease and other dementias. *The Gerontologist.* 25:232–236.

Goldberger, L. & Breznitz, S. (eds.). (1982). *Handbook of stress.* New York: The Free Press.

Goldstein, A. (1999). Clinton budget to boost aid for long-term care; kin of severely ill, disabled could get $1,000 tax credit. *The Washington Post.* p. A19 Jan 4, 1999.

Golembiewski, R. T. & Proehl, C. W. (1980). Public sector application of flexible work hours: A review of available experience. *Public Administration Review.* 40:72–85.

Gonyea, J. G. (1997, Summer). The *real* meaning of balancing work and family. *The Public Policy and Aging Report.* 8(3):1, 6–8.

Gonyea, J. G. & Googins, B. K. (1992). Linking the worlds of work and family: Beyond the productivity trap. *Human Resource Management.* 31:209–226.

Goode, W. J. (1960). A theory of role strain. *American Sociological Review.* 25:483–496.

Goodman, W. (1995, August). Boom in day care industry the result of many social changes. *Monthly Labor Review.* 3–12.

Googins, B. K. (1997). Shared responsibility for managing work and family relationships: A community perspective. In Parasuraman, S. & J.H. Greenhaus, (eds.). *Integrating work and family: Challenges and choices for a changing world.* (pp. 220–231). Westport, CT: Quorum Books.

Googins, B. & Burden, D. (1987). Vulnerability of working parents: Balancing work and home roles. *Social Work.* 32:295–300.

Googins, B., Gonyea, J. & Pitt-Catsouphes, M. (1990). *Linking the worlds of family and work: Family dependent care and workers' performance* (Final report). Boston, MA: Center on Work and Family.

Gorey, K. M., Rice, R. W. & Brice, G. C. (1992). The prevalence of elder care responsibilities among the work force population: Response bias among a group of cross-sectional surveys. *Research on Aging.* 14:399–418.

Grad, J. & Sainsbury, P. (1963). Mental illness and the family. *The Lancet.* 1:544–547.

Green, M. & Widoff, E. (1990). Special needs child care: Training is a key issue. *Young Children.* 45:60–61.

Greenberg, J. S., Seltzer, M. M. & Greenley, J. R. (1993). Aging parents of adults with disabilities: The gratifications and frustration of later-life caregiving. *The Gerontologist.* 33:542–550.

Greenhaus, J. H. & Beutell, N. J. (1985). Sources of conflict between work and family roles. *Academy of Management Review.* 10(1):76–88.

Groginsky, S. & McConnell, L. (1998). Subsidizing success with child care: With the need for more and better child care becoming urgent, state lawmakers are deciding how to help. *State Legislatures.* 24(April):28–31.

Gunby, P. (1993). Adult day care centers vital, many more needed. *Journal of the American Medical Association.* 269:2341–2342.

Gutek, B. A., Searle, S. & Klepa, L. (1991). Rational versus gender role explanations for work-family conflict. *Journal of Applied Psychology.* 76:560–568.

Hagen, S. (1999, March). *Projections of expenditures for long-term care services for the elderly.* Washington, D.C., Congressional Budget Office.

Haley, W. E. (1989). Group intervention for dementia family caregivers: A longitudinal perspective. *Gerontologist.* 29:478–480.

Haley, W., Brown, L. & Levine, E. G. (1987). Experimental evaluation of the effectiveness of group interventions for dementia caregivers. *The Gerontologist.* 27: 376–382.

Haley, W. E., Roth, D. L., Coleton, M. I., Ford, G. R., West, C. A. C., Collins, R. P. & Isobe, T. L. (1996). Appraisal, coping, and social support as mediators of well-being in Black and White family caregivers of patients with Alzheimer's Disease. *The Journal of Consulting and Clinical Psychology*. 64(1):121–129.

Hareven, T. K. & Adams, K. (1996). *The generation in the middle: Cohort comparisons in assistance to aging parents in an American community. Aging and generational relations over the life course: A historical and cross-cultural perspective.* University of Delaware Family Research, Symposium Essays, 272–293.

Harrick, E., Vanek, G. & Michlitsch, J. (1986, Summer). Alternate work schedules, productivity, leave usage and employee attitudes: A field study. *Public Personnel Management*. 15:159–169.

Harrington, C. & Pollock, A. M. (1998). Decentralisation and privatisation of long-term care in UK and USA. *The Lancet*. 351:1805–1808.

Hartford, M. & Parsons, R. (1982). Groups with relatives of dependent older adults. *The Gerontologist*. 22:376–382.

Harvey, E. (1999). Short-term and long-term effects of early parental employment on children of the national longitudinal survey of youth. *Developmental Psychology*. 35(2):445–459.

Hausenstein, E. J. & Boyd, M. R. (1994). Depressive symptoms in young women of the Piedmont-Prevalence in rural women. *Women and Health*. 21:105–123.

Hayes, C., Palmer, J. & Zaslow, M. (1990). *Who cares for America's children? Child care policy for the 1990's* (Report of the Panel on Child Care Policy, Committee on Child Development Research and Public Policy, Commission on Behavioral and Social Sciences and Education, National Research Council). Washington, D.C.: National Academy Press.

Hayghe, H. V. (1990). Family members in the work force. *Monthly Labor Review*. 113(3):14–19.

Haynes, S. G., Eaker, E. D. & Feinleib, M. (1984). *The effect of employment, family, and job stress on coronary heart disease patterns in women: An epidemiologic approach.* Lexington, MA: DC Heath.

Health Insurance Association of America. (1997). *Long-term care insurance: An employer's guide.* Washington, DC: Author.

Hedges, J. (1977, October). Absence from work—measuring the hours lost. *Monthly Labor Review*. 100(10):16–23.

Heiss, J. (1981). Social roles. In M. Rosenberg & R. H. Turner (eds.), *Social psychology: Sociological perspectives* (pp.94–129). New York: Basic Books.

Helburn, S. & Howes, C. (1996). Child care cost and quality. *Financing Child Care*. 6:62–82.

Helburn, S., Culkin, M., Morris, J. Mocan, N. Howes, C., Phillipsen, L., Bryant, D., Clifford, R., Cryer, D, Peisner-Feinberrg, E., Burchinal, M., Kagan, S.L. & Rustici, J. (1995). *Cost, quality and child outcomes in child care centers. Final report.* Denver: University of Colorado.

Heller, T. (1993). Aging caregivers of persons with developmental disabilities: Changes in burden and placement desire. In Roberto, K.A. (ed.), *The elderly caregiver: Caring for adults with developmental disabilities* (pp. 21–38). Newbury Park, CA: Sage Publications, Inc.

Heller, T. & Factor, A. (1988). Permanency planning among Black and White family caregivers of older adults with mental retardation. *Mental Retardation*. 26: 203–208.

Hendrickson, M. C., Jewett, A., Emerson, S. & Seck, E. T. (1988). *State tax incentive programs for informal caregivers and the elderly.* Center for Health and Social Services Research. Washington, D.C.: U.S. Government Printing Office.

Hewitt Associates. (1993, February). Employer response to family and medical leave legislation. *On employee benefits.* Lincolnshire, IL: Hewitt Associates.

Hewitt Associates. (1997). *Work and family benefits provided by major U. S. employers in 1996.* Washington, D.C.: Hewitt Associates.

Heymann, S. J., Earle, A. & Egleston, B. (1996). Parental availability for the care of sick children. *Pediatrics.* 98:(S pt. 1), 226–230.

Higgins, C. A., Duxbury, L. E. & Irving, R. H. (1992). Work-family conflict in the dual-career family. *Organizational Behavior and Human Decision Processes.* 51:51–75.

Higgins, C., Duxbury, L. & Lee, C. (1994). Impact of life-cycle stage and gender on the ability to balance work and family responsibilities. *Family Relations.* 43:144–150.

Hill, M. (1979, Fall). The wage effects of marital status and children. *Journal of Human Resources.* 14:579–594.

Hiller, D. V. & Dyehouse, J. (1987). A case for banishing "dual-career marriages" from the research literature. *Journal of Marriage and the Family.* 49(4):787–795.

Himes, C. L., Jordan, A. K. & Farkas, J. I. (1996). Factors influencing parental caregiving by adult women. *Research on Aging.* 18(3):349–370.

Hirsch, B. J. & Rapkin, B. D. (1986). Multiple roles, social networks, and women's well-being. *Journal of Personality and Social Psychology.* 51:1237–1247.

Hirst, M. (1985). Young adults with disabilities: Health employment and financial costs for family carers. *Child Care, Health and Development.* 11:291–307.

Hobfoll, S. E. (1989). Conservation of resources: A new attempt at conceptualizing stress. *American Psychologist.* 44:513–524.

Hochschild, A. R. (1989). *The second shift: Working parents and the revolution at home.* New York: Viking Press.

———. (1997). *The time bind: When work becomes home, and home becomes work.* New York: Metropolitan Books.

Hofferth, S. (1992). The demand for and supply of child care in the 1990s. In Booth, A. (ed.). *Child care in the 1990s: Trends and consequences.* Hillsdale, NJ: Lawrence Erlbaum.

———. (1996). Child care in the United States today. *The Future of Children.* 6(2):41–61.

Hofferth, S., Brayfield, A., Deich, S. & Holcomb, P. (1991). *National child care survey, 1990* (A National Association for the Education of Young Children (NAEYC) Study. Urban Institute Report. (pp. 91–95). Washington, D.C.: Urban Institute Press.

Hoffman, L. (1989). Effects of maternal employment in the two-parent family. *American Psychologist.* 44:283–292.

Hoffman, C., Rice, D. & Sung, H. (1996, November). Persons with chronic conditions: Their prevalence and costs. *Journal of the American Medical Association.* 276: 1473–1479.

Holmes, D. K. & Friedman, D. (1995). *The changing employer-employee contract: The role of work and family issues.* New York: Families and Work Institute.

Holroyd, K. A. & Lazarus, R. S. (1982). Stress, coping and somatic adaptation. In Goldberger, L. & S. Breznitz, (eds.). *Handbook of stress.* New York: The Free Press.

Hooyman, N. R. & Gonyea, J. (1995). *Feminist perspectives on family care.* Thousand Oaks, CA: Sage Publications.

Horowitz, A. (1985a). Family caregiving to the frail elderly. In Lawton, M. P. & G. Maddox, (eds.). *Annual review of gerontology and geriatrics.* Vol. 5 (pp. 194–246). New York: Springer.

————. (1985b). Sons and daughters as caregivers to older parents: Differences in role performance and consequences. *The Gerontologist.* 25(6):612–617.

Horowitz, A. & Dobrof, R. (1982). *The role families in providing long-term care to the frail and chronically ill elderly living in the community.* Final report submitted to the Health Care Financing Administration, U.S. Washington, D.C. Department of Health and Human Services.

Horowitz, A. & Shindleman, L. (1983). Social and economic incentives for family caregivers. *Health Care Financing Review.* 5:25–33.

House, J. S. (1981). *Work, stress and social support.* Reading, MA: Addison-Wesley.

Howes, C., Smith, E. & Galinsky, E. (1995). *The Florida Child Care Quality Improvement Study.* New York: Families and Work Institute.

Hu, T., Huang, L. & Cartwright, W. S. (1986). Evaluation of the costs of caring for the senile demented elderly: A pilot study. *The Gerontologist.* 26:158–163.

Huff-Corzine, L., Corzine, J. & Moore, D. C. (1991). Deadly connections—Culture, poverty and the direction of lethal violence. *Social Forces.* 69:715–732.

Hughes, D. & Galinsky, E. (1988). Balancing work and family lives: Research and corporate applications. In A. E. Gottfried & A. W. Gottfried, (eds.). *Maternal employment and children's development.* New York: Plenum Press.

Hunt, R. G., Near, J. P, Rice, R. W., Graham, T. D. & Gutteridge, T. G. (1977). Job satisfaction and life satisfaction: Survey results on work and nonwork-related correlates. *Journal Supplement Abstract Service.* 7:55–56.

Ingram, P. & Simons, T. (1995). Institutional and resource dependence determinants of responsiveness to work-family issues. *Academy of Management Journal.* 38(5): 1466–1482.

Institute of Medicine. (1996). *Quality of long term care services in home and community based settings.* Washington D.C., National Academy Press.

Is your work/life service earning its keep? (1995, September). *Employee Benefit News.* 76:1.

Jacobs, E.E. (1998). *Handbook of U.S. Labor Statistics.* Lanham, MD: Bernan Press.

Jacobson, M., Kolarek, M. H. & Newton, B. (1996, October). *Business, babies & the bottom line: Corporate innovations and the best practices in maternal and child health.* Washington, D.C.: Washington Business Group on Health.

Jacobson, E., Charters, W. W. & Lieberman, S. (1951). The use of role concept in the study of complex organizations, *Journal of Social Issues.* 7:18–27.

Johnson, A. A. (1995). The business case for work-family programs. *Journal of Accountancy.* 180:53–58.

Jones, S. L. & Jones, P. K. (1994). Caregiver burden: Who the caregivers are, how they give care, and what bothers them. *Journal of Health and Social Policy.* 6:71–89.

Josselson, R. (1992). The space between us: Exploring the dimensions of human relationships. San Francisco, CA: Jossey Bass Publishers.

Kahne, H. (1993). Part-time work: A Reassessment for a changing economy. *Social Service Review.* 68(3):417–436.

Kamerman, S. B. (1989). Child care, women, work, and the family: An international overview of child care services and related policies. In Lande, J.S., S. Scarr & N. Gunzenhauser, (eds.) *Caring for children: Challenge to America.* Hillsdale, NJ: Lawrence Erlbaum Associates, Inc.

————. (1991). Child care policies and programs: An international overview. *Journal of Social Issues.* 47(2):179–196.

————. (1996). The new politics of child and family policies. Special Issue: Social work in an era of diminishing federal responsibility. *Social Work.* 41(15):453–465.

Kamerman, S. B. & Kahn, A. J. (1995a). Innovations in toddler day care and family support services: An international overview. *Child Welfare*. 74(6): 1281–1300.

Kamerman, S. B. & Kahn, A. J. (1995b). *Starting right: How America neglects it's youngest children and what we can do about it*. New York: Oxford University Press.

Kamerman, S. B. & Kahn, A. J. (eds.). (1997). *Child care in the context of welfare reform*. New York, NY: Columbia University School of Social Work.

Kane, R. A. (1995). *Quality, autonomy, and safety in home and community-based long-term care: Toward regulatory and quality assurance policy*. Report of a national mini-conference officially recognized by the White House Conference on Aging. Minneapolis, MN: National Long Term Care Resource Center.

———. (1998). Assuring quality in nursing home care. *Journal of the American Geriatric Society*. 46:232–237.

Kanter, R. M. (1977). *Work and family in the United States: A critical review and agenda for research and policy*. New York: Russell Sage Foundation.

Karasek, R. (1981). Job socialization and job strain: The implications of two related psychosocial mechanisms for job design. In Gardell, B. & G. Johanson, (eds.). *Working life*. Chichester, England: John Wiley & Sons.

———. (1987). *Selection of job stress questionnaire items for NHANES III*. Los Angeles, CA: University of Southern California.

Kasl, W. V. & Cooper, C. L. (eds.). (1987). *Stress and health: Issues in research methodology*. Chichester, England: John Wiley.

Kasper, J. D., Steinbach, U. & Andrews, J. (1990). Factors associated with ending caregiving among informal caregivers to the functionally and cognitively impaired elderly population. *Final report to the Office of the Assistant Secretary of Planning and Evaluation, Department of Health and Human Services* (Grant # 88 ASPE 209A), Washington D.C., US Government Printing Office.

Kates, N., Grieff, B. S. & Hogen, D. Q. (1990). *The psychosocial impact of job loss*. Washington, D.C.: American Psychiatric Press.

Katz, S., Ford, A. B., Moskowitz, R. W., Jackson, B. A. & Jaffee, M. W. (1963). Studies of illness in the aged. The index of ADL: A standardized measure of biological and psychosocial function. *Journal of the American Medical Association*. 185:914–919.

Keita, G. P. & Sauter, S. L. (eds.). (1992). *Work and well-being: An agenda for the 1990s*. Washington, D.C.: American Psychological Association.

Kelly, R. F. & Voydanoff, P. (1985). Work/family role strain among working parents. *Family Relations*. 34:367–374.

Kemper, P. (1988). Overview of findings. *Health Services Research*. 23:161–174.

Kemper, P. & Murtaugh, C. M. (1991). Lifetime use of nursing home care. *New England Journal of Medicine*. 324(9):595–600.

Kingston, E. R. & O'Grady-LeShane, R. (1993). The effects of caregiving on women's social security benefits. *The Gerontologist*. 33(2):230–239.

Kinnear, D. & Graycar, A. (1984). Aging and family dependency. *Australian Journal of Social Issues*. 19:13–25.

Kinney, J. M. & Stephens, M. A. (1989). Caregiving hassles scale: Assessing the daily hassles of caring for a family member with dementia. *The Gerontologist*. 29:328–332.

Kisker, E. E., Hofferth, S. L., Phillips, D. A. & Farquhar, E. (1991). *A profile of child care settings: Early education and care in 1990*. (Vol. I). Princeton, NJ: Mathematica Policy Research.

Kisker, E. E. & Maynard, R. (1991). Quality, cost, and parental choice of child care.

In Blau, D. M., (ed.). *The Economics Of Child Care*. (pp. 127–143). New York: Russell Sage Foundation.

Kisker, E. E., Maynard, R., Gordon, A. & Strain, M. (1989). *The child care challenge: What parents need and what is available in three metropolitan areas.* Princeton, NJ: Mathematica Policy Research.

Klein, B. W. (1986). Missed work and lost hours, May 1985. *Monthly Labor Review*. 109(10):26–30.

Klein, N. & Sheehan, R. (1987). Staff development: A key issue in meeting the needs of young handicapped children in day care settings. *Topics in Early Childhood Education*. 7:13–27.

Kline, M. & Cowan, P. A. (1988). Re-thinking the connections among "work" and "family" and well-being (Special issue: work and family: theory, research, and applications). *Journal Of Social Behavior & Personality*. 3(4):61–90.

Kodner, D. L. (1996). Foreseeing the future of long-term care: The highlights and implications of a Delphi study. In Binstock, R. H., L. E. Cluff, and O. Von Mering, (eds.). *The future of long-term care*: Social and Policy Issues. Baltimore, MD: The Johns Hopkins University Press.

Komarovsky, M. (1976). *Dilemmas of masculinity: A study of college youth.* New York: W. W. Norton.

Korenman, S. & Neumark, D. (1991, Spring). Does marriage really make men more productive? *Journal of Human Resources*. 26:282–307.

Kossek, E. (1990). Diversity in child care assistance needs: Employee problems, preferences, and work-related outcomes. *Personnel Psychology*. 43:769–791.

Krajicek, M., & Moore, C. (1993). Child care for infants and toddlers with disabilities and chronic illnesses. *Focus on Exceptional Children*. 25(8):1–16.

Kramer, B. J. & Kipnis, S. (1995). Eldercare and work role conflict: Toward an understanding of gender differences in caregiver burden. *The Gerontologist*. 35(3): 340–348.

Krause, N. M., Herzog, A. R. & Baker, E. (1992). Providing support to others and well-being in later life. *Journals of Gerontology*. 47:300–311.

Laabs, J. J. (1993). Family issues are a priority at Stride Rite. *Personnel Journal*. 82(7): 48–55.

———. (1998). Two steps forward for domestic-partner benefits. *Workforce*. 77(1): 13–14.

Labor Project for Working Families. (1994, Fall). The case for paid leave. *Labor News for Working Families*. pp. 1–2.

Labreque, M. S., Peak, T. & Toseland, R. W. (1992). *American Journal of Orthopsychiatry*. 62:575–588.

LaCroix, A. & Haynes, S. (1987) Gender differences in the health effects of workplace roles. In Barnett, R., L. Biener & G. K. Baruch, (eds.). *Gender and Stress*. (pp. 96–121). New York: Free Press.

Lair, T. (1992). *A profile of nursing home users under age 65. National Medical Expenditure Survey, Research Finding 13.* AHCPR Pub. No 92–0060. Rockville, MD: Agency for Health Care Policy and Research.

Lambert, S. J. (1990). Processes linking work and family: A critical review and research agency. *Human Relations*. 43:239–257.

———. (1993). Workplace policies as social policy. *Social Services Review*. 67:237–260.

Landis, S. & Earp, J. (1987). Sick care options: What do working mothers prefer? *Women & Health*. 12:61–77.

Lawlor, J. (1995, May). Where are the women? *Working Mother*. 18(5):32.

Lawton, M. P. & Brody, E. M. (1969). Assessment of older people: Self-maintaining and instrumental activities of daily living. *The Gerontologist.* 9:179–186.

Lawton, M. P., Moss, M., Fulcomer, M. C. & Kleban, M. H. (1982). A research- and science-oriented multilevel assessment instrument. *Journal of Gerontology.* 37: 91–99.

Lawton, M. P., Rajagopal, D., Brody, E. & Kleban, M. H. (1992). The dynamics of caregiving for a demented elder among Black and White families. *Journals of Gerontology.* 47:156–164.

Lazarus, R. S. (1966). *Psychological stress and the coping process.* New York: McGraw-Hall.

Lazarus, R. S. & Folkman, S. (1984). *Stress, appraisal and coping.* New York: Springer.

Lechner, V. M. (1993). Racial group responses to work and parent care. *Families in Society: Journal of Contemporary Human Services.* 74(2):93–103.

Leibowitz, A. (1996). Child care: Private cost or public responsibility? In Fuchs, V.R., (ed.). *Individual and Social Responsibility: Child care, education, medical care, and long-term care in America.* (pp. 33–58). Chicago: University of Chicago Press.

Levitan, S. A. & Conway, E. (1988). *Raising America's Children: How Should We Care?* Washington, D.C.: Graduate Institute for Policy Education and Research, George Washington University, Graduate School of Arts and Sciences.

Lerner, S. (1994, March). The future of work in North America: Good jobs, bad jobs, beyond jobs. *Futures.* 26:185–196.

Lewis, F. M. (1986). The impact of cancer on the family: A critical analysis of the research literature. *Patient Education and Counseling.* 8:269–289.

Lewis, S. (1997). An international perspective on work-family issues. In Parasuraman, S. & J. H. Greenhaus, (eds.). *Integrating work and family: Challenges and choices for a changing world.* (pp. 104–114). Westport, CT: Quorum Books.

Lewis, S. & Lewis, J. (1996). *The work-family challenge: Rethinking employment.* Thousand Oaks, CA: Sage Publishing.

Lezak, M. D. (1978). Living with the characterologically altered brain injured patient. *Journal of Clinical Psychiatry.* 39:592–598.

Linsk, N. L., Keigher, S. M. & Osterbusch, S. E. (1988). States' policies regarding paid family caregiving. *The Gerontologist.* 28(2):204–212.

Locke, E. A. (1976). The nature and causes of job satisfaction. In Dunnett, M. D., (ed.). *Handbook of industrial and organizational psychology.* Chicago: Rand McNally.

Loomis, L. S. & Booth, A. (1995). Multigenerational caregiving and well-being: The myth of the beleaguered sandwich generation. *Journal of Family Issues.* 16(2): 131–148.

Lucas, T. (1986). *Employer support for employee caregivers* New York: Business Group on Health.

Macklin, E. D. (1988). AIDS: Implications for families. *Family Relations.* 37:141–149.

Maddox, G. L. & Douglass, E. B. (1973). Self-assessment of health: A longitudinal study of elderly subjects. *Journal of Health and Social Behavior.* 14:87–93.

Mahon, R. (1997). Child care in Canada and Sweden: Policy and politics. *Social Politics.* 4:382–418.

Manton, K. G., Corder, L. S. & Stallard, E. (1993). Estimates of change in chronic disability and institutional incidence and prevalence rates in the U.S. elderly population from the 1982, 1984, and 1989 national long-term care survey. *Journal of Gerontology.* 48:S153–S166.

Marks, N. F. (1995). Caregiving across the lifespan: A new national profile. *NSFH Working Paper, 55,* Center for Demography and Ecology. Madison, WI: University of Wisconsin-Madison.

Marks, S. (1977). Multiple roles and role strain: Some notes on human energy, time, and commitment. *American Sociological Review.* 42:921–936.

———. (1994). What is a pattern of commitment? *Journal of Marriage and Family.* 56:112–115.

Marks, S. R. & MacDermid, S. M. (1996). Multiple roles and the self: A theory of balance. *Journal of Marriage and Family.* 58:417–432.

Marra, R. & Lindner, J. (1992). The true cost of parental leave: The parental leave cost model. In Friedman, D.E., E. Galinsky & V. Plowden (eds.). *Parental leave and productivity.* New York: Families and Work Institute.

Marriott considers employee problems at home problems they take to work. (1995, October 27). *The National Report on Work and Family.* p. 1.

Marshall, N. (1991). *The bottom line: Impact of employer child care subsidies.* (Working Paper Series, No. 225). Wellesley, MA: Wellesley College, Center For Research on Women.

Marshall, N. L., Barnett, R. C., Baruch, G. K. & Pleck, J. H. (1990). Double jeopardy: The costs of caring at work and at home. In Able, E. K. & M. K. Nelson, (eds.). *Circles of care: Work and identity in women's lives.* Albany: State University of New York.

Martin, G. T. (1997). An agenda for family policy in the United States. In Arendell, T., (ed.). *Contemporary parenting: Challenges and issues.* Thousand Oaks, CA: Sage Publications.

Martin, J. (1990a). Deconstructing organizational taboos: The suppression of gender conflict in organizations. *Organization Science.* 1(4):339–359.

———. (1990b). *Rereading Weber: Searching for feminist alternatives to bureaucracy.* Paper presented at the annual meetings of the Academy of Management, San Francisco.

Marx, K. & Engels, F. (1939). *The German ideology.* New York: International Publishers.

Mason, M. A. (1992). Standing still in the workplace: women in social work and other female-dominated occupations. *Affilia Journal of Women and Social Work.* 7(3): 23–24.

Matthews, L. S., Conger, R. D. & Wickrama, K. A. S. (1996). Work-family conflict and marital quality: Mediating processes. *Social Psychology Quarterly.* 59(1):62–79.

Matthews, K. A. & Rodin, J. (1989). Women's changing work roles: Impact on health, family, and public policy. *American Psychologist.* 44:1389–1393.

Matthews, S. H., Werkner, J. E. & Delaney, P. J. (1989). Relative contributions of help by employed and nonemployed sisters to their elderly parents. *Journal of Gerontology.* 44:36–44.

Maume, D. (1991). Child care expenditures and women's employment turnover. *Special Forces.* 70:495–508.

Maume, D. & Mullin, K. (1993). Men's participation in child care and women's work attachment. *Social Problems.* 40:533–546.

McBride, A. B. (1990). Mental health effects of women's multiple roles. *American Psychologist.* 45:381–384.

McCubbin, H. I., Cauble, E. & Patterson, J. M. (1982). *Family stress, coping, and social support.* Springfield, Ill: Thomas.

McEnroe, J. (1991). Split-shift parenting. *American Demographics.* 13:50–52.

McFall, S. & Miller, B. H. (1992). Caregiver burden and nursing home admission of frail elderly persons. *Journal of Gerontology.* 47:73–79.

McGuire, J. & Liro, J. (1987, Spring). Absenteeism and flexible work schedules. *Public Personnel Management.* 16:47–59.

McKinlay, J. B., Crawford, S. L. & Tennstedt, S. L. (1995). The everyday impacts of providing informal care to dependent elders and their consequences for the care recipients. *Journal of Aging and Health*. 7:497–528.

McLanahan, S. S. & Monson R. A. (1990). Caring for the elderly: Prevalence and consequences. *A National Survey of Families and Households*. Madison, WI: Center For Demography And Ecology, Department of Sociology, University of Wisconsin-Madison.

Meeker, S. E. & Campbell, N. D. (1986, June). Providing for dependent care. *Business and Health*. 18–22.

Meichenbaum, D. & Jeremko, M. (eds.). (1982). *Stress prevention and management: A cognitive behavioral approach*. New York: Plenum.

Meisenheimer, J. (1990, August). Employee absences in 1989: A new look at data from the CPS. *Monthly Labor Review*. 113(8):28–33.

Meisenhelder, J. B. (1986). Self-esteem in women: The influence of employment and perception of husband's appraisals. *Image: Journal of Nursing Scholarship*. 18: 8–14.

Menaghan, E. G. & Parcel, T. L. (1995). Social sources of change in children's home environments: The effects of parental occupational experiences and family conditions. *Journal of Marriage and the Family*. 57:69–84.

Merton, R. K. (1957). *Social theory and social structure*. Glencoe, IL: The Free Press.

Milkman, R. (1987). *Gender at work: The dynamics of job segregation by sex during World War II*. Urbana, IL: University of Illinois Press.

Miller, A. (1990). Earning bread and baking bread: Reconciling welfare and family life. *Employee Assistance Quarterly*. 5(4):83–88.

Moen, P., Robison, J. & Fields, V. (1994). Women's work and caregiving roles: A life course approach. *Journal of Gerontology*. 49:S176–S186.

Monat, A. & Lazarus, R. S. (1985). Psychoanalytic perspectives on normality. In Offer, D. & M. Sabshin, (eds.), *Normality and the life cycle: A critical integration*. New York: Basic Books.

Montgomery, R. & Borgatta, E. F. (1989). The effects of alternative support strategies on family caregiving. *The Gerontologist*. 29:457–464.

Morgan, D. L., Schuster, T. L. & Butler, E. W. (1991). Role reversals in the exchange of social support. *Journals of Gerontology*. 46(5):S278–S287.

Morris, B. (1997, March). Is your family wrecking your career? (and vice versa). *Fortune*. 71–90.

Morycz, R. K. (1985). Caregiving strain and the desire to institutionalize family members with Alzheimer's disease. *Research on Aging*. 7:329–361.

Moskowitz, M. (1996, October). 100 best companies for working mothers. *Working Mother*, 19(9):1–30.

Mui, A. C. (1992). Caregiver strain among Black and White daughter caregivers: A role theory perspective. *The Gerontologist*. 32:203–212.

Mukherjee, S. (1997, April 4) Employers ditch family coverage. *Minneapolis/St. Paul CityBusiness*. pp. 12, 40.

Mulroy, E. A. & Pitt-Catsouphes, M. (1994). *Single parents at the workplace*. Policy Paper Series. Boston, MA: Boston University, Center on Work and the Family.

Mutschler, P. H. (1994). From executive suite to production line: How employees in different occupations manage elder care responsibilities. *Research on Aging*. 16(1):7–26.

Muurinen, J. (1986). The economics of informal care: Labor market effects of the national hospice study. *Medical Care*. 24:1007–1017.

Myers, C. D., Borthwick, S. A. & Eyman, R. (1985). Place of residence by age, ethnicity, and level of retardation of the mentally retarded/developmentally disabled population of California. *American Journal of Mental Deficiency*. 90:266–270.

Nathan, R. P. (1995). *Hard road ahead: Block grants and the "devolution revolution."* Unpublished manuscript, Nelson Rockefeller Institute of Government, Albany, N.Y.

National Alliance for Caregiving & American Association of Retired Persons (NAC/AARP). (1997). *Family caregiving in the U.S.—Findings from a national survey*. Bethesda, MD: NAC/AARP.

National Association of Child Care Resource and Referral Agencies (NACCRRC). (1992). *Facts from the field: agencies tell us that. . . .* Washington, DC: NACCRRC.

National Association for Home Care (NAHC) (1993). *Basic statistics about home care, 1993*. Washington, D.C.: NAHC.

National Council on the Aging, Inc. (NCOA) (1997). *Caregiving across the miles: Findings of a survey of long-distance caregivers*. Washington, D.C.: NCOA.

National Council of Jewish Women (NCJW) (1987, November). *Accommodating pregnancy in the workplace*. (National Council of Jewish Women Center for the Child report). New York: NCJW.

National Research Council. (1990). In Ferber, A. & B. O'Farrell, (eds.). *Work and family: policies for a changing work force*. Washington, D.C.: National Academy Press.

Neal, M. B., Chapman, N. J., Ingersoll-Dayton, B. & Emlen, A. C. (1993). *Balancing work and caregiving for children, adults, and elders*. Newbury Park, CA: Sage.

Near, J. P., Rice, R. W. & Hunt, R. G. (1980). The relationship between work and nonwork domains: A review of empirical research. *Academy of Management Review*. 5:415–429.

Netemeyer, R. G., Boles, J. S. & McMurrian, R. (1996). Development and validation of work-family conflict and family-work conflict scales. *Journal of Applied Psychology*. 81:400–410.

NEWFA Survey: Family and Medical Leave Act. (1993). Boston, MA: New England Work & Family Association.

New Ways to Work. (1995). *Balanced lives: Changing work patterns for men*. London: New Ways to Work (NNW) London.

New York Business Group on Health (NYBGH). (1986). *Employer support for employee caregivers*. New York: New York Business Group on Health.

Noelker, L. S. & Poulshock, S. W. (1982). *The effects on families of caring for impaired elderly in residence*. Final report submitted to the Administration on Aging. Cleveland, Ohio: The Margaret Blenkner Research Center for Family Studies, The Benjamin Rose Institute.

Nollen, S. (1982). *New Work Schedules in Practice*. New York: Van Nostrand Reinhold.
———. (1989, September/October). Does flextime improve productivity? *Harvard Business Review*. 57(5):12, 16–18, 22.

Northhouse, P. & Swain, M. (1987). Adjustment of patients and husbands to the initial impact of breast cancer. *Nursing Research*. 36:221–225.

O'Connell, M. (1990). Maternity leave arrangements: 1961–1985. Bureau of the Census. Current Population Reports, Special Studies Series P-23, No. 165. Washington, D.C.: U.S. Department of Commerce.

Oktay, J. S., Steinwachs, D. M., Mamon, J., Bone, L. R. & Fahey. (1992). Evaluating social work discharge planning services for elderly people: Access, complexity and outcome. *Health and Social Work*. 17(4):290–298.

Older Women's League. (1989). *Failing America's caregivers: A status report on women who care*. Washington, D.C.: Older Women's League.

Olson, D. & Hamilton McCubbin & Assoc. (1983). *Families: What makes them work*. Beverly Hills, CA: Sage Publishing.

Olson, E. (1998, February 16). *U.N. Surveys paid leave for mothers*. New York Times, (pp. 1, 3).

O'Neil, R. & Greenberger, E. (1994). Patterns of commitment to work and parenting: Implications for role strain. *Journal of Marriage and the Family*. 56:101–118.

Orthner, D. K. (1980). *Families in the blue: A study of married and single parent families in the Air Force*. Washington, D.C.: Department of the Air Force.

Orthner, D. K. & Pittman, J. F. (1986). Family contributions to work commitment. *Journal of Marriage and the Family*. 48:573–581.

Osterbusch, S. E., Keigher, S. M., Miller, B. & Linsk, N. L. (1987). Community care policies and gender justice. *International Journal of Health Services*. 17(2):217–232.

Ozer, E. (1995). The impact of childcare responsibility and self-efficacy on the psychological health of professional working mothers. *Psychology of Women Quarterly*. 19:315–335.

Paid Leave for AFSCME. (1995, Summer). *Labor News for Working Families*. III(3).

Palley, H. A. & Oktay, J. S. (1983). The chronically limited elderly: The case for a national policy for in-home and supportive community-based services. *Home Health Care Quarterly*. 4(2):3–141.

Parcel, T. & Menagham, E. (1994). *Parents' jobs and children's lives*. New York: Aldine & Gruyter.

Parker, S. K. & Smith, M. A. (1976). Work and leisure. In Dubin, R., (ed.). *Handbook of work, organization, and society*. Chicago: Rand-McNally.

Parkinson, D. (1995). Employee assistance programs. *The Conference Board Work-Family Roundtable*. 5(3):3–14.

Parsons, T. (1970). *Social structure and personality*. New York: Free Press.

Pavalko, E. K. & Artis, J. E. (1997). Women's caregiving and paid work: Causal relationships in late midlife. *Journal of Gerontology*. 52B(4):S170–179.

Payton-Miyazaki, M. & Brayfield, A. H. (1976). The good job and the good life: Relation of characteristics of employment to general well-being. In Bideman, A. D. & T. F. Drury, (eds.). *Measuring work quality for social reporting*. New York: Wiley.

Pearlin, L. I. (1983). Role strains and personal stress. In Kaplan, H.B., (ed.). *Psychosocial stress: Trends in theory and research*. New York: Academic Press.

Pearlin, L. I., Mullan, J. T., Semple, S. J. & Skaff, M. M. (1990). Caregiving and the stress process: An overview of concepts and their measures. *The Gerontologist*. 30:583–594.

Pearlman, D. N. & Crown, W. H. (1992). Alternative sources of social support and their impacts upon institutional risk. *The Gerontologist*. 32(4):527–535.

Peckman, J. A. (1990, March). Future of the income tax. *The American Economic Review*. 80(1):1–20.

Petty, D. & Friss, L. (1987). A balancing act of working and caregiving. *Business and Health*. 4:22–26.

Phillips, D. (1987). *Quality in child care: What does the research tell us?* Washington, D.C.: National Association for the Education of Young Children.

Piotrkowski, C. (1979). *Work and the family system*. New York: Free Press.

Piotrkowski, C. S. & Katz, M. H. (1983). *Research in the interweave of social roles: Families and jobs*. (Vol. 3). Greenwich, CT: JAI Press.

Pittman, J. F. (1994). Work/family fit as a mediator of work factors on marital tension: Evidence from the interface of greedy institutions. *Human Relations.* 47(2):183–209.

Pittman, J. F & Blanchard, D. (1996). The effects of work history and timing of marriage on the division of household labor. *Journal of Marriage and the Family.* 58:78–90.

Pleck, J. (1984). The work-family role system, work and family: Changing roles of men and women. In Voydanoff, P., (ed.). *Work and Family.* (pp. 8–19). Palo Alto, CA: JAI Press.

Pohl, J. M., Boyd, C., Liang, J. & Given, C. W. (1995). Analysis of the impact of mother-daughter relationships on the commitment to caregiving. *Nursing Research.* 44(2):68–75.

Polakow, V. (1997). Family policy, welfare, and single motherhood in the United States and Denmark: A cross-national analysis of discourse and practice. Special Issue: Children, families, and change: International perspectives. *Early Education and Development.* 8(3):245–264.

Poulshock, S. W. & Deimling, G. T. (1984). Families caring for elders in residence: Issues in the measurement of burden. *Journal of Gerontology.* 39:230–239.

Powell, W. W. & DiMaggio, P. (1991). *The new institutionalism in organizational analysis.* Chicago: University of Chicago Press.

Pruchno, R. A. & Potashnik, S. L. (1989). Caregiving spouses: Physical and mental health in perspective. *Journal of the American Geriatric Society.* 37:697–705.

Pruchno, R. A. & Resch, N. L. (1989). Aberrant behaviors and Alzheimer's disease: Mental health on spouse caregivers. *Journal of Gerontology.* 44(5):177–182.

Putman, R. D. (1995). Bowling alone: America's declining social capital. *Journal of Democracy.* 6(1):65–78.

Putting families first: AFL-CIO Working Family Resource Guide. (1992). Washington, D.C.: AFL-CIO.

Quinn, R. P. & Stains, G. L. (1979). *The 1977 quality of employment survey: Descriptive statistics with comparison data from the 1969–70 and 1972–73 surveys.* Ann Arbor, MI: Survey Research Center.

Raber, M. (1996). Downsizing of the nation's labor force and a needed social work response. *Administration in Social Work.* 20(1):47–58.

Rabiner, D. J., Mutran, E. & Stearns, S. C. (1995). The effect of channeling on home care utilization and satisfaction with care. *The Gerontologist.* 35(2):186–195.

Rabins, P., Mace, N. & Lucas, M. J. (1982). The impact of dementia on the family. *Journal of the American Medical Association.* 248:333–335.

Ramey, C. & Ramey, S. (1992). Early educational intervention with disadvantaged children—to what effect? *Applied and Preventative Psychology.* 1:131–140.

Ransom, C. & Burud, S. (1986). *Productivity impact study. Conducted for Union Bank Child Care Center.* Unpublished manuscript. Available from Burud & Associates, 56 East Holly Street, Pasadena, CA 91103.

Repetti, R. L. (1989). Effects of daily workload on subsequent behavior during marital interaction: The roles of social withdrawal and spouse support. *Journal of Personality and Social Psychology.* 57(4):651–659.

Repetti, R. L., Matthews, K. A. & Waldron, I. (1989). Employment and women's health: Effects of paid employment on women's mental and physical health. *American Psychologist.* 44:1394–1401.

Repetti, R. L. & Wood, J. (1997). Effects of daily stress at work on mothers' interactions with preschoolers. *Journal of Family Psychology.* 11(1):90–108.

Reschovsky, J. (1996). The demand for and access to institutional long-term care: The role of Medicaid in nursing home markets. *Inquiry*. 33:15–29.

Rexroat, C. & Shehan, C. (1987). The family life cycle and spouses' time in housework. *Journal of Marriage and the Family*. 49:737–750.

Ribbe, M. W., Ljunggren, G., Steeel, K. & Topinkova, E. (1997). Nursing homes in 10 nations: A comparison between countries and settings. *Age and Ageing*. 26(6):S3.

Robins, P. K. (1988). *Federal financing of child care: Alternative approaches and economic implications*. Paper presented at the conference sponsored by the Child Care Action Campaign: Economic implications and benefits of child care, Racine, WI.

Robison, J., Moen, P. & Dempster-McClain, D. (1995). Women's caregiving: Changing profiles and pathways. *Journal of Gerontology*. 50B:S362–S373.

Rocha, C. J. (1994). *The effects of poverty on working families: Comparing models of stress by race and class*. PhD diss. Washington University.

Roche, S. E. & Camasso, M. J. (1993). Parental preferences and considerations of cost in the selection of school-age child care. *Children & Youth Services Review*. 15:53–70.

Romeis, J. C. (1987). *Caregiver strain: Toward a role theory perspective with societal implications*. Paper presented at the 39th Annual Scientific Meeting of the Gerontological Society of America, Chicago, IL.

Rosenfield, S. (1989). The effects of wives' employment: Personal control and sex differences in mental health. *Journal of Health and Social Behavior*. 30:77–91.

Roy, F. H. & Russell, C. (1992). *The encyclopedia of aging and the elderly*. New York: Oxford Univ. Press.

Ruben, D. (1991, February). Daycare: How do you spell relief? *Parents*. 96–102.

Ruhm, C. J. & Teague, J. L. (1993). *Parental leave policies in Europe and North America*. Greensboro, N.C.: Department of Economics, University of North Carolina.

Ruhm, C. J. & Teague, J. L. (1997). Parental leave policies in Europe and North America. In Fr. Blau & R. Ehrenberg, (eds.). *Gender and family issues in the workplace*. New York: Russell Sage Foundation Press.

Ryff, C. D. (1986, November). *The failure of successful aging research*. Paper presented at the Meeting of the Gerontological Society, Chicago, IL.

Sahoo, F. M. & Bidyadhar, S. (1994). Critical factors of work-family linkage: An application of lens model to generate indigenous dimensions. *Psychology and Developing Societies*. 6(2):169–185.

Sancier, B. & Mapp, P. (1992). Who helps working women care for the young and old? *Affilia*. 7(2): 61–76.

Sarbin, T. R. (1954). Role theory. In Lindzey, G. (ed.). *Handbook of Social Psychology* (pp. 223–258). Cambridge, MA: Addison-Wesley.

Savasta, M. A. (1997). Into the mainstream?: Employers examine domestic partnership benefits. *Risk Management*. 44(9):70–74.

Scanlon, W. (1998). Long-term care: Baby boom generation presents financing challenges. U.S. General Accounting Office (GAO/T-HEHS-98-107), Washington D.C.: U.S. Government Printing Office.

Scarr, S. (1998). American child care today. *American Psychologist*. 53(2):95–108.

Scarr, S., Eisenberg, M. & Deater-Deckard, K. (1994). Measurement of quality on child care centers. *Early Childhood Research Quarterly*. 9:131–151.

Scarr, S., Phillips, D. & McCartney, K. (1989). Working mothers and their families. *American Psychologist*. 44:1402–1409.

Scharlach, A. (1988). *Survey of caregiving employees*. Los Angeles, CA: Transamerica Life Companies.

Scharlach, A. E. (1994). Caregiving and employment: Competing or complementary roles? *The Gerontologist.* 34:378–385.

Scharlach, A. E. & Boyd, S. L. (1989). Caregiving and employment: Results of an employee survey. *The Gerontologist.* 29(3):382–397.

Scharlach, A. E. & Fredriksen, K. I. (1994). Elder care versus adult care: Does care recipient age make a difference? *Research on Aging.* 16:43–68.

Scharlach, A. E., Lowe, B. F. & Schneider, E. L. (1991). *Elder care and the work force: Blueprint for action.* Lexington, MA: Lexington Books.

Scharlach, A. E., Midanik, L. T., Runkle, M. C. & Soghikian, K. (1997). Health practices of adults with elder care responsibilities. *Preventive Medicine.* 26:155–161.

Scharlach, A. E., Runkle, M. C., Midanik, L. T. & Soghikian, K. (1994). Health conditions and service utilization of adults with elder care responsibilities. *Journal of Aging and Health.* 6:336–352.

Scharlach, A. E., Sobel, E. L. & Roberts, R. E. (1991). Employment and caregiver strain: An integrative model. *The Gerontologist.* 31:778–787.

Scharlach, A. E. & Stanger, J. (1994). *Mandated family and medical leave: Boon or bane?* (Unpublished manuscript). Available from Andrew Scharlach, University of California, Berkeley, CA 94720.

Schor, J. (1991). *The overworked American: The unexpected decline of leisure.* New York: Basic Books.

Schultz, J. B., Chung, Y. L. & Henderson, C. G. (1988). Work/family concerns of university faculty. *Journal of Social Behavior and Personality.* 3:249–264.

Schultz, R., O'Brien, A. T., Bookwala, J. & Fleissner, K. (1995). Psychiatric and physical morbidity effects of dementia caregiving: Prevalence, correlates, and causes. *The Gerontologist.* 35(6):771–791.

Schultz, R., Tompkins, C. A. & Rau, M. T. (1988). A longitudinal study of the psychosocial impact of stroke on primary support persons. *Psychology and Aging.* 3:131–41.

Schwartz, R. (1989). Management women and the new facts of life. *Harvard Business Review.* 1:65–76.

Scott, W. R. (1992). *Organizations: Rational, natural, and open systems.* N.J.: Prentice Hall.

Secord, P. F. & Backman, C. W. (1964). *Social psychology.* New York: McGraw-Hill.

Secret, M. & Greeen, R. G. (1998). Occupational status differences among three groups of married mothers. *Affilia.* 13(1):47–68.

Seitel, S. (1997, April). *Emergency and sick care.* Speech given to a gathering of business executives in Indianapolis, IN. Unpublished manuscript. Available from Work & Family Connections, Inc., 5197 Beachside Drive, Minnetonka, MN 55343.

Sekaran, U. & Hall, D. T. (1989). Asynchronism in dual-career and family linkages. In Arthur, M. B., D. T. Hall & B. S. Lawrence, (eds.). *Handbook of career theory* (pp. 159–180). Cambridge, MA: Cambridge University Press.

Seligson, M. (1997, Spring). Before and after school child care comes of age. *The Wellesley Centers for Women Research Report.* 1(2):1–2.

Seligson, M. Fersh, E., Marshall, N., Marx, F. & Baden, R. (1990). School-age child care: The challenge facing families. *Families in Society.* 71:324–332.

Seltzer, M. M. & Krauss, M. W. (1989). Aging parents with mentally retarded children: Family risk factors and sources of support. *American Journal on Mental Retardation.* 94:303–312.

Selye, H. (1950). *The physiology and pathology of exposure to stress.* Montreal, Canada: Acta.

Shamir, B. & Salomon, I. (1985). Work-at-home and the quality of working life. *Academy of Management Review.* 10:455–464.

Shellenbarger, S. (1993, June 23). Employers band together for better elder care. *The Wall Street Journal.* pp. B1.

Sheppard, M. (1994). Childcare, social support and maternal depression: A review and application of findings. *British Journal of Social Work.* 24:33–51.

Shinn, M., Galinsky, E. & Gulcur, L. (1990). *The role of child care centers in the lives of parents.* New York: Families and Work Institute.

Shinn, M, Wong, N., Simko, P. & Oritz-Torres, B. (1989). Promoting the well-being of working parents: Coping, social support, and flexible job schedules. *American Journal of Community Psychology.* 17:31–61.

Sizemore, M. T. & Jones, A. B. (1990). Elder care and the workplace short-term training preferences of employees. *Educational Gerontology.* 16:97–104.

Slaughter, D. (1983). Early intervention and its effects on maternal and child development. *Monographs of the Society for Research on Child Development.* 48(4, Serial No. 202).

Small, S. A. & Riley, D. (1990). Toward a multidimensional assessment of work spillover into family life. *Journal of Marriage and the Family.* 52:51–61.

Smith, B. (1991). Back to school: Work-family conflicts. *Personnel.* 68:1–2.

Soloman, C. (1994, March). Special report: Latchkey Kids. *Parents.* 42–46.

Sonnenstein, F. (1991). The child care preferences of parents with young children: How little is known. In Hyde, J. S. & M. J. Essex, (eds.). *Parental leave and childcare: Setting a research and policy agenda.* (pp.337–353). Philadelphia, PA: Temple University Press.

Spalter-Roth, R. & Hartman, H. (1990). *Unnecessary losses: Costs to Americans of the lack of family and medical leave.* Washington, D.C.: Institute for Women's Policy Research.

Spector, W. D. (1991). Cognitive impairment and disruptive behaviors among community-based elderly persons: Implications for targeting long-term care. *The Gerontologist.* 31:51–59.

Spector, W. D., Reschovsky, J. & Cohen, J. D. (1996). Appropriate placement of nursing home residents in lower levels of care. *Milbank Quarterly.* 74(1):139–160.

Spillman, B. C. & Kemper, P. (1995), Lifetime patterns of payment for nursing home care. *Medical Care.* 33(3):280–296.

Spitze, G. & Logan, J. (1990). More evidence of women (and men) in the middle. *Research on Aging.* 12(2):182–198.

Staines, G. L. (1980). Spillover versus compensation: A review of the literature on the relationship between work and nonwork. *Human Relations.* 2(33):111–129.

Staines, G. L. & Pleck, J. H. (1983). *The impact of work schedules on the family.* Ann Arbor: Institute for Social Research, University of Michigan, Survey Research Center.

Starrels, M. E., Ingersoll-Dayton, B., Dowler, D. W. & Neal, M. (1997). The stress of caring for a parent: Effects of the elder's impairment on an employed, adult child. *Journal of Marriage and the Family.* 59:860–872.

Starrels, M., Ingersoll-Dayton, B., Neal, M. & Yamada, H. (1995). Intergenerational solidarity and the workplace: Employees' caregiving for their parents. *Journal of Marriage and the Family.* 57:751–762.

Statham, A. (1986). Family or career first: How professional women fare in making the choice. *Affilia.* 1(4):22–38.

Steil, J. M. & Turetsky, B. A. (1987). Is equal better? *Applied Social Psychology Annual.* 7:73–97.

Stephens, M. A., Norris, V. K., Kinney, J. M., Ritchie, S. W. & Grotz, R .C. (1988). Stressful situations in caregiving: Relationships between caregiver coping and well-being. *Psychology and Aging*. 3:208–209.

Stern, S. (1996). Measuring child work and resilience adjustments to parents' long-term care needs. *The Gerontologist*. 36:76–87.

Steuve, A. & O'Donnell, L. (1984). *Interactions between daughters and aging parents: Conditions and consequences of daughters' employment*. (Working Paper, No. 146). Wellesley, MA: Wellesley College Center for Research on Women.

Stipek, D. J. & McCroskey, J. (1989). Investing in children: Government and workplace policies for parents. *American Psychologist*. 44(2):416–423.

Stoiber, S. A. (1989). *Parental leave and woman's place: The implications and impact of three European approaches to family leave policy*. Washington, D.C.: Women's Research and Education Institute.

Stoller, E. P. (1983). Parental caregiving by adult children. *Journal of Marriage and the Family*. 45:851–858.

Stoller, E. & Pugliesi, K. (1989). Other roles of caregivers: Competing responsibilities of supportive resources. *Journal of Gerontology*. 44:S231–S239.

Stone, R. (1991). Familial obligations: Issues for the 1990s. *Generations*. 15(3):47–50.

Stone, R., Cafferata, G. L. & Sangl, J. (1987). Caregivers of the frail elderly: A national profile. *The Gerontologist*. 27(5):616–626.

Stone, R. I. & Short, P. F. (1990). The competing demands of employment and informal caregiving to disabled elders. *Medical Care*. 28:513–526.

Stroh, L. K., Brett, J. M. & Reilly, A. H. (1996). Family structure, glass ceiling, and traditional explanations for the differential rate of turnover of female and male managers. *Journal of Vocational Behavior*. 48:99–118.

Stull, D. E., Bowman, K. & Smerglia, V. (1994). Women in the middle: A myth in the making? *Family Relations*. 43:319–324.

Stull, D. E., Bowman, K. & Smerglia, V. (1991, October). *Women in the middle: A myth in the making?* Revised version of paper presented at the 1990 annual scientific meeting of the Gerontological Society of America, Boston, MA.

Swanson, J. L. (1992). Life-span career development and reciprocal interaction of work and nonwork. *Journal of Vocational Behavior*. 41:101–161.

Tax Management. (1998). Public employers lead in extending benefits to domestic partners. *Tax Management Financial Planning Journal*. 14(9):250–252.

Tennstedt, S., Cafferata, G. L. & Sullivan, L. (1992). Depression among caregivers of impaired elders. *Journal of Aging and Health*. 4:58–76.

The Conference Board. (1994). Family and Medical Leave. *Work-Family Roundtable*. 4(4):7.

The National Report of Work & Family (1999). Silver Spring, MD: Business Publishers, Inc.

Thomas, E. J. (1968). Role theory, personality and the individual. In Borgatta, E. F. & W. W. Lambert, (eds.). *The handbook of personality theory and research* (pp. 691–727). Chicago: Rand McNally.

Thomas, L. T. & Ganster, D. C. (1995). Impact of family supportive work variables on family conflict and strain: A control perspective. *Journal of Applied Psychology*, 80:6–15.

Thomas, L. T. & Thomas, J. E. (1990, Winter). The ABCs of child care: Building blocks of competitive advantage. *Sloan Management Review*. 31(2):31–41.

Thompson, L. & Walker, A. J. (1989). Gender in families: Women and men in marriage, work, and parenthood. *Journal of Marriage and the Family*. 51:845–871.

Torres-Gil, F. M. (1992). *The new aging: Politics and change in America*. New York: Auburn House.

Toseland, R. W. & Rossiter, C. M. (1989). Group interventions to support family caregivers: A review and analysis. *The Gerontologist*. 29:438–448.

Toseland, R. W., Rossiter, C. M., Peak, T. & Smith, G. C. (1990). Comparative effectiveness of individual and group interventions to support family caregivers. *Social Work*. 35:209–217.

Travelers Corporation. (1985). *A survey of caregiving responsibilities of Travelers employees for older Americans*. Hartford, CT: Travelers Corporation.

Turner, H. A., Pearlin, L. I., & Mullan, J. T. (1998). Sources and determinants of social support of caregivers of persons with AIDS. *Journal of Health and Social Behavior*. 39(2):137–151.

UAW/Long Term Care. (1995, Fall). *Labor News for Working Families*. III(4)

UNCO, Inc. (1975). *National childcare consumer study: 1975* (vols. 1–4). Washington, DC: UNCO.

U.S. Bureau of the Census. (1987). *Who's minding the kids. Child care arrangements: Winter 1984–85, Data from the survey of income and program participation* (Current Population Reports, Series P-70, No 9.). Washington, D.C.: U.S. Government Printing Office.

———. (1990). *The need for personal assistance with everyday activities: Recipients and caregivers. Current population reports, household economic studies* (Series P-70, No. 19). Washington, D.C.: Department of Commerce.

———. (1991). *Childcare arrangements: Population profile of the United States 1991*. (Current Population Series P-23, no. 173). Washington, D.C.: U. S. Government Printing Office.

———. (1992a). *Current population reports: Households, families, and children: A 30 year perspective*, P23-181. Washington, D.C.: U.S. Government Printing Office.

———. (1992b). *Current population reports: Marriage, divorce, and remarriage in the 1990s*, P23-180. Washington, D.C.: U.S. Government Printing Office.

———. (1993a). *Current population reports: Household and family characteristics*, P-20, No. 477. Washington, D.C.: U.S. Government Printing Office.

———. (1993b). *Statistical abstract of the United States: 1993* (113th edition). Washington, D.C.: U.S. Government Printing Office.

———. (1994a). *Current population reports: Geographical mobility: March 1993 to March 1994*. P20-485. Washington, D.C.: U.S. Government Printing Office.

———. (1994b). *Statistical abstract of the United States*. Washington, D.C.: U.S. Government Printing Office.

———. (1995a). *Current Population reports: Population profile of the United States*, P23-190. Washington, D.C.: U.S. Government Printing Office.

———. (1995b). *The nation's Asian and Pacific Islander population—1994*. SB/95-24 U.S. Department of Commerce, Economics and Statistics Administration.

———. (1996a). *Current population reports, special studies: 65 + in the United States*, P23-190. Washington, D.C.: U.S. Government Printing Office.

———. (1996b). *Statistical abstract of the United States: 1996* (116th edition). Washington, D.C.: U.S. Government Printing Office.

———. (1997a). Household and family characteristics: March 1997. *Current Population Reports*, P20-509.

———. (1997b). *One in 10 Americans report a severe disability in 1994–95)*. Washington, D.C.: Department of Commerce.

———. (1998). Statistical Abstract of the U.W., 1998 (118th edition). Washington, D.C.: U.S. Government Printing Office.

U.S. Bureau of Labor Statistics. (1985). *Employee benefits in medium and large firms, 1984* (Bulletin 2237). Washington, D.C.: US Department of Labor.

———. (1989) *Employee benefits in medium and large firms, 1988.* (Bulletin 2336). Washington, D.C.: U.S. Department of Labor.

———. (1997). *Employee benefits in medium and large private establishments, 1995.* (Bulletin 2496). Washington, D.C.: U.S. Department of Labor.

———. (1998). Employment characteristics of families: March, 1998. Washington, D.C.: U.S. Government Printing Office.

U.S. Bureau of National Affairs (BNA). (1989a). *Corporate work and family programs for the 1990s: Five case studies.* Washington, D.C.: U.S. Bureau of National Affairs.

———. (1989b). *Long distance eldercare: Spanning the miles with a new benefit.* (Special Report #22 Series on Work & Family). Washington, D.C.: U.S. Bureau of National Affairs.

———. (1994). *Majority of workers unaware of rights provided by Family and Medical Leave Act, BNA survey finds.* Washington, D.C.: U.S. Bureau of National Affairs.

U.S. Chamber of Commerce. (1988). *Employee benefits: Survey data from benefit years, 1987.* Washington, D.C.: U.S. Chamber of Commerce Research Center, Economic Policy Division.

U.S. Department of Labor. (1992). *Work and family provisions in major collective bargaining agreements.* (Bureau of Labor-Management Relations and Cooperative programs BLMR 144). Washington, D.C.: U.S. Department of Labor.

U.S. Department of Labor, Women's Bureau. (1994). *1993 Handbook on Women Workers: Trends and Issues.* Washington, D.C.: U.S. Government Printing Office.

———. Women's Bureau. (1995a). *Care around the clock: Developing child care resources before nine and after five.* Washington, D.C.: U.S. Government Printing Office.

———. Women's Bureau. (1995b). *Working women count!: A report to the nation.* Washington, D.C.: U.S. Government Printing Office.

———. (1997). *Report on the American Workforce.* Washington, D.C.: U.S. Government Printing Office.

U.S. General Accounting Office (GAO). (1991). *Workers at risk: Increased numbers in contingent employment lack insurance, other benefits.* Report to the Chairman, Subcommittee on Employment and Housing, Committee on Government Operations, House of Representatives, (GAO/HRD-91-56 Contingent Workers March, 1991). Washington, D.C.: U.S. General Accounting Office.

———. (1992a). *The changing Federal workforce: Comparison of Federal and nonfederal work/family programs and approaches.* (GAO/GDD-92-84). Washington, D.C. U.S. General Accounting Office.

———. (1992b). *The changing workforce: Demographic issues facing the federal government.* (GAO/FFD-92-38). Washington, D.C.: U.S. Government Accounting Office.

———. (1994a). *Long-term care: Private sector elder care could yield multiple benefits* (GAO/HEHS-94-60). Washington, D.C.: Author

———. (1994b). *Long-term care: Support for elder care could benefit the government workplace and the elderly.* (GAO/HEHS-94-64). Washington, D.C.: U.S. General Accounting Office.

———. (1994c). Long-term care: Other countries tighten budgets while seeking better access: Report to the Special Committee on Aging, U.S. Senate (GAO/HEHS 94-154). Washington, D.C.: U.S. General Accounting Office.

———. (1998). *Welfare reform: States' efforts to expand child care programs.* (GAO/HEHS 98-27). Washington, D.C.: U.S. General Accounting Office.

———. (1995a). *Long-term care: Baby boom generation presents financing challenges.* (GAO/HEHS 98-107). Washington, D.C., U.S. General Accounting Office GAO.

———. (1995b). *Long-term care: Current issues and future directions.* (GAO/HEHS-95-109). Washington, D.C.: U.S. General Accounting Office.

U.S. Health Care Financing Administration. (1996). Administration, financing, services, recipients, benefits, and eligibility; various periods through the year 1994. Washington, D.C.: U.S. Government Printing Office.

U.S. House of Representatives, Committee on Ways and Means. (1993). *Overview of Entitlement Programs: 1993 Green Book.* Washington, D.C.: U.S. Government Printing Office.

———. Committee on Ways and Means. (1994). *Overview of Entitlement Programs: 1994 Green Book.* Washington, D.C.: U.S. Government Printing Office.

———. Committee on Ways and Means. (1996). *Hearing before the Subcommittee on Health.* Serial 104-85. Washington, D.C., U.S. Government Printing Office.

———. Committee on Ways and Means. (1998). *The 1998 Green Book.* Washington, D.C.: U.S. Government Printing Office.

U.S. Internal Revenue Service (1997). Your Federal Income Tax. Washington, D.C.: U.S. Government Printing Office.

U.S. Senate, Special Committee on Aging in conjunction with the American Association of Retired Persons, the Federal Council on the Aging, and the U.S. Administration on Aging. (1987–1988). *Aging America: Trends and Projections.* Washington, D.C.: U.S. Government Printing Office.

———. Special Committee on Aging (1992). *Developments in aging: 1992.* From the Senate Reports Online via GPO Access (<wais.access.jpo.gov>).

———. (May 9, 1994). *Hearing before the Special Committee on Aging,* 103rd Congress, 2nd session, Milwaukee, WI. Serial No: 103-20.

———. Special Committee on Aging (1996). *Developments in aging: 1996.* From the Senate Reports Online via GPO Access (<wais.access.jpo.gov>).

———. (1998). *Hearings before the Special Committee on Aging.* Serial No. 105–14. Washington, D.C.: U.S. Government Printing Office.

U.S. Small Business Administration. (1987). *The state of small business: A report of the president.* Washington, D.C.: U.S. Government Printing Office.

Urdent, L. (1987). Ethical analysis of scarce resources in pediatric home care. *Children's Health Care.* 15(4):253–258.

Vitaliano, P. P., Schultz, R., Kiecolt-Glaser, J. & Grant, I. (1997). Research on physiological and physical concomitants of caregiving: Where do we go from here? *Annals of Behavioral Medicine.* 19:117–123.

Vogel, C. (1992). Levi Strauss and Co.—A work/family program in action. *Family Resource Coalition Report.* 11(2):4–5.

Voydanoff, P. (1984). *Work role characteristics, family structure demands and quality of family life.* Paper presented at the annual meeting of the National Council on Family Relations.

Voydanoff, P. (1988). Work role characteristics, family structure demands, and work/family conflict. *Journal of Marriage and the Family.* 50:749–761.

Voydanoff, P. & Donnelly, B. W. (1989). Work and family roles in psychological distress. *Journal of Marriage and the Family.* 51:923–932.

Wagner, D. L. (1997, June). *Comparative analysis of caregiver data for caregivers to the elderly 1987 to 1997.* Bethesda, MD: National Alliance for Caregiving.

Waldron, I. & Herold, J. (1986). Employment, attitudes toward employment and women's health. *Women and Health.* 11:79–98.

Waldron, I. & Jacobs, J. (1989). Effects of multiple roles on women's health: Evidence from a national longitudinal survey. *Women & Health.* 15(1):3–19.

Wallace, R. W. & Noelker, L. S. (1984, November). *Conceptualizing family caregiving: An application of role theory.* Paper presented at the 37th Annual Scientific Meeting of the Gerontological Society of America, Boston, MA.

Warren, J. A. & Johnson, P. J. (1995). The impact of workplace support on work-family role strain. *Family Relations.* 44: 163–169.

Weber, M. (1947). *The theory of social and economic organization.* (Henderson, A.M. & T. Parsons, Trans.). Glencoe, IL: Free Press.

Wellisch, D. K., Jamison, K. R. & Pasnau, R. O. (1978). Psychosocial aspects of mastectomy: II. The man's perspective. *American Journal of Psychiatry.* 135:543–546.

Wetzel, J. R. (1990). American families: 75 years of change. *Monthly Labor Review.* 113(3):4–13.

Whitebook, M., Howes, C. & Phillips, D. (1990). *Who care? Child care teachers and the quality of care in America: Final report of the National Child Care Staffing Study.* Oakland, CA: Child Care Employee Project.

Whitfield, S. & Krompholz, B. (1981). *Report to the General Assembly on the family support system demonstration program.* Baltimore, MD: State of Maryland Office on Aging.

Wiatrowski, W. J. (1995, June). Who really has access to employer-provided health benefits? (Limitations of health insurance plans). *Monthly Labor Review.* 118(6): 36–44.

Wilensky, H .L. (1960). Work, careers, and social integration. *International Social Science Journal.* 12:543–560.

———. (1990). Common problems, divergent policies: An 18-nation study of family policy. *Public Affairs Report.* 31(3):1–3.

Willer, B., Hofferth, S., Kisker, E., Divine-Hawkins, P., Farquhar, E. & Glantz, F. (1991). *The demand and supply of child care in 1990: joint findings from the 1990 national child care survey, 1990 and a profile of child care settings.* Washington, D.C.: National Association for the Education of Young Children.

Williams, K. J. & Alliger, G. M. (1994). Role stressors, mood spillover, and perceptions of work-family conflict in employed parents. *Academy of Management Journal.* 37:837–868.

With First Hawaiian, care begins at home. (1993, October). *Bank Marketing.* 25(10):6, 8.

Wohl, A., Morgenstern, H. & Kraus, J. F. (1995). Occupational injury in female aerospace workers. *Epidemiology.* 6:110–114.

Wolf, D. & Sonenstein, F. (1991). Child-care use among welfare mothers. *Journal of Family Issues.* 12:519–536.

Woodworth, R. S. (1934). *Psychology.* (3rd ed.). New York: Henry Holt.

Work/Family Directions. (1998). *Financing child care in the private sector.* [online] available internet: http: <www.pewtrusts.com/docs/childcare/child037.html>.

Wyatt Company. (1988). *A survey of health and welfare plans covering salaried employees of U.S. employers.* Washington, D.C.: Wyatt Company.

Young, R. F. & Kahana, E. (1995). The context of caregiving and well-being outcomes among African and Caucasian Americans. *The Gerontologist.* 35(2):225–232.

Youngblood, S. & Chambers-Cook, K. (1984, February). Child care assistance can improve employee attitudes and behavior. *Personnel Administrator.* 45–46:93–95.

Zambrana, R. & Hurst, M. (1984). Interactive effects of health status on work patterns among urban Puerto Rican women. *International Journal of Health Services*. 14:265–277.

Zaretsky, E. (1976). *Capitalism, the family & personal life*. New York: Harper & Row.

Zarit, S. H. (1989) Do we need another "stress and caregiver" study? *The Gerontologist*. 29:147–148.

———. (1990a, June). *Concepts and measures in family caregiving research*. Paper presented at the Conference on Conceptual and Methodological Issues in Family Caregiving Research, University of Toronto, Toronto, Canada.

———. (1990b). Interventions with frail elderly and their families: Are they effective and why? In Stephens, M., J. Crowther, S. Hobfall & D. Tennenbaum, (eds.). *Stress and coping in late life families*. (pp. 241–265). Washington, D.C.: Hemisphere Publications.

Zarit, S., Reever, K. E. & Bach-Peterson, J. (1980). Relatives of the impaired elderly: Correlates of feelings of burden. *The Gerontologist*. 20:260–266.

Zedeck, S. & Mosier, K. L. (1990). Work in the family and employing organization. *American Psychologist*. 45(2):240–251.

Zigler, E. F. & Finn-Stevenson, M. (1995). The child care crisis: Implications for the growth and development of the nation's children. *Journal of Social Issues*. 51(3):215–231.

Zigler, E. F. & Muenchow, S. (1992). *Head Start: The inside story of America's most successful educational experiment*. New York, NY: Basic Books.

Zucker, L. G. (ed.). (1988). *Institutional patterns and organizations: Culture and environment*. Cambridge, MA: Ballinger Publishing Company.

Author Index

Subject Index

315